Praise for DARING TO STRUGGLE, ~~DARING TO WIN~~

"I salute my good friend and comrade Helen Shiller for the broad vivid picture of her extraordinary life's journey, filled with personal challenges, and her decades of exceptional social justice work with and for the poor and oppressed communities. Helen worked tirelessly with the Illinois chapter of the Black Panther Party and its Intercommunal Survival Committee for racial and social justice during the 1970's. She is as a true servant of the people." —**Emory Douglas**, revolutionary artist, Minister of Culture, the Black Panther Party 1967–1980

"Helen Shiller has led no ordinary life: A witness to history, a crusader for justice, and deeply loyal to the women and men whose lives and predicaments cry for fairness, she has dedicated herself to righteous warfare, whether in the streets or in the hallowed halls of government. Her story is profoundly human and profoundly personal, but also a clarion call to the rest of us to join her." —**Achy Obejas**, author of *Boomerang/Bumerán*

"As a journalist who has covered Helen Shiller, off and on, throughout her half-century of community activism, I have long wondered how she would tell her own epic story. *Daring to Struggle, Daring to Win* answers that question poignantly and powerfully. Her epic journey takes us from the era of SDS, Black Panthers and school desegregation, through both Mayors Daley to the rise of Mayor Harold Washington, President Barack Obama and finally her own election to Chicago City Council—for 24 years. From outside agitator to insider alderperson, Shiller earned respect even from her political rivals for her savvy and resilience. For those who wonder whether they can "buy in" to the system without selling out, this story is a great place to start." —**Clarence Page**, Pulitzer-prize-winning columnist and editorial board member at the *Chicago Tribune*

"This book is a must read for today's organizers working to connect their neighborhoods to a vision of transformative, anti-racist politics. Daring to Struggle expands our knowledge of New Left organizers who rarely grabbed headlines, yet set a high standard for radical street-level and electoral activism." —**Amy Sonnie and James Tracy**, coauthors of *Hillbilly Nationalists, Urban Race Rebels and Black Power: Interracial Solidarity in 1960s–70s New Left Organizing*

"For more than a half century, Helen Shiller has been the radical's radical. She has led countless progressive causes, from the battle against police brutality; to bureaucracy busting; to fighting against poverty; to fighting for racial equity. Her story is a go-to-battle blueprint for the fights of today, and for those to come. It is a dare well worth taking." —**Laura S. Washington**, political analyst, ABC 7-Chicago

"Helen Shiller carefully weaves together her personal life story with the events that show her unflagging support and advocacy for grass roots communities in Chicago's Uptown. From Campus radical to long term alderwoman in Chicago's 46th Ward Shiller maintains her principles and effectiveness in fighting racism and building community led coalitions that took on and gained power against Chicago's political machine. A story of personal and political triumph against all odds." —**Jeffrey Haas**, author of *The Assassination of Fred Hampton*

"The only way NOT to repeat history and mistakes of the past is to share it, honor it, and learn from it. . . . and *Daring to Struggle, Daring to Win* does just that and talks about REAL CHANGE & REAL ALLIANCES." —**Jeanette Taylor**, Alderwoman, Chicago's 20th Ward

"Helen Shiller's work inside and out of the Chicago City Council is a model for all those seeking to make real change in the world. From her tireless work challenging gentrification, police abuse, and homophobia, Shiller never lost sight of her roots, and always put the struggles of poor and working class people first. No matter where you live and organize there is much to be learned from Helen's inspiring and courageous life story. Read this book!" —**Rossana Rodríguez Sánchez**, Alderwoman, Chicago's 33rd Ward

"From coping with sexual abuse, experiencing life before *Roe v Wade*, committing to support Black liberation, and taking on the brass knuckle Chicago politics, *Daring to Struggle Daring to Win* is interwoven with historical milestones. Shiller chronicles her life as a radical founder of All Chicago City News, a recipient of vote tampering and intimation, and the challenges of new thinking in parenthood. The call to fight white supremacy and the erosion of human rights with intentional solidarity is more relevant than ever. Shiller fills in significant information gaps and provides much to think about in our elusive search for an equitable and anti-racist future." —**Sylvia Ewing**, media personality, nonprofit executive, poet

"In 1969 Helen Shiller, already a young radical (revolutionary? community?) activist, heard inspirational Illinois Black Panther Chairman Fred Hampton proclaim that a serious revolutionary must "dare to struggle, dare to win." For the next five decades, Shiller pursued Fred's credo with unparalleled energy and commitment, daring to struggle, and daring to win. Her excellent book chronicles, in compelling historical detail, that journey, from Brooklyn to Madison, from Racine to Chicago, from Cuba to Zimbabwe, but most centrally from the streets of Chicago's Uptown to the chambers of Chicago's City Council, and documents how she relied on the 'power of the people' to speak truth to power in her tireless pursuit of Chairman Fred's uncompromising and timeless command." —**Flint Taylor**, author of *The Torture Machine*

"Regardless of the era, fighting for justice and marginalized people and principled positions in the public arena is difficult and challenging. *Daring to Struggle* contains numerous lessons for electeds, community leaders, and others on how to fight and win in the political arena without compromising those principles." —**Kim Foxx**, Cook County State's Attorney

"Helen Shiller has written a much needed, past due, historical account of her life as a community organizer and Council woman representing the poor in Uptown Chicago. Shiller has provided a voice for those poor residents who had little power to fight for their survival in a city that would only recognize them as irrelevant and refused to let them assimilate. *Daring to Struggle Daring to Win* is a much needed read for those who want to organize in poor communities." —**Hy Thurman**, cofounder, Young Patriot Organization, cofounder, Original Rainbow Coalition, author, and revolutionary hillbilly

"Helen Shiller's voice is direct, personal and accessible. This quality makes for a tale that others can take as an example and inspiration for their own community development and fight for justice." —**Lewis Watts**, co-author (with Elizabeth Pepin) of *Harlem of the West: The San Francisco Fillmore Jazz Era* Professor Emeritus UC Santa Cruz

DARING TO STRUGGLE, DARING TO WIN

FIVE DECADES OF RESISTANCE IN CHICAGO'S UPTOWN COMMUNITY

HELEN SHILLER

Haymarket Books
Chicago, Illinois

Published in 2022 by
Haymarket Books
P.O. Box 180165
Chicago, IL 60618
773-583-7884
www.haymarketbooks.org
info@haymarketbooks.org

ISBN: 978-1-64259-842-1

Distributed to the trade in the US through Consortium Book Sales and
Distribution (www.cbsd.com) and internationally through Ingram Publisher
Services International (www.ingramcontent.com).

This book was published with the generous support of
Lannan Foundation and Wallace Action Fund.

Special discounts are available for bulk purchases by organizations and
institutions. Please call 773-583-7884 or email orders@haymarketbooks.org
for more information.

Cover and text design by Eric Kerl.

Library of Congress Cataloging-in-Publication data is available.

10 9 8 7 6 5 4 3 2 1

Printed in Canada

Dedicated to my son, Brendan

CONTENTS

PART III: BUILDING A BASE OF OPERATIONS

PART IV: CHICAGO JOINS THE COUNTRY AT A CROSSROADS

PART V: 1983-1987: THE WASHINGTON YEARS

PART VI: ALDERMANIC YEARS: FROM MAKING THE MAJORITY TO BEING THE MINORITY VOICE

ACKNOWLEDGMENTS

There are very few things we do in life that are not a product of the hard work and struggles of those that came before us and on whose shoulders we all stand. The justice we seek takes commitment, sacrifice, passion, heart, and so much more. It is not just a cliché to say that failure to know and understand history condemns us to repeat it. But knowing and understanding history is no easy feat, and yet so necessary to any quest for justice.

In the United States, this is highlighted by the continuing impact of compromises made centuries ago, during the founding of our country. We still struggle for that illusive right of all people to life, liberty, and the pursuit of justice—a pursuit made all the more difficult by the codification of slavery and the ensuing legal and cultural embedding of white-skin privilege in all facets of our lives. However, justice does not have a color or gender: it is a universal concept and demand.

There is nothing more impactful than this ongoing demand and the protracted struggle it has engendered.

We live in a complicated world where loyalties are easily divided and fact is all too often mixed with fiction, making it hard to sort out what the true history is. Truth matters. The task of learning from the past to avoid repeating the actions that have prevented the pursuit of justice for all is impeded when actual facts are perverted. By our nature, human beings make mistakes; that is how we learn. But when an atmosphere is created where mistakes (or the perception of mistakes) are used as tools of attack, an environment is created that engenders the opposite of truth: in fact, it is the kernel that opens the door to the fascism my father warned me to be wary of.

During my early forays into electoral politics, my supporters were labeled "Shilleristas"—an allusion to the Sandinistas of Nicaragua (and a not-so-veiled attempt to defame me.) I bore it as a badge of honor. This book is my nod to all the Shilleristas and an expression of my pride of being able to make even the smallest of contributions to the ever-ongoing pursuit of justice.

This book would never have been written without the nudging of George Atkins and Tom Johnson or the ever-present support of my son, Brendan. We tragically lost Tom along the way when he and his wife were brutality murdered in their home in April 2020. I had last seen him at a fundraiser for the Uptown People's Law Center just over a month earlier. We had briefly talked about the book, which was just a collection of stories at the time. He wanted me to make it more personal and was concerned that his saying so might have offended me. I took his and Leslie's deaths hard and dedicated the next year (which was also the first year of the COVID-19 pandemic, entailing near-total lockdown) to heeding his message.

A big thank you to Achy Obejas for her friendship and encouragement and to Patrick Reichert (whom Achy brought into my orbit) for providing invaluable editing assistance, without which I may never have finished my first draft. Thanks to Marilyn Katz and Maggie Marystone, each of whom gave me quick edits and reminders of major events and/or people I had failed to mention or write about. A special thanks to Roberto Lopez, who took up slack for me as I put aside other responsibilities to focus on this effort. And thanks to all my friends who encouraged me along the way, shared their experiences, helped me remember a piece of history here and there, and most importantly for their views of the slice of history we shared together: Michilla Blaise, Billy "Che" Brooks, Jacinda Hall Bullie, Jim Chapman, Ann Cline, Steve Cole, Emory Douglas, Mary Driscoll, Sylvia Ewing, Jackie Grimshaw, Jack Hart, Phoebe Helm, Cha Cha Jiménez, Marc Kaplan, Susan Klonsky, Joy Lindsay, Stan McKinney, Jeri Miglietta, Alan Mills, Kari Moe, Prexy Nesbitt, Henry Nesbitt, Laurie Odell, John "Oppressed" Preston, Jane Ramsey, Diane Rapaport, James Ratner, Lani Ravin, Renault Robinson, Susan Rosenblum, Suzie Ruff, Paul Siegel, Susan Solovy, Justice Stamps, Tara Stamps, John Taylor, Dorothy Tillman, Harriet Trop, Lewis Watts, John Yolich, and Karen Zaccor. Thanks to Jim and Reem Dababneh at whose restaurant so many of these stories were written, Evan Reifman, who helped with some early editing, and of course the staff and editors at Haymarket: Julie Fain, Eric Kerl, Nisha Bolsey, Ashley Smith, Rachel Cohen, and editor extraordinaire Sam Smith.

To my ever-supportive family as well, a big thank you: my brother Ed (himself a published author and publisher) and his wife, Rosemary

Shiller; my brothers Larry Shiller and Albert Brutko; and my nieces and nephews David, Jenny, Lisa, Sophia, Olivia, and Johnny—all with the last name "Shiller." My dad's phonetic spelling of the name at Ellis Island will have a long legacy. My son Brendan is an integral part of this story and has been an integral part of my process creating this manuscript. He is my heart, and I have dedicated this book to him. With his wife and partner Brenda, they have raised three offspring, each extraordinary in their own right: Britteney, Justice, and Ricky. Britteney, this immediate family's first published author, has been a true inspiration and cheerleader.

There are so many people who contributed to the stories in this book that it is impossible to mention them all, let alone give them credit for their impact and contributions. Besides all the historical figures, this includes so many from Uptown, members of the Intercommunal Survival Committee, numerous activists in the many coalitions included and not included in the scope of this book, and a long list of my staff during my twenty-four-year stint as alderman. I apologize in advance to those not included—it is not for a lack of appreciation.

More than fifty people worked on my aldermanic staff. Their acknowledgment in this book was determined by the stories I chose to include, not by their value or my appreciation for their work. The same goes for the hundreds of volunteers who worked on my multiple election campaigns.

My primary involvement since leaving the city council (where this book ends) has been to help develop and manage the building that has become known as the Westside Center for Justice. Initially housing the two laws firms that were part of the ownership (Brendan, his partner April Preyar, and Anthony Burch), it became the home to other attorneys with a social justice bent and a growing number of nonprofits engaged in the pursuit of justice by providing access to legal assistance while challenging some of the most pernicious policies of the system.

In 2018, marking the fiftieth anniversary of the founding of the Illinois Chapter of the Black Panther Party, members Stan McKinney, Henry Nesbitt, John Preston, Billy "Che" Brooks, Harold Bell, Billy Dunbar, and Diana Nesbitt spearheaded a photo exhibit at the Westside Center for Justice. It was my honor to give them full access to the archives of *Keep Strong* magazine and *All Chicago City News* (in effect the archives of the Intercommunal Survival Committee, of which I somehow became the minder). It quickly became a source of history realized through hundreds of tours with high school and college students, led primarily by Stan, Henry, John, and Che (sometimes with the added voice of Jack Hart), and with the support of the nonprofit Westside Justice Center and the Crossroads Fund. Although these tours have been limited since the pandemic, the exhibit has been greatly expanded, largely through Henry's efforts.

The photos in this book are from the archives of the Keep Strong Publishing Company and Justice Graphics. While many were taken by members of the Intercommunal Survival Committee and a host of volunteers, we often received press releases from the city of Chicago that included unattributed photos. While I am unable to identify the photographers for all the photos we have included, I would like to acknowledge the Harold Washington Collection at the Harold Washington Library, Antonio Dickey, Michelle Agins, Marc Pokempner, Bob Black, John Gunn, Paul Sequeira, Pat Cummings, Kim Nash, James Ratner, and of course revolutionary artist Emory Douglas. Photographers and graphic artists create the images that can tell a thousand words. I apologize for any I have left out.

While we can't know for sure what the future will bring, through political education (knowing our past) and political action (in and out of the electoral arena), the sea will be created as often as necessary to ensure that the arc of justice expands its reach to its ultimate realization. Lest we forget: change does not come without friction, but justice is well worth the trouble.

INTRODUCTION

A LIFE OF STRUGGLE,
A FIGHT FOR JUSTICE

When I arrived in Chicago's Uptown neighborhood in 1972, it teemed with people. A port of entry for immigrants from everywhere, the neighborhood was characterized by unkempt and poorly maintained housing. Many of the original six-flats had their large apartments converted into multiple sleeping rooms with shared baths. The plumbing and electricity in most buildings had been untouched for generations. Electrical fires were common, as was salmonella poisoning from compromised water and sewer pipes. Lead from flaking paint flowed through the veins of children.

City planners wanted to tear down what they could. "What's the harm?" they asked. "The conditions are horrific." However, they never recommended replacing this dilapidated housing with decent and affordable units. While no one wanted to live in these "horrific" conditions, the truth was that in the absence of plans for replacement housing, the people living there had few choices. Any housing to which they could move would likely be in the same or worse condition.

Uptown is one of seventy-seven formally recognized neighborhoods in Chicago—a city of communities that are, for good and for bad, both segregated and distinctive, mostly built around commercial strips based on the local ethnic culture. The Uptown community is located right on the lakefront, a little more than halfway up the North Side. In the 1960s and '70s, it was surrounded by middle-class and upper-middle-class communities on all sides. There is more than one way to think of Uptown's geographical borders. Street-wise and officially, Uptown is bounded by Ashland Avenue on the west, Foster Street on the north, Lake Michigan on the east, and Irving Park Road on the south. But, like most Chicago communities in the 1960s, more practical geographic boundaries were defined by geographic barriers. St. Boniface Cemetery on Lawrence

Avenue separated the Asian part of Uptown to the north from the rest of Uptown, while Graceland Cemetery was the natural barrier that cut off the poorer part of Uptown from some of its more well-off residents to the south. In the 1970s, the elevated train that tracked the somewhat-diagonal Broadway was the barrier that determined most of the racial segregation, and therefore gang territory as well.

I had arrived that summer with plans to join the Intercommunal Survival Committee, a cadre of young white activists operating under the direction of the Black Panther Party. Numbering between twenty and twenty-five, about half of us were Jewish. We shared our paltry incomes, working 24/7 around the issues we held in common with other poor and working people—particularly people of color. We participated in weekly political education classes and agreed with W. E. B. Du Bois that "the problem of the twentieth century is the problem of the color line."[1] Acknowledging our white-skin privilege, we accepted the responsibility to win over the hearts and minds of those willing to get past their own sense of entitlement. These were not merely the expression of heady ideals or an outlet for youthful polemic: our efforts would ultimately result in the creation of a political power base in Uptown that would directly affect the direction of politics—and the city's future.

Some of us had been college students, but others were not. We were joined by single moms, high school dropouts, ex-offenders, and military veterans politicized by the Vietnam War. Some of us thought the revolution was imminent; many of us came to understand the prolonged nature of the path we were on. All of us were committed to transforming our world.

Following the model created by the Black Panther Party, we developed programs to assist in "survival pending revolution," based on a foundation of love and respect for the people. In Uptown, our programs served everyone who could benefit, with a focus on engaging white people who otherwise avoided contact with people of color. However, the change to which we dedicated our lives would not come swiftly: rather, it would happen only when demanded by too many to be ignored. The words of legendary abolitionist Frederick Douglass rang clear, "Power concedes nothing without a demand. It never did and it never will."

---

1   Still true in the twenty-first century, this statement was made by Du Bois in London in 1900 at the Pan-African Congress.

My mantra was to leave no stone unturned. Make no assumptions. Discard no one. We would move this mountain shovelful by shovelful. We would knock on every door, speak with everyone we encountered, shy away from nothing in our path. We were foot soldiers in a war against racism, anti-Semitism, and all forms of inequality and oppression. Every day, I reminded myself that it was only step by step that we would achieve the change to which we committed ourselves. This aim required sacrifice, courage, discipline, study, criticism/self-criticism, growth, and development. We had a specific role: to follow the leadership of the vanguard of the struggle for Black liberation and win over poor and working white people to our cause.

On Saturdays, we were each tasked with selling one hundred *Black Panther* papers[2] on street corners in Uptown and throughout the North Side. And we did. However, that was a higher bar for some of us to reach than it was for others. The paper was a key source of updates from the front lines of the day-to-day struggle to survive. During the week, we established home distribution routes that gave us an opportunity to talk to those subscribers while reaching out to new people on a weekly basis. Each week, we reserved time for Country Music Sundays—a gathering that combined music, food, and political education. Through all of these efforts ran a through line: our job was to confront racism. And to do so, we knew we had to challenge the assumptions that we had repeatedly seen lead to conflict and thwart unity.

The heart of Uptown was an ideal place for our political efforts. At that moment in time, this geographically compact community, home to some fifty thousand people, was probably the largest concentration of poor white people in an urban area—many of whom had moved there from the South. There were as many Native Americans here as on some reservations. Following the mass internment of Japanese Americans during World War II in California and Arizona, many came to Chicago via Uptown as they searched for new homes. After urban renewal forced Puerto Ricans out of Lincoln Park and the near–North Side community that would become the Carl Sandburg Village, a significant number of them moved to Lakeview and Uptown. Soon Uptown also became the

---

2   Officially, the *Black Panther Intercommunal News Service*. The papers cost 25 cents. We paid the Party for the papers we distributed and were each responsible to bring in the $25 for our papers at the end of the day.

port of entry for refugees from several war-torn African and Southeast Asian countries.

The oldest Black community, apart from Chicago's "Black Belt," was here as well, its origins reflecting the influence of Jim Crow in the postbellum North. The first Black person to live in Uptown was a chauffeur whose employer left him his home in his will. This would be the catalyst for a city restriction that read, "No Negro person can buy, own, or rent property in this district except on that block which is inhabited entirely by Negros." The district to which it referred was the Uptown community. The block was the 4600 block of Winthrop Avenue.[3]

While several of those original Black families still lived here when I first moved to Uptown, most had moved on. The Jones family was a mainstay, still living in the two-flat that housed them for half a century, as was Eddie Qualls, known as "Big Daddy" and for his barbeques at his single-family home. It would not be long, however, before Big Daddy moved to the HUD-mortgaged building at 4848 Winthrop, a couple of blocks north. Joanne Jones, a fifty-something mainstay of our organizing efforts, took care of her elderly mother. After her mother died Joanne remained outspoken, joining our fights against plans to displace Uptown residents until she herself succumbed to a host of health problems.

In the decade before I had come to Uptown, developers in Chicago had taken advantage of federal subsidies to erect high-rise buildings that were intended to serve low- and moderate-income households. Nearly four thousand of these high-rise units were built in or near Uptown—the largest concentration of such units in any community in the country. They attracted tenants from many Chicago communities, as well as immigrants and refugees from virtually every continent.

Most of the people then living in the heart of Uptown had the common experience of displacement. Some were forced from their homes for economic reasons; some were escaping war; some were from other Chicago communities. Some migrated from other states. Some were

---

3   In her book *Legends and Landmarks of Uptown*, journalist Jacki Lyden noted that in 1940, "[t]he Central Uptown Chicago Association spent $14,000 to get this restriction. To obtain a legal injunction, the association needed 90 percent of the neighborhood's property owners to sign a petition. It took several years to collect the necessary number of signatures, since many property owners lived outside the neighborhood."

refugees from other countries. All had been ripped from communities they had known as home and made new homes in Uptown.[4] This was now their home, and many were prepared to fight to keep it that way.

Even with the displacement of entire blocks designated for urban renewal, housing was dense. The most prominent housing was three-story apartments. These were initially built as stand-alone six-flats or courtway buildings, which were essentially six-flats attached to each other in a *u*-shaped configuration with multiple entrances. As veterans had returned from fighting in World War II twenty-five years earlier, Chicago faced a housing crisis. In Uptown, apartments were divided into smaller units, often with shared baths. Many six-flats became twelve- or fifteen-unit buildings. Those that remained untouched had three and four bedrooms and were coveted by the large families now living in Uptown. Hotels built during Uptown's heyday to service the 1920s theater scene were transformed into small studio apartments as likely to be rented to a family as to a single person. Fifty years later, their electrical wires were fraying, their elevators unsafe, their plumbing compromised.

The Chicago Democratic machine thrived in this environment. Precinct captains who were counted on to bring in votes on election day did whatever it took. Meals were promised. Cash was exchanged. Liquor flowed. Threats were made. Manipulation and coercion were common and the most pernicious. Some voters were threatened with loss of jobs or welfare and sometimes even eviction.

In the 1960s the state of Illinois closed all its mental health facilities, sending their residents back to their "home" communities. Many former patients ended up in Uptown and its collection of nursing homes. Some found shelter in myriad residential hotels that had been transformed into one-room apartments, while others simply wandered the streets, making them their home. These nursing homes (for both low-income seniors and low-income mentally ill people) and apartment buildings became the site of some of the most insidious and gross misconduct, in which owners or managers were payees for various forms of government income and held access to the money as a means of voter coercion.

---

4 It did not escape me that the conditions that had brought most to the States, to Chicago, and to Uptown could often be traced to one or another foreign or domestic US policy that had not served them well.

To keep them in line, precinct captains (or one of their minions) accompanied potential voters to vote. The election judges would then allow the machine worker to accompany the voter into the voting booth to watch and make sure they voted as they were told—usually for a straight Democratic ticket.

A few years before I had arrived in Chicago, Mayor Richard J. Daley's planning commissioner, Lew Hill, and his chairman of the City Colleges, Oscar Shabat, announced their intention to build a new City College in Uptown. The location they chose was entirely residential. It also included some of the densest blocks of poor people in the community. Initially, the two most affected square blocks were North Clifton and North Racine, and the blocks of West Sunnyside and West Wilson that bordered them. Six-flats and court-way buildings standing shoulder to shoulder filled these blocks to capacity. The Black community had spilled over from Winthrop to Clifton, while Racine was primarily white. Rooming houses adorned Wilson Avenue, housing mostly white and Native American single men and women. Despite superficial gestures toward compromise, ultimately the plan for the construction of the college meant thousands would be displaced with no hope of finding comparable housing they could afford. The powers that be rejected all suggestions for alternative sites.

By the time we filed a lawsuit in federal court in 1975 challenging the city's planning policies, development plans for the City College that would become Truman College, a middle school[5], and a health clinic run by the Chicago Board of Health were all completed, or soon would be. Each of these held a promise for educational opportunities and health benefits. Each had led to the displacement of thousands of families and collectively contributed to years of destabilization of the housing stock, and therefore all the people who had been relying on that housing—not to mention more than a decade of unchecked arson-for-profit schemes that had cost many lives. Named after one of the named plaintiffs, the lawsuit would become known as the Avery suit.

At the heart of our discontent was the sacrifice of home and stability that the community was being forced to bear while the city steadfastly

---

5   The middle school would become Arai Middle School. Later the young activists of my son's generation would take over that middle school, transform it into a high school, and rename it Uplift, making a school in their vision.

refused to provide replacement housing. Circa 1975, the Chicago Housing Authority built three 3-flats across the street from the college. When the lot was initially purchased for the college, circa 1968, Bud Salk was the broker for the sale. Bud had joined the Abraham Lincoln Brigade fighting against fascism in Spain three decades earlier before becoming a mortgage broker. Our paths crossed many times in the 1970s. On one of these occasions, he told me he put a clause in the sales contract requiring that the land be used for housing. This caveat was apparently missed by the City College's attorneys. This was to be the only replacement housing for all sixteen hundred units demolished for the first of two college buildings. And for the units lost to the second college building, the health clinic, and the middle school, there would be no replacement at all.

Two lawsuits—one filed in 1975 and another a little more than thirty years later, in 2009—provide bookends to forty years of struggle against displacement. In 1975 the Avery suit charged that the city engaged in a conspiracy with a private developer and the Department of Housing and Urban Development to destroy an economically and racially integrated community. The developer was Bill Thompson, the mayor's son-in-law. Purchasing existing low-income housing from HUD, he proceeded to evict everyone who lived there. Black, white, Latino, and Native American, the tenants were the epitome of Chicago's working poor.

A federal judge accepted racial discrimination as a cause of action and ruled the Avery suit could continue. He threw out our allegation of economic discrimination as there was no requirement of economic fairness in the US Constitution. It would be nearly two decades before settlements with each of the defendants would be realized.

The 2009 lawsuit, brought by a group calling itself "Fix Wilson Yard," argued that the city (they meant me) was engaged in a conspiracy with a local developer to *maintain* an integrated community. They were political opponents vehemently against my efforts to preserve and create housing for poor and working families. Their argument before the court was a typical NIMBY ("not in my backyard") response, charging that the addition of 178 units of housing affordable to people living up to 60 percent of the metropolitan area median income (about half the people living in Chicago at the time) would have a negative impact on the

Uptown community. Arguing they feared their property values would decline, their lawyer's arguments echoed the racially charged fearmongering that was a staple of the political debate in Uptown. Meanwhile, many of the proponents of the housing at Wilson Yard considered these 178 units a pittance in the face of the thousands that were lost to urban renewal. The "Fix Wilson Yard" lawsuit was unceremoniously dismissed.

◊ ◊ ◊

The chapters that follow tell my story through the lens of my experience in Uptown and in Chicago's city council where I served from 1987 to 2011. It is a story about the resegregation of one of Chicago's only racially and economically diverse communities. It is the Chicago story of the multiracial class resistance to the Nixon- and Reagan-inspired retrenchment of the gains of the civil rights movement that led to the election of Harold Washington as mayor of Chicago in 1983—and ultimately, some say, to the election of Barack Obama as president. It is the story of the impact of the changing federal policy on taxation and public services (Social Security, Medicare, welfare, housing, transit, education) as it played out in Chicago.

At the same time, this book is a story about my growth and development as I tried to be a soldier in the class and race struggles the United States faced in the second half of the twentieth century and the beginning of the twenty-first. It would be impossible to fully compartmentalize my personal struggles, pains, and growths from my participation in the larger issues and struggles of the years through which I lived and the people with whom I joined in this larger world of ours.

PART I

BIRTH AND GROWTH IN THE CRUCIBLE

1.

BEWARE OF FASCISM

On a gray day in March 1954, my father kept me home from school. On most school days, he would have been at work, and my parents rarely allowed me to miss school. In my first-grade classroom, I would have been at my desk, most likely daydreaming. Instead, I was sitting on the floor of my dad's study that doubled as our family's TV room. The weather was beginning to turn. It was cold outside, but our Long Island house was heated through the floor, so I felt warm and comfortable.

I knew that whatever was happening on TV was important to my dad. He was a chemist, and when he worked at home he would sit at his desk in a big blue armchair, writing formulas (none of which I ever understood) on a desk covered with matzo crumbs and stained from weak black coffee. I was rarely permitted in this room when my dad was home, so I knew something special was happening.

This was the early 1950s, and the black-and-white TV was one of those big brown boxes that sat on the floor. Like most middle-class families in those days, we had only one TV in the house. Together, we watched the first day of the Army–McCarthy hearings before the House Un-American Activities Committee.

My father told me he knew I might not understand, I might be bored, I might not even remember much of it. "Except," he said, "this is an important event that is happening, and when you get older, remember it. Then find out about it." While much of the country was enthralled by the apparent exposure of communists, from my family's point of view (and countless others), those hearings were about fascism. "You need to know about fascism and how to recognize it," he told me, adding, "and when you see it, you must fight against it."

I was six years old. I didn't know yet that hundreds had already been the target of this Joe McCarthy–inspired (and mostly conjured) fear campaign. Nor did I know that some of the most iconic actors, writers, and artists of the time had become targets. Some had testified before the subcommittee. Others had refused. Some had been blacklisted and lost their jobs, creating waves of fear and intimidation in their wake. These hearings were designed to do just that.[1] Now, Senator McCarthy was claiming the Army too was rife with communists who had to be exposed.

It was an experience I would remember ten years later when the documentary film *Point of Order* came out, which brought the disturbing scenes from these hearings into public view. I made sure to see it.[2] It was not, however, until my last visit with my father, nineteen years after that day in his study, that I learned our family secret that had haunted my early childhood and made these hearings so personal for him.

. . . .

2.

MY IMMIGRANT PARENTS

Both my parents immigrated to the United States in 1921.

The previous year, the Nineteenth Amendment had passed, giving women the right to vote. Meanwhile the Ku Klux Klan, experiencing an insurgence and spreading into the north, was dramatically enlarging its membership. In the previous two decades, fourteen million immigrants

---

1   For the four years prior to these hearings, Joe McCarthy, a senator from Wisconsin, traveled the country insisting communists (and by direct implication Russian spies) were everywhere—often holding up blank sheets of paper upon which he claimed were long lists of communists. Congressional hearings were held where people with some celebrity and or government jobs were identified as having connections to leftist organizations or activities. Threatened with contempt and incarceration if they refused, they were required to name names of others they knew or suspected to be communists. People lost their jobs, their livelihoods, and sometimes their liberty and even their lives. The only proof required was that somebody had said your name.

2   Coincidentally, I was reading excerpts from the book *Point of Order*, a summary of the Army-McCarthy hearings, days before watching the Donald Trump impeachment hearings before the Congressional Committee on Intelligence in November 2019. The tactics of diversion were hauntingly familiar.

had entered the United States, welcomed as cheap labor.[3] Labor conditions were intolerable, and income inequality reigned.[4] Workers began to resist, resulting in turmoil.

With the emergence of the Communist Party and an insurgence of strikes and successful union organizing after the war, the political reaction against immigrants and communists was swift. Congress was on the verge of changing the rules.[5]

My father was born in Latvia in 1908.[6] He came from Liepāja, formerly Lebov, Latvia's second-largest city, a major seaport located on the east coast of the Baltic Sea, 150 miles southwest of Latvia's capital city of Riga. My grandfather was a tailor who traveled to Russia to purchase textiles. Shortly before Latvia was occupied by German troops in the early years of World War I, he went to St. Petersburg. While he was there, the German army invaded Latvia, taking over most of the country. My grandfather was unable to return to Liepāja until the war ended, leaving my seven-year-old father to support his mother and three siblings by selling trinkets from his father's tailor shop on the streets of Liepāja.

Shortly after the war ended and my grandfather returned home, the family received an offer of passage for one to America from a cousin living in the United States. Partly as a reward, partly out of concern that

---

3   Howard Zinn, *A People's History of the United States*, rev. ed. (New York: HarperCollins, 1999).

4   "One tenth of 1 percent of the families at the top received as much income as 42 percent of the families at the bottom, according to a report of the Brookings Institution. Every year in the 1920s, about 25,000 workers were killed on the job and 100,000 permanently disabled. Two million people in New York City lived in tenements condemned as firetraps." Zinn, *A People's History*, 382–83.

5   The law established quotas that "favored Anglo-Saxons, kept out black and yellow people, limited severely the coming of Latins, Slavs, Jews. No African country could send more than 100 people; 100 was the limit for China, for Bulgaria, for Palestine; 34,007 could come from England or Northern Ireland, but only 3,845 from Italy; 51,277 from Germany, but only 124 from Lithuania; 28,567 from the Irish Free State, but only 2248 from Russia." Zinn, *A People's History*, 382.

6   The Republic of Latvia was established in 1918. Prior to that it was ruled by the German Empire. In 1940, at the outset of World War II, it was incorporated into the Soviet Union before being occupied by Nazi Germany in 1941. It became part of the Soviet Union again and remained so until 1991.

the burden of taking care of the family would continue to fall unfairly on my dad, the family decided to send him—hoping for a brighter future for their eldest son. Having just turned twelve, he had to pass for sixteen. The passage was fourteen days on the SS *Hudson*, which landed at Ellis Island in New York on November 19, 1921.

Upon his departure from Latvia, my dad's name was Moiszei Schumazer. When he left Ellis Island, he was Morris Shiller. According to the SS *Hudson*'s manifest, he was one of seven hundred passengers who crossed the ocean in third class. The island was the port of entry for more than half of the immigrants entering the United States between 1892 and 1924. It was here that those hoping to enter the country were inspected for diseases, screened for work history and prospects, sometimes quarantined, and then passed for entry or returned home. As such, it was a place of both hope and fear. Corralled like cattle, thousands of expectant immigrants passed through checkpoint after checkpoint hoping to make it through. Accompanying long waits and pushing and shoving was a constant cacophony of voices, in multiple languages, conjuring images of the Tower of Babel. If passengers were fortunate enough to have crossed the ocean in first or second class, their papers were checked onboard the ship, allowing them to avoid the bleak immigration process on Ellis Island.

My father's sister Rosa and her son Kirov were the only members of his family to have survived the Holocaust. As the Nazi army approached in June 1941, her husband, who was in the Russian army, had put them on the last train out of Latvia toward the Ural Mountains. Their remaining family members had perished, along with an estimated ninety thousand other Latvian Jews, slaughtered by their Nazi occupiers while fellow Latvians, for the most part, watched or ignored the mass killings. Kirov's father had died in combat during the battle for Latvia, a few days after putting his wife and son on the train. They returned after the war, joining the one thousand Jews who had also survived.

In 1959 Rosa hired a private detective to find my father. He was successful, and a letter-writing communication between our families began. Because Latvia was still behind the Iron Curtain, writing was their only means of communication.

More than eighty years after my dad crossed the Atlantic, in March 2002, I sat in the lobby of a hotel in the historic section of Riga with my brother Ed and my first cousin Kirov. As Ed, Kirov, and I caught up with each other, I asked why his parents had sent my dad to the United States. Kirov (from his mom's perspective) and Ed (from my dad's perspective) responded at the same time. Ed: "As a punishment." Kirov: "As a reward."

I burst into tears. Hearing the conflict between these opposing views dovetailed with my own sense of betrayal and abandonment when, as a teenager, I had been sent away to school "for my own good." I know the pain my dad felt from being sent, at age twelve, to the United States. Indeed, I feel it deeply.

◊ ◊ ◊

My mother was born into a Jewish community in a place called Baranovichi, in what is now Belarus. Her mother, Rae, was a dentist, and her father, Hyman, a Talmudic scholar.

My mother's birth corresponded to the beginning of World War I, a time when the sound of planes meant bombs overhead. The constant change of occupying armies—one day Russian, the next German, and then Polish—was dizzying and anxiety-provoking. The presence of soldiers meant hostility and loss of life or property.

For a short while during the war, Baranovichi was occupied by the German army. Following the conclusion of World War I, borders were redrawn, and the town fell within Poland. When my mother was born in 1914, it was with a Russian birth certificate. However, her sister Gertrude, born in 1916, had a German birth certificate, and her sister Miriam, born in 1918, had a Polish one. I grew up with the understanding that my mother's family was from Poland but never considered to be Polish citizens. My family were Jews without a country.

Motivated by the insecurity of war and threats of anti-Semitic violence, my Grandpa Hyman felt that there was no future for Jews in Europe. He wanted to emigrate. Rae, however, was not so sure. They lived in a community they knew well, with generations of history. As the only dentist, she was highly respected in the community, and even with all the threats, she felt she had a good life. In spite of her reservations, and encouraged by her sister who had already emigrated, she agreed to go. Like my father, my mother and her family arrived at Ellis Island in 1921. She was six and a half.

Once in America, with the fear of violence behind them, they moved to the Bronx, where they lived in close quarters in a succession of rat- and roach-infested tenement apartments. Finding herself faced with one barrier after another that prevented Grandma Rae from legally practicing dentistry, according to my mom, she "despaired and became bitter about their decision to have come in the first place." However, after learning of the death of her sister Rifka, who chose to emigrate to Germany instead of the states, Grandma Rae later wrote in a memoir that had they not come, they "would have surely perished in Hitler's gas chamber with the rest of the millions of Jewish men, women, and children."

As the eldest child, my mother had responsibility for her four siblings. Anxious to be on her own, she jumped at the chance to continue her education after high school. In spite of her mother having achieved a dental degree in tsarist Russia, my mother was convinced a girl could not become a doctor, instead setting her sights on becoming a nurse. She often told me about her grueling and intense days and nights in training, filled with long hours and little sleep. She glowed with energy and excitement whenever she spoke of this experience. I assumed she worked in a public hospital serving the poor, as her deep passion for nursing often accompanied an equally passionate expression of concern for the underdog.

● ● ●

In 1936, my mother had just graduated from nursing school when she met my dad. By now, they were both US citizens.[7] They married six months later.

My favorite photo of my parents is of them sitting at a bar in New York City during the Depression, circa 1936. She would have been twenty-two, and he would have been twenty-eight, give or take. In a pose reminiscent of Clark Gable (or so I thought), handsome with a well-groomed mustache, he sports a fedora, with a glimmer of a smile gracing his face. Beside him, my mom is stylishly outfitted with a veiled hat and fur-collared coat, dainty earrings, and an angelic expression on her face. She must have saved up a long time for that outfit.

---

7   My mother's citizenship application from 1925 listed her race as "Caucasian." My father's citizenship was awarded in 1933 with "Hebrew" as his race.

My parents circa 1936.

In fact, my father was of average height, five foot eight with broad shoulders and barrel chested. His skin was fair, his eyes brown, and his black hair never turned gray. He always had a mustache—surely one of the reasons he was able to pass as sixteen when he made the Atlantic crossing by himself.

My mother was petite, standing five feet for most of her adult life, though she would lose several inches by her death at the age of ninety-six. Her eyes were green and deep set, complemented by brown hair and smooth, olive-toned skin. She was as likely to be mistaken as being from India as she was to be identified as Jewish. She was an attractive woman with a deep sadness radiating from her eyes.

By the time the Second World War broke out in Europe, it became known within the New York Jewish community that Jews were being rounded up and disappeared. Despite this common knowledge in the Jewish community, the mass executions in Europe were initially disputed and denied by the United States government and others. Still feeling the hurt of his childhood and faced with the possibility of never seeing his family again, my dad was deeply affected.

After the United States entered the war, my dad tried to enlist, only to be rejected because his legal age made him too old for the armed forces. Looking for work as a chemist, he rejected offers from the large chemical companies such as DuPont and Dow—all of whom he believed had ties to Nazi Germany—and opted to set up his own business. Not coincidentally, he found it hard to work for anyone else, a character trait that he inflicted upon his children and their children.

Founded in 1941, M. Shiller Corp. manufactured paints, inks, and lacquers for textiles. My father spent his days running a factory and his nights doodling away at new formulas to be tried and tested for any number of products. For instance, he created the adhesive for flock that would be the forerunner of fake suede-like fur and the stuff of which Swiss-dots fabric is made.[8]

My mother lived with a deep fear of authority—likely a vestige from her childhood in Baranovichi. She both accepted and rebelled against these feelings of insecurity. Craving education, she read always and, whenever she could, returned to school. She often worked part time, nursing at one hospital or another. Every chance she got, she took college courses, eventually receiving a master's degree in education. She then became a school health education teacher and nurse, working first for the Catholic Archdiocese of New York and then the Roslyn Public Schools. As a woman who never talked about sex at home (at least with me), it always amused me that she developed the sex education curriculum for the Archdiocese.

My parents were communists in the 1930s and '40s. The primary evidence of this, besides my mother's many stories of organizing for better work conditions when she was a nurse during the Depression, was their art, books, and music. Through these things, I learned of the many "coffees" they (or, at least, my mother) attended where the likes of Paul Robeson, Diego Rivera, Howard Fast, and Alice Neel came to sell their art while talking politics. According to family lore, my father (who could be very argumentative and mercurial) was kicked out of their cell. My mother simply stopped participating.

Immediately after World War II, the American public's war weariness led to broad support for demobilization and disarmament. The left

---

8 Swiss-dots fabric was popular in the 1950s, when it was used in curtains and some clothing.

embraced this sentiment. Following the hardships of the Great Depression and the successful fight against fascism, the left was influential in the United States. Some were communists, some socialists, and many others simply leftists who supported humanist ideals.

When the Soviet Union and the United States divided up Germany at the war's end, they declared the economic and political rivalries that laid the foundations of the Berlin Wall. In 1949 Chinese communist forces successfully ousted Chiang Kai-shek's government. Concurrently, anti-imperialist movements grew throughout the world. (Notable among these was the small country of Vietnam.) For the most part, these were locally inspired, not Russian-directed. However, they threatened American business interests and therefore required an American military response. The declaration of the Korean War a year later marked a crossroads in the conflict between demobilization and disarmament on one hand, and militarization and the sustenance of an arms economy on the other. In choosing militarism over demobilization, the Truman administration contributed to an atmosphere of fear and hysteria about Communism. The Cold War had begun.

At this time, anti-Communism was sufficiently entrenched to break any remaining loyalties between the traditional liberals and the left. President Truman, with his liberal allies in Congress, led the way with executive orders on loyalty oaths, Justice Department prosecutions, and anti-Communist legislation: one was either 100 percent behind a capitalist economy or clearly under the influence of Russia. The stage was set for the next phase of anti-Communist repression, spearheaded by Senator McCarthy.

Though by the fall of 1950 my parents were no longer active in any organized political activity, they were in for a scare—the incident that would become our family secret. An unexpected knock on a fall day turned to fear and confusion when FBI agents visited our apartment in connection with charges against Julius and Ethel Rosenberg of sharing high-level US military secrets with the Soviet Union.[9]

---

9   Julius Rosenberg was charged with sharing atomic bomb secrets with the Russians in July 1950. A month later, so was his wife Ethel. Testimony against them came primarily from Ethel's brother, a confessed spy. They were found guilty in February 1951, leading to their execution on June 19, 1953, but not before a great hue and cry against it. Nevertheless, an

The FBI asked about my dad's relationship with a chemical engineer named Abraham Brothman who was under indictment for espionage and indirectly connected to the now-infamous Rosenbergs. Based on the testimony of Harry Gold—an admitted spy who was also giving evidence against the Rosenbergs—Brothman was accused of transmitting information to the Soviet Union in the early 1940s. He was convicted in November 1950 on charges of conspiracy to obstruct justice and obstruction of justice.

The factory my father operated in 1941 had a small lab. Very cluttered, it contained his worktable, shelves containing chemicals used in the production of the paints, inks, and lacquers his company produced, and a sole piece of equipment: a miniature hand-operated press used to test his new adhesive formulas. It was six years since my father had seen Brothman, whom he knew as a fellow chemist and who, for a three-month period in 1944, had made an agreement with my father to use his lab.

Following the FBI visit, my father suffered a heart attack that nearly killed him. Although no longer affiliated with the Communist Party, he continued to keep up to date with current events by reading all the daily newspapers, including the *Daily Worker*.

My mother reacted by removing virtually all their "political" books from our apartment, leaving behind *Freedom Road* by Howard Fast, which became the first chapter book I read. Fast's description of the betrayal of northern politicians and financiers during Reconstruction after the Civil War was haunting and stayed with me. The inhuman impact of slavery, and white supremacist reaction to ending it, resonated with my family's historic experience with anti-Semitism and the Holocaust.

The FBI stopped their visits after my father's heart attack, but a shadow of fear emanating from their visit became part of my family's DNA.[10]

All of this had a chilling effect on my two older brothers, who found it difficult to navigate what was safe conversation with their friends, classmates, and casual acquaintances in an environment that was becoming increasingly hostile toward anyone with a connection, past or

---

international campaign of prestigious personalities and millions of ordinary people did not stop, or even delay, their execution.

10 After acquiring my father's FBI files, I discovered that the FBI had received a letter suggesting he was a communist and should be investigated.

present, to the Communist Party. At the same time, it passed over my head. Only later would I learn from my brother Ed of their fears and tribulations.

When we moved to Long Island in 1952, I was four. Oblivious to the problems of the world, I was happy to have a backyard and streets I could ride on with my supersized tricycle.

Dinner as a family was a ritual we rarely missed. Personal tensions and political discussions ruled. Memories of the Holocaust intermingled with paranoia about McCarthyism. Interest in the fledgling civil rights movement merged with my parents' frustrations with anti-Semitism—especially in my father's business activities. However, if my brothers were home and if it was baseball season, sports took a front seat.

Huge fans of the Brooklyn Dodgers, we lived in Brooklyn when I was born, not quite a mile from Ebbets Field. My brothers and father listened to the radio and later watched every game on TV, when they did not go in person. To us, the Dodgers represented regular working people, and their first baseman, Jackie Robinson, was a hero for breaking the color line, which he did just months before my birth. The Yankees—one of two other New York City teams—represented the elite, the moneyed interests, and the status quo. We hated the Yankees. When the Dodgers moved to California in 1958, it broke our hearts.

My parents were American leftists. They hated fascism, believed in socialist principles, and saw the ideal of democracy through that lens. To them racism was equivalent to anti-Semitism, and they detested them both—although not equally. They also argued incessantly, and as time passed their political debates became surrogate arguments reflecting their increasing disaffection toward each other.

3.

CHILDHOOD TRAUMA, ADOLESCENCE, FAMILY SECRETS

During his freshman year in high school, my oldest brother, Bob, was in a head-on car collision. Riding shotgun, he miraculously survived, although, several operations later, he was left with a long, jagged scar running down the right side of his face, a great deal of pain, a lifelong addiction to heroin, and a diagnosis of manic depression.

My parents sent him and my second-oldest brother, Ed, to a boarding school in Vermont shortly thereafter. I have no idea how they found the school, but my guess is they were attracted by its reputation as avant-garde and experimental. While Ed flourished in the Woodstock Country School environment, Bob lasted all of three months.

A few years later, Bob had a near-fatal heroin overdose. Afterward, my mother reached out to Jack Royce, a Manhattan psychiatrist, who agreed to work with him—but only if he could treat the entire family. He would see both of my parents, my brother Ed whenever he was home from school, and even my brother Larry, who was six or seven at the time.

Although he had sessions with all of us (individually and as a family unit), Jack's focus was always Bob. In fact, he became the most influential decision maker for our family for the next seven-plus years, and my mother never finalized a decision until she ran it by Jack. My dad appeared to go along quietly, but he never seemed happy about it. In retrospect, I don't think Jack liked women very much. In my joint visits with my mother, he was dismissive of her perspective. And in all my sessions, he was disdainful of any independent thought I had. In 1965, during my Christmas break from college, I would discover that Jack Royce had been spying on me using his nephew who went to the same college. I never went back to see him again.

I'm pretty sure Jack was aware of Bob's sexual abuse of me. This was something I never talked about to anyone—at least not until I was in my forties. The abuse had started when I was nine, shortly after his car accident. After that, I had a lot of difficulty with food. Sunny-side-up eggs had been a favorite for breakfast. I could no longer stand eating them. The loose white part of the eggs reminded me of semen and made me feel sick. I couldn't explain why I no longer wanted sunny-side-up eggs—which seemed to anger my mom. She suspected I was keeping a secret. And I was. Bob had told me not to tell anyone about his abuse (not what he called it), and I complied. I was sufficiently scared and felt an inexplicable shame. I had been convinced that I would be at fault if I uttered a word, but it was never far from my mind.

Most days, I got sick a couple of hours after breakfast, and after lunch. A year later, when I started attending Hebrew school every day after public school, I had trouble staying awake and complained of stomach aches. My mom insisted there was nothing wrong and it was all psychosomatic.[11] I just wanted to take a nap.

In the spring of 1962, I was an adolescent navigating a growing interest in boys and new friendships with a growing group of girlfriends. More often than I could manage, Bob interfered. My mother—wittingly or not—often facilitated him. It was very confusing. No doubt I acted out, and after being caught shoplifting a 45 RPM record of Richie Valens version of "Donna," my mother informed me that I was going to Woodstock in the fall. I was not happy about this.

My mom made it clear that I was being sent away for my own good. That it was because I was acting like a delinquent was implied. But a part of me was sure that they were sending me away to protect me from Bob. It would be forty years before I confirmed this, and questioned why sending him away was not an option.

Until I went away to school, I lived with my parents and three brothers. This was the 1950s and '60s. In spite of the abuse (or maybe because of it), I felt close to my older brothers. Ed was away at school from the time I was nine, but he loomed large in his absence.

All the males in our family were infected by the chauvinism of the times—especially with regards to accepted practices of objectifying women. My brothers regularly talked openly in my presence of their sexual exploits, often with denigrating references to any girl or woman who refused or ignored their advances. On rare occasions, my father joined in.

---

11 Years later I was diagnosed as having had an ulcer at that time.

As a teenager, Bob took me to see sexually explicit films, from *Lolita* to pornographic movies in Greenwich Village, while he railed against a sexually repressed society and for the legalization of drugs.

◊ ◊ ◊

The Woodstock Country School was founded in 1945 by David Bailey and Ken Webb. Ken came from a Quaker background, while David brought an ideal that was aspirational and dynamic, steeped in a strong sense of community. Three years later, Ken moved on and David remained as headmaster and a personality larger than life itself.

After a fire destroyed the main classroom building in 1954, the school was moved to a four-hundred-acre property in South Woodstock, Vermont. The school became relatively well known. Considered among the best alternative, coeducational boarding schools, it had a challenging curriculum and good college acceptance rate.[12] It was characteristically small, intimate, and personal, with a student body that hovered around one hundred. Most of the maintenance was done by students. Everyone was assigned daily jobs: washing dishes, serving food, sweeping and mopping floors—whatever.

My beginning at Woodstock was inauspicious. I was assigned to a girls' dorm, in one of three bedrooms on the second floor of a small farmhouse. I had two roommates. The dorm master, Larry Roberts, lived on the first floor with his family. Larry had a soft step and would often come upstairs without notice, catching us unaware and in varying degrees of dress.

My parents sent my brothers to boarding school in part because there was no public school in Roslyn Heights. By the time I was ready for seventh grade, however, a new junior/senior high school was built and operating, and I enrolled, expecting to continue the rest of my secondary education there. In ninth grade, I took algebra and was in an experimental science program that switched up the traditional order in which the curriculum was taught. I also took biology that year and looked forward to taking chemistry the following year. That expectation did not change when I arrived at Woodstock as a sophomore.

---

12 For more on the school, see William Boardman, *Woodstock Country School: A History of Institutional Denial* (Toronto: Yorkland Publishing, 2016).

Larry was the chemistry and algebra teacher that year. He refused to let me take his chemistry course. "It's not for sophomores," he told me. "Furthermore, you will have to take algebra." He didn't care that I had already taken it my freshman year. I was furious.

In the fall it was tradition to collect apples, put them through a press (worms and all), and voila: we would have cider for days. Seeing an opportunity to go a step further and turn the cider hard, I snuck into the chemistry lab collecting everything I would need for a still. My roommates and I set the still up in our closet and carefully tended our project until the night before Thanksgiving break when we threw a party, enjoying the fruits of our labor. Before leaving for the long weekend we dismantled the still, leaving all the components in full view at the bottom of the stairs.

While home for Thanksgiving break, I had a run-in with Bob. My mom was out running errands with Larry. Ed, home for the holiday, was out and about with friends. My dad was on the first floor in his study. I was upstairs, on my bed in my room, when Bob came in and got on top of me. He started to pull my pants down, and I started screaming. My dad came running upstairs and pulled him off me, throwing him out of the room. We never spoke of this incident, and I have no idea if he told my mother. I did not. But in my experience, this was the first and only time anyone protected me.

My relationship with Bob was complicated. He was manipulative and hurtful, and I both feared and loved him. He and my mother had an unusually close bond, while he and my father engaged in a volatile and antagonistic life dance.

At Woodstock music, art, and drama were taken seriously; in fact, the entire second floor of the main building was a huge arts loft and a theater. When Mary Hull, a friend and classmate, introduced me to weaving, I was hooked. I often sewed my own clothes. Also, I would pick up tans of leather when I was in New York to make sandals and purses. I began getting requests from my classmates. I would sew any-thing—as long as there were no sleeves involved. Mary and I wanted to go to Europe after our senior year, and we earned enough money making clothing and bags to do so.

I often felt out of place at Woodstock. While the school was con-sidered experimental for its time, it was nevertheless a prep school with mostly white Anglo-Saxon students and teachers. Up until this point in my life, my family had lived and socialized in entirely Jewish communities. Here, however, there were only a handful of Jewish students, even fewer Black students, and no Latinos that I can recall. I had a strong Long Island accent and received a lot of teasing about it. Tuition was significant. My father had one of his economic downturns while I was there, meaning my parents could no longer afford the tuition. However, I was led to believe I got a de facto scholarship.

In spite of its shortcomings, Woodstock was where I got the confidence to believe in myself, value knowledge in the service of change, and to believe that anything was possible. But none of this came easily. The headmaster's wife, Peggy Bailey, was born in South Africa. A slightly built woman, she usually wore a scowl of disapproval, rarely interacted with students outside of her classroom, and taught a notoriously difficult English class, which every senior had to pass to graduate. I was terrified of her, especially after the end of my sophomore year when she sent a letter to my parents (as my "advisor") telling them that I was "not college material." I was convinced I would not make the cut.

My junior-year English teacher, Peter Sauer, changed all that for me. He was young—just a few years older than me—and served as master for the boys' farmhouse dorm, where he lived with his wife and two children. When I met him, I thought I was a terrible student: I was insecure and had a great deal of difficulty expressing myself. With a great deal of patience and an attitude that clearly assumed I could do anything put in front of me, he taught me to have confidence in my abilities.

My time at Woodstock (1962–65) occurred during a series of violent events domestically and abroad. The Cuban Missile Crisis made nuclear war appear imminent; the war in Vietnam intensified; four girls were killed in a Ku Klux Klan bombing of the Sixteenth Street Baptist Church in Alabama; John F. Kennedy was assassinated; three civil rights workers, engaged in voter registration, were abducted and burned to death in Mississippi by a KKK mob during Freedom Summer; Malcolm X was assassinated as he spoke in Harlem.

In 1961, the Student Nonviolent Coordinating Committee, under the leadership of Stokely Carmichael, organized sit-ins after diplomats from newly independent African countries were denied service in the many roadside restaurants in Maryland and elsewhere. Now a student in Baltimore, Ed joined them. He would become involved in sit-ins at lunch counters and in the early days of Students for a Democratic Society.[13] During our vacations from school he would regale me with stories of these experiences.

At Woodstock, I was classmates with children of civil rights movement activists—a proximity that made me painfully aware of the dangers and necessity of the struggle raging across the country, bringing me into new worlds I would not have otherwise experienced. I attended Pete Seeger's concerts with my roommate and his daughter Mika (who often scoffed at the necessity to be there). More than anything, I was enamored of her ability to pick up her flute and make haunting music. I read the *I. F. Stone's Weekly* report, which my history teacher gave me. I hung on every word of conversations generated by the *Monthly Review* magazine (published by the father of a classmate). With another roommate, Sheila, on a visit with her mom to a shantytown in New Jersey serving mostly Black migrant workers, it was apparent that poverty and racial injustice was not just a problem south of the Mason-Dixon Line.

Emulating the participation of some of my schoolmates, I begged my parents to let me spend the August before my senior year in Tennessee at the Highlander Research and Education Center's youth camp. Founded by Myles Horton, the father of my classmate Thorsten, Highlander began as a "school in the South where teachers will work with both black and white students to address community problems"—a dangerous mission during Jim Crow. Troubled by threats of violence, including the Klan's expressed intent to "burn the center down" (which they actually achieved that July), my parents refused my pleadings. But the effort, and the accompanying disappointment, awakened a lifelong commitment to racial justice.

---

13 Considered to represent the "New Left" and focused on participatory democracy and support for the civil rights movement, SDS pivoted quickly to criticism of the war in Vietnam.

4.
MEETING THE MOB

My replacement for a summer month at Highlander was a summer commuting between Roslyn Heights and New York City, where I took classes at Columbia University. I was also enrolled in a weaving class at a studio in Greenwich Village and had a summer romance—losing my virginity and becoming pregnant in the fall (during breakup sex). In denial for the next couple months, and far away from my family—with whom I knew I would ultimately have to share my predicament—I avoided confirming my pregnancy until my winter vacation. I had just turned seventeen and was close to twelve weeks pregnant when I finally told my mother.

My mother assumed I would have an abortion and acted accordingly. After all, I was in no way prepared to care for another person, and she clearly had no intention to do so. My brother Bob and Jack Royce, the family shrink, were brought into the conversation. I have no recollection of my father participating in these discussions. I resented everyone acting like they knew what was best for me and that this was their decision to make for me. I quickly came to the conclusion that this was my body and my decision to make.

Nevertheless, how it was to be done remained in my mother's hands. This was 1964—almost a decade before *Roe v. Wade*. Abortions were illegal in most states, including New York. She told me she had found a doctor—whose name I can't remember, in a town whose name I don't recall—who was known to do safe abortions. I suspect she got his name from Jack. He had started performing abortions to save the lives of the women in the Pennsylvania coal town where he lived and worked. For these women life was tough and resources were short. Unable to cope with another mouth to feed, it was all too common for a woman to take a coat hanger or any number of chemical substances to try and abort herself. Sometimes they had sought help from inexperienced friends, sometimes unscrupulous strangers. Often, they had been desperate enough to risk humiliation, pain, sterilization, and even death. It was the tragedy of such deaths that had led this doctor to offer safe abortions, illegally but in the spirit of "Do no harm."

I liked this aspect, as I had heard a lot of horror stories of women who had died, or never been the same, after an abortion in unsafe and dangerous circumstances. I wasn't so sure about the rest of it.

The New York City mob had become aware of the doctor's activities: abortions were just another opportunity for them to make money off so-called morality laws, much as prohibition had been a boon for organized illegal activity in the 1920s, and drugs, sex, and gambling would continue to be fertile ground for organized crime.[14]

The doctor was allowed to operate his practice with the mob's "protection" (apparently they had the political and financial ability to do so). However, in return he was required to provide abortions for women they brought him from the city. They handled the payment, schedule, and all arrangements related to these women.[15]

At the end of a four-hour drive, my mother pulled into an alley in the small southern-Pennsylvania town and told me to get out of the car. "Wait here. Someone will come get you. I'll see you when it's done," she said as she pulled away. I looked to my left and saw a large man with broad shoulders and a gruff exterior, wearing a dark overcoat and a scowl on his face as he lumbered toward me. There could not have been a more stereotypical version of a mob enforcer. I was terrified.

Fortunately, this turned out to be a very straightforward interaction. Silently, apart from a no-nonsense expression that served as my greeting, he brought me to a car and drove a few blocks where we entered a nondescript back door. I was brought down a dark, narrow hallway and unceremoniously handed off to a nurse who scurried me into an examining room. With gaunt white faces and ragged clothes, the handful of women and children waiting to be seen glanced my way, as if to say,

---

14 All of these activities are ones politicians decided the state should ban. Once illegal, these activities were pursued underground without the threat of supervision or healthy standards. In the name of morality, the misery of others became the source of new illicit economic activity. In such underground economies, the rules are blurred, and law enforcement can and does use a subjective lens to determine who is prosecuted, often meaning the most vulnerable become the target. In short, making vice illegal usually means making it illegal for poor people.

15 In 1970, three years before the *Roe v. Wade* decision, New York state made abortions legal, turning the state into a magnet for women looking for a safe ending to their unintended pregnancies.

"What are you doing here? How do you get to go before us?" My privilege did not escape me.

Once I was in the examining room, the atmosphere completely changed. No frenzy. No tension. In fact, the doctor had the best bedside manner of any doctor I have known in my lifetime. Lying on the examining table, my eyes immediately went to the ceiling, where they were met with a collection of cartoons that had me laughing out loud. He explained what was to happen, how long it would take, and what I should do in the next few days. He made sure I was ready before he proceeded.

My mother picked me up at a designated time. With a supply of antibiotics and instructions in case of complications, we left together through the front door. No mobster in sight.

· ·

5.

COLLEGE YEARS
INDEPENDENCE AND EPIPHANIES

When it was time to apply for college, I was interested in getting away from the East Coast (read: my family) and attending a school with tens of thousands of students (there had only been one hundred of us at Woodstock) that had a good history department. My only other requirement was that the application form be short and require no essay. Buffy, our resident music teacher, school treasurer, and full-time bohemian, helped me sort out my choices. She provided me with applications to the University of Michigan at Ann Arbor and the University of Wisconsin at Madison. I received my acceptance letter from Madison first. It was farther away, had thirty-six thousand students, and a renowned history department. I was good to go.

During the summer break after my first year at Madison, my father expressed concern that I wasn't more involved in anti-war activities. "Search out the organizations that are active on campus. Find one you like and do something!" he implored, adding, almost as an afterthought, "but don't get arrested." For once my mother agreed. Her warning, "Remember your studies, and don't get suspended or expelled" was not so much an afterthought.

My father's exhortations to fight fascism and to challenge the war in Vietnam always came along with a vision of a future just society where everyone had what they needed and contributed what they could. He called on me to share his vision. Still, he was clear it would be neither easy nor quick; rather, this was a calling to a lifetime of commitment and protracted struggle.

My brother Ed's civil rights organizing and activities with Students for a Democratic Society (SDS) served to give me additional encouragement. His travels through Europe as a reporter covering the democratic movements in Greece and Ireland intrigued me and engendered pride. At the same time, my brother Bob's oft-expressed ideal of "Live and let live" struck a chord and stayed with me. And my mother's many stories about her time as a nursing student and later as a union organizer at Lebanon Hospital in New York City always came along with a moral calling to pay attention to the needs of the underdog which stayed with me.

In Madison, during the 1966–67 school year, supporters of the Committee to End the War in Vietnam were producing a play to raise funds. Given my experience sewing my own creations while I was at Woodstock, I thought, "I can sew. I know about clothing. I could make costumes," and volunteered. It would be my entrée into organized anti-war activism. I loved working on the

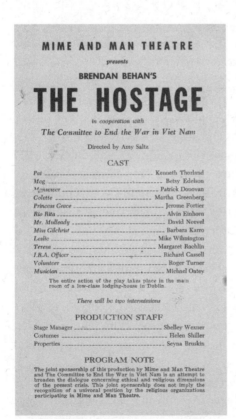

MIME AND MAN THEATRE

presents

BRENDAN BEHAN'S

THE HOSTAGE

in cooperation with

The Committee to End the War in Viet Nam

Directed by Amy Saltz

CAST

Pat	Kenneth Thorland
Meg	Betsy Edelson
Monsewer	Patrick Donovan
Colette	Martha Greenberg
Princess Grace	Jerome Fortier
Rio Rita	Alvin Einhorn
Mr. Mulleady	David Neevel
Miss Gilchrist	Barbara Karro
Leslie	Mike Wilmington
Teresa	Margaret Rachlin
I.R.A. Officer	Richard Cassell
Volunteer	Roger Turner
Musician	Michael Oatey

The entire action of the play takes place in the main room of a low-class lodging-house in Dublin.

There will be two intermissions

PRODUCTION STAFF

Stage Manager	Shelley Wexner
Costumes	Helen Shiller
Properties	Seyna Bruskin

PROGRAM NOTE

The joint sponsorship of this production by Mime and Man Theatre and The Committee to End the War in Viet Nam is an attempt to broaden the dialogue concerning ethical and religious dimensions of the present crisis. This joint sponsorship does not imply the recognition of a univocal position by the religious organizations participating in Mime and Man Theatre.

The playbill for the production of *The Hostage* that assuaged my father and was my first direct foray into activism.

play. The actors, crew, and director comprised a community I had been missing. Up until now, I had been opposed to the war but not intentionally involved; most of my interactions had been limited to debates and discussions. Until now, I had not been involved in any action upon which I could build a sense of purpose. This venture into the theater world was a different experience.

Born in Dublin in 1923, the play's author, Brendan Behan, was a volunteer in the Irish Republican Army at the age of sixteen, and an active participant for twenty-four years. He spent time in a youth detention prison in the United Kingdom and an adult prison in Ireland. Known for his huge drinking habit and flamboyant lifestyle, he died young, in March 1964.

His play, *The Hostage*, addressed moral dilemmas and the righteous indignation of a fight for independence and self-determination, of haves and have-nots—but mostly the fate of the have-nots. It was not far-fetched for us to be enamored of and to romanticize the Irish Republican Army's struggle for independence and self-determination from the United Kingdom. Indeed, the play forecast what would be a lifetime of internal debates and conversations, out of which the core of my plumb line[16] is intertwined, dovetailing seamlessly with the lesson my parents had taught me about the importance of walking in the shoes of others.

My own journey into adulthood was a cacophony of thoughts and experiences drawing me to social change as I grappled with competing notions of how to get there. The concrete experience I had during the year I spent with this acting community was the perfect transition into the person I was becoming.

By 1967 resistance to the war in Vietnam had taken a turn. Tens of thousands of people from all walks of life participated in peace marches, demanding an end to this unpopular war. Student teach-ins

---

16 I learned of this concept many years later from Nancy Jefferson, an amazing woman who led the Midwest Community Council on Chicago's West Side for decades. While serving coffee and cake at her dining room table in the aftermath of Harold Washington's death, Nancy told me: "Your house can't stand without its core, its plumb line. Everything is built around it and dependent on it. We all need a plumb line as well. It is the core of our essence of who we are—the place from where all our actions come, have value, and make sense. It is our core and our sense of being. It is what allows us to be accountable."

and demonstrations were in full force in universities across the country. For young men between eighteen and twenty-five, the draft defined their lives. Some with money and influence were able to escape it. Others found ways to resist it. Returning veterans came home disillusioned—some joining the anti-war movement and the Black liberation struggle. Others found themselves in poor physical and mental health without a support system, met upon their return by a community ambivalent about their service. Some brought with them stories of chemical weapons, including Agent Orange and napalm, wondering if their use by the American armed forces could be related to the elusive ailments many of them were suffering.

I understood that Vietnam was a small country on the other side of the world that had been fighting for its freedom from colonial domination for decades—successfully forcing the withdrawal of French colonial forces. While the US government incited fear of the spread of Communism as justification for the war, it seemed to me the actual reason for its involvement had more to do with a small group of business interests who hoped to get access to the country's oil and mineral deposits—not a good reason, in my view, for either Americans or Vietnamese to die.

I was not alone. The same year, a coalition of organizations opposed to the war organized "Vietnam Summer." Over twenty-six thousand volunteers working in about seven hundred local projects throughout the United States informed, educated, and protested the war, while providing counseling on draft resistance.[17] I spent the summer in Cambridge, Massachusetts. While taking summer classes, I attended teach-ins and cemented a relationship with a group of fellow UW students. Back at Madison that October, we joined thousands of our classmates to demonstrate against the Dow Chemical Company's production of napalm and Agent Orange.

We were young, facing the rest of our lives at a time when the future was insecure. The draft was on everyone's minds. Students held a privileged position and often were able to get deferments. But how long would that last? The more I learned about the war, the more I became aware of the atrocities being committed by our government. Both napalm and Agent Orange were routinely reigned down upon civilian

---

17 See "Vietnam Summer: Activism during the Vietnam War," American Friends Service Committee, September 25, 2017, https://www.afsc.org/story/vietnam-summer-activism-during-vietnam-war.

targets. And American soldiers were almost as likely to be in its path as were the North Vietnamese guerrilla armies they fought.

The Dow demonstration was my first personal confrontation with lies from the highest levels of government, many of which we suspected but could not confirm until Daniel Ellsberg released the Pentagon Papers four years later. The papers proved that the congressional vote giving President Johnson war powers in Vietnam had been based on lies and misrepresentations. And while Johnson and his secretary of state, Robert McNamara, claimed that the US Navy destroyer *Maddox* had been fired upon, unprovoked, by Vietnamese torpedo boats in international waters, the Pentagon Papers told a different story. They disclosed that the *Maddox* had in fact been in Vietnamese waters; that the CIA had been engaged in secret operations targeting installations along the North Vietnam coast; and that the *Maddox* was not on a routine patrol but a special electronic spying mission.[18]

A few weeks before the Dow demonstration, a group of friends made a display of burning their draft cards, founding the Wisconsin Draft Resistance Union. I had met Jane Segal, Betsy Strausberg, and Claire Steinman when I moved into the house they also stayed in. They were a tight-knit threesome who, along with their boyfriends, were worried about the dramatic expansion of the draft that was feeding American involvement in the war. I had met David Goldman, Bob Zwicker, and Max Samson (another close-knit group) in Cambridge during the Vietnam Summer. A month later, we all joined the Dow action.

---

18 Commissioned by Secretary of State Robert McNamara in 1967, the Pentagon Papers, officially titled *Report of the Office of the Secretary of Defense Vietnam Task Force*, is a United States Department of Defense history of the United States' political and military involvement in Vietnam from 1945 to 1967. Daniel Ellsberg was a military analyst working on this study for the Rand Corporation. Driven by concern over the contents of the study, he released a copy of this secret report to various media outlets. In a 1996 *New York Times* article titled "25 Years Later; Lessons From the Pentagon," R. W. Apple wrote that the Pentagon Papers had demonstrated, among other things, that the Johnson administration had "systematically lied, not only to the public but also to Congress"—a pattern that was to be repeated when President George W. Bush's false claims about evidence of mass weapons of destruction led to the invasion of Iraq in 2003.

I believed in what we were doing: incontrovertibly, Dow was making weapons of choice for use in Vietnam, without regard for human life. Napalm, a highly flammable sticky jelly that causes second degree burns when touched to human skin, was used in munitions dropped by B-52 bombers.[19] While the stated objective of its use was to burn down sections of forests and bushes, the collateral effects were as likely to be felt by enemy guerrilla fighters as any civilians who may be unfortunate enough to be within its path. The iconic picture of a young Vietnamese girl naked with her arms covered in burns, clearly terrified, running and screaming with the image of smoke and destruction behind her, confirmed all I needed to know about the inhumane effects of napalm and the nature of the war the United States was fighting in Vietnam.[20]

Agent Orange—a toxic chemical combination of herbicides and defoliants fifty times more concentrated than herbicides used for normal agricultural uses—was used to eliminate forest cover and crops. More than twenty million gallons were sprayed over fields and forests in Vietnam. Given such vast distribution, it is likely that all 2.8 million US troops serving in the Southeast Asia theater were exposed,[21] along with an estimated four hundred thousand Vietnamese who were sickened or killed by its toxic effects.

Fifteen of us gathered at the bottom of Bascom Hill at 9:00 a.m. At a meeting the night before, a group of one hundred had committed to sit in and block anyone trying to get to the Dow recruitment tables. While we waited and wondered when the rest were going to show up, someone approached and told me, "Take your earrings off. They could be ripped from your ears."

That got my attention. Our intended action could be dangerous. We could be hurt. We could be arrested. We could be expelled from school. I recalled Dad's exhortation to get involved, and his simultaneous

---

19 By the war's end, eight million tons of bombs were dropped over Vietnam by the US military (more than three times the number of bombs used in World War II).

20 The Pulitzer Prize–winning photograph of nine-year-old Kim Phuc was taken at Trang Bang during the Vietnam War by AP photographer Nick Ut.

21 While denied by the Veteran's Administration for many years, the devastating effects of Agent Orange were ultimately acknowledged, even as there are reports that it is still in use.

warning: "Just don't get arrested." Meanwhile, my education and the diploma that came with it were among my mom's top priorities. For what might have been the first time in my life, I was on my own, making a decision with real-life consequences, and I was doing so intentionally and in spite of my parents' wishes.

As I affirmed my commitment to participate in this act of civil disobedience, I made a promise to myself: I would live my life taking action and making decisions based on what spoke to my core—on what was the right thing to do, not the expedient thing.

By 10:00 a.m. on October 18, 1967, two hundred of us had entered the lobby of the Commerce Building at the top of Bascom Hill. Another thousand picketed outside. For the next several hours, our numbers continued to increase. Ultimately more than three hundred strong inside, we sat shoulder to shoulder in a cramped area, doing our best to disrupt Dow's efforts to entice our fellow students to join their war games, until the campus police and administration lost their patience.

Outside, the crowd swelled to at least five thousand supporting picketers, along with a guerrilla theater group passing out literature and explaining—or demonstrating—to our fellow students and passing faculty why we were there and what we were protesting. All of us inside were grabbed and thrown through a gauntlet of baton-wielding police as we were clubbed and pushed through a revolving door and out of the building. This action resulted in some arrests, more demonstrations, and a flurry of activity initiated in the state legislature (the capitol being a stone's throw from the Madison campus) geared toward repression of future student activism.

David Goldman, my boyfriend at the time, was at the center of this effort, having been one of eight who was targeted by the administration. Although he was hit by batons and thrust from the sit-in against Dow, he was not arrested that day. He was, however, an SDS leader and therefore in the crosshairs of the special state senate committee that was investigating the October 18 demonstration. Concurrently, at the university's behest, the Wisconsin state attorney general issued a restraining order against eight students and teaching assistants (including David), restricting them from demonstrating on campus.

In response, a federal lawsuit was filed charging violation of their rights to freedom of speech. There was a flurry of hearings, newspaper articles, and pressure from the university. Seven students were expelled or quit school. The threats and intimidation were the first of its kind felt by us—otherwise-privileged white students. After all, we believed that free speech meant you could express unpopular opinions. We believed in justice and were shocked and angered by an unjust war. However, we were unprepared for the repression targeting us. What was a relatively short-lived—albeit intense—relationship with David did not survive the emotional strain of those times.

Ten days after the Dow action, Black Panther Party chairman Huey Newton was chained to a hospital gurney charged with the murders of two Oakland police officers.[22] Cries of "Free Huey" reverberated in urban areas throughout the country and on college campuses—including ours in Madison. That morning, we learned, officer John Frey had ordered Huey out of the car he was driving. Soon after, Huey was found unconscious with a bullet in his stomach, and Officer John Frey was dead. Another officer, Herbert Heanes, was wounded. The officers must have shot each other while they were shooting at Huey, he insisted. Frey was well known as a racist cop who liked to roam the Black community, and against whom many had lodged charges of brutality. Few in the Black community of Oakland believed the police version of the story: that Huey had done all the shooting. The same skepticism permeated the student movement.[23]

The parallel realities of the war in Vietnam and the civil rights struggle at home, highlighted in this moment by the Free Huey movement,

---

22 Formed by Bobby Seale and Huey Newton in 1966 in Oakland, California, the Black Panther Party for Self-Defense raised the ire of the police when they began patrolling the streets armed with a law book and (initially while it was still legal) a shotgun to observe and inform Black people while stopped by the police. They quickly added a host of survival programs including the iconic Free Breakfast for Children Program to their activities. The BPP Ten-Point Platform and Program is reprinted in the appendix to this book.

23 Huey was convicted of voluntary manslaughter for Frey's death and acquitted for shooting Hearns. His conviction was reversed in May 1970. After two subsequent trials ended in hung juries, the charges were dropped. A good description of the facts in the case and the trial by Huey himself can be found in his autobiography, *Revolutionary Suicide* (New York: Harcourt Brace, 1973).

resonated with me and had a lasting impact. I read everything I could, developing a growing discomfort with what I perceived as a disconnect of many anti-war activists from the civil rights movement. After all, they seemed to me deeply and inextricably connected.

In July 1968 a trip to Cuba was organized by SDS, following the same path as senior members of the Black Panther Party who had recently attempted a trip to the island nation. Planning to fly there from Mexico, the Panthers were intercepted by US intelligence agents and held for a few days before being returned to the opposite coasts in the States from which they originally came. SDS, in turn, sought to make a statement with its delegation of thirty students from across the country. All of us were white except for Irmgard Yglesia, a Puerto Rican activist from New York City, who I got to know in Madison during the month leading up to the trip. I was otherwise traveling with a group of people I did not know, but with whom I assumed I had an agreed purpose: to challenge the US State Department's ban on travel to Cuba, and to do so in a manner that was clearly defined by some as being illegal.

The first week of our journey took us to Dallas, Texas, where we met as a group for the first time. The house we stayed in was large (probably six or seven bedrooms that we shared), with a large living area that we adapted to be our meeting space. We also used it as our workout room, since we knew we would spend some of our time in Cuba doing physical labor but were not all physically prepared to do so. We did not know the city and were advised to stay inside to avoid the police surveillance we assumed we were under. During the week we were there, we did our best to brush up on Cuban history, and especially on the course of Cuba's developments in the almost ten years since the revolution.

Among us were several leaders from different local chapters of SDS. But most of us were young activists seeking answers and a direction for our lives. Marilyn Webb, a feminist who had recently left Chicago where she went to school and was now living in Washington, DC, posed a striking presence. But after she teamed up with Tom Mosher, who was from Chicago, I did my best to avoid them both. I had not met Mosher before, but he came off as a loudmouth know-it-all who was erratic and unpredictable.[24] I found his many antics to be both juvenile and em-

---

24 Mosher was from Chicago's North Side. He got involved with JOIN (Jobs Or Income Now) when a group from SDS went to Uptown to organize

barrassing. Sue Jankowski, friendly, jovial, and easy to travel with, was from the national SDS headquarters in Chicago and enjoyed what I considered to be movement gossip. In Cuba, as we rode the bus from one to another scheduled activity, Sue would exercise this passion. I particularly remember her telling her version of talks that were in progress between Stokely Carmichael and Black Panther Party leadership. Would he join the Party? Would he not? Huey Newton's trial had just been getting underway as we had prepared to leave Dallas for Cuba, leaving lots of room for speculation.

We arrived in Havana the third week of July—just in time to hear Fidel speak for hours at Revolution Square on Cuba's Independence Day. For two months, in some of the hottest weather I have experienced, we traveled the country visiting newly built factories, health centers, and schools. We met with volunteers who returned from the literacy campaign through which many Cubans traveled in youth brigades to the mountains and other isolated areas of the island, and we visited farms where cows were being bred for milk and beef, observing new efforts at artificial insemination.

We met with representatives of freedom fighters from several African countries—all of whom would gain their independence during the next several years—and sat with representatives from North Vietnam and the Viet Cong, who gave us their side of the story about the war. The United States had its hand in supporting (financially and militarily) many of the colonial governments throughout Africa, Asia, and Latin America. Cuba, on the other hand, may not have had money to support the liberation movements, but they had made it possible for freedom fighters from around the world to find respite. Consequently, we had the opportunity to meet with many combatants who were clear that it was the US government that was their enemy—not the people of the United States.

I studied Che Guevara and his commitment to "building a new man and a new woman," which was very much present as a goal during our time in Cuba. The notion that change is a constant that needs to be respected, revered, and channeled toward the improvement of people's

---

white youth a few years earlier. By most accounts, he was an agitator and hanger-on there but had garnered enough credibility to be invited to go on this trip to Cuba after one of the national SDS leaders had to cancel, leaving a slot open.

lives, and that to do so a society must nurture an ever-changing path of renewal, captured my imagination and has stayed with me to this day.

At this moment in Cuba, the possibilities when this idea was put into practice seemed endless. As we explored this island country struggling with their own form of socialism, we were excited by the energy we experienced. We spent time in every one of its regions, visiting new health clinics that were being built in even the most remote communities. Having heard about the literacy campaign that was just ending, having reached the goal of nearly 100 percent literacy, we were encouraged by the many day care centers and schools newly built and operating—again throughout the country in rural and urban areas.[25] For decades, the Cuban economy had been tied to sugarcane production. These plantations, built on the backs of an early slave trade, were now nationalized. In the ten years since the revolution, an effort had been made to diversify the economy, paid for in part with large loans from Soviet bloc nations.

Following our trip, SDS organized the first Venceremos Brigade (in part with a goal of raising the funds to pay back these loans). Students from the United States would spend six weeks cutting sugarcane, contributing to Cuba's Ten Million Ton Harvest Campaign. Its goal was to commemorate the tenth anniversary of the Cuban Revolution by doubling Cuba's sugar output. This brigade of over two hundred activists, the first of many, would prove more effective as a symbolic and educational tool than it would as an efficient way to cut sugarcane.[26]

Similar to my experience a year earlier, the participating activists experienced the US blockade of Cuba from another perspective. Seen through this lens, the stranglehold the blockade created on the Cuban people made no sense. We knew the history of the brutality and neglect of the Batista regime that preceded the Cuban Revolution, so when we saw new infrastructure that supported the housing, health, and

---

25 I have Cuban friends who left Cuba with their families after the revolution who tell me the literacy campaign was a sham and that most Cubans had access to education and could read in the years leading up to the revolution. I don't argue with them. I was not there then. But when I was there in 1968, there were too many ordinary people I talked with who told me their stories of the literacy campaign to believe these were made up.

26 Cutting sugarcane is not simply hard work—which it is in spades. It also requires some technique to reap the maximum sugar product. The American volunteers had neither the experience nor the technique.

education needs of the majority of people who had previously had little if any access to them in the past, we were energized by the possibilities.

Several years later, when Tom Mosher outed himself as an informant by testifying in front of a congressional intelligence committee, I was not surprised. I learned many years later that he had grown up in Uptown, been a protégé of Preston Bradley[27] and was involved in the early organizing of JOIN (Jobs or Income Now), an SDS project in Uptown seven years before I arrived there in 1972. In 1983, after Harold Washington was elected mayor, Tom Mosher showed up in Uptown again, where he would stalk me from time to time. But more on him later.

On the heels of my return to Madison from Cuba in October 1968, Black students at the university went on strike. Their target was racism. Their demand was an African American studies program. When these requests fell on the deaf ears of the administration, they called for a student boycott. This was the first effort in which I was involved that was conceived and led by Black students—something that did not always sit well with many of the white students who had been involved in previous student-inspired demonstrations. Their discomfort was an embarrassment for me and numerous others. Some of us who were involved in the anti-war movement responded to the strikers' challenge, supporting them with our feet and taking responsibility to organize our fellow white students. We went building to building at the university, marching into classrooms to explain the strike and why the (mostly white) students we encountered should be supporting it. Ultimately, the university would agree to changes in the curriculum to include African American studies, but the repression felt by the Black students who were involved far outweighed any experienced by other students engaging in protest.

Representing SDS, I made several presentations about Cuba and attended SDS conventions in Michigan and Texas in the months leading to the end of my senior year. During a return trip to Madison from Austin in March, I was the sole driver in a car four of us were riding in. Marc Zalkin, an organizer from Racine who had been in Madison for the Black

---

27 Preston Bradley (1888–1983), a pastor and founder of the People's Church in Uptown, had a radio program with a wide listenership. While considered a liberal reformer, he maintained close ties to Chicago's political machinery and the administration of Richard J. Daley.

student strike, stayed up all night to help me stay awake during the long drive. In Madison, he and I had run in and out of classrooms together.

On the first Saturday in May 1969, a block party was planned for an area of Madison where many students lived off campus, just behind the block where most African American students who lived off campus rented apartments. It had been a long winter, and we welcomed the opportunity to celebrate the spring. Madison's new Republican mayor, who was not a fan of the university's out-of-state and "hippie" students, refused to issue a permit for the block party.

The party proceeded nevertheless, and by the end of the evening it had turned into a police-inspired riot. In the week that followed, most of the area was cordoned off by the police. Three days later, those of us living in the area were still sneaking through alleys to go to campus, dodging tear gas and police. Some of us were not so lucky. When I asked Paul Siegel (a college friend and teacher's assistant who later joined us in Racine and in Chicago) what he remembered about that weekend, he reminded me that he was arrested the day after the block party while walking in the area, probably on his way home, with a briefcase full of student exams.

"They jumped out of the car and handcuffed and arrested me, threw me in the car," he later remembered. "It was shortly after those events that it was revealed that since around 1964 the Madison PD had been keeping files on campus radical activists, including photos. I think that's how they picked me out to be arrested." Paul recalled that there were initially fifteen or so people in the cell, but that "as the night went on, more and more people were thrown in." The unlawful-assembly charges on which everyone had been arrested were dropped when they went to court.

In another incident, a popular history professor, Harvey Goldberg, was accosted by police as he sat in an armchair in his living room.

I made a lot of spaghetti that week. Our house became a place for people to come for medical attention and a warm meal. Marc was visiting from Racine. We spent most of every day that week transporting friends (some new, some old) to the hospital emergency room for split-open skulls, chemical burns from pepper spray, and other various ailments—a result of enthusiastic police pursuing anyone who dared show their face on streets within a couple-block radius of Mifflin Street.

Many arrests and protests later, just weeks before the school term ended, the city relented.

6.

THE PATH TO RACINE AND THE BLACK PANTHER PARTY

In May 1969, a young Black organizer named Fred Hampton was capturing hearts and minds on the West Side of Chicago and its western suburbs, which contained some of Chicago's most concentrated Black communities. At that very moment I was deciding whether to move and organize in Racine, Wisconsin, or to go to either Sweden or Mexico and realize my dream of becoming a master weaver. Fred came to campus to an overflow crowd in the social sciences building located across the street from the school's commerce building where we had protested recruitment efforts by Dow Chemical Company nineteen months earlier.

Flanked by Black Panther security, dressed in black leather and wearing stern expressions, Fred entered the room, raised his fist, and greeted us with "All power to the people!" As these profoundly serious and disciplined Panthers surrounded him on stage, facing a group of spectators more familiar with academic lectures than challenges to the status quo, Fred called out racism and economic injustices, leaving no room for confusion.

Fred was dynamic. He was challenging, strong, confident, and undeniable. It had barely been six months since he, along with Bobby Rush, had established the Illinois Chapter of the Black Panther Party. He lived up to his reputation. Formerly the head of the Maywood, Illinois NAACP, Fred was young and insightful. The hall overflowed with students anxious to get a glimpse of this young leader.

Fred schooled us on the ten-point platform of the Black Panther Party, and its survival programs. He challenged us: "Dare to struggle, dare to win. If you don't dare to struggle, you don't deserve to win." And he admonished: "You can't have theory without practice. You can have as many degrees as a thermometer and still cannot walk across the street and chew gum at the same time. People learn by observation and participation."

"The people will observe the Black Panther Party feeding children in people's power programs," he explained. "We will open the door and ask for their participation. When they participate, they will learn what we are talking about. When the power structure comes down on these programs, the people will defend them."

He had me at "You don't fight fire with fire, you fight fire with water. You don't fight racism with racism. You fight racism with international working-class solidarity." Fred's sense of justice painted a picture that was to inform my vision of a future I felt to be worth fighting for. His explanations for practical application were a blueprint: I knew where I was going next and what I was going to do. Weaving would have to wait.

One of the initiatives of the Wisconsin Draft Resistance Union in the summer of 1968, as they organized in communities around the state, was to connect with people's everyday struggle to survive. In the fall, cadres of students (who had dropped out or graduated) moved from Madison to three cities—Milwaukee, Racine, and Waukegan, Illinois—to work in factories and organize workers.

Marc Zalkin joined Jody and Susie Chandler in planning to go to Racine. As I was approaching the end of my senior year, he recruited me to join them. I didn't know anything about Racine. And I didn't really choose to go there; it chose me.

Marc and I had spent a lot of time together since that drive from Austin and were now a couple. We would ultimately get married and have a son named Brendan, after the playwright Brendan Behan. Without informing his parents, Marc dropped out of Madison during his sophomore year. So that his father continued to send him tuition money, Marc would register and then withdraw before the deadline for returning full tuition. This is how he survived until we both started working in factories that summer.

Marc took a job in a foundry working with fifty- to one-hundred-pound auto parts in unbearably hot temperatures. I was at Western Publishing Company, working on an assembly line packaging board games. That didn't last long. We were working two different shifts. Marc made a connection with workmate Nate Long but rarely had the time or energy to talk to anyone else. We spent many Sundays with Nate and his family. Originally from Memphis, Nate's path in life had not been easy. He was determined that his young son would grow up prepared to survive as a Black male in America, and Nate believed that to do so he would have to toughen him up. I respected that, and it was clear to me that he loved his son dearly, even if I was conflicted about the methods he chose to do so. But I had not walked in his shoes—who was I to judge?

Marc began drinking a pint of gin a day, becoming increasingly discouraged about whether this was the path to organizing that made sense for him. I felt pretty much the same way, and by the end of the summer we both quit, turning our attention to organizing youth at Racine's two local high schools.

This was 1969. During the national convention of Students for a Democratic Society held in Chicago that June, there was a split in the organization that exposed many fissures in the student movement. Race, class, and feminism were at the vortex of most disagreements in strategy and ideology. The role of the Black liberation movement—and specifically the vanguard role of the Black Panther Party—came to a head, splitting the organization.

Feminists were split along the divide of the color line as well. There were those who made no distinction between the challenges faced by women of different classes and races. They were primarily white middle-class women who took the position that women's liberation should be the priority of the movement. Others, many of whom were already working closely with the Panthers and multiracial working-class feminist groups, insisted race and economic status were the first determining factors in striving for the advancement of women's interests. I stood with the second group. The tension between these two different orientations would inform my approach to feminism for years to come—a dynamic that some twenty years later would be called intersectionality.

A month later, the Black Panther Party held in Oakland the conference that established the National Committees to Combat Fascism. We attended them both. By September, we were out of factories and organizing young white people at the two local high schools, connecting with the Milwaukee National Committee to Combat Fascism (NCCF),[28] and selling *Black Panther* newspapers. We also produced our own newsletter and newspaper with the aid of a handful of high school students.

At the time, Black Panther Party chairman Bobby Seale was on trial in Chicago, along with seven white activists, for mob action and other

---

28 The NCCFs were a creation of the Black Panther Party as pre-vehicles for people interested in forming BPP chapters.

charges from demonstrations a year earlier during the Democratic National Convention. Charles Garry was the Panthers' attorney, but he had his hands full with another trial in California. When Judge Julius Hoffman refused to accommodate Gary's schedule, Bobby Seale decided to represent himself. Hoffman was not on board and ordered Bobby bound and gagged in the courtroom as the trial proceeded.[29] We loaded up our car with high school students and drove to Chicago to attend a rally on the Federal Plaza. For us, Fred Hampton was the main attraction.

Several weeks later, on October 8, we joined the Revolutionary Youth Movement faction of SDS (RYM II)[30] in Chicago to protest the closing of the International Harvester plant and its conversion into Cook County Jail.[31] We again loaded up our car and drove to Chicago to join the march that would wind through the city's North Side and end up at the Harvester plant, located at Twenty-Sixth and Sacramento. The Chicago police, the city's Red Squad, and the FBI all disrupted this march—not to be confused with a second march the same day, organized by the Weathermen (another faction of the SDS Revolutionary

---

29 A couple of months later in November, Seale was severed from this trial (which by then had earned the defendants the name "Chicago Seven") and tried separately. Judge Hoffman sentenced Seale to forty-eight months in prison for sixteen acts of contempt—all of which would be later dismissed. His trial otherwise ended up in a hung jury.

30 SDS, originally founded in 1960, was a mass organization that grew rapidly on campuses throughout the United States. Initially inspired by the civil rights movement and rejecting anti-Communism, it became a primary vehicle for mostly white students to protest the war in Vietnam as well as US military interference in emerging countries throughout Latin America and Africa. As the organization grew, it had a large umbrella. In 1969, at its national convention held in Chicago, the organization began to show its fissures, initially splitting between its members who called themselves the Revolutionary Youth Movement and those identifying with the Progressive Labor Party. We identified with the Revolutionary Youth Movement which later split into the Weathermen and Revolutionary Youth Movement II or RYM II. For more on SDS, see the Freedom Archives (freedomarchives.org).

31 During my first forty years in Chicago, I witnessed the jail expand and the population of Black and Brown people continue to grow. It was not until my fifth decade in Chicago, when I was out of political office, that people power moved in ways that decreased its population.

Fred Hampton speaking at a rally in front of the Federal Building in Chicago where Bobby Seale was being bound and shackled, September 1969.

Youth Movement, following the SDS split that had occurred in June.) As a result of police action, the Cobra Stones—a North Side gang—were encouraged to attack the march while the police, who were keeping a close eye on us, looked the other way. Following a brief skirmish with the gang, we managed to complete our journey.

After Thanksgiving, all of us who had left Madison to organize in the three cities convened in Milwaukee to compare notes. Jody and Susie decided to move to Detroit. Marc and I were having issues and considering leaving Racine to go our own separate ways. Then we woke up in the morning on December 4 to the devastating news that Fred Hampton and Mark Clark (chairman of the Panther's Peoria Illinois branch) had been killed by police in Chicago.

Joined by Steve Gold, a college friend ready to leave the campus for the "real world," we vowed to forget our personal issues, return to Racine, and continue to organize white people to join the struggle for racial and social justice.

7.

CEMENTING OUR COMMITMENT IN RACINE

Before returning to Racine, we took a short detour to Chicago to attend Fred's funeral. By then, thousands of people had walked through the apartment where Fred and Mark Clark were murdered. After doing so, one could have no doubt this was an assassination.

In the early hours of December 4, 1969, police had raided the apartment where Fred Hampton was staying—2337 West Monroe, on the city's West Side. The police conducting the raid were in a detail assigned to the office of Edward Hanrahan, the highest prosecutor in Cook County and a protégé of Mayor Richard J. Daley.

With the complicity of the Chicago police command, and armed with a diagram of the apartment provided by the FBI, Hanrahan ordered the raid killing Fred Hampton and Mark Clark and seriously wounding four other Panthers: Verlina Brewer, Ronald "Doc" Satchel, Blair Anderson, and Brenda Harris. Along with Harold Bell, Louis Truelock, and Akua Njeri (née Deborah Johnson), they were arrested on charges of aggravated assault and the attempted murder of police officers. Each was held on $100,000 bail.

After gleefully removing Mark's and Fred's bodies and arresting the survivors, the police left the apartment unattended. They left no yellow tape. In their arrogance, they engaged in virtually no collection of forensic evidence—though they had a police photographer take photos of the front door and of several smiling police carrying Fred's body out of the building.

In their absence, attorneys for the Panthers did their own forensic collection—all of which was filmed and documented, and all of which contradicted the story being peddled by Hanrahan and the police raiders. At least two media outlets covered Hanrahan's version in its totality—the *Chicago Tribune* and CBS News.

Hanrahan immediately presented his version of events to the media, describing a Panther-inspired shootout with the police. He had his police officers do a mock reenactment of his fictional version of the raid for the media, describing what later turned out to be nailheads in the door as evidence of shots fired by the Panthers.

Almost everything they said was contradicted by the physical evidence in the apartment. The police claimed they were responding to gunfire coming from inside the apartment when they returned fire. In fact, between eighty-two and ninety-nine shots were fired—all but one from police guns. Mark Clark was providing security, sitting at the front door shotgun in hand, when a bullet fired by a Chicago police officer came through the door, hitting him in the heart. As he fell, the shotgun went off, representing the lone shot fired from a BPP weapon.

Fred was asleep when the police raid occurred. They showered bullets from the doorway of his bedroom before entering. When Akua Njeri, eight months pregnant with Fred's child, couldn't wake him up, she covered Fred's body with her own as shots flurried around them.[32] The police then forced her from the bedroom, leaving an unconscious Fred Hampton alone with the police. They took her to the kitchen, from which she heard someone say, "He's barely alive, he'll barely make it." Then she heard shots fired and, "He's good and dead now."[33]

This was not going to go away quietly.

While in Chicago, and before beginning what would be another two-and-a-half-year foray into Racine, Wisconsin, we connected with SDS friends and RYM II leaders Slim Coleman and Cathy Archibald. Both heavy smokers, Slim, whose given name was Walter, stood a lanky six foot three and could spin a tale that would capture your imagination. Cathy had long red hair, brooked no nonsense, and was dedicated to detail and averse to talking about herself. They both had come to Chicago a year or two earlier to work at the SDS national headquarters, having each crossed paths with James Forman, cofounder and executive secretary of the Student Nonviolent Coordinating Committee (SNCC), who had encouraged them to do so. They had both grown up in the South—Slim in Texas and Cathy in Arkansas—and their worldview put the color line, and therefore racism, at the center of all of America's

---

32 An independent autopsy would reveal that Fred was dosed with barbiturates.

33 From testimony by Akua Njeri (then Deborah Johnson) in federal court during the Hampton/Clark civil suit.

With the police failing to secure 2337 W. Monroe, the Black Panther Party secured the building and did their own forensic review before opening it up for the public viewing—putting the lie to Hanrahan's version of the raid that killed Fred Hampton and Mark Clark.

woes. They developed a close working relationship with Fred Hampton and Bobby Rush.

Since there was no Black Panther Party chapter in Racine, and the NCCF chapter in Milwaukee was suspended, our intention was to connect with someone we knew from Madison who had been in leadership of the Black student strike. We told Slim and Cathy of our plan, and they offered to put us in touch with Ray Lewis and Harold Bell,[34] the leadership of the Rockford branch of the Illinois Chapter of the Black Panther Party. When our college contact was exposed as a police informant a few months later, Lewis and Bell became our primary lifeline to the BPP. We got our papers to sell each week from them, and they came to Racine from time to time to lead political education classes.

The Racine I knew seemed straight out of a sociology textbook. With a majority-white population, African Americans composed a little over 10 percent of the population, while the (mostly Mexican) Latino

---

34 Harold Bell survived the police attack while staying overnight at Fred Hampton's apartment the night of the raid.

population amounted to 4 percent. It was a working-class town built largely around the auto industry. There were small tool and die plants and foundries serving American Motors and International Harvester. SC Johnson's headquarters and research division were housed in a Frank Lloyd Wright–designed building located just south of downtown Racine. Along with Western Publishing, these were the city's largest employers.

Class and race organized the geography of Racine. Working people lived closer to the city center—although skilled workers tended to live in segregated communities. Professionals—teachers, social workers, first responders—lived in a ring around the central area of the city and along the lakefront. The captains of industry resided within a tax island that had been carved out north of the city proper.

Marc, Steve, and I lived just north of downtown in an area of poor working people—Black, white, and Latino. During the time I lived in Racine from June 1969 through June 1972, I stayed in seven apartments.

Marc was probably the best organizer I have known. He was also a good investigative reporter. In Racine we organized a free breakfast program and held food and clothing giveaways. We provided rides for family members to visit their loved ones incarcerated in several of Wisconsin's state prisons and advocated for welfare rights while organizing local attorneys to take on cases of all sorts pro bono. We demonstrated against the War in Vietnam and the increasing bombings in Laos and Cambodia, and opened a movement bookshop we named the People's Bookstore.

In addition to distributing the *Black Panther* paper, we produced our own literature and published a newsletter and then our own newspaper, the *Midnight Special*. The name was inspired by the Creedence Clearwater Revival version of "The Midnight Special," a traditional folk song originally recorded by Lead Belly that told the story of a prison train. Its chorus was "Let the midnight special shine its ever-loving light on me." This name for the paper won out over "Bad Moon Rising," a song by the same artists with the refrain "There's a bad moon on the rise."

We rented an office in downtown Racine. It was a large space allowing for many activities. We had the People's Bookstore; a large meeting space we used for political education as well as forums and organizing activities around legal and welfare rights; and a basement area, providing us with the space to collect clothing and food for the giveaways we regularly held in public parks and on school grounds.

Our crew of volunteers pose for a picture following a successful clothing program. We are outside the People's Bookstore. Racine, Wisconsin circa 1971–1972.

Shortly after the People's Bookstore opened on Main Street, the Racine City Council had passed a law making it a loitering offense for any two people to be standing on that particular sidewalk downtown. It was obvious harassment, and we were arrested for loitering while chatting outside our bookstore. To my recollection, nothing much came of the arrest, but that day I had a chance to get a nap and eat a bologna sandwich. Little did they know they were doing us a favor—I was hungry and tired with no other prospect for lunch. When the local newspapers wrote about this arrest, they only identified Marc Zalkin and Steve Gold, along with two teenage girls, as being arrested. I was twenty-one at the time.[35]

We had our own personal FBI agent who followed us wherever we went. Apparently we had gotten the feds' attention with our demonstrations against the increased bombing in Vietnam, Laos, and Cambodia, our promotion of the Black Panther Party and the establishment of a

---

35 *Journal Times* (Racine, Wisconsin), May 18, 1970, 6.

free breakfast program on the city's North Side, and our fledgling welfare defense and legal program.

Marc and Steve were both questioned and investigated by the FBI after the bombing of Sperling Hall at the University of Wisconsin in August 1970, and again after draft offices in several other cities were bombed. This was the FBI's fallback—something going on in the Midwest? "Go see those radicals in Racine."

Katherine Ann Power was an anti-war activist who, along with four others, was wanted by the FBI for a September 23, 1970, Boston bank robbery during which a policeman was killed. Raised in Denver, Colorado, and a student at Brandeis University, she had been the getaway driver. None of us had ever met her but likely had heard of her exploits. Jane Segal, my college roommate and BFF, visited us in Racine on her way to California. Jane, who was raised in New Jersey, had stayed in Madison for a couple of years after I moved to Racine, during which time we would visit each other occasionally. Jane had dark hair. The FBI picture of Katherine Ann Power shows a woman with shoulder-length hair that looks to be light brown. There is nothing similar about their facial features. Nevertheless, the FBI was convinced that Jane was Katherine Ann Power and that I was aiding her in evading capture.

We owned a commercial van—a yellow metal box with no windows besides the windshield and front passenger's and driver's sides. It was the perfect vehicle for transporting clothing and people to any number of rallies and demonstrations. The back area was big enough to carry up to ten or eleven people, which proved advantageous during trips to the Great Lakes naval base for demonstrations against the escalating war in Vietnam. We loved it.

I was planning a trip to the East Coast, so when it was time for Jane to move on, we left for the airport in Milwaukee together. Returning from dropping us off, after pulling our yellow van into the driveway at our home, Marc, Steve, and one of our volunteers were surprised by two FBI agents. They were looking for Powers.

It was a warm fall day. The agents shoved the threesome into the back of the van—which by this time of the day would have been a hotbox—where they held them captive and threatened them for hours before bringing them upstairs to our apartment for further interrogation. The agents were disinclined to accept that Jane was not Katherine Ann Power.

According to an FBI document dated October 21, 1970, "Racine, Wisconsin, police department informant advised October twenty last, Katherine Ann Power was with Helen Shiller on October Five last in Racine . . . info available to informant is that Power left Racine in company of Shiller and may have traveled to California." The document went on, "BU [Bureau] Agents strenuously interviewed Marc Stephen Zalkin, Steven Alan Gold, Michael Norman Christensen. . . . Zalkin claims Shiller left town with friends . . . claims female . . . not subject Power."

Neither Marc nor Steve would say much about the incident. However, while our level of paranoia moved up a notch, our commitment grew stronger.

. . . .

8.

CONFRONTING THE POLITICS OF GERMAN MEASLES

In 1969 the federal government initiated a $50 million campaign to vaccinate forty to sixty million children between the ages of one and twelve against German measles. They were expecting a national outbreak of the virus in 1970–71. While generally mild by comparison, the disease has a potentially devastating impact on unborn children when contracted by pregnant women. During the previous outbreak of German measles in 1963–65, fifty thousand children born to women who had the virus during their pregnancy were born with serious defects[36] or were stillborn. At the same time, there was concern among public health experts that the vaccination could mirror the disease and cause defects to an unborn fetus.

Amid preparations for the expected new outbreak, it circulated that the Racine Department of Health planned to have pregnant moms be among the first to be immunized. We were awed by the ignorance.

---

36 Thirty thousand children were born with defects such as cataracts, intellectual disabilities, deafness, and cardiovascular defects. Twenty thousand were stillborn.

Clarifying that they would not immunize pregnant women but would focus on children, the health department announced its intention to provide vaccines to children in kindergarten, first and second grades, even as the federal government recommended *all* children between the ages of one and twelve receive the vaccination. Racine's Board of Health cried poverty and insufficient vaccine supplies, insisting they could only immunize this much smaller group of children.

There was an uproar. Why weren't they including children aged one through five and eight through twelve? Where had all that federal government money gone? Hadn't Racine received their fair share? Why weren't they fighting for it? The Racine County Board of Health acknowledged the danger of German measles to an unborn child and confirmed that they would not inoculate pregnant women. Otherwise, they were intractable.

Charging that those most affected were the poor who could not afford to go elsewhere for the vaccinations, we insisted that the city find a way to expand their reach to all children. We challenged representatives from the Department of Health, Education, and Welfare and the Racine United Fund to be part of the solution by rising to the challenge and ensuring all children were protected—and by extension all women of child-bearing age, meaning they would no longer have reason to fear being exposed to this potential killer of unborn fetuses.

We picketed the downtown public health office—a new experience for Racine's downtown. We also crashed the Racine United Fund's meetings, bringing with us a swarm of scared and angry parents, along with the science to back up our demands. Two months later the public health departments in Kenosha and Racine agreed to expand their outreach to vaccinate all children ages one to twelve. We had won, and, in so doing, firmly established our presence—and, more importantly, that every child had the right to a responsive public health system. We were energized by this very real material impact.

9.

I BECOME A MOTHER

When I became pregnant in the summer of 1970, I was surprised by my positive response to the thought of becoming a mom. I had previously vowed not to have children. Influenced in large part by my relationship to my brother Bob, I had clung to a notion that this was not a world into which I would want to bring a child. But committing my life to making change had shifted my worldview. I now understood that we needed a new generation to carry on the fruits of our labor.

I had been driving a cab for several months. While the FBI was effective at notifying most employers in Racine that we were radicals not to be hired, the local cab company apparently did not care. However, as a woman I was only allowed to work during "daylight hours"—7:00 a.m. to 3:00 p.m. Neither Marc nor Steve were able to secure a job, leaving me as our primary breadwinner.

By this time, we had opened the People's Bookstore on Main Street in downtown Racine, but we were lucky if it broke even. Neither selling our newspaper, the *Midnight Special*, nor selling *Black Panther* papers were money-making activities. When Paul Siegel joined us that summer, he had completed his master's degree and was looking forward to completing a PhD in history (a goal he would finally achieve thirty years later). He had no better luck in securing a job in Racine.

We lived on fried dough—a creation of Marc's—sweetened in the morning for breakfast, and spiced in the evening for dinner. We had friends from our factory days who bought us coffee and a sweet roll during the day from George Webb's (our local fast-food chain.) The cab company would not let me work while pregnant, and I went on welfare. We continued to eat fried dough, but at least once each month we had enough for a week's worth of square meals.

I was involved in many welfare rights activities in Racine, advocating for policy changes while also addressing the individual issues faced by people navigating the bureaucracy. It was common for a woman on welfare to have her check amount decreased without notice, to have her medical access limited, or to receive the wrong food when she went to pick up her allocation at the local welfare distribution center.

In Wisconsin at the time, instead of food stamps, monthly allocations of flour, cornmeal, some canned vegetables, eggs, butter, and cheese were available for pickup in amounts based on household size. Often this was arbitrary—designed to discourage people from welfare. As advocates, we joined others in challenging the system to serve their clients with dignity and respect.

I was a young white woman with a bachelor of arts degree. This rankled some of the social workers, prompting them to challenge my status on welfare. However, their supervisor apparently stopped this action from proceeding any further. "I suggested that if you were kicked off welfare, I would bring you to work here, replacing one of those complaining," he later told me. "After all," he said, "You do more for our clients than all of them combined." I doubt I would have taken him up on the offer, but I appreciated the support.

A big issue for many of the women was health care. A growing number (most of whom were poor and on welfare assistance) complained of having miscarriages after seeing a particular doctor. They each had a similar experience that included receiving a shot of some kind during their visit, feeling poorly after, and then miscarrying their child. Obviously anecdotal, I checked it out.

Early in my pregnancy I went to this doctor. Maybe he suspected me of having an ulterior motive, or, more likely, he treated me differently because of my white skin. In any case, he did not offer me any shots. He did, however, prescribe tetracycline for my nausea. I took one dose before learning that tetracycline was becoming known to cause birth defects in unborn children. I threw out the pills, worrying for the next eight months that I might have caused permanent damage to my child.

I wanted a natural childbirth—no sedatives or pain medications. I convinced Marc to attend Lamaze classes with me—no easy feat. I wanted Marc to be in the delivery room when our child was born. That was a harder sell, but not as hard as finding a doctor and hospital where this would be allowed. I found only one gynecologist who was open to the idea. He was Jewish, and the city's protestant hospital, Saint Luke's, agreed, although not enthusiastically.

I went into labor early in the morning on Easter Sunday. We got to the hospital to learn that my new, carefully chosen doctor was not available. He was out of town for the weekend. "Not to worry," I was told. "Another doctor will be substituting for him." I went into a panic when I learned they were talking about the doctor that I suspected was causing Black and Brown mothers to miscarry. Dispatching our friends to wait in front of my doctor's house for his return, I was determined to wait for him. I immediately stopped dilating. The next day at 10:00 a.m.—more than twenty-four hours later—my doctor arrived. By then, several other women had given birth while I roamed the hospital floor, cajoled and coaxed by nurses who thought activity would get my contractions back on track.

My newly arrived doctor insisted I take muscle relaxers. It took some convincing and a promise that the medicine would not impact my child before I agreed. Finally, I was in real labor. One of the ladies I shared the "labor room" with was on her seventeenth child. She was there for less than an hour. Ten hours of contractions and unimaginable pain later (and thirty-six hours after my labor began), Brendan was thankfully born.

Marc stood behind me as Brendan emerged into this world, looking blue and with a cone-shaped head. He was not breathing. In all our studying about childcare we missed that part. Marc took one look and started screaming, "What's wrong?" as he almost fainted and was led out of the delivery room. Meanwhile, I was trying to figure out what was going on as they slapped Brendan, got him screaming (more like a screech), cut his umbilical cord, swaddled him and brought him to me for a quick moment.

A few hours later when they brought Brendan to my room, I was struck by the miracle of this event that up until then I had imagined but never really grasped. He was born almost two weeks past his due date. He weighed nine pounds, five ounces, and was tall (twenty-one and a half inches long) and reminded me of an old man, but with fists and feet like those of a lion cub. As I held him to my breast, I was overwhelmed with love, with amazement, and more than an ounce of fear.

Bringing a child into this world meant being responsible for that child's growth and development. It meant reflecting on all the "I'll never do that when I have a kid" moments of my own life. It meant learning how to love without judgment or manipulation. I did not feel up to the task, but I didn't question for a minute that was what I was going to do as best I could.

Marc and I agreed that we each had baggage that we didn't want to pass on to our child. We didn't exactly know how, but we knew we would do things differently than we had ourselves experienced. We wanted our son to have the chance to realize his full potential without negative influences—no matter how well intentioned—discouraging him or standing in his way. In our concern for his safety and well-being, we wanted him to have the freedom to reach beyond what appeared to be safe and not be inhibited by fear.

Marc and I with baby Brendan.

PART II

EARLY DAYS IN UPTOWN

10.

TRANSITION AND GROWTH

The fifteen months that followed Brendan's birth were a time of growth and transition. Our numbers in Racine expanded as we grew our organizing efforts. Shortly after our son was born, Richie "Curly" Cohen joined us in Racine; Joy Seaman, Tom Lindsay, and Marc Kaplan, just out of high school and looking for someplace to organize, joined us shortly after. We were excited about adding young activists to our growing community. Kaplan later told me that they made the choice to move to Racine, rather than Chicago,[1] because they "thought that the practice in Racine was more along the lines of what we wanted to be involved in."

In Racine we continued to agitate against the War in Vietnam and bombings in Cambodia, in the process meeting veterans who were against the war and wanted to do something about it. Randy Saltz, born and raised in Racine, found us and brought knowledge of the legal issues facing veterans to our fledgling legal program, and of the unique survival needs facing veterans to our welfare-defense work.

Our first foray into electoral politics came when we supported a Black candidate running for alderman in the ward where we lived, a local election campaign with a heavy emphasis on empowerment. As we defended against an effort to close our breakfast for children program, we enlarged our survival programs, drove families to visit loved ones in prisons throughout Wisconsin, organized lawyers to represent people who could not afford to pay them, distributed clothing and food in organized giveaways, held political education classes, and sold papers.

During those fifteen months, I came to Chicago on several occasions to help on various survival programs of the People's Information Center, which Slim Coleman and Cathy Archibald had organized while

---

1 Had they moved to Chicago, they would have worked with Rising Up Angry—another group of young predominantly white students and former students who were organizing. The group had roots in Uptown and the original Rainbow Coalition from the '60s and were now printing a newspaper, *Rising Up Angry*, which then turned into an organization. Our paths occasionally crossed.

we were getting our feet wet in Racine. Based in the Lincoln Park community, they had worked closely with the Young Lords and José "Cha Cha" Jiménez, supporting their survival programs and joining them in efforts to resist the city's urban renewal plans. Unlike today, in the late '60s Lincoln Park was a diverse community of poor and working families. Puerto Rican families made up the majority of residents living there, alongside a number of Black and white families. The median income was barely above poverty level.

In addition to raising financial support for the Black Panther Party, the People's Information Center organized a clinic and a free breakfast program, and developed enough contacts to organize several mass survival programs. They distributed the *Black Panther* through a home distribution network in Lincoln Park and Lakeview.

I was there for the 1971 Christmas Survival Program, when the focus was on shoes for every child of the families signed up for the program. An important feature of the program was that it was a community-survival program organized by and with people from the community. I was tasked with finding a pair of shoes for and with one of our most dedicated volunteers at the children's breakfast program, Mrs. Williams, whose son James was thirteen and in desperate need. We were not looking for hand-me-downs but for a new pair he would be proud to wear. We shopped at many stores that day before finding the combination of a desired pair of shoes and a store whose manager was willing to donate them.

Several months later, I returned to Chicago to help with a mass distribution of milk at Lathrop Homes, which was, along with Cabrini-Green, one of only two Chicago Housing Authority (CHA) developments for families on the North Side. When it opened in 1938, Lathrop Homes housed 925 families in a combination of two-story townhouse structures and four-story walk-ups on thirty-two acres straddling Diversey Parkway, adjacent to the Chicago River, and bordering the neighborhoods of Bucktown and Roscoe Village. An eight-story senior building was added in 1959.

Lathrop was one of four projects built in Chicago prior to World War II, and the city's first public housing.[2] Each of these developments

---

2   The Chicago Housing Authority was founded in 1937 to be responsible for all public housing in Chicago, after the federal Public Works

was administered according to the federal Public Works Administration's neighborhood segregation policy. Called the "Neighborhood Composition Rule," the policy required that the tenants moving into a public housing unit be of the same race as the people who live in the area where it is located. Three of these four original public housing projects, including Lathrop, were designated for whites only.[3] The fourth, Ida B. Wells, had the largest number of units on the smallest footprint and was designated for African American families only. The CHA later officially abandoned the rule, circa early 1950s, introducing a short-lived policy of racial integration which was followed by de facto twin policies of racial segregation and benign neglect.

Despite this, by 1972 Lathrop Homes was the only CHA property where Black, white, and Latino families all lived. It had not, however, escaped the CHA's policy of benign neglect. The conditions were poor, and most people living there were unemployed or working low-paying jobs. The People's Information Center established a home distribution route for the *Black Panther* at Lathrop. This weekly contact with people living there meant organizers became aware of one particularly acute economic hardship faced by residents: there was only one grocery store in the area near Lathrop, and the price of milk there had spiked. The organizers' response was to address this immediate material need by launching a mass milk distribution program.

A few months later, as June came to an end, Slim and Cathy asked me to move to Chicago and join them in the newly formed Intercommunal Survival Committee. The ISC was a cadre of white activists organizing white people under the direction of the Black Panther Party—pretty much what we were doing in Racine but in a big city and with a clear relationship to the BPP. They wanted me to come right away to work on a clothing program planned for that August.

I was ready to move on. At heart, I was a big city girl. I had spent a good chunk of time in New York City, where I found the energy from all the people somewhat overwhelming at times; Racine, on the other

---

Administration built the first four developments in the city. The four initial developments were Jane Addams Houses, Lathrop Homes, Trumbull Park Homes, and Ida B. Wells Homes.

3   The exception to this was Jane Addams Houses, where 2.5 percent of the 1,027 units were assigned to Blacks.

hand, was too small. Not quite ninety-five thousand people lived there, and I was feeling claustrophobic. I packed up Brendan (then fifteen months old) and headed to Chicago.

By then, our original group of three organizing in Racine had grown to nearly twenty. Within six months, almost everyone moved to Chicago. Marc Zalkin, Paul Siegel, and Steve Gold—our mainstay Racine crew from our Madison days were in Chicago by summer's end. Joy and Tom Lindsay had since married. With Kaplan, they would join us the following January, along with Randy Saltz, Lynn Tremelling, Jerry Cleveland, Joannie Wallace, and Dean Loumos—all Wisconsinites we had met through our organizing. Curly came after clearing up his legal problems with the Selective Service, as did Steve Cole, who had been organizing in Milwaukee.

Working with Bobby Rush and the Illinois Chapter of the Black Panther Party in 1972, Slim recruited cadres to join Chicago mainstays Cathy, Jack Hart, Laurie Odell, and Pat Spaulding. Besides Racine, Rush reached out to a group of white activists working with Black Panthers in East St. Louis. He asked them to come to Chicago and join the Intercommunal Survival Committee. Four of them did—George Atkins, James Ratner, Susan Rosenblum, and Kim Nash.

Kim was a free spirit and musician—a guitar-playing singer who often wrote her own songs. When I think of her, I think of "Ninety-Nine Shots," a song she wrote about the murder of Fred Hampton and Mark Clark. She made sure our Country Music Sundays always had a music feature—including Gil Scott-Heron—who would be interviewed in *Keep Strong* magazine once we began publishing it three years later.

From the beginning, James was an information cadre who taught himself how to print as we ultimately formed Justice Graphics. He and George Atkins had been students together at Michigan State before dropping out. After trying organic farming—an unsuccessful effort—they ended up in East St. Louis running errands for the local chapter of the Black Panther Party. George would later become my partner through all my political campaigns and a person I would come to rely on deeply.

Susan was our ace paper seller, researcher, and, for many years, breadwinner. She had more degrees than the rest of us, was a great fundraiser, and took her commitment to the movement seriously. For several years she worked at the League of Women Voters, where she met Betty Willhoite, a strong, active, independent woman who became a true friend and supporter. Susan and I were roommates early in our shared Chicago experience.

Over the next decade, dozens more comrades would come and go, including Cathy Shanley, Ann Cline, Suzie Ruff, Barbara Schleicher, Mary Masterson, Sheila McMacken, Jeri Reed, Jeri Miglietta, Anne Toomey, Susan Gevatoff, Mary Masterson, Hannah (Ann) Hayes, Maureen Grey, Denise Reynolds, Karen Zaccor, and Alan Mills.

· ·

11.

WELCOME TO CHICAGO

My first assignment in Chicago was an August 1972 clothing give-away. The clothes had been accumulating in an empty industrial loft not far from Lathrop Homes. I was brought to the loft to sort out the usable clothes and discard the rest. We were only giving away new or almost-new duds. Respect was the guiding concept. "No problem," I thought to myself, until I got there. The loft must have been a good ten thousand square feet, with clothes piled everywhere. "You have ten days, and you'll be on your own." Welcome to Chicago.

Brendan was fifteen months old, and we were staying on Linda Turner's couch. Linda introduced me to the writings of Maya Angelou—her daughter's namesake. She was a wiz typist at a time when all documents had to be typed on an old-fashioned typewriter—no electricity, no autocorrect, just whiteout and carbon paper for copies. She worked long hours on legal cases for movement lawyers representing the Black Panther Party and others and volunteered with the People's Information Center.

Soon after, we moved to the basement of a house owned by the brother of one of the early members of the Intercommunal Survival Committee. This two-bedroom garden apartment would serve as our temporary home for the rest of the year. A crash pad for everyone else who had come to Chicago from Racine and East St. Louis, it was to become the home of our fledgling information-cadre activities, beginning with a hand-cranked mimeo machine and several light tables. Here we prepared leaflets and posters using press-on letters and became experts at making the mimeo machine hum, as we also did with the small printing press we eventually bought and brought to our basement.

Brendan and I shared a mattress on the floor, where we both also occasionally took naps. Brendan, because that's what toddlers do. Me, because I rarely got more than a few hours' sleep. Sandwiched between preparing for the clothing giveaway program, preparing flyers through the early hours of the day, collecting names on a petition to "Dump the butcher Hanrahan," selling one hundred *Black Panther* papers on Saturdays at one of many preferred North Side locations, and delivering papers on any one of numerous distribution routes to people's homes, sleep didn't seem that important—until it was.

That's how I happened to be home taking a nap midmorning one Sunday. Wiped out from a week of activities, I thought I'd grab a few winks while Brendan was taking his own nap. Unbeknownst to me, he woke up, got bored, and did what any engaged sixteen-month-old would do: try to get his mom's attention. He grabbed the nearest object—a glass diamond-shaped ashtray—and hit me in the head just over my right eye.

Suddenly, without warning and out of a deep sleep, a sharp pain penetrated my consciousness, and I was up in a flash sitting over my child, whose arms I had pinned down, watching blood drip onto his face. It was the blood that brought me into the reality of the moment. Releasing my grip and sobbing through tears, I jumped back, grabbed and hugged Brendan, and then called for help. The twentysomething doctor in the emergency room at Augustana Hospital told me I'd have a small scar over my eyebrow before informing me that he had done the same thing to his mom at about the same age.

We obviously needed a better plan. A balance between raising kids and making revolution had to be an organizational priority. While there had been no other cadres with children when I first came to Chicago, that would soon change.

As we were joined by others from Racine, the number of children grew as well, and by the beginning of the new year we had rented an entire

Left to right: Yvonne, Tania, Brendan, Anton, and Lisa (hidden behind Anton) with Joannie leading, show off their yoga at the Fred Hampton Memorial Hall.

apartment for the babies. Starting with three, there were six within a year. We organized the place literally from their point of view—complete with kid-sized tables and chairs for them to sit and play at. Whatever it took, we were going to raise the first generation of "intercommunal children." The security of our children, their health, and their development were the top priorities of our child development operation—or, as we all called it, CD. Depending on our various activities and responsibilities, two adult cadre were with the children at all times. Additionally, one cadre was overall in charge of coordinating all things CD related and making sure there was a schedule that reflected this. Parents participated, but all cadre were assigned to do child development.

We often found ways to integrate the children's activities with ours. Following the example of the Black Panther Party's exercise program for their kids, we began our own. Joannie, who was coordinating CD, enthusiastically engaged our kids in a daily dose of yoga- and tai-chi-inspired moves, often displaying their progress to us in a series of demonstrations. They showed a bit more progress than any of our own efforts at exercise.

Ultimately, our 24/7 child development was a work in progress. Balancing our organizational commitments and our quite-different perspectives on raising children was difficult. Nevertheless, we were united by our commitment to the future. It was becoming clear that ours was a prolonged struggle. Indeed, the world was not going to be changed in a year or two. We were in it for the long haul, and we understood that at the least we had the responsibility to ensure the best outcome for our children. Becoming thoughtful, committed adults capable of realizing their full potential and contributing to a humane and just world was our goal for them—and for ourselves. For inspiration, we looked toward the example of the Black Panther Party. However, this did not mean we always agreed on policy—or, even when we did, with how it was implemented.[4]

. . . .

12.

SUMMER 1972

Each of us who joined the Intercommunal Survival Committee in Chicago at this moment was energized by and committed to organizing poor white people under revolutionary Black leadership. Slim's history with the Black Panther Party afforded us this unique opportunity.

At the time, urban renewal was having a heavy impact on Lincoln Park. It was therefore far from an ideal site for outreach to educate white people in marginalized communities about the nature and goals of the Black Panther Party, about struggle with racism in the community, and to bring out that "in unity there is survival." For the newly minted Intercommunal Survival Committee, Uptown was the place for us to go, as it had a significant concentration of poor white people with zero political power.

The clothing program I initially came to Chicago to work on would be our last mass giveaway outside of Uptown. We would continue the *Black Panther* home-distribution routes that the People's Information

---

4 After April 1979, our children began spending more time with their parents, and shortly after a new crop of children were born with a greatly altered plan for child development.

Center had started in Lincoln Park, Lakeview, and Lathrop Homes, but our focus turned to Uptown.

In August we knocked on doors preparing for the Uptown Rally to End Police Brutality and Establish Community Control, which was to be held in October. In between, we had to get food together for the August Survival Conference, organized by the Black Panther Party on the South Side, which we hoped would give us the experience we needed to host a successful conference in October.

Uptown teemed with poverty programs, also having its fair share of street preachers and all sorts of "do-gooders." Leftists and student activists had preceded us, as did the Young Patriots and JOIN, who had made their mark but were now more or less gone from Uptown. The community was likely to be suspicious of us. We knew that we were going to have to prove ourselves.

We were armed with our own sense of purpose and determination. Door to door, we talked about the three thousand bags of groceries we planned to distribute in October, police brutality, the Black Panther Party August Survival Conference, and the effort to defeat Hanrahan, who was running for reelection as state's attorney in November. We asked residents if they wanted to get the *Black Panther* delivered to their home weekly and did our best to follow up on medical, welfare, and housing problems that they shared with us.

Police misconduct was a common complaint, allowing us the opportunity to explain the origins of the Black Panther Party for Self-Defense and their mission to patrol the police in the community (with legally acquired weapons) following a spate of police violence against Black people in Oakland, California.[5] Complaints of misconduct were common in Uptown, where, regardless of race, poor people were often victims of police brutality.

I had been doing home distribution for months when I knocked on a door in the heart of Uptown. Many times before I had this door slammed in my face. The apartment, however, was in the same building

---

5   Shortly after the BPP began patrolling the streets of Oakland with a
    firearm and a law book *Policing the Police*, a Republican state legislator
    introduced a bill banning the open carry of loaded firearms in California.
    Easily passed in the Democratic-dominated state legislature, the new law
    was instantly signed by then-governor Ronald Reagan. For Reagan, the
    right to bear arms was not a right extended to people of color.

as other regular subscribers. Whenever I did this route, I knocked on every door, hoping to add another subscriber. It was getting harder and harder to knock on this door, but our motto was "Leave no rock unturned," and I was not about to give up. My job was to win the hearts and minds of the people.

This time, a big guy with a scruffy face and well-toned muscles pulled the door open. As I steeled myself, he grabbed the paper out of my hand before I could even say a word, demanding "Give me that! You've been here seventeen times. Let me see what you think is so important!" Having broken the ice, I highlighted some of the articles in that week's paper that seemed relevant. And then we just talked. "Come back next week," he growled, "and bring that paper with you!" He stayed on the home distribution route for many years.

We learned from these daily interactions about the needs of people, as well as the barriers created by the bureaucracies they encountered. And it was on the basis of this learning that we developed the survival programs and engaged members of the community collectively in addressing the day-to-day struggles everyone faced. This was our lifeblood.

. . . .

13.

RALLY TO END POLICE BRUTALITY AND ESTABLISH COMMUNITY CONTROL

It was October 1972, and we had been bagging groceries on the first floor of the Aragon Ballroom for what felt like days. We had bagged even more than the three thousand bags of groceries we had promised, with a chicken in every bag.

The Aragon Ballroom was one of a number of elegant theaters built during the roaring 1920s that was rundown by the early '70s. Named for a region in Spain, it was designed in the Moorish architectural style, with an interior resembling a Spanish village. The theater was adjacent to the elevated (or "L") train and less than a block away from similarly

Aragon Ballroom marquee; October 12, 1972.

storied venues such as the Riviera Theater and the Uptown Theatre. In between those two large and elegant movie houses lies another infamous venue: the Green Mill lounge. Rumor had it that in between the Aragon and the Green Mill were underground tunnels used by Al Capone to run alcohol during prohibition.

Those four venues—the Aragon, the Riviera, the Uptown Theatre, and the Green Mill—all lay less than eight hundred feet from each other, surrounding the corner of Lawrence and Broadway in Uptown. This corner and those venues would later become a focal point for the re-creation of an Uptown entertainment district.

In October 1972, the Aragon was a cavernous, beautiful, but underutilized and slightly neglected ballroom, surrounded by housing where oppressed people of all races and cultures lived. This was one year before the Aragon would be sold to a couple of Latino promoters who would rejuvenate the space, first as a boxing venue and then as a concert hall.

In October 1972, however, it was the scene of the Rally to End Police Brutality and Establish Community Control. With Bobby Rush, deputy minister of defense of the Illinois Chapter of the Black Panther Party, as the headliner, we truly did not know what to expect from the three thousand mostly poor white people who would attend—largely transplants from mining country in states like Kentucky, Tennessee, Ohio, Pennsylvania, and West Virginia. In fact, the level of disrespect, brutality, and corruption practiced in Uptown by the police was like that being experienced in Chicago's Black and Latino communities. One of the announced speakers was Peggy Terry, who had been a political activist in Uptown since she moved there after World War II. She organized with JOIN, and her son was involved with the Young Patriots.[6] We hoped for the best but prepared for the worst.

In addition to the eight of us who had come to Chicago in the last few months from Racine and East St. Louis, another eight would join the following January. A few of them had come up to help prepare for and attend the rally. You could pick us out in a crowd because of the duds picked up wholesale from stores on Roosevelt Road in the weeks leading up to the rally: baby-blue silk shirts and Stetson hats for the guys, and I can't remember what for the sisters. But no one would be able to say we were shoddy looking. We would be cool!

We were joined by nearly one hundred volunteers from the community as, over the course of several days, we bagged groceries, set up chairs, and prepared for the big event—our first major activity in Uptown!

In the previous year, as the People's Information Center, shoes were given away in Lincoln Park, milk in Lathrop Homes, and clothing in Lakeview. Now, as the Intercommunal Survival Committee, we were staking out our territory in Uptown, and planned to do so with flair—challenging the power of racism over the power of common needs and desires. We began with the force at the heart of so many injustices throughout Chicago: the demand for an end to police brutality and the establishment of community control of policing. This wasn't a first for Uptown.

In 1960, eight Chicago police officers had been caught in a massive corruption scandal. Uniformed police officers stationed in Uptown had been caught plotting and carrying out burglaries while on patrol and in collusion with a known thief who had often served as their lookout. Although many considered this revelation to be the catalyst for one of

---

6   Peggy was the Peace and Freedom Party's vice presidential candidate with Eldridge Cleaver in 1968, as well as a participant in the Southern Christian Leadership Conference's Poor People's Campaign. She was interviewed by Studs Terkel for several of his books.

the largest shake-ups and reform efforts in Chicago Police Department history, these initiatives had made little impact on how the residents of Uptown were treated. Five years on, the scandal had become folklore with little if any impact on the behavior of police officers. This would be a recurring cycle for the next six decades in Chicago.

When Students for a Democratic Society had come to Uptown in 1964 and organized under the banner of JOIN, they had interacted with the Goodfellows, a local gang. The Goodfellows had become politically active and would soon reorganize as the Young Patriots. Along the way they had organized several actions to bring attention to the mistreatment of young people in Uptown by the police. In 1965, in a joint action with JOIN, they had demonstrated in front of the Summerdale police district.[7]

Among their demands had been the firing of Sergio "Sam" Joseph.[8] Nothing had come of these demands, but members of the Young Patriots still remember the impacts of the consequential repression that followed—especially after they were recruited to join the Black Panther Party and the Young Lords Organization in the Rainbow Coalition.

Police misconduct had been rampant for years and included allegations that evidence was planted, demands that guns be found and left in dumpsters twenty-four hours later for the cops to pick up, and sexual

---

7   Uptown is divided between two police districts—Town Hall and Summerdale. While their boundaries, and even their designations, have changed over the years, this fact has remained constant. In 1972, Town Hall was located in an aging building at the corner of Addison and Halsted Streets and was also called the Twenty-Third District. Today, it is housed in a new building a half block away and is part of the Nineteenth District. In 1972, Summerdale was located to the west on Foster Avenue in a cramped one-story building. Today it is located in a new building a mile northwest and is referred to as the Twentieth District.

8   Several years later, Joseph was charged with "excessive abuse", but the charges were dropped after an outcry of support from several aldermen, led by Joseph P. Burke (father of Alderman Ed Burke, who would later, along with Ed Vrdolyak, lead the opposition to all reforms proposed by Harold Washington) and Judge Saul Epton (the brother of Bernard Epton who would later be the Republican candidate against Harold Washington in 1983). Decrying the decision to suspend "the most highly decorated officer in Chicago history," they demanded to know "how the word of a criminal could be taken against his."

Left to right: Harold Bell, Bobby Rush, and Stan McKinney on stage at the Aragon for the Rally to End Police Brutality and Establish Community Control, October 1972.

harassment and assault of women. Few victims of this behavior were willing to come forward with official complaints.

As people arrived at the Aragon, we went to our previously assigned positions for security, crowd control, grocery distribution, and so on. The main event was in the ballroom on the second floor, where the huge dance floor that could accommodate up to four thousand people was prepared for the rally, with three thousand chairs set up theater-style facing a stage filled with and surrounded by bags of groceries. As we anxiously awaited the arrival of our guest speakers, the hall began to fill with throngs of Uptown residents looking for food, a glimpse of the leaders of the Black Panther Party, or an answer to their troubles with the police, as well as those who came out of sheer curiosity.

From the bottom of the Aragon's glamorous binary staircase, where I was stationed doing first-floor security with George Atkins, our only clue as to what was going on above us was what we could hear. There we stood, listening attentively. The place was full before Bobby Rush and his entourage arrived and were ushered up the stairs. That's all we knew until we heard a huge commotion. Our hearts in our throats and adrenaline rushing, we ran up the stairs, taking two steps at a time, ready for the worst, only to find the audience giving Rush an enthusiastic standing ovation.

When it was built a half century before, the main floor of the Aragon had been ornate. Now it was a shadow of itself, but the room we entered was alive. The crowd of three thousand were mostly on their feet, clapping, whistling, and hollering. Rush was on stage, flanked by Stan McKinney and Harold Bell, and surrounded by thousands of bags of groceries.

During the two weeks leading up to this moment, few of us had gotten much sleep. We had been busily soliciting donations and arranging for the assembly of the bags of groceries, which had taken several days to bag. Our hopes and our faith that white people could come together with people of color in a common struggle for justice were more than gratified.

The color line may be America's defining dynamic, but there are moments in which its rule can be challenged. We had come to understand that it was possible to change the context, create a new set of rules, and find common ground. In that moment, the way forward was clear. It would not, however, be easy.

· ·

14.

DUMP HANRAHAN!

In summer 1972, Edward Hanrahan was running for reelection as the Democratic Party's nominee for Cook County state's attorney. But his role in the murders of Fred Hampton and Mark Clark had not been forgotten. He would face a serious challenge, even though many pundits believed it would be a fool's errand to oppose him.

Cook County encompasses not only Chicago but also more than one hundred suburbs and municipalities whose combined population outnumbers those living in the urban core. Nevertheless, Chicago is the dominant political force. And the suburbs (both then, but even more so now) comprise a wide mix of poor and rich, and Black, Latino, and white communities. Although the Chicago mayor is the most powerful politician in the county (perhaps in the state of Illinois), the county officials—including the board president, sheriff, and state's attorney—are all relatively well known. The Democratic machine controlled them all. Jumping right into the campaign to defeat Hanrahan, we hit the streets with "Dump Hanrahan" petitions, which were already being circulated throughout the city and county by the Black Panther Party and thousands of others angered by Hanrahan's lies and the murders he had authorized and—along with the FBI—put in motion.

We also found support in Uptown, where three years earlier Fred had reached out to the Young Patriots to join the Black Panther Party and the Young Lords Organization in forming the Rainbow Coalition. Soon before I first set foot in Uptown, they had been organizing a series of survival programs, including a free health clinic that was still functioning.[9]

The Young Patriots had been organized by young people who, like the Young Lords, had started as a local street gang. Indeed, Chicago's history is rife with stories of street gangs organized by young people to "protect their community"—often glorified social clubs.

Richard J. Daley was famously a part of one such group in his own neighborhood of Bridgeport when he was a teenager. As a newcomer to Chicago, I was struck by how references on the part of media and politicians alike, including Daley, to street gangs in Black, Latino, and poor white communities dramatically differed from those to Daley's boyhood gang affiliation.

Meeting our goal to collect ten thousand signatures, the Intercommunal Survival Committee enthusiastically joined the Black Panther Party, South Side and West Side community organizations, independent Black politicians, and progressive-minded whites in an all-out drive to defeat Hanrahan. Citywide, hundreds of lawyers, poll watchers, and election judges were trained to protect the vote on Election Day that November.

In the end, the effort proved successful. When Hanrahan was defeated, it was a rare blow to Daley's political organization, as the Democratic Party had been able to rely on considerable support from Chicago's Black wards since the 1930s—which often had a decisive impact in countywide races where the suburban vote usually went to

---

9   The clinic would lose its lease in the fall of 1973. Several attempts to find an alternative location were unsuccessful.

Republican candidates. Now, however, a Republican state's attorney had been elected to replace Richard J. Daley's protégé. Message sent!

· ·

15.

MODEL CITIES ELECTION
A SURVIVAL TICKET

As the last leaves fell in autumn 1972, we were on a roll. And with elections for the Model Cities councils scheduled for December, we already had another opportunity to try to shift the landscape of Chicago's electoral politics. A creation of Lyndon Johnson's Great Society and War on Poverty, the Model Cities councils were hyped as an experiment to develop new anti-poverty programs and alternative forms for municipal government. In Chicago the program provided an infusion of federal capital into Richard J. Daley's well-oiled Democratic machine. Daley rarely saw a federal program he didn't like, and whatever the legislative intent, he would first and foremost find a way to use such initiatives to enhance his patronage army.

The Illinois Chapter of the Black Panther Party was running their own slate against the machine-endorsed slate for the Model Cities Council in the Grand Boulevard community on Chicago's South Side. We did the same in Uptown. Peggy Terry joined Jack Hart and Slim Coleman on what we called the "Survival Ticket." Originally from the South, Peggy had been active in Uptown since the JOIN days and was well known and respected. Jack and Slim were by then leading members of the Intercommunal Survival Committee.

Authorized in 1966, Model Cities planning grants had been awarded the following year to sixty-three cities, of which Chicago had been one. Federal regulations attached to these funds required citizen participation in each of the neighborhoods chosen. In Chicago, the neighborhoods chosen by Daley and Lou Hill, his planning czar, for participation in Model Cities were Woodlawn, Grand Boulevard,

Lawndale, and Uptown, and in every one of them Daley controlled the appointments. While elections were held to choose representatives to sit on the Model Cities community council in each of the four neighborhoods, those individuals chosen and endorsed by the regular Democratic Party usually won. In Uptown, most people had no idea when or where these elections were held.

Decisions made by the Model Cities Uptown Council rarely reflected the concerns of most people living in Uptown. Usually skewed to the benefit of real estate interests, the council had resources that could be used to improve housing conditions, educational resources, or activities for young people, but rarely did so. Instead, the council became another rubber stamp for the city's efforts to use the promise of new construction of public institutions to "urban-remove" those they did not want to include in the urban renewal of the community.

When the city announced the plan to locate a new City College in the heart of Uptown on a densely populated four square blocks, people were enraged and organized. Residents weren't against the college coming to Uptown; they were against how it would be done. Rather than just campaign against city planners' obvious intention to remove poor people from the community, the people most affected came up with their own plan that enhanced their housing and included new recreational and job-training opportunities. The proposal for the Hank Williams Village, with the aid of a supportive neighborhood architect, put to paper their vision for their future in Uptown. It was handily rejected.

After the Model Cities Council failed to endorse the Hank Williams Village proposal presented by a broad coalition of Uptown residents and organizations, many had had enough. The time seemed ripe for a challenge to the makeup of Uptown's Model Cities Community Council, as our flyer explained:

> Vote so you can put people's candidates into a position to tell you what is going on behind those closed doors! $66 million dollars is supposed to be coming into Chicago this year, to help upgrade the standard of living of the people in four communities. Uptown-Lakeview is one of these. The money is to come into Model Cities-Urban Progress programs. The people should know what happens to these funds, so they can demand control of them. The Intercommunal Survival Committee is supporting

3 candidates (the Survival Ticket) for the Uptown-Lakeview Community Council which helps plan Model Cities-Urban Progress programs around housing, medical care, food, education and other areas of our survival.

Emphasizing the need for people to have decent affordable housing, the campaign called for funding by the federal government, with the goal of ownership by the tenants. The Survival Ticket was clear that:

Whether the survival ticket is elected or not, the Intercommunal Survival Committee is going to go on organizing survival programs—free food and clothing, free health care, free legal and welfare counseling, free housing maintenance and other programs that are needed in our community. . . . But we just feel that Model Cities programs could be Mayor Daley's way of wiping us out while feeding us a little candy. We don't want a little candy, we want all $66 million put into programs that righteously serve the people. That is why we are working on the Survival Ticket—Hart, Terry and Coleman.

While the Survival Ticket did not win the election, the slate came in second to the machine candidates. The liberal candidates, representing people who lived in the single-family homes and mansions looping the heart of Uptown, came in third. For the first time a coalition of poor and working families from Black, white, Puerto Rican, Native American, and Japanese American households came out and voted in an election many had previously not even known existed.

Even so, we were going to have to get real and work harder. The 46th Ward had voted to dump Hanrahan and we took this as a victory. The Model Cities election was not so clear-cut. We did not meet our goals and did not beat the machine. They had received a little over 55 percent of the vote. We split the remaining votes with the liberal slate coming out just four hundred votes ahead. We needed to strengthen our depth in the community.

16.

THE 1973 COMMUNITY CONTROL OF POLICE CONFERENCE

At a rally in August 1972, the Illinois Chapter of the Black Panther Party had launched a Campaign for Community Control of Police. Our ISC Rally to End Police Brutality and Establish Community Control in October had been part of this campaign. The campaigns had worked in parallel during the successful effort to oust Hanrahan in November of 1972. For the next nine months, a BPP–led drafting committee developed some general principles for a humane, effective, community-controlled police force. This all led to a citywide conference held on June 1 and 2, 1973.

Having joined the Illinois Chapter of the BPP in 1969, Yvonne King was a field secretary and had been one of the party members who ran for the Grand Boulevard Model Cities Council the previous December. She was now assigned to oversee communications and the media for this event. I was assigned to assist her. The flyer leading up to the conference charged:

> In 1969–70 at least 70 civilians were killed by police in Chicago, the highest rate in the nation. In a city at least one-third black, 55.5 percent of all those arrested are black people. And yet, 70 percent of all black applicants to the police department are turned down. If figures for Latino, Native American and other people of color were available, the evidence would prove even more clearly the racism of the Chicago Police Department. Facts like these have brought about the movement for Community Control of Police.

Keynote speeches by Julian Bond, Reverend Ralph Abernathy, Archie Hargraves, Fannie Lou Hamer, Gary mayor Richard Hatcher, Benjamin Spock, and BPP chairman Bobby Seale highlighted the conference. Renault Robinson and other local Chicago leaders participated in workshops. Aimed at educating participants on the elements of an ordinance for community control of policing and what it would take to get one passed, the workshops were billed as the main event.

For me, however, the main event was Fannie Lou Hamer's speech. A decade earlier, she had risked her life for the right to vote. Now I was responsible for picking her up from the airport and getting her to her hotel, and to the conference. I knew of the challenge of the Mississippi Freedom Democratic Party to have their delegates—including Ms. Hamer—seated at the 1964 Democratic Convention and of the beatings and many threats she and her family received from white supremacists and police. Her humility, her strength of commitment, determination, refusal to back down, and grace in the face of intimidation and violence stirred me to the core.

Since the beginning of the year, in Uptown and Lakeview, we met with a wide variety of organizations, church groups, and community leaders about community control of policing. We (the ISC) also gained a position of respect within the liberal independent organizations because we had more contacts in the community than they did and our position on community control of policing appealed to more people than they thought it would. Canvassing, expanded home distribution, and survival services continued right up to the conference. As a result of these face-to-face interactions, we brought several hundred people to hear Seale and Hamer, among others, speak.

Over nineteen hundred people registered during the two-day conference, which was held at the University of Illinois campus at Chicago Circle. Most left with a goal of building a citywide campaign for an ordinance for community control of policing. To get there required a voter registration campaign to reach the thousands of unregistered voters. As a brochure for the citywide conference noted, "Since the majority of unregistered voters in Chicago are young, registering them for community control of policing is a key issue for the survival of young blacks, young whites, and young Latinos."

This was the focus. But the avenues for registration had to be opened. The June conference was the kickoff of phase two of this campaign— registering to vote for community control. We identified strategies to force the board of election commissioners to have more in-precinct registration days, or to empower deputy registrars to go door to door to register people to vote. Meanwhile, we also engaged with allies in the independent political movements of the city to advance this effort.

These efforts to pass an ordinance for community control of policing did not succeed in 1973. However, the campaign to register to vote for community control had a significant impact. The groundwork it laid would make it possible, a decade later, to register over two hundred thousand new voters, leading to the election of Harold Washington as Chicago's first Black (and progressive) mayor.[10]

Additionally, our organizing in 1973 led directly to the creation of the Office of Professional Standards—later renamed the Independent Police Review Authority, and subsequently the Civilian Office of Police Accountability. As with these successor agencies, the creation of the OPS would be a pyrrhic victory. Indeed, it would ultimately become just another layer in the bureaucracy that prevented police accountability.[11]

---

10 Our community organizing would also foreshadow further campaigns for police accountability—activism which would lead, in July 2021, to the historic passage of a new citywide civilian oversight ordinance. This followed an extensive period of debate during which a compromise version was agreed to. It remains to be seen how effective this new attempt will be at finally bringing legitimate civilian oversight to the Chicago Police Department, or whether new changes in the most recent bargaining agreement between the city and the Fraternal Order of Police will have a positive effect or if reforms in discipline, supervision, training, and recruitment required by a 2019 federal consent decree will ultimately be implemented. As of mid-2022, very little has been done to begin the implementation of this ordinance, while deadline after deadline established in the consent decree continues to be missed.

11 According to a *Washington Post* investigation published on March 9, 2022, Chicago paid nearly $528 million in police misconduct claims between 2010 and 2020. More than $380 million was tied to officers who were targets of multiple claims. It is rare for an officer to be separated from service following a judgment in a civil suit.

17.

PERSONAL TRAGEDY STRIKES

As our campaign for community control in Uptown kicked off, personal tragedy struck. My father died.

He had moved his factory from Greenpoint, Brooklyn, to an industrial park near Scranton, Pennsylvania, in 1965, taking advantage of financial incentives to do so. He stayed in Pennsylvania during the week, returning to our home in Long Island most weekends. Signs that my parents' thirty-year marriage was coming to an end abounded. By the time of their divorce in 1968, my brother Bob felt my father owed him his business. My mother agreed. My father, not so much. My own relationship with all three of them was complicated. My mother had never acknowledged Bob's abuse, while my father's relationship with him had been compromised by it. Even so, I loved all three of them.

When I received a call in late August 1972 that my father had had a stroke, the first person I called for help was Bob. In spite of our history, he was the only person I could think of who could help me with the money I needed to get a plane ticket. He declined. My brother Ed was out of the country. Larry was still a high school student. My mother and my father were estranged. I called Jane, who by now was living on the West Coast. As always, she came through.

Taking a break from petitioning to dump Hanrahan and organizing for the rally to end police brutality, I flew to Pennsylvania in October to tend to my dad. Bob beat me to it. By the time I got there, while Dad was still in the hospital, Bob had changed the locks on the doors of the factory and locked him out. It would be a few months before he got back in. Somehow, my father had a check for his salary through the end of the year.

The stroke turned out to be a cancerous tumor in his brain. He had had a cancerous section of one of his lungs removed several years earlier, and apparently a cluster of cancer cells had escaped the scalpel and traveled to his brain. The use of his left side began to return quickly, and he was out of the hospital in a few days and ready for me to drive him to New York City for specialized medical treatment.

First, though, we visited with his new family. Since moving to Pennsylvania, my dad had fathered three children with Carla. Albert was the oldest; Lisa, the youngest, was just a year older than Brendan. Carla was still married, and the children knew my dad only as "Uncle Morris." It would be almost two decades before Lisa figured this out and spilled the beans to her siblings.

His doctors gave him six months to live. He stretched that to ten. During that time, he restructured his business and brought me onto the board. This would be an open declaration that I'd taken sides in the feud between my parents, clearly putting myself at odds with my brother Bob, who I had never challenged before.

My dad and I were in touch often that year. He came to visit in Chicago, and I saw him in Pennsylvania just days before he died. I got a chance to say goodbye. But even so, his death hit me hard.

. . . .

18.

REGISTERING TO VOTE FOR COMMUNITY CONTROL OF POLICING

We taped the speech Bobby Seale gave at the Citywide Conference for Community Control of Police, subsequently setting up fifty listening sessions in people's homes. Usually between five and fifteen people came, listened, and discussed the Panthers' concept of "the human movement" and community control of policing—the Seale-Brown program emanating from their Oakland joint campaign for mayor and city council, respectively.

While Elaine Brown had not made it past the April 1972 primary in her bid for city council, Bobby had forced the incumbent mayor into a runoff election in May. Their joint campaign focused on Oakland as a base of operations, and many aspects of this analysis were reported weekly in the *Black Panther*, which we continued to distribute and study. Leading members of the Party described the campaign as another survival program, and it was influential to our own actions in Chicago. Analyzing the two electoral campaigns in which we had been involved in 1972 through this lens, we looked toward this new voter-registration drive in the same way.

Through the Northside Campaign for Community Control, organizing meetings for precinct committees were held in Uptown precincts, located in the 46th and 48th Wards. Chicago's fifty wards were roughly equal in population and were usually drawn along ethnic or community lines. Each ward's alderman is more local mayor than legislator. Each ward is split up into between forty and sixty precincts, usually of between five hundred and one thousand voters, and people came together in each of these precincts to discuss the problems they faced.[12]

We brought copies of the draft ordinance for community control of policing for discussion. In addition to police corruption and misconduct, issues with housing, legal assistance, welfare, food, and health care were popular topics. In one precinct meeting, there was a proposal to mobilize against a particularly vicious slumlord; in another, to organize a new children's breakfast program before school started; and in another, where there was racial tension, one to bring about unity between the Black and white people in the community.

Voter suppression was a well-used tool of the Daley machine. Cynicism ("You can't beat city hall") added to a sense of powerlessness that discouraged many from making the effort to vote. The machine rarely advertised opportunities to register, often outright suppressing the vote—for instance, by requiring more identification than was actually required by law, and which for some was difficult to access—to limit new, "unreliable" voters. Thus, it was no surprise that most of the hundreds of people participating in these meetings that summer were

---

12 These precincts should not be confused with police districts, sometimes referred to as precincts. Chicago has fifty wards, which are redrawn every ten years after the census results. The number of people in each ward is one-fiftieth of the city's population. After the 1970 and 1980 census, there were about sixty thousand people in each ward. Since this number includes children, immigrants, and others not eligible to vote in Chicago, the number of eligible voters in each ward varies. For voting purposes, each ward is divided into precincts. One location in each precinct is designated as the polling place for that precinct. The number of precincts in a ward varies as they are designed to accommodate an average of five hundred voters.

not registered to vote. "Until now," they said, "there was no reason to vote." The people they knew who voted often did so for the favors being offered by the precinct captain—sometimes a dollar, or a meal, a bottle of wine, or a promise of one sort or another. Others they knew voted to ward off threats made to their survival, including eviction (if they lived in buildings controlled by the machine), or their access to a job at the day-labor line, or even their ability to collect welfare. The politicians they knew of had done nothing for them.

Again and again, people agreed that the only time they saw their precinct captain was around election time or when they wanted something. Many people didn't know how to register to vote. "The Daley precinct captain takes care of a hundred or so people and keeps the rest of us in the dark, and that is how Daley stays in power," was a commonly expressed sentiment.

I did an analysis of voter registration in the 46th Ward, which we published. What we learned was that less than half the eligible voters in Uptown were registered, while in more affluent areas of the ward, 75 percent of eligible voters were registered. Between the low number of eligible voters registering and the low turnout to elections of voters that were registered, the alderman of the 46th Ward was elected in 1972 with less than 14 percent of the eligible voters and just over 23 percent of the registered voters voting for him.

In 1973, the only time someone could sign up to vote in their community was during in-ward registration. These occurred in two locations per ward, thirty days before an election. These dates and locations were poorly publicized—except to those voters the Democratic precinct captain could depend on for their vote. The only other alternative for registration was to take off work during the workweek and go downtown to register. It was my experience that most people living in the heart of Uptown were more likely to visit family in Kentucky or Tennessee than they were to go to downtown Chicago.

That summer we began a regular practice of weekly trips in vans and buses to city hall to bring Uptown residents to "register to vote for community control." The Northside Campaign for Community Control became the place people gathered to brainstorm solutions to common problems.

Illegal lockouts were rampant. Despite a state law that required a landlord to go to court before evicting a tenant, tenants often found their belongings thrown out on the street or sold without notice, and certainly without a court order. When police were called, they rarely helped the tenant; more often than not, in fact, they assisted the landlord in their illegal evictions.

Building conditions were often horrific—something that was particularly true on streets near proposed city-sponsored developments. Plans for the new City College that would later be named Truman College had already leveled one square block, but rumors of plans to expand the college's footprint were affecting the surrounding blocks. On Racine Street, Sunnyside Avenue, and Clifton Street, landlords continued to rent out their apartments while "milking" the buildings. They collected rents but did no repairs, stopped paying for garbage collection, and fell behind on water, electric, and gas bills. If anyone complained, they were put out.[13] The pattern continued as plans for a city health center and a middle school at Wilson and Hazel became public knowledge.

These were three major institutions being planned to "revitalize" Uptown's 46th and 48th Wards, approved by the respective aldermen. They were supported by the Model Cities Council, but not so much by the people who lived in the heart of Uptown, where all these improvements were to occur.

The new City College was to be built on land that had housed nearly three thousand people until it was cleared,[14] lying empty for several years before ground was broken. In fact, by the time I arrived in 1972,

---

13 This was before the Chicago City Council imposed any regulations or requirements for notice to tenants. Today, there must be notices posted before a building's utility can be cut off for nonpayment, giving tenants an opportunity to go to court and rectify the situation. No such requirements were in place in 1972.

14 The original footprint for the college was ultimately limited due to the strong resistance from the community. In place of the original plan to displace three thousand people, sixteen hundred people were displaced to build the first and main Truman College building. Another twelve hundred people were displaced for the second building that houses the gym and swimming pool and skills center, and for tennis courts that would later become a surface parking lot and eventually the Larry McKeon Administration Building and parking facility.

the entire block had become a dumping ground for abandoned cars—and the rats that came with them.

Joan Arai Middle School was built to accommodate sixth, seventh, and eighth grades. When the students who were transferred from four elementary schools arrived in 1975, the library was without books, and the new Olympic-sized swimming pool went unused because doors had not been installed on the locker rooms. It took almost two years, a great deal of community pressure, and some embarrassing news stories to get locker-room doors and books into the school.

Meanwhile, the highly touted Uptown Health Center failed for years to provide much health care.

A developer named Peter Tomase, who was also a machine precinct captain and on the Model Cities Council, floated an idea for a shopping center to be located between Broadway to Sheridan and Wilson to Lawrence. His request for a $5,000 planning grant from Model Cities was opposed by the Campaign for Community Control, the advocacy organization Voice of the People, and the Uptown People's Action Project and was temporarily shelved by the city. However, Daley then announced that fifteen new shopping centers would be built across the city, with one designated for Uptown.

As the Voice of the People had done five years earlier when the city was confirming plans for what would become Truman College, our coalition now proposed a people's plan alternative to the shopping center proposal we feared—with history as our insight—would reappear.

It was clear that the decision makers were not going to listen to anyone who they didn't need to listen to. We would have to work to get their attention, and Register to Vote for Community Control was a good place to start: indeed, it afforded an opportunity to educate and organize ourselves and our community to challenge the machine, block by block and precinct by precinct. To be successful we would need to leave no stone unturned as we endeavored to win the hearts and minds of enough people to challenge racism, police misconduct, inadequate and unsafe housing, poor health, and so much more.

19.

HOUSING WIPEOUT IN UPTOWN

The Northside Campaign for Community Control began publishing a newspaper, *Community Control*, that summer. Voice of the People, a local grassroots organization and ally in the campaign, had been active in Uptown since the late '60s.[15] Voice leaders Dovie Coleman and her niece Dovie Thurman, (popularly referred to as Big and Little Dovie respectively), Virginia Bowers, Mary Hockenberry, and Irene Hutchison were engaged in fighting for welfare rights as well as decent housing. Black, white, and Native American—all were committed to creating the space for poor and working people to have a voice in their community and their future. In addition to opposing the location identified for the City College, they spearheaded the Hank Williams Village plan that was ignored and dismissed by the Model Cities Council, the City Colleges, the alderman, and the mayor's planning department.

"The college was a gimmick, developed through the efforts of the Chicago Uptown Commission. They had been working for several years at that time and had succeeded in having Uptown declared an urban renewal area," Irene Hutchison told *Community Control* in 1973. "The college was the extra added attraction to interest people in investing in Uptown," she continued. "And also, it would serve the purpose of getting rid of quite a large number of 'undesirable people'—the Appalachians, Black people, Indians, Spanish speaking—that were 'messing up the neighborhood.' As we were told, the land here is like gold and we just don't qualify to live on it."[16]

Taking their opposition to the streets, Voice went door to door informing people living in the target area of what the city planned for them. They demonstrated, confronted the local powers that be, recruited a local architect who helped them design an alternative plan, and identified several alternative sites. In Irene's words, "We weren't against the

---

15 It would be nearly a decade before Voice became the affordable housing provider it is known as today.

16 *Community Control*, Vol. 1, No. 3 (October 1973), published by the Northside Campaign for Community Control.

Left to right: "Big Dovie" Coleman, "Little Dovie" Thurman, Irene Hutchison, Mary Hockenberry, and Edna Johnson.

idea of the college or improving our education. We were only against the idea of the college tearing down the places where we lived." But their suggestions fell on deaf ears.

Speculators saw their chance to make a buck. Maintenance on most buildings ceased. Utility bills were not paid. Garbage collection became a thing of the past. In short, conditions became dire. "The city started a campaign of harassment," Irene recalled, "where the urban renewal workers would come and tell them, 'We're going to tear down your buildings, you've got to get out.'"

In response, Voice of the People went door to door, telling tenants they had rights. Federal regulations required them to have replacement housing, money to move and a subsidy to help pay their rent. While the city blatantly ignored these regulations, more and more tenants were forced out. "Most of them got scared," Irene explained. "The wreckers would knock down a building and knock out windows or bricks in the building next to it. When the people would come out to complain, they'd say, 'Why aren't you out? You better get out because tomorrow morning we're going to come and wreck your building.'"

Buildings began to burn at an unusual rate. Although the fire station was less than a block away, a response to fight the fires often took as long as twenty or thirty minutes. "We pulled people out of burned-out buildings. Sometimes they'd be the last family or the last two families in a building that caught fire. We were told by the people in the neighborhood that they knew who was getting paid fifty dollars for each fire they set. They wouldn't tell us their names because they were too scared."

The failure to protect people living here was so blatant that the Department of Housing and Urban Development withheld some urban

(Top) The process of demolishing apartment buildings was often a lengthy one with piles of debris left for weeks at a time becoming the primary playgrounds in the community. (Bottom) Speculators were not the only problem. This playlot at Buena and Kenmore had a swimming pool until the Park District decided to demolish it. After tearing down the fence that had surrounded it, workmen began the demolition, taking their time in doing so and leaving a gaping hole and dangerous debris for children coming to the playground to have easy access to.

renewal money. "They didn't care. They had so much to gain by wiping the people out of this area which they saw as the gold coast, that they were willing to lose $15 million in federal money to carry out their purpose," Irene concluded. A city promise to provide replacement housing never came to fruition.

Once again speculators were circling the blocks rumored to be the site of the college expansion. A second building, designed to house a technical skills center, was to be located adjacent to the first, expanding the college's footprint to the alley west of Racine. We further suspected that the college intended to expand south another block to Montrose as they argued additional land was required to create a proper campus environment.

In a repeat of history, landlords collected rents while failing to pay for basic utilities. Unknown men would show up to collect rent claiming they were the new owners. They had bought the building on a contract, they said, insisting that the rent must now be paid to them. These inscrutable figures took tenants' money and brought zero services back to them in return. Sometimes the water or electricity would be turned off the very next day. For those families who had lived in housing previously located on the city block where the first college building was to be constructed, this was literally their second round.

The home-distribution route in this area included every building that was still occupied. During our rounds, we were bombarded with requests for assistance and greeted again and again with heavy doses of cynicism. Our antidote was to build avenues for empowerment: a tenant union controlled by those most affected; a support network for landlords who were trying to do the right thing; legal assistance for tenants;[17] and voter registration. In time, our efforts would also extend to the Avery lawsuit, which would challenge the public policy that encouraged displacement of tenants living in a racially integrated community.

In the end, the expansion of the college campus south of the main building was only partially successful. West Sunnyside Avenue between the L tracks and North Racine was relocated about two hundred feet south of its original location. Tennis courts were built on the southern

---

17 While we always considered legal action one of the tools for survival, this was a clear instance where it was also a vehicle for political education. At this time, tenants had few if any protections. It would be another ten years before a tenants' bill of rights would be passed by the Chicago City Council.

In the mid 1970s tenants at 4425–27 N Racine took a stand when the wrecking ball came to tear down their home. This last stand is pictured here. Following numerous arrests, police entered the building to clear it out, paving the way for the demolition. While the tenants were not successful in stopping the wrecking ball, the expansion of the college southbound did not claim any further apartments on this block. The property remained vacant for years. A decade later Deloris Jones, a Voice of the People tenant who lived next door and whose job at the University of Illinois Cooperative Extension Service was to create community gardens, did just that on this still vacant lot. For another decade, this space was transformed into a place of community growth and development and the source of much needed fresh vegetables.

end of this new border, adjacent to a small parking lot that could barely accommodate thirty cars. A green space was created between these courts and the building. I don't know where the idea for tennis courts came from, but they went largely unused before being repurposed in the 1990s as parking.[18] The green space became a popular spot for neighborhood kids to play football each fall and for Brendan and his friends to play their annual "Turkey Bowl" every Thanksgiving, well into their thirties.

The "technical skills" center, built on the West Side of Racine, included facilities to teach automotive repair and cosmetology, a sports complex complete with an Olympic-sized swimming pool and a gym, and, in a nod to the demands of the nearby middle-class community, a theater complex that would for many years house the Pegasus Theatre.

. . . .

20.

THE COMMUNITY SAYS, "DON'T SELL GRAPES"

One of my favorite foods has always been table grapes. Red grapes, green grapes—I love them all. Between 1965 and 1970, in solidarity with striking farmworkers in Delano, California, I had given them up. When I did so again in 1973, I knew, as before, that it was hardly a sacrifice compared to those made every day by the workers who picked them.

Farmworker migrants rarely lived past forty. During childbirth, infants and their mothers died at a rate 125 times higher than the country's average. The average wage of a farmworker was $2,400 a year (about $15,500 in 2022). Regular exposure to the insecticide DDT caused what farmworkers called "the walking death," a condition that was eerily familiar to ex-miners and their families living in Uptown. Whether the cause was caustic chemicals or fine coal dust, the outcome

---

18 Three decades later, in 2010, it was redesigned again as a new administration building, and a parking lot was built.

Big chain stores were not the only ones selling grapes and lettuce. National Foods, a local Chicago store located at Sunnyside and Sheridan, was the primary grocery store in the heart of Uptown in the 1970s and was refusing to take grapes and lettuce off their shelves. They became a target.

was the same—terminal lung failure. It was a no-brainer that we were paying attention.

Organizing a rally in the fall of 1973 to show support for the farmworkers' boycott, we filled the orchestra section of the Palacio Theater. By then known as a place to see mostly Spanish-language movies, the venue, originally called the Sheridan, seated over twenty-six hundred people. It had been built in 1927, during the period of Uptown's heyday. After the Sheridan closed in 1951, the building had a second life as a Jewish synagogue that lasted fifteen years. Subsequently shuttered for a few years, it was reopened as the Palacio Theater (Teatro El Palacio) for another decade before being shut down for good and ultimately demolished, making room for hard-won low-cost senior housing.

The well-attended rally cemented our relationship with United Farm Workers organizer Marcos Muñoz, who had come to Chicago to lead the UFW's efforts in the city to build support for their boycott. We joined the boycott, organizing support that culminated in the rally at the Palacio a year later and a commitment to join the boycott of any Chicago store that continued to stock California grapes, lettuce, or wine.

Taking on the boycott as an action of the Campaign for Community Control, we sent joint letters to most North Side grocery stores requesting they stop selling lettuce and grapes. Many did—mostly the smaller ones. Jewel did not. We would focus on Jewel and any other store on the north lakefront that would not honor the boycott. All over the country, people were doing the same—standing outside stores discouraging shoppers from buying lettuce, grapes, and California wine, while shopping at stores that refused to stock them.

Demanding improvements in their working conditions, migrants—primarily in California and Texas, and largely from Mexico and the Philippines, but including African American and Puerto Rican workers—fought for a decade to have representation and improve their working conditions.

Since 1962 Cesar Chavez and Dolores Huerta were organizing the National Farmworkers Organization in Delano, California. In September 1965 they joined mostly Filipino American members of the AFL-CIO-affiliated Agricultural Workers Organizing Committee's strike against the Delano-area grape growers, in what would become a five-year strike.

Garnering broad support across the country, the Delano boycott was successful, ending after the UFW Organizing Committee was recognized by the growers as the bargaining unit for the migrant workers in 1970. In Racine and then in Uptown, we had gone back to eating grapes.

But then things had taken a turn. Most Salinas Valley growers, determined to break the back of Cesar Chavez and Dolores Huerta's United Farm Workers Organizing Committee and to keep them out of the California lettuce and vegetable fields, made a deal with the Teamsters to break the fledgling union. While acknowledging their actions were likely unlawful, without the benefit of a vote and amid an outbreak of violence and intimidation, the growers signed so-called sweetheart contracts with the Teamsters.

The UFW reinvigorated their organizing effort, launching a national campaign. Some ten thousand farm workers walked off their jobs in protest. It was Chavez's subsequent call for a consumer boycott of lettuce and resumption of the grape boycott, in fact, that had led to Marcos's relocation to Chicago and our efforts to support the campaign.

The boycott would not end until laws were changed to require the cooperation of the growers, and this required political action. To get there, organizing activities initiated in cities throughout the country built an effective boycott, causing noticeable losses to the growers and contributing to the pressure on the growers that would ultimately lead to change.

Rudy Lozano and CASA would become one of our coalition partners. Here I am at a CASA meeting circa 1978–79. Rudy is far left, Jesús "Chuy" García is between us.

After fifteen thousand people marched 110 miles from San Francisco to Modesto, California, in 1978, the California Agricultural Labor Relations Act passed. It would be a few more years, and hundreds more elections under the law, before the UFW ended its successful boycott in February 1978.

José "Cha Cha" Jiménez, having recently returned to Chicago to reestablish the Young Lords Organization's presence, joined us as our organizing efforts connected us with fellow activist Rudy Lozano and the beginnings of the Center for Autonomous Social Action (CASA), the fledgling organization he and others organized to defend the rights of undocumented workers.[19]

These would be long, lasting relationships, as would be our ongoing efforts to support the UFW and their boycotts of lettuce and grapes—with some success, As the farmworkers turned their attention to political action, in Uptown we joined the Young Lords in our own political venture.

---

19 Rudy, as local coordinator of CASA, declared at their initiating press conference, "We are workers, we have rights, we create the wealth, with or without documents." Like us, CASA developed coalitions with other immigrant groups, labor, religious representatives, and community organizations.

PART III

BUILDING A BASE OF OPERATIONS

21.

CHA CHA RUNS FOR ALDERMAN

During the two years since I had arrived in Chicago from Racine, we had been involved in two elections and an extended voter registration drive—not to mention many run-ins with Democratic party machine minions. Given this history, when José "Cha Cha" Jiménez decided to run for alderman, it was not such a big leap to transition our priorities in Uptown to his 1974 electoral campaign.

It hadn't taken long for me to have my first run-in with a precinct captain upon arriving in Uptown. While canvasing to expand our home-distribution route in summer 1972, I couldn't believe the conditions in which people were living. I spent as much time as possible talking with people on the route. Many of my conversations ended up with my sharing ideas about how tenants could organize to improve their housing. Usually these were well received—at least at first.

The next time I did the rounds, my experience was quite different. I learned that the Democratic precinct captain had followed behind me the previous week, telling everyone that if they continued to talk to me, they would lose their housing, their welfare, or something else they desperately needed. All those running home distribution had similar experiences. The lesson couldn't have been clearer: in Chicago, everything is political.

Urban renewal (the engine behind what we now call gentrification) was a tool commonly used by Richard J. Daley's planning department to reconfigure communities, moving the people who lived in them around like pawns. This had been the pattern surrounding the development of the site that is now the University of Illinois Circle campus. It had been the pattern leading to the construction of Robert Taylor Homes, an ill-conceived public housing complex that was so poorly designed and constructed that it was demolished just forty years later. Urban renewal had also been the vehicle that moved an entire Puerto Rican community from the area surrounding Clark and Division, clearing the way for the construction of the Carl Sandburg Village. From "La Clark," many families moved to Lincoln Park. Cha Cha's family was among them.

Cha Cha had been the leader of the Young Lords when it was a Puerto Rican street gang. In 1968, however, he had reorganized the Young Lords into a political organization committed to Puerto Rican independence and neighborhood empowerment. They had subsequently established a free health clinic, day care center, and children's breakfast program. Fighting the city's plans for urban renewal in Lincoln Park, the Young Lords had coined the term "urban removal." Their slogan: "Tengo Puerto Rico en mi corazón." The Young Lords'

Cha Cha in 1975.

political transformation had led to heavy police surveillance and harassment, the attention of the FBI's Counter Intelligence Program (COINTELPRO),[1] the killing of YLO member Manuel Ramos by an off-duty police officer, and the racially motivated killing of José "Pancho" Lind. In 1969, when Eighteenth district police commander Clarence Braasch[2] planned a meeting of senior citizens about the dangers of

---

1   COINTELPRO was an initiative inspired by J. Edgar Hoover, the FBI's director, that began with surveillance of radicals and communists. Its focus broadened to include the civil rights movement, with the clearly stated purpose to "prevent the rise of a Black messiah." It now had a laser focus on the Black Panther Party. The leadership qualities of Fred Hampton did not escape the FBI. They developed schemes to thwart the many attempts that Fred made to develop relationships across racial lines, as well as his efforts to organize leaders of street gangs in Chicago and convince them to transform their groups into political organizations and "serve the people," as Cha Cha and the Young Lords had done.

2   Four years later, in 1973, Braasch, along with eighteen police officers who worked under him, was convicted in federal court of extorting hundreds of thousands of dollars from nightclubs and bars located in the Eighteenth

gangs—and specifically the Young Lords—they caught wind of it and decided to mobilize for it as well. The turnout filled the community room at the Chicago Avenue station, with broad attendance by people from the community.

Unceremoniously, Cha Cha later told me, "we took over the meeting, pushing Braasch to the side." Speaking directly, especially to the seniors who were in a majority, the newly political Young Lords experienced the power of their demands: Cha Cha was well received. Their action was reported in the news, and the next day Fred Hampton approached Cha Cha. This would be the embryonic beginnings of the Rainbow Coalition between the Black Panther Party, the Young Lords Organization, and Uptown's Young Patriots.

In a six-month period during 1969, Cha Cha accumulated eighteen felony charges—mostly for disorderly conduct and mob action during protests. During one of his times in lockup, Reverend Bruce Johnson—the pastor of the Armitage United Methodist Church where the Young Lords had their health clinic, a day care center, and other survival programs—and his wife, Eugenia Johnson, were found viciously stabbed to death in their home. Johnson had been outspoken on behalf of the Young Lords, leading them to believe his and his wife's deaths were the consequence of that support. No one was ever charged in their murders.

One of the charges Cha Cha had faced was for stealing twenty-three dollars' worth of lumber. At the time, he had pled guilty to a misdemeanor charge of theft. "There were so many charges being thrown at us, and I needed to be on the streets. It seemed like a good idea at the time," Cha Cha later told me. Soon after, Cha Cha had gone underground. Several years later, when he returned to Chicago, turning himself in at the Town Hall police station, this would be the sole charge on which he was convicted. He was sentenced to, and served, the maximum time—one year. Thus having resolved his legal status, more or less, he announced his intention to run for alderman in January 1974. We were all in.

By then, many of the Puerto Rican families who had lived in Lincoln Park when the Young Lords were active there in 1968 and 1969

District between 1966 and 1970—covering the same period of time the Young Lords were active. He received a six-year sentence. A few months later, Cha Cha announced his run for alderman.

had been "urban-removed"; many of them ended up a mile north, in Lakeview. Puerto Ricans now comprised a good 75 percent of the people living in the Lakeview precincts of the 46th Ward.

While many argued that he would not be able to take office if elected because of his felony conviction, the Young Lords, and we along with them, persisted. Our primary goal was to educate the people and build support for systemic change. If we won the election, that would be the icing on the cake, and we would cross the bridge of figuring out how Cha Cha could take his seat.[3] If elected, Cha Cha would have been Chicago's first Puerto Rican and Latino alderman.

The Young Lords opened an office at 835 West Grace, on the corner with Wilton Street. The storefront office, which doubled as the Young Lords' headquarters and Cha Cha's campaign office, was the first floor of an apartment building. The corner was known as a drug corner, and the police were in the habit of harassing everyone living in the area and busting into the apartments of people living above the YLO office.

At a pre-campaign press conference in January 1974, the Young Lords and the Campaign for Community Control released a statement documenting the police harassment of a Latina woman who was eight months pregnant. The police had raided Gladys Mercado's home three times within a six-week period without presenting a warrant. Nothing illegal had been discovered, and no arrests made, but they kept coming back. She was told by her obstetrician that any more excitement would cause her to lose her child.

In fact, there had by that time been over a dozen warrantless raids on homes in the neighborhood, with similar outcomes. On the street, however, a different story was playing out. The police were sending undercover agents to make buys from local small-time dealers and to

---

3   While his conviction was for a misdemeanor, he served the maximum time of one year, which some argued made this a felony. If he were to have won, it was apparent that this would have been litigated. Twenty years later, a candidate with a felony conviction (for a more serious crime) would win election and serve as the alderman of the Twenty-Seventh Ward. Walter Burnett had the support of George Dunne, the head of the Democratic Party and ward committeeman of the Twenty-Seventh Ward. Dunne used his clout to assist Burnett in receiving clemency from the governor, making him eligible to take office—and proving it possible for someone with a felony conviction to serve on the Chicago City Council.

harass anyone near the corner when their raids took place. The result of the combination of drug activity and police action was destabilization. Five houses were put up for sale, and most tenants were moving out of 835 West Grace.

Following the press conference, a community tribunal was held to dramatize the two-sided problem of drugs and police. The youth were engaged to force the drugs off the corner. Landlords and tenants were brought together to discuss the problem. The apartments at 835 West Grace were rented with two-year leases, and its tenants formed a union to work with the landlord to upgrade the building. Every effort was made to get a change in direction and cooperation from the police for it.

Cha Cha proposed the police take a different course of action: he suggested they stop harassing the youth and go after the people behind the drugs available in the community. He requested a squad car be temporarily stationed on the corner to scare away addicts and distributors. "The youth on the corner are victims of the whole drug industry," Cha Cha said at the time. "The police should prevent the big dealers from trapping the brothers into selling for them, taking all the risks, and going to jail."

Alternatively, the Young Lords, working with the Illinois Drug Abuse Program, planned a local program for the area. Tensions began to ease, and the drug traffic began to stabilize.

In response, the commander of the local police district called Cha Cha his "natural enemy," refusing to post a squad car and claiming that Latinos were responsible for the drug problem. This narrative echoed the police response to demonstrations against police misconduct by the Young Patriots almost a decade earlier in Uptown and was a common refrain whenever citizen review or control was raised over the course of the next four decades.

Angie Lind was the Young Lords' communications secretary. Her husband, Pancho Lind, had been killed six years earlier, leaving her with four young children. Along with Cha Cha and other Young Lords, she had gone underground. We became fast friends. Together we were responsible for literature, outreach, and all media and press conferences. For me that meant twenty-hour days preparing literature, interspersed with staffing press conferences and networking with independent organizations that were open to supporting an independent running against a machine-endorsed candidate.

One of Cha Cha's early supporters was Jim Chapman, an attorney who was involved in independent political activities in the Lakeview and Lincoln Park communities. The trio of Cha Cha, Slim Coleman, and Jim coordinated the campaign. With Jim's help we made forays into both the Independent Voters of Illinois and the Independent Precinct Organization,[4] ultimately getting their endorsements for Cha Cha. Jim, a brilliant attorney, became one of our fiercest supporters and defenders.

The campaign needed a logo. In my mind's eye, I saw a sunburst. I enlisted the volunteer assistance of a graphic designer who lived in the ward and supported Cha Cha. Because his time was limited, he agreed to take me under his wing (much like an apprentice). He was true to his word and together we designed a campaign graphic theme, incorporating purple and yellow colors, the campaign slogan "Dawning of a new day" with a shot of Cha Cha, and the Young Lords' slogan, "Tengo Puerto Rico en mi corazón" that became the basis for all literature I designed, printed, and made available during the campaign.

My primary source of relaxation came on Friday nights, when a few of us from the Intercommunal Survival Committee and the Young Lords went out drinking and dancing at one of a number of bars along Halsted and Lincoln Avenue. That is, until one Friday in December, just two months before the election. Cha Cha, José "Cosmos" Torres, and Eddie Ramirez were with us that night. Eddie was a Vietnam veteran with PTSD,[5] susceptible to flashbacks. I had not experienced one with him and did not know how violent they could become.

While dancing at the old Town Hall Pub on Halsted, the music was loud and there was some kind of light show action, when something set Eddie off. While trying to restrain him, fists went flying, along with a beer bottle or two. My only thought was, "Get Cha Cha out of here now!" And we did—out the backdoor into the alley and away. Worried that this moment would come back to haunt us, that was the end of our Friday outings.

Between the YLO cadre, the ISC cadre, and a growing list of volunteers—not just from Uptown but from Lakeview and the high-rises along the ward's lakefront—we had a vibrant campaign filled with purpose, dedication, and commitment.

---

4   This was before the two merged, becoming IVI-IPO.
5   We didn't know much about PTSD at the time. It was widely rejected as being a myth.

In 1971, Chris Cohen was elected alderman after being handpicked by the ward's Democratic ward committeeman. Chris was considered by some to be a maverick. However, he had run with the active support of the Daley-machine-controlled regular Democratic Party. He may have been considered by many to be the next generation of Chicago pol, but to us he was part and parcel of the so-called North Side Donkey Club[6] and in lockstep with the mayor's plans to continue the "urban removal" that started along Clark and Division and was quickly approaching Lakeview and Uptown to the north.

While this was our first foray into a ward-wide election taking our organizing efforts beyond the confines of Uptown, we had come up against the Democratic machine on numerous occasions before. We would adopt their structure of campaigning: door-to-door canvasing, running voters to the polls on election day, registering our voters. However, we would challenge the manipulations the machine traditionally used to coerce voters into voting as the precinct captain demanded.

Most of all, we told our story everywhere. In every corner of the ward, we recruited volunteers to talk to voters. We provided them with information to dispel the lies and innuendo being passed on by the machine precinct captains about Cha Cha, his history fighting urban renewal and leading the Young Lords Organization, and his vision for the 46th Ward. In doing so we took their structure, added our content, and fought for every potential vote—in the process, changing the way politics would be conducted in the Forty-Sixth Ward for the next thirty-five years.

That February there were three candidates running for alderman of the 46th Ward. Chris Cohen was the incumbent, and Cha Cha his most renowned opponent. Cohen handily won reelection with 63 percent of the vote, while Cha Cha won five precincts and was competitive in another eight, receiving 27 percent of the vote. A third candidate got 10 percent of the vote, winning one precinct.

An aldermanic campaign fit in well with the line of the Black Panther Party to build a base of operations in Oakland; indeed, it was

---

6 The Donkey Club was the name for Jewish machine politicians who had originated on the West Side's Twenty-Fourth Ward before relocating on the north lakefront, along with much of the Jewish community, as Black families moved in.

shortly after the Citywide Conference to Stop Police Brutality and Establish Community Control that members of the Party from all over the country were called to Oakland to work on the Seale-Brown campaign.

Four of the five precincts Cha Cha won were in the heart of Uptown, as were many of the eight where he was competitive. We knew this election would be a long shot. We also knew that we had surprised the machine, and that they were not happy to have lost even one precinct—especially in Uptown.

Cha Cha's 1975 aldermanic campaign brought a renewed focus on the position of Latinos in Chicago and the state of Illinois. His leadership, and the story of the Young Lords, served to expand awareness of Puerto Ricans' basic struggles to survive in Chicago while projecting the Puerto Rican struggle for independence to the forefront.

. . . .

22.

STRUCTURES FOR SURVIVAL
THE ROAD TOWARD COMMUNITY CONTROL

It was time to refocus. We knew that we needed to expand our interaction with the community and make it consistent. It was time to find ways to integrate political education, which had been so critical to the internal development of the Intercommunal Survival Committee, into our mass work. This next phase in our organizational development would lead to new beginnings, including weekly community meetings, the founding of the magazine *Keep Strong*, and what would ultimately become the Heart of Uptown Coalition.

In between his law practice and Cha Cha's campaign for alderman, Jim Chapman worked with us to expand our community service and advocacy programs, and especially our tenants' rights and legal assistance capacity. We had a growing list of people looking for help with minor and major criminal cases—a significant number of which resulted from interactions with police that turned into violent confrontation, beatings, and/

or arrests. We knew that not everyone was innocent, but none of them deserved beatings. And we believed all of them should have a legal defense.

While the Legal Assistance Foundation was active in Uptown at the time, their services were limited to help with civil cases; they could not even touch a criminal complaint. In addition to LAF, there were movement lawyers who would take on cases, but they were often busy representing prison cases, the civil suit that had resulted from the police killings of Fred Hampton and Mark Clark, and ensuring their own survival.

Our door-to-door activity uncovered issues people had with every city, state, and federal bureaucracy. Through the Northside Campaign for Community Control, we fast became advocates at the welfare office, the Social Security office, the Department of Human Services, Veterans Affairs, and in courts.

With Jim's support and mentoring, the Forty-Sixth Ward Community Service Center was established, opening its doors on Sheridan Road as the campaign got underway. Our cadres were joined by community volunteers.

After being sued by the Forty-Sixth Ward regular Democratic Party over the use of the phrase "Forty-Sixth Ward," we changed our name as multiple organizations grew from our work. Our survival programs would grow under the umbrella of the Uptown Community Service Center. Our members included people with passions of their own. Both Marcs recruited attorneys to respond to the growing needs for legal representation we found in the community. Walter Tunis wouldn't let a bad welfare decision go unchallenged, and Randy Saltz did the same with Veterans Affairs. Know-your-rights forums were integrated into our other activities. We facilitated a tenants union, a food co-op, and other entities as the need for them arose.

Retired coal miners suffering from the effects of black lung disease, as well as their wives and widows, used our space and volunteers to form a club that would become the Chicago Area Black Lung Association (often referred to as CABLA), with Paul Siegel volunteer-staffing them.

A few months into 1975, Stan McKinney and other members of the Illinois Chapter of the Black Panther Party, who had relocated to Oakland for the party's consolidation, returned to Chicago. A few years earlier, before opening the Community Service Center on Sheridan, the Campaign for Community Control had rented an office on Lawrence

Avenue. We often had meetings there, and we stored our file copies of the *Black Panther*, as well as all our photo negatives. The returning Panthers made our office their temporary home.

Late that summer, a fire broke out in the office, spreading quickly to the twelve apartments above us, which were left uninhabitable. It was soon determined that the fire had been set intentionally, though the culprits were never identified. The barbershop next door, a fixture in the community, was burned out and forced to close. Almost everyone who lived in the remaining houses on Winthrop and Leland had been customers there for decades. Although no lives were lost that day, a piece of the fabric of the community was gone forever, as were some of our historic files and most of our photo history.

Following Cha Cha's campaign, we felt the need to reconnect the Intercommunal Survival Committee to the community. When we celebrated the ISC's fifth anniversary in June, we used the event as a kickoff for weekly mass meetings. We started that summer with meetings of the Uptown Tenants Union at the Uptown Hull House.

We continued to sell the *Black Panther* but needed something that was closer to home as well. With the Black Panther Party's ten-point platform in mind, we settled on a magazine format that would provide local examples of how each point in the platform reflected the realities of everyday people's lives. *Keep Strong* magazine delivered news through the lens of ordinary people's day-to-day struggle to survive, including stories from all Chicago communities, national and international news, and a cultural section. We aspired for it to be a vehicle through which the oppressed white community could identify its common experience, needs, and desires with the growing Black and Third World struggle for social justice.[7]

The magazine would now become my primary focus.

In order to produce literature for Cha Cha's campaign—and to do so with few resources—I spent my daytime hours running between a typesetting company in what is now the West Loop and other places located along the way to produce printed literature. My evenings were spent laying out copy and preparing to start the entire process over again the next day. After a year of this, I was well acquainted with all aspects

---

7 While *Third World* was the vernacular of the day in the 1970s, today the term *Global South* is preferred.

of printing flyers and newsletters; however, publishing a magazine presented new challenges.

Until recently, the text of newspapers and magazines had been prepared using linotype—a labor-intensive process that required bulky machinery. However, the printing industry was changing.[8] Phototypesetting equipment—a precursor to today's personal computers and laptops—was just becoming available to smaller operations. To produce pamphlets and flyers during the campaign, I would go to Compugraphic[9] with my copy and specifications for size, font, and format. I would sometimes have to return several times to get corrections made.

This was not going to work for the production of a sixty-four-page magazine. I spent a good part of the next three months learning everything I could about this new technology; I needed to know what was on the market, what the learning curve was, and, of course, how we were going to pay for it. We bought what we could afford, formed the Keep Strong Publishing Company, and joined the Typographic Union.

Our first issue was published in July 1975. The cover, with a photo of Richard J. Daley wearing a ball cap emblazoned with the City of Chicago insignia, declared "Four More Years of Daley?" In a nod to the Black Panther Party, whose literature was often in blue and black, the border and logo letters were a royal blue. Our next issue came out in September, and for the next five years, we would publish monthly (with a few exceptions). Five or six of us worked on production. Slim Coleman coordinated the editorial content, and if we didn't know how to write a coherent article or how to get a graphic that worked well with our content, we learned by doing—and redoing. We were all over the city following stories and making connections between the common

---

8   Linotype, patented in 1884, was the primary method of setting copy for newspapers, magazines, and other publications until the early 1970s, when phototypesetters became more readily available. With linotype, characters were cast in hot metal and prepared for print. With phototypesetters, heat and metal were removed from the equation. Within just two decades, the transition to computers would be complete.

9   Located just west of Greek Town on Chicago's Near West Side, Compugraphic was one of the few businesses with typesetting equipment and where one could go to have their copy typeset. Today, that area is completely gentrified and considered part of the trendy West Loop; back then it was simply the Near West Side.

struggles of people from widely different communities. During production, we were all hands on deck.

During the week of production, I would not sleep for six days and nights while we put the magazine to bed. I would then sleep for three days before going back to my regular schedule. Sometimes I would spend this time at the apartment where our children stayed. I was told that Brendan would come in and check on me from time to time while I slept. This was an improvement over my schedule during Cha Cha's campaign, when I rarely got more than two hours of sleep a night. While I never questioned my sleep patterns during those days—in fact I thought sleeping was a waste of time interfering with the work I felt needed doing—I wouldn't recommend them to anyone.

That fall, in between issues, I spent two weeks in Oakland, California, at the headquarters of the Black Panther Party. During that time, I contributed to the work required to put out two issues of the paper, learned how to write international briefs, and was privileged to work with the extraordinary team of Michael Fultz, David Du Bois, Emory Douglas, and JoNina Abron.[10]

I visited the Oakland Community School and the Party's child development operation. Their approach to child-rearing and education was impactful. The school was open not only to the Party's children but to the whole community. They were laser focused on the development of each child and their unique needs to reach their full potential. We may not have fully realized this ideal in Chicago (or even come close), but from then on, I had the confidence to believe it was possible.

Our survival programs kept us in touch with the issues families faced in the course of everyday survival in Chicago. Our initiatives (Uptown Tenants Union, Black Lung Association, veterans forums, and legal strategies) were in direct response to these issues. Our weekly

---

10 David Du Bois, stepson of W. E. B. Du Bois, was the editor of the *Black Panther Intercommunal News Service*. Emory Douglas was minister of information of the Black Panther Party and artist in chief. Each issue of the *Black Panther* paper included his artwork, usually adorning the outside back page. Michael Fultz was the managing editor who taught me a great deal about writing shorts and finding information on international Third World struggles. JoNina was in charge of the layout room and kept me on task, teaching me technique along the way.

meetings became "Country Music Sundays." Held in the Fred Hampton Hall, with portraits of Huey P. Newton and Fred adorning the space behind our small stage area, this Sunday activity was complete with music, food, and conversation, and was to become a key component in our efforts to build a community of people committed to their collective survival.

. . . .

23.

THE AVERY LAWSUIT

In August 1975 we filed a lawsuit charging the City of Chicago with engaging in a conspiracy with local developer William Thompson to destroy an integrated community. Attending the press conference (held in front of one of Thompson's three newly acquired apartment buildings) were tenants that had been displaced, as well as community members concerned about the city's urban renewal policies. This effort would become known as the Avery lawsuit, after the name of the first plaintiff listed.

Leroy Avery was the head of household of one of thirty families that had lived for many years in three court-way buildings (essentially six-flats attached to each other in a *u*-shaped configuration with multiple entrances) on North Broadway between West Buena and West Montrose. The Maremont Foundation, with assistance from the Department of Housing and Urban Development, provided low-income housing in these buildings for over twenty years. Apparently, a year or so earlier, they had decided to get out of the business of providing affordable housing, and their properties had been added to HUD's inventory.

Thompson had acquired these buildings from HUD, with whom he had an in through his close relationship with the Daley family (he married the mayor's daughter and future mayor's sister.) He also purchased the largest rental apartment building in HUD's portfolio (655 West Irving Park Road), making it private market-rate housing and renaming it Park Place, and built the Boardwalk (a 300-apartment building that would later become a condo) nearby on vacant land located at Montrose and Clarendon.[11] There was good reason to believe this was a well-connected developer playing his own personal game of Monopoly—one in which he showed no concern that real people's lives were being impacted.

Having evicted most long-term tenants from the Maremont buildings, Thompson took advantage of Uptown's reputation for being a port of entry to Chicago, as well as government programs that facilitated rentals for immigrants, by quickly filling the empty apartments with as many as three Vietnamese families at a time. We understood that as refugees fleeing the war, these families were receiving from the federal government as much as $3,000 a month to cover their rent and living expenses; Thompson got a good chunk of this from each family. About six months later, nothing had been put into the buildings, but much had been squeezed out of them; the buildings were in disarray. The buildings were declared uninhabitable, and the families forced elsewhere. These buildings were now ripe for a massive overhaul, setting the stage for market-rate housing with rents out of the range of all those displaced. Thompson called these buildings Scotland Yard.

Thompson also acquired as much of the property as he could lay his hands on to the north of these buildings. Although he failed to acquire a building owned by the Salvation Army that they used for their resale shop, he managed to acquire virtually everything else north of the court-way buildings. He was negotiating with the city to acquire Pensacola Place—a city street only one block long between Hazel and Broadway. He bought up everything else on the block bordered by West Pensacola, North Hazel, West Montrose, and North Broadway—property with five hundred units of housing as well as a bowling alley and the Montrose Urban Progress Center. He announced an ambitious plan to build a twin high-rise development on this property while concurrently rehabbing the court-way buildings.

The housing along Montrose was reminiscent of that lost on Wilson for the first Truman College building. The bowling alley on Broadway

---

11 In 1975, there were no condominiums. It would be a few more years before massive conversions of rental properties became popular. Initially unregulated, the newly minted condos presented many issues to both the original renters and the purchasers, and it took some time for the most egregious of these to be addressed. But at this time all the development was rental. Thompson's plan was to build luxury housing.

had been an important recreational facility in Uptown matched in popularity only by the Rainbo skating rink a mile away on the corner of Clark and Lawrence. The razing of the Urban Progress Center, on the southwest corner of the land Thompson acquired at Hazel and Montrose, raised a whole new set of concerns. The Urban Progress Center had housed all of the services available to the community from the Model Cities program, all city social service departments, and a wildly popular array of GED classes. He called this plan Pensacola Place, after one of the streets vacated for the development.

We weren't the only ones opposed to this development concept. In fact, it was pretty much panned by residents and community leaders across the board. The twin-tower high-rise was too dense for the area; the plan contained retail for the exclusive use of those living in the development—in an area that was crying out for retail for the general public. Recreational and social services important to many would be gone. We were particularly concerned with the additional demolition of existing housing; at the same time Thompson planned to transform a historic low-income housing site down the block into market-rate housing.

The tenants who had lived in the Maremont buildings before Thompson acquired them were African American, Latino, Native American, and white. They were all low-income. The three buildings were their home and comprised a small, stable community. All that changed quickly when ownership changed from Maremont to Thompson. But the tenants didn't intend to stand by quietly.

Jim Chapman, who was then working with us to grow our legal program, had experience representing a suburban developer and was familiar with the limitations tenants faced due to a strong property-rights bias in Illinois state law. After meeting tenants being displaced from the Maremont buildings, Jim came up with a legal theory to challenge this development in federal court and hopefully secure replacement housing.

When our lawsuit went to court that fall, the federal judge hearing the case ruled that there was a legitimate cause of action but removed the claims of economic segregation. We were thankful that the lawsuit moved forward but disappointed that there was not a way to make a claim for equal treatment under the law based on economic disparity. For me, this has always stood as a stark reminder that addressing

The federal judge hearing the lawsuit ruled there was a legitimate cause of action but removed claims of economic segregation. The remaining Avery plaintiffs pose with attorney Jim Chapman (dark suit) after one of their many court dates.

economic disparity has no place in the Constitution of "our perfect union."[12]

We understood that Thompson owned or controlled these properties. Their value, however, was tied to their zoning, given that zoning changes were required to allow him to build the high-rise. If the city were to approve these changes, his land would immediately become significantly more valuable.

While Thompson acquired the land from HUD in a series of sweetheart deals, the Chicago Housing Authority stood by as tenants living in the Maremont Apartments lost their housing subsidies. Indeed, the city acted quickly to facilitate all zoning changes and vacation of the alley at Pensacola Place. All of this increased Thompson's personal wealth, while the affected community and those most negatively impacted got nothing and were shoved to the side. His plan sought to transform a city block, significantly changing the demographics, and ultimately the dynamics, of the community.

---

12 Unfortunately, while racial discrimination may have been finally outlawed in the US Constitution by amendment, by no means has it been addressed fully, and the current disparity is unacceptable.

Surrounded by tenants and plaintiffs, Slim Coleman answers questions during the press conference announcing the filing of the Avery lawsuit.

We were rarely in a fight where legal, community, and political action wasn't required. When Jewel reneged on promises to hire locally in the construction and the operation of the supermarket once it was built, community action was called for.

Soon we added HUD and CHA as defendants in the lawsuit.

Over the course of the next few years, plans for Pensacola Place underwent a metamorphosis. In response to demands for less density, the reality of market forces, and a broad community insistence on a supermarket, the development was downsized, retail was changed to include a supermarket, and a commitment was made that 20 percent of the units would be subsidized for low-income tenants, with former residents getting the first shot at them. The court-way buildings, by now rehabbed, would also contract with HUD for 20 percent of units to be subsidized. Based on these agreements, the displaced tenants agreed to settle with Thompson.

Thompson promised that community residents would get jobs in the construction of Pensacola Place and in the supermarket. As construction began, however, it appeared they reneged on this promise. We went back to the streets, demonstrating and temporarily closing down the work site as hiring agreements were renegotiated. While we were successful in ensuring access for community residents to the jobs at the Jewel supermarket when it opened, our efforts to have construction jobs open to community residents were less effective. But the lessons learned informed actions I took three decades later in the development of Wilson Yard.

Later, when Thompson again reneged on a key component of the agreement—giving former tenants priority for the Section 8 apartments—Jim Chapman and another attorney, Alan Mills, went back to court to enforce it.

With the developer now settled out of the lawsuit, it continued with the city, CHA, and HUD. We wanted resources and policy changes to improve housing for those displaced and others facing a similar fate. However, a settlement with HUD, CHA, and the city would not be finalized until I became alderman more than a decade later.

24.

COINTELPRO AND THE HAMPTON/CLARK LAWSUIT

The families of Fred Hampton and Mark Clark, along with the survivors of the December 4, 1969 police raid that had resulted in their murders, filed a civil suit against the police involved in the raid. As 1975 drew to a close, their day in court was near.

Leading up to the trial, I interacted with the December 4 Committee as they provided support for the plaintiffs and the attorneys preparing the case. As the trial got underway, my responsibility was to attend the trial, take notes, and write articles weekly for the *Black Panther* and monthly for *Keep Strong* magazine.

The People's Law Office had been involved in the case since the morning of the assassination. They had stayed at the building on Monroe Street protecting the evidence the police had left behind; in so doing, they preserved the proof that showed Hanrahan was trying to pass off nails as bullet holes in order to justify the assassination.

Now, the civil lawsuit concerning the raid was ready for a jury. Attorney James Montgomery joined Flint Taylor and Jeff Haas in bringing the case before Judge Joseph Sam Perry.

Coincidentally, Perry was the same judge who had heard the case against Harold Washington in 1972 for failing to file income tax returns. In that instance, he had appeared to agree with Harold's attorney that there was likely political influence afoot. Harold had failed to file income tax returns over a twenty-year period. But it was not clear that he even needed to for most of those years, given that his income rarely exceeded the threshold that required the payment of taxes. In total, Harold owed the IRS for $500 of income over the threshold. Perry sentenced Harold to forty days in Cook County Jail. Harold would later tell me his time at County only served to strengthen his resolve.

The Hampton/Clark civil trial began on January 5, 1976. It was tough going. Judge Perry often acted more as an advocate for the police and other government defendants than an adjudicator.

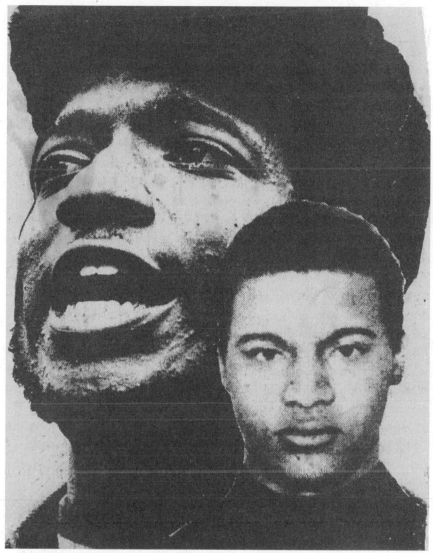

Fred Hampton and Mark Clark. Graphic created by Emory Douglas.

A critical point in the trial occurred when an FBI agent alluded in his testimony to documents that up until then the FBI had denied existed. The FBI's Counter Intelligence Program (COINTELPRO), designed by J. Edgar Hoover to "prevent the rise of a Black Messiah who could unify and electrify the Black nationalist movement," was a specter that had loomed over the case. While information about this program was not readily available at the time, knowledge of it was spreading outside the courtroom. There was reason to believe that access to the program's documents would provide evidence of the FBI's role in the raid and consequent murder of Fred Hampton and Mark Clark. Judge Perry had refused to allow any mention of it in his courtroom, ruling that it was irrelevant to the case. However, the agent's testimony changed all that. Angry that he had been lied to, the judge changed direction and ordered the documents released.

The FBI produced several shopping carts of files, but these were subsequently sealed by the judge. Two hundred thirty documents were ultimately approved as exhibits for the trial. Some of the documents that were allowed to appear tell stories of lies and deception. They show a government agency intent on destroying those who challenged their authority—efforts for which J. Edgar Hoover had the support of the Johnson, Nixon, and Ford administrations.

The exhibits that were made public during the trial showed a pattern that was repeated again and again. First, a directive was sent to all agents requesting suggestions on how to destabilize actions being taken by the Black Panther Party, with the goal of undermining their support. Then, responses would come in. Some proposals would be accepted, while others would not. For instance, a proposal to poison food served at the breakfast for children program was rejected. However, the proposal to do the same at the Revolutionary People's Convention in Philadelphia in 1970 was approved. (A member of the BPP attending the convention told me he got sick from the food but had no idea why until he saw this directive many years later.)[13]

---

13 In 2018, while preparing an exhibit commemorating the fiftieth anniversary of the founding of the Illinois chapter of the Black Panther Party, John "Oppressed" Preston and I were reviewing copies of FBI directives that were allowed by Judge Perry. Among them were three that referred to poisoning of food at the Revolutionary People's Constitutional Convention in 1970. As I was reviewing them with John, he exclaimed, "I was there. I got sick!" John got his nickname from Fred Hampton, who took one look at this fourteen-year old recruit to the BPP and began calling him Oppressed "because that's how I looked to him—young, poor, shabbily dressed, and much skinnier than I am today." John was in charge of distribution of the *Black Panther* paper in Illinois and, after a while, for the country.

As Chairman of the Black Panther Party, Elaine Brown visited Chicago to attend the Hampton Clark civil trial. Here she is addressing reporters outside the Federal building. (I'm on the left.) A year earlier she had visited and participated in a forum at PUSH and another in Uptown with Flint Taylor, Jeff Haas, Daniel Ellsberg, Renault Robinson, and Lu Palmer that was focused on COINTELPRO and the FBI's efforts to destroy the BPP.

Favorite targets for COINTELPRO in Chicago were the relationships Fred worked at developing with the gangs and with leftist whites. Agents developed cartoons, attributed to Students for a Democratic Society, ridiculing the Black Panther Party. They also were given the go-ahead to scheme friction between Jeff Fort, leader of the Black P. Stone Nation, and Fred Hampton, who was trying to organize Fort to engage in service to the people. A letter was composed and sent to Jeff Fort with the intent of sowing division, born of a desire to incite violence.

But the most damning document in the context of the trial and the charges of conspiracy to take the life of Fred, and any other Panther who might stand in the way of this objective, was the floor plan provided to the FBI by an informant named William O'Neal. O'Neal had successfully inserted himself into the Illinois Chapter of the Black Panther Party, becoming chief of security, and is believed to have drugged Fred on the night of the raid. The floor plan (for which O'Neal received $300) was given by the FBI to Edward Hanrahan, who gave it to Chicago police officers, instructing them to conduct the raid.

On April 15, 1977, Judge Perry dismissed the charges against twenty-one of the original twenty-eight defendants. A week later he directed verdicts of innocence for the remaining defendants and excused the jury.

Two years on, a federal appeals court reinstated the $47 million lawsuit against Hanrahan and returned the case to Chicago for a new trial with a different judge. Hanrahan, the police involved in the raid, and others (including Chicago FBI office head Marlin Johnson and informant William O'Neal) were reinstated as defendants. Although the court upheld dismissal of charges against four defendants and a portion of the charges against two others, it said that evidence was presented in the eighteen-month-long trial to suggest that a conspiracy existed and that therefore this evidence should have been weighed by a jury for their determination, not by the judge.

In 1983, following thirteen years of litigation, a settlement of $1.85 million provided some monetary remuneration to the families of Fred Hampton and Mark Clark and the survivors of the 1969 raid.[14] Judge Perry's order remains intact, keeping the FBI files—likely thousands of pages—hidden from public view.

. . . .

25.

FIGHTING THE MASTER PLAN

Our relationship to the Black Panther Party and our responsibility for distribution of the paper put us in touch with organizations throughout Chicago. The more stories we covered in *Keep Strong* about housing and urban renewal, the more the similarity of issues facing Chicago's other neighborhoods became apparent. Black, Brown, white, Latino, Asian,

---

14 Thirty-nine percent of the settlement went to the attorneys, organizations, court reporters, and experts as reimbursement for expenses and legal fees that had accumulated since the 1969 raid. For a fuller description of the entire saga, see *The Assassination of Fred Hampton* by Jeffrey Haas and *The Torture Machine* by Flint Taylor.

Native American—if you were a community of poor and working families and households, you were on someone's chopping block, or you were being left out there alone to fend for yourself.

Major cities across the country were developing master plans. It made us think, "Chicago must have one as well." With Susan Rosenblum as our researcher, we learned of the Chicago 21 Plan. The 125-page plan had been drafted for the city by the architectural firm Skidmore, Owings, & Merrill, and released in May 1973. Providing a vision for Chicago in the twenty-first century, it laid out a $15 billion plan for overhauling downtown Chicago.

The plan envisioned a downtown where upper-middle-class families could live and thrive, while targeting surrounding communities where poor and working people (often of color) lived, and where we were in touch with activists who were equally determined to stabilize their own communities of Cabrini-Green, Pilsen, Kenwood Oakland, Uptown, Westtown/Humboldt Park, and East Garfield Park—all of whom were concerned that the 21 Plan would lead to the urban renewal (increasingly referred to as gentrification) and displacement of their community and the people who lived there. Joined by the Chicago Housing Tenants Organization (CHTO), the Kenwood Oakland Community Organization (KOCO), the Puerto Rican Socialist Party (PSP) in Westtown, and CASA in Pilsen, the Heart of Uptown Coalition formed the Campaign to Stop the Chicago 21 Plan.

We saw the Chicago 21 Plan as an intention to develop a two-tiered city to further segregate Chicago economically and racially. Plans for tunnels downtown envisioned a private walkway that would separate the general populace from those privileged enough to live and/or work in the buildings with access to the weather-protected walkways. A third walkway would be for deliveries. It looked like the downtown was being fortified to protect the privileged while providing a catalyst to take on surrounding neighbors to whiten the inner city.

The plan envisioned the restructuring of the industrial base in Pilsen into market-rate housing. The area on the North Side that included Cabrini Green had the same intention, albeit with its priority to remove the pesky problem of more than ten thousand poor and Black people. If successful, the waves of development going north, south, and west would greatly disrupt the existing communities.

Downtown Chicago has a few different geographic definitions. "The Loop," a term which some use interchangeably with "downtown," specifically refers to the square that is made by the elevated trains that run along Van Buren on the south, Wabash on the east, Wells on the west, and Lake on the north. Downtown in the 1970s was mostly considered to encompass the Loop, going from the Lake on the East to the Chicago River on the west, and from the river on the North to Congress Parkway (now Ida B. Wells Parkway) on the south. Over time, however, and due to so-called urban renewal, the southern and northern borders kept expanding.

In 1971, the powers that be thought downtown needed a buffer between the city's center and the overwhelmingly Black South Side. The majority of the forces behind the 21 Plan were focusing their attention on a large vacant tract of land in the South Loop.

While today the South Loop is a swanky neighborhood, that was far from the case in 1975. Nearly a century earlier, Dearborn Station, located in the South Loop, was built to serve the many railroads coming to downtown Chicago from the south. In 1971, however, it was abandoned as Amtrak consolidated their trains at Union Station, leaving a fifty-one-acre site of rail-covered vacant land.

Dearborn Park was a development pushed by the 21 Plan's visionaries and directors as a vision of the future. Located directly across from Eleventh and State, where the police headquarters was then located, it was to be the catalyst for the reinvention of the South Loop. Dearborn Park was to be a model community of owner condominiums in low-rises and townhouses. By 1977 plans for the first of two phases were nearing completion.

In the 1970s, in each of our communities, members of the coalition had to deal with a growing trend of condominium conversions. Often with little or no notice, tenants were informed that they had to move because their building was going condo. In the early days, many of these conversions were "as is." The tenants were long-term, the managements were responsible, and the buildings relatively well maintained. Sometimes tenants were given an option to buy their unit, which they usually could not afford; more often, though, they were simply told to get out. What repairs needed to be done on the units were often superficial. There was no real regulation. And complaints were growing.

We were familiar with the impacts of this growing trend through our legal programs and stories we covered in *Keep Strong*. There was pressure on state legislators to do something about them. The conversions led to a great destabilization in many people's lives, as many of the new owners were speculating and had bought multiple units for investment purposes. Consequently, they were rarely around, took little responsibility for those units, and raised rents often—all of which resulted in a constant turnover of tenants.

Among the suggestions we offered to legislators were requirements that purchasers of condominium units be owner-occupants for a period of time; that investment properties in any given building be limited; that all new developments receiving assistance from the city (zoning, financing, street or alley vacation, direct financial assistance) be required to insure a minimum number of subsidized units; and that educational resources expended to accommodate an influx of new families to the area include the nearby schools, then largely attended by Black and Brown students.

The coalition was continually active, garnering attention and support for our demand that Dearborn Park be reenvisioned and the Chicago 21 Plan stopped. Instead, we argued, the city should take alternative action in the communities that would provide a future for people already living there.

The Dearborn Park developers took notice. In response to some of their critics, they promised to require all owners to live in their units for at least two years. They promised diverse ethnicities. In fact, they argued this would be a new opportunity for Black middle-class families to live in a safe, integrated community near the heart of Chicago's downtown. In such a segregated community, how could anyone object? For those concerned about affordable housing, they promised an affordable senior high-rise building. They also promised to build a model public school in the Dearborn Park Station.[15]

---

15 This school, which the developers originally planned to open in 1978, was scrapped by the developers in 1980, leading to their abandonment of the Dearborn Park station and any plans to renovate it. In place of this plan for a school, the Dearborn Park Corporation sold five adjoining townhouses to the board of education. Designed to teach one hundred students, there were still not that many children living in Dearborn Park. Between the price the board paid for these townhouses and the cost of converting them into classrooms, the board had spent almost $1.35 million. This was on top of the funds required by the city to acquire the

We weren't swayed, although we did find it ironic that realtors who were now touting these promises for their model community lobbied against them elsewhere in the city. We were opposing Dearborn Park to raise the bigger question of how and for whom development in Chicago was taking place. We wanted policies to change. We wanted people of color and those with lower incomes to be welcome in our city, and to have policies that protected us and improved our lives.

In 1979, I became the executive director of the Employment Action Coalition, with my office at the Community Renewal Society. That must have given me some legitimacy, because soon after I was invited by the architects of the Chicago 21 Plan to participate in a tour through the South Loop, Pilsen, and the near West Side, where Cook County Hospital was surrounded by multiple other medical facilities. By now, Phase I of Dearborn Park was completed with planning for Phase II well underway.

It was symbolic to me that as we passed this burgeoning medical district, all the institutions were identified except for Cook County Hospital. The original hospital, a majestic building with historic significance (architecturally and as an important community institution) was still operating and took up an entire city block.[16] To me the omission was deafening. In hindsight, however, it was no surprise that an institution important primarily to the poor would not be considered worthy of consideration for comment on a tour designed to highlight planners' vision for this side of town's entrance into the twenty-first century.

During the wrap-up at the end of the tour, I joined the group to hear a brief presentation by members of the Dearborn Park corporate board. Somewhere along the line, a year or so earlier, we had concluded that we had lost this particular battle to stop this first phase of Dearborn Park and the redevelopment of the South Loop; we therefore turned our attention elsewhere. Suddenly I heard the words, "There was significant opposition to this development. We came close to being stopped." The speaker was looking directly at me, and I realized in that moment that we had given up too soon.

Dearborn station from the Dearborn Park Corporation and for its future development. See *All Chicago City News*, Introduction Issue, (1980), 1.

16 A new Cook County Hospital would later be built a couple blocks away. After a decade of fighting its demolition, the original hospital building was transformed into a hotel.

In *Keep Strong* we covered stories of survival in Uptown and those of resistance throughout the city, expressing in so many ways the common ground between Chicago's poor and working communities. Everything we were doing in Uptown led us to some coalition work with others in the city (if not the rest of the country and the world.) We learned, we followed, and we were sometimes led down a path challenging racism and for renewal and social justice.

The Coalition to Stop the Chicago 21 Plan solidified our efforts for welfare and employment rights as well as access to quality and afford-able health care, our struggle for affordable housing and tenants' rights, school reform, an end to police brutality and community control; at the same time, it brought us into a close working relationship initially with Marion Stamps, Bob Lucas, Rudy Lozano, Art Vazquez, Mecca Sor-rentini, and later Nancy Jefferson, Dorothy Tillman, and many other talented organizers and activists. Solutions to everyday struggles of sur-vival were being implemented in communities throughout Chicago. We reported on many of them and found common ground.

Although we couldn't claim any victory in battling the Chicago 21 Plan, we gained a lot. Virtually all our partners engaged in one or more survival programs in their communities—not unlike the programs in which we engaged in Uptown. There was synergy with the work of the Intercommunal Survival Committee and our fledgling mass organiza-tion, the Heart of Uptown Coalition. We bonded, building trust and a close working relationship with others doing similar work—largely because we were each based in our own communities, doing the work and bringing that practice and experience to the table.

The Chicago 21 Plan was as much a vision as a plan. For me, that vision of Chicago was representative of the divergent realities Chicago-ans live with every day. It would dovetail seamlessly with the Demo-cratic machine's opportunism (and the emerging "me first" Republican agenda) as the 1970s drew to a close, signaling the turn in national pol-itics and Ronald Reagan's trickle-down economics view, which stressed an antipathy to the social programs of FDR's New Deal and Johnson's War on Poverty. Everything from the national passenger-train system to public education, local public transit, public housing, and welfare—even Social Security and Medicare—faced derision and privatization.

26.

EARLY DAYS OF THE HEART
OF UPTOWN COALITION

In Uptown, following the end of Cha Cha's aldermanic campaign, we were in constant motion. Our consistent door-knocking became a tried and tested way to develop new survival programs and community institutions. This activity gave us tremendous input into the needs and desires, frustrations and challenges of individuals throughout Uptown. However, we were not interested in just "doing good"; we wanted to create the environment and infrastructure that would allow the community to collectively solve problems. In this manner, we proceeded to found food co-ops, a tenants union, multiple recreation programs, and a learning center, while forging a relationship with Shimer College.

Housing was always an issue. The city planners and decision makers saw no place in the future for the mostly poor and working people living in Uptown. It was an added disdain for the significant number of poor, and often disabled, whites who had made their way to Uptown, as well as the large Native American population residing there.

The Sunnyside Mall was created upon the recommendation of the Uptown Model Cities Council in the late 1960s. After rejecting a community proposal for the Hank Williams Village, the council decided instead to close off two blocks of Sunnyside Avenue. Located where residents of those blocks used to park, the street turned "mall" was now a slab of cement with poorly designed play equipment, faded markings apparently intended for games of horseshoes and shuffleboard, and a bunch of ill-fated planters. The cement play equipment was not safe, as it chipped in many places, leaving jagged edges. The soft padding placed beneath could not compete with Chicago's weather and had pretty much disappeared by the time I had arrived. The cement structures mimicking various sea animals were more likely to be used as urinals than for play. The planters placed throughout the mall were built with their freeze line in the wrong place, so hardly anything planted in them could survive. Consequently, the planters were mostly empty vessels on which a great

(Top) Beginning in July 1976 Survival Day became an annual event in Uptown. Our survival programs were integral to the day's events. (Bottom) The Uptown People's Law Center, featured in this photo, continues to fight for a fair and just criminal justice system.

deal of graffiti—often racially explicit—could be found. Neither horse-shoes nor shuffleboard had ever actually been played there.

There was not much to do at the mall, but it was the front yard to several buildings and attractive as a gathering place. Fights were common.

The police often drove over the curb separating the mall from the intersecting streets. Sometimes, without warning, their cruisers flew down the length of the mall at high speeds. Garbage trucks—both city and private—were constantly driving on the mall, often paying little attention to people (young and old) who might be there.

In July 1976, we held our first Uptown Survival Day—a symbolic taking back of the mall. Ahead of the event, we mobilized for weeks, going door to door to encourage everyone who lived in the area to join us.

On the day of the gathering, the police tried to shut us down, citing our lack of a permit; however, we held our ground; after all, we didn't need one, given that the street was already closed. Once several hundred people showed up, the police decided to leave us alone. We had music, speakers, and a karate demonstration. Our survival programs were on full display, providing information about their services and how people could get involved. The local fire station was a block away. They came and helped us put up our banner between streetlights, letting the children climb on their fire truck and then play in the fountain of water they sprayed from it. Everyone came—families with their children; white, Black, Native American; dope dealers and machine precinct captains.

Every July or August for the next ten years, Survival Day would continue, including sports, music, animals, and food. Volunteers would staff tables filled with information about survival programs and recruit many to volunteer and or problem solve. Health screenings became a staple. We held boxing exhibitions by then Golden Glove champion Johnny Lira, and Stan McKinney, a karate teacher and Black Panther, held demonstrations by his students, which would become a staple of Survival Day. He would become a sensei to hundreds of Uptown youth (including eventually both of my granddaughters), providing lessons in self-defense, focus, and responsibility at Truman College, Arai Middle School, Clarendon Park, and any other place we could find for him. One year, we had a pony to provide rides to children—some of whom had never seen a horse before.

By now we were well on the way of developing our own structures for accountability. If the government wouldn't take responsibility, we would force the issue and do for ourselves what they wouldn't. Eventually, the annual Survival Day would be coordinated by the Heart of Uptown Coalition and the various institutions that grew out of the work of the Intercommunal Survival Committee, including the Uptown Tenants Union, the Uptown Community Service Center, the Uptown People's Law Center, the Chicago Area Black Lung Association (CABLA), and the Uptown Community Learning Center with their partners from Daniel Hale Williams University to Shimer College to North Park College.

Housing, health, education, a true safety net, and the role of policing were all critical survival concerns. Many people in Uptown were not healthy. The infant mortality rate was among the highest in the city, tuberculosis and lead poisoning were at epidemic levels, and diabetes and heart disease were common, as was black lung disease (often found in former coal miners).

Our consistent day-to-day work had brought us into contact with many whose primary and most immediate issue was health care. In my early days in Uptown, we would take them to the Fritzi Engelstein Free People's Health Center run by Rising Up Angry, or to the Young Patriots' clinic that was still operating in Uptown. By 1976, both had closed. Our efforts turned toward advocacy at the Uptown Board of Health Clinic and a number of storefront clinics. Very few of our visits with ill people resulted in their gaining access to adequate health care. We decided we had to do more.

CABLA started out as an idea—a dream, really—born of loss, fear, discouragement, plain old stubbornness, and a heavy demand for justice and fair play. Coal miners worked the mines for decades breathing in the coal dust that destroyed their lungs and took away their breath. When they could no longer breathe, they could no longer work, and they were left to fend for themselves. A militant union successfully won many improvements for miners, but there was more to do.

Union men, displaced coal miners, and their families in Uptown and the Chicago area demanded acknowledgment of this disease and action to protect them before they got sick and to ensure access to treatment after. This was an elusive demand. Miners, ex-miners, and their wives and widows who came to Chicago from West Virginia, Kentucky, and southern Illinois had heard of people in coal-mining country forming their own clubs to fight this plague. They found their way to the Uptown Community Service Center. There they found support, encouragement, and a host of volunteers who helped them form CABLA.

Black lung associations in coals fields located in West Virginia, Kentucky, Virginia, Tennessee, Pennsylvania, and Ohio predated CABLA and were instrumental in winning federal acknowledgment of the disease through the Federal Coal Mine Health and Safety Act of 1969 that established federal black lung benefits and a commitment to dust control. The black lung associations kept up their organizing efforts, and CABLA joined in. The mining companies were forced to take some responsibility as a national trust fund for victims of black lung was established by Congress in 1978. It was funded in large part by the coal companies behind the unsafe conditions that had led to so much misery for miners. While cadre from the Intercommunal Survival Committee (particularly Paul Siegel) played an important support role, CABLA was organized and directed by ex-miners and widows of miners who had died from black lung disease.

In 1976 Illinois congressman Sidney Yates joined CABLA at a hearing on the impact of black lung to many of his constituents living in the Ninth Congressional District. He was clearly impacted by the two days of testimony held in Fred Hampton Memorial Hall at the Uptown Community Service Center on Wilson Avenue.

Shortly after, we began our campaign to establish a full-service family health clinic in Uptown with a dedicated facility for treating black lung. Health surveys and screenings quickly became a staple at Survival Day.

· ·

27.

UPTOWN PEOPLE'S COMMUNITY HEALTH CENTER

So long as we are breathing, health, and its associated struggles, remains a constant in all of our lives. For me this was always personal. My father had a heart attack when I was three. My brothers had asthma. My mother was a nurse who tried but often failed to protect her children. My preteen ulcer was dismissed as the complaints of a silly girl wanting to get out of going to Hebrew school. When I was twelve, the two arm bones I had broken when I fell on them in a ditch were not, in fact, broken—or so the doctor said. The pain and swelling was psychosomatic, my mother said. "It had to be. The doctors said so." Finally, after a week, she grudgingly took me back to the doctor, who admitted his mistake. My brother Bob's addictions, sexual assaults, and manic behavior had manifested themselves every day. Migraine headaches and depression had been steady fare at Woodstock, and female issues about which I was fearful to talk to anyone lived silently within me.

In Racine, the policies of the city's health department threatened the lives of friends and neighbors, highlighted by their inadequate response to the German measles epidemic. Some of the private doctors we encountered asserted their power over their patients without the benefit of collaboration and informed consent.

In Uptown, everyone had health issues—most often serious, life-and-death ones. The free clinics initially open when we arrived in Chicago in 1972 were gone by the mid-'70s, and the Intercommunal Survival Committee had stepped into an organizing role in Uptown as the Young Patriots disappeared. The expansion of our home-distribution network and canvassing around community control of policing had brought us in touch with a wide variety of people and issues. Health care was at the center of a great many.

Black lung disease afflicted many of the families now living in Uptown. Poor health, however, was not restricted to those who worked in the mines. People in Uptown were poor and had inadequate nutrition. Every generation was impacted. There was virtually no dental health available. Prenatal care was a concept few had heard of. Infant mortality was at 25 percent, exceeding most Chicago communities. Poor housing conditions meant lead paint, obsolete plumbing, rodents, roaches, and mold, all of which contributed to poor hygiene, high levels of lead poisoning, and multiple forms of bacterial and viral infestation. For instance, salmonella poisoning from improper sewage disposal was common. High blood pressure and tuberculosis were epidemic, as was diabetes.

We became health educators by necessity, helping people get to the few remaining free health clinics for diagnosis and treatments. For the most part, health insurance was only available to those who could get access to an Illinois Public Aid medical card. The working poor had no access to health insurance, earned too much to qualify for Medicaid, and were pretty much out of luck when it came to health care. It was hard to find a doctor who offered a sliding scale for payment or would see someone without the full payment up front.

After our first Survival Day in 1976, for the next three years, the event included a health fair—screening for common health issues, providing educational material about health issues, and conducting health surveys. While the number of storefront clinics, hospitals, and even the board of health's own data indicated that this was a well-served community, our anecdotal information, said otherwise. By 1977 we were on a mission to prove that despite appearances, Uptown was a medically underserved community. And once this assertion was proved, we were going to change it!

After years of allegations of inefficiencies and corruption, the state legislature created the Health and Hospital Governing Commission to run Cook County's health care system. Dr. James Haughton was hired to be in charge. At this time the highest-paid African American official in the state of Illinois, Haughton had jockeyed on occasion with the county's physicians who were organizing to form a union. Quentin Young, head of the medical staff at Cook County Hospital, had gone toe to toe with Haughton, and there had been bad blood between them ever since. It was within this dynamic that we approached both Quentin and Haughton about the possibility of a county clinic for Uptown: to realize our goal, we would need support from them both.

Haughton was up for an arrangement that would bring new financial resources into the Cook County health system he managed. Quentin, for his part, was aware of the health challenges we faced in Uptown and had helped us with some of the health screenings. He seemed anxious to work with us to open an Uptown clinic that would be staffed in part by his medical staff. "Get the designation as a medically underserved area, and we can make this happen," he told us. Along with this designation would come doctors and dentists paid by the federal government.

By now, the Chicago Area Black Lung Association was in full organizing mode and looking for resources geared toward black lung disease. CABLA was bringing disabled miners to Cook County Hospital for diagnostic testing for their federal black lung claims, working with

To proceed with the Uptown clinic, approval of the Cook County Health and Hospital Governing Commission was necessary. Hundreds of Uptown residents and ex-coal miners filled the meeting room the day they made their decision. (Top) Then-state senator Harold Washington was present (fourth from right). On the left I am standing between Slim Coleman and Jack Hart.

(Bottom) Lawrence Zornes (back row third from right) and Richard Ricono (second from right) sit close by holding their signs, "I'm proud to be an ex-coal miner." Dr. James Haughton is pictured on the left with his notebook open. This was just the beginning of the ties that would grow strong between Harold Washington and the Chicago Area Black Lung Association (and Lawrence Zornes).

the Occupational Medicine Division at Cook County Hospital, and educating the doctors about the federal black lung program and the history of associated struggles. Frustrations for miners with the mammoth and confusing hospital confirmed the need for a community-based health center. Quentin and others told us where there were likely to be additional federal and private resources, but first we needed that "critical manpower shortage area" designation. There was little expectation that we could get such a designation for Uptown. The health indicators were there: high infant mortality, severe lead poisoning, heart disease, kidney disease. But Uptown was a magnet for storefront clinics. How could we prove the deficiency that we saw in reality?

To solve a problem, you must first see it, analyze it, and identify its most serious manifestation, then start from there. We needed to show that the doctors in our community were not responsive to those among us whose medical problems were most urgent.

We knew anecdotally that if they were on Medicaid, they could see a doctor, and if not, they probably could not afford to see one. We also knew that just because one had a medical card didn't mean they would get adequate health care. There were many storefront providers that were "welfare mills" organized first and foremost for the Medicaid payment—and only secondarily (if that) for health care. Health care thus became an arena of anger and frustration for many. Those who made little enough to qualify for a medical card were frustrated by the state of their health. Those who made just enough not to qualify were equally frustrated, often turning their anger toward those they perceived to be less worthy of getting this advantage. ("Why them and not me?" was a common refrain.)

We wanted to stop the cycle of blaming the victim and create the opportunity for everyone to get quality health care they could afford. To do so we would have to prove these "welfare mills" were not in fact delivering the health services they purported to provide.

There was no shortage of cadre to go visit every doctor and clinic. Joy Lindsay gathered her two daughters and presented herself as a single mother with a sick child and no insurance. Other parent volunteers did the same, but with welfare insurance. Others presented as a sick, elderly man or woman who couldn't afford to have their infected tooth or their high blood pressure treated. Or they presented as a woman who was eight months pregnant having had no prenatal care and no place to go to give birth. There were many scenarios and many results. We documented them all.

Combining this anecdotal information with census information, city and state health statistics, the results of our many health surveys, and other statistical information, we were confident we now had enough proof that the "welfare mills" were not providing the health services they were being paid to provide. We applied to have the Uptown community designated a critical manpower shortage area.

For months I had lived and breathed this effort. A full-service clinic with a special facility for black lung was our end game. Now, we were well on our way, with a designation we almost couldn't believe.

Meanwhile, the organizing to make this vision a reality was frenetic. We needed political support where, at least on the surface, there would be none. We were at odds with the regular Democratic machine. But Senator Charles Percy, Illinois's relatively liberal Republican senator, gave us his support, as did Art Telcser, a liberal Republican state representative. CABLA had a working relationship with our congressman, Sidney Yates—a liberal Democrat with a reputation for occasionally acting independent of the machine. Yates, who was supportive of the clinic, had participated in community hearings sponsored by CABLA a year before. Another ally, Ross Harano, was the executive director of the Uptown Chamber of Commerce. As a boy he had moved to Chicago with his family after being interned in a camp in Arizona for Japanese Americans during World War II. While his vocation was banking, his avocation was politics. Deeply involved in the Japanese American community of Uptown, he displayed his independence when he wrote a letter in support of the clinic. Harold Washington, now a state senator, added his support, joining us at the Health and Hospital Governing Commission meetings to help plead our case.

The Chicago Department of Public Health was caught unaware, having failed to pursue the designation of critical manpower shortage for any other Chicago neighborhood up till now. As we were gearing up for the clinic's grand opening, I received a call from someone at the Chicago Board of Health. They wanted to know if they could adopt my research for the city's application for critical-manpower-shortage designation in the rest of Chicago. Amused, I said yes.

Meanwhile, plans continued for the clinic, slated to open in August 1978. We spent a good part of the summer holding health fairs and pre-screenings and identifying a multitude of health problems on which anyone with abnormal test results would now have a means to follow up. By the day of the opening, nearly two thousand patients had preregistered.

We now had a community board, a medical director, an administrator, and a full medical staff for our clinic in Uptown, funded by the federal and county governments. Our application for funding for a black lung facility in the clinic was under review. We were good to go—though, as we would continually be reminded, nothing in Chicago comes easy.

. . . .

28.

THE 1978 SPECIAL ELECTION
JUMPING IN FEET FIRST

Chris Cohen resigned as alderman of the Forty-Sixth Ward in late 1977. By the beginning of 1978, with the clinic now slated to open that August, it was announced that there would be a special election in May to choose Cohen's successor.

Aldermen in Chicago are like mini-mayors. Your alderman can make sure your garbage is collected and your street is swept of debris and cleared of snow, and can determine if, when, and where you can have a block club or a rummage sale. Your alderman votes on funding for the police, and has a say in which curfews and other misdemeanors they are called upon to enforce. Your alderman votes for mental health and other health resources and where they are allocated. An alderman can make or break the construction of affordable housing in your community. In Chicago in 1978, if you wanted something from the city, you were likely to need your alderman to support you getting it.

Cohen was leaving the city council to become the regional director of the federal Department of Health, Education, and Welfare. The two community areas now known as Uptown and Edgewater were in

My 1978–79 campaign photo. Truman College is in the background as is the clearing of the adjacent block of housing (bottom right) for construction of the second college building.

1978 designated as Uptown. Our focus was on the southern end, which we often referred to as the heart of Uptown. The ward boundaries in Chicago often do not follow community boundaries. For instance, the Forty-Sixth Ward included just over half of the heart of Uptown and included parts of the Lakeview community to the south. The rest of Uptown (including most of what would later become Edgewater) was in the Forty-Eighth Ward.[17]

While the clinic was in the Forty-Eighth Ward, most of the heart of Uptown was in the Forty-Sixth. Following Cohen's resignation, a special election was scheduled for May 1978 for the Forty-Sixth Ward.

We garnered the support of Congressman Yates, Senator Percy, and state legislators Art Telcser and Harold Washington. More powerful than any of them when it came to what happens in Chicago, an alderman could trump them all. Support of either the Forty-Sixth or Forty-Eighth Ward alderman would make our path easier.

While we now knew we had community support for the clinic, we were certain we would need political support as well. We also knew that

---

17 Coincidentally, the alderman of the Forty-Eighth Ward also resigned, leading to a special election there at the same time.

unless the clinic could function independently of the existing political machinery, it would never properly serve the people. Moreover, we had learned from the Campaign to Stop the Chicago 21 Plan that our issues were not exclusive to our community.

Arson for profit was a plague in Uptown. For almost a decade, since the site for Truman College was confirmed, fires had been a common occurrence. They appeared to be a habitual way for landlords to force people out or to take advantage of insurance payouts. In any case, hundreds of tenants were displaced, injured, and/or killed by fires in buildings located in the heart of Uptown in the mid-1970s.

Our ongoing efforts to redefine city policies for safe and affordable housing clearly cried out for political support, so we decided we needed to run someone for alderman of the Forty-Sixth Ward. I had no intention of being that person. While accepting political activity as one of many tools in our toolbox for survival programs, I was disdainful of politics as a career path.

In 1978, the Forty-Sixth Ward meandered from a long strip along Lake Shore Drive, where a good ten thousand registered voters were middle class and mostly Jewish, to a handful of western precincts encompassing the heavily working-class Catholic parish surrounding St. Andrews Church. Among the leadership of the Intercommunal Survival Committee and the Heart of Uptown Coalition, we explored our options. Someone, we agreed, should run. I had a presence in the heart of Uptown. I had never been arrested (the loitering charges in Racine were dropped.) I had a bachelor's degree from the University of Wisconsin. I was a woman, a mother, and Jewish. In short, I was it. I was also very shy. Anxiously but without hesitation, I agreed.

Uptown precincts made up about a third of the voters in the election. The time between the date to begin collecting petitions to get on the ballot and the election was four months, leaving a small window for me to introduce myself to the rest of the ward and recruit volunteer campaign workers outside of my Uptown base area.

I would be running against Ralph Axelrod, a foot soldier for the machine for many years and most recently Chris Cohen's ward secretary. The Forty-Sixth Ward aldermanic and Democratic Party offices were in Uptown, but Axelrod lived in Graceland East. Located just west of the heart of Uptown, this enclave of mostly single-family homes was considered to be part of Uptown by the city map of community areas, but not by the people who lived there. This was a stable middle-class community where we had had little previous contact.

To win an aldermanic race outright, a candidate must receive at least 50 percent plus one vote. In spite of our best efforts, when the election rolled around, I didn't do well enough in the special election to force a runoff. I received 35 percent of the vote to Axelrod's clear majority, while a small share went to a third minor candidate.

However, this was only the beginning of what would be a year of aldermanic campaigns. The regularly scheduled municipal elections would come just nine months later, in February 1979. I never stopped campaigning.

• •

29.

A YEAR OF ELECTIONS AND COMMUNITY PRIDE

By now the Heart of Uptown Coalition was in full swing. Organized on a block-by-block basis, it was a block club coalition in the twelve-block area surrounding Truman College. We developed a block by block plan that was revised to fit the entire heart of Uptown area, and then took it back for review and approval of a majority of residents and building owners on each block. We went to community development hearings, forced meetings with the commissioner of development and planning, and impacted the direction of city-directed funds to include 90 percent of the Heart of Uptown Block Club Coalition plan.

The Uptown People's Community Health Center was becoming a reality. However, Alderman Ralph Axelrod opposed it. We were challenging the city to do something about the blatant arson for profit that was scarring the community—killing and maiming people as buildings they lived in were destroyed. But we couldn't get any traction. At best, the fire and police departments were either uninterested in solving these murderous crimes or just incompetent. But we suspected collusion. City Hall and Alderman Axelrod ignored this crisis.

Our legal program was taking off as the Uptown People's Law Center. Food co-ops started through the Heart of Uptown Coalition were now everywhere, bringing fresh fruits and vegetables along with basic staples to households on most blocks.

Our Community Pride Campaign turned the focus on our youth. Toluene, the sweet-smelling chemical found in most airplane glue, was known as Tolly on the street and had become the most popular high among the young. Its fumes, when sniffed, not only provided a quick high but attacked brain cells that would never recover. The campaign demanded local stores remove toxic glue made with toluene from their shelves as a nontoxic version was available.

There was, however, an even bigger concern: teenage boys were disappearing without a trace. One of the most active members of this campaign was Bessie Stapleton, whose son was one of the disappeared. We established a child safety network in hopes of saving other children from the same fate. Years later it would be proven that several of serial killer John Wayne Gacy's victims were some of these missing boys—including Bessie's son. Over time others were identified as victims of Larry Eyler and Jeffrey Dahmer. Uptown was their hunting grounds.

The municipal elections on February 20, 1979, included Republican and Democratic primary elections for mayor, city treasurer, and city clerk. They were also the nonpartisan election for alderman in each of the city's fifty wards. The general election for mayor, city treasurer, and city clerk would be held in April, along with runoff elections between the two highest vote-getters in any ward where no aldermanic candidate had received more than 50 percent of the vote.

Richard J. Daley had died in December 1976, just a year and a half into his sixth term as mayor. His was a sudden death resulting from an unexpected heart attack. Wilson Frost, alderman of the Thirty-Fourth Ward[18] and president pro tempore of the city council, had been expected

18 The Thirty-Fourth Ward encompasses the Black part of the Beverly community on the city's far Southwest Side, a community with spacious homes and large yards that saw an influx of Black middle-class and upper-middle-class families in the 1960s and '70s without total white flight. Because of its unique status as a stable middle-class Black

We campaigned hard for state senator Harold Washington in Uptown during his first run at mayor. Howard Saffold (to Harold's right) provided security as he did in Harold's future campaigns and as Harold's chief of security once he was mayor.

by many—especially in the Black community—to become the acting mayor. He had been loyal to Daley and the machine, but his race made him unacceptable to the majority-white Daley loyalists. Tom Donovan, Daley's chief of staff, locked the doors of the mayor's office, met behind closed doors, and made a deal that, while embraced by Frost, became a bitter pill to swallow for many.

Michael Bilandic, the alderman of Bridgeport—Daley's home ward—became the acting mayor, while Frost became chairman of the City Council Finance Committee. Bilandic's appointment led to an outcry from the Black community, encouraging the growth of an already-nascent independent political movement.

Six months later Bilandic won the full title of mayor following a special election. Bilandic had five challengers, of whom State Senator Harold Washington was one. We worked hard for Harold, coordinating the Forty-Sixth Ward and organizing campaign activities and events in

community in the city, it was also one of the stronger Democratic machine wards (along with the Eighth, representing the Chatham community on the mid-Southeast Side).

Westtown and Humboldt Park, where we had many contacts from our coverage of stories in *Keep Strong*.[19]

The 1979 municipal elections, and especially the mayoral race, would be impacted by Bilandic's incompetent response to a major blizzard. Chicagoans simply wanted to be able to come and go to work, but the streets were clogged, L trains were redirected (with stops eliminated in the city), and parking was virtually impossible. Bilandic held a press conference announcing that he had arranged for roads and parking lots to be cleared of snow for city residents to park their cars. In most cases, however, they had not been touched.

What was considered incompetence in many areas of the city incited charges of racism in the Black communities where there was little evidence of snow removal. At 4:00 p.m. on a workday, as snow was falling hard and everyone was trying to get home (leaving work early to do so), Bilandic ordered the Chicago Transit Authority to streamline train service by skipping many stops in the Black community. On the West Side, trains were ordered to leave downtown and go directly to Oak Park, leaving passengers waiting at all stops in between stranded and unaware that trains would not stop for them.

Amid the madness, mayoral hopeful Jane Byrne seized the opportunity, later going to the same train stops that were impacted, where she reminded passengers there how Bilandic failed them while promising to be their champion. Citywide she ran as an independent, implying that she was the candidate for equity and justice. Byrne had worked in city government for years with the blessing of Mayor Daley, but she had been dismissed as the commissioner of consumer affairs by Bilandic after challenging a taxi fare rate increase. Now she was running against him. She campaigned against the "evil cabal" of old-guard aldermen and said she would be a different kind of mayor, laying out a series of policies that spoke to people's frustrations.

It was in this context that I announced my second campaign for alderman. Declaring "independent is not enough," I explained: "I have long considered myself an 'independent.' But being independent came to be known simply as being opposed to Richard J. Daley and his political machine. While I continue to actively support the drive

---

19 Harold Washington would later reciprocate by campaigning for me in my
   three 1978–79 elections.

for honesty in government and accountability in city services that has characterized the independent movement, I feel that time has come to take another bold step. We must challenge not only the process of city government in Chicago, but its direction. Innovation and effective action must be added to protest if we are truly to find solutions to the problems of the city."[20]

During the summer of 1978, we launched a series in *Keep Strong* on what we were calling the "new opposition." A new class of freshmen elected in 1978 entered the state legislature in 1979. Among them was Carol Moseley Braun, who would later become the first African American woman in the US Senate. Another newcomer with fresh energy and insight, Art Turner, would join her in Springfield two years later. Representing the South and West Sides of Chicago, they were committed to justice. Their targets were the critical problems of racism, unemployment, poor health service, and inadequate educational opportunities that had been sidestepped and that continued to make city life unstable, dangerous and increasingly expensive for everyone. I wanted to bring that new opposition to city hall.

We worked every corner of the ward, door to door, bringing with us a vision of the future that people could embrace. We didn't just talk about the problems but displayed their solutions. We registered over three thousand new voters, and when the machine challenged most of them, we did our best to protect their right to vote.

We opened a small campaign office on the southern boundary of the ward, just off Broadway, with our front window open onto Cornelia. To accommodate the late hours of the ISC cadre and campaign volunteers working there, we rented one of the twelve apartments that was above the campaign office. Marc Zalkin, George Atkins, Barb Schleicher, and other campaign volunteers were often there working late.

---

20 Not much has changed since 1978. There continues to be tension in Chicago between the good-government liberals who prioritize process, ethics, and transparency over equity and social justice issues championed by others on the left. Contradictions abound and, like change, are inevitable. This tension played out as recently as the 2019 mayoral race, when the good-government left swept Lori Lightfoot into office over Toni Preckwinkle.

In the early morning, just a couple weeks before the election, Marc, George, and Barb had stayed up late crunching numbers. Someone smelled smoke and went to investigate. The problem was immediately obvious: the building was on fire, and it was spreading quickly. Rushing through the building, pounding on doors and dodging smoke, they managed to get everyone up and out of the building—probably saving a bunch of lives. We soon learned that a Molotov cocktail, thrown through the front window of the office, had ignited the fire. "All the other tenants in the building were asleep," Marc told me. Indeed, there was no reason for the person who bombed the office to expect anyone in the building would be awake. If Marc, George, and Barb had not been up, people would have died that night.

A fire's trail can be sinuous, and does not always follow an obvious path—unless you happen to be an expert in these matters—so we were surprised to learn that while all the upper-floor apartments were beyond repair, the first-floor office was largely intact. We had to move, but the street-level retail space of the building was saved after the apartments above were demolished. While we lost campaign literature and some of the number crunching and paperwork on field operations, Marc and George had pretty much everything in their heads. Rather than slowing us down, the attack energized the campaign.

On the evening before the primary election, February 27, 1979, one of my precinct workers checked in at his polling place in a vintage high-rise rental building in the heart of Uptown. In 1979 voting took place in booths that you walked into, pulling the curtain behind you. Once inside, you pulled a lever after picking your candidates. This would record your vote on a paper ballot and deposit it in the machine. At the end of the day all ballots would be collected from each voting booth and counted by the election judges. Every vote cast was recorded on a counter that could be viewed from the outside of the voting booth. When the polls opened in the morning, the machine should always have a zero count. As a rule, we asked all our precinct volunteers to check the machine count before voting began.

"It was the night before the election," campaign volunteer John Taylor later recalled. "The polling place was in the lobby of 4278 Hazel. At about 9:00 p.m., I was doing last-minute canvassing in the building, reminding our voters about the importance of tomorrow. As I was coming

Defacing my posters was common as was racist graffiti during my 1978 run for alderman.

down the stairs, I heard voices in the lobby. As I got to the bottom of the stairs, there was [machine precinct captain] Paul Hamilton directing the five judges to open the voting machine." John intervened.

"Paul Hamilton was not alone," John continued. "As I approached the judges, he and three or four of his guys circled around me. I continued to remind the judges that they are violating the law. Just then, I was knocked to the floor. I learned later that Hamilton had hit me over the head with a chair. As I lay there, Hamilton or one of his guys started kicking me in the face and body. I remember the women yelling to stop." Fleeing to the manager's office, John was able to get a ride to the hospital. Released early the next day, he was recuperating at home when he was called by Paul Siegel to get to the polling place. John and Paul tried to get criminal charges filed against Hamilton. It was a struggle, as the police initially refused. Eventually Hamilton was arrested. As John recalled, "Paul said that Hamilton being gone for most of the day at the Belmont station was beneficial to our results, especially in that precinct." No charges were ever filed.

We ended that day almost eight hundred votes ahead of all other candidates. However, I had only received 46 percent of the vote in a three-
way race; therefore, I would have to face Ralph Axelrod in a runoff in
April. My mother, who was now retired and living in midtown Manhattan in New York City, pitched in to help. She came to Chicago, moved
in with friends living on Lake Shore Drive, and worked her heart out on
the campaign for the next six weeks. Meanwhile, my opponents had a
heyday spreading rumors, innuendos, and lies about me to discourage the
growing support for my campaign. In some precincts, I was apparently
"married to a Puerto Rican in jail for murder," or I "had five Black babies
and lived on Lake Shore Drive." Along the heavily Jewish Lakefront precincts, I had "lied about being Jewish" or I "was the wrong kind of Jew"—
there was a significant Jewish vote in the ward. My mother's presence and
active participation served to challenge some of these lies.

In March I was invited to a forum at the ward's conservative Anshe
Emet Synagogue that drew several hundred people. I spent a lot of time
answering questions about the Black Panther Party and my relationship
to them, explaining the survival programs, and stating clearly, "I support the programs of the Black Panther Party." After a few questions
about city services in Chicago and the Forty-Sixth Ward, the questions
pivoted to Israel.

Most of my mother's extended family in Baranovichi, Belarus, had
emigrated to the United States and to Palestine (settling there and remaining after the State of Israel was established in 1948.) These were my
mother's aunts and uncles, and they kept in touch. During my first year
in college at Madison, my mother's first cousin Zipporah, her husband,
and five children had been studying in Chicago, where I would often
come on the weekend to visit and babysit. They subsequently returned
to Jerusalem, where Zipporah later practiced medicine in a hospital that
catered to Jewish and Arab patients. Peace—the possibility and hope for
it—in Israel was an important topic of conversation. I had difficulty seeing the way forward for democracy unless all citizens (Jews and Arabs)
had equal footing in the law. I naively viewed our differences of opinions
as I had viewed the differences expressed at our nightly dinners at home
when I was growing up: as political ideas to be explored.

To one of the questions about Israel—I have no idea now what it
was—my answer included a reference to my family members "who left

Europe for Palestine in the 1920s" (nearly thirty years before the state of Israel was established). While we went on to the next topic without comment, this use of the term "Palestine" would generate quite a tempest after the event.

In the mail the day before the runoff election, ten thousand Jewish voters along the lakefront (and heavily concentrated in the First Precinct) received a letter from the rabbi of an Orthodox synagogue located north of us in the Forty-Eighth Ward who also had deep ties to the Donkey Club. Referring to the Anshe Emit forum, the letter quoted me as saying, "I support the programs of the PLO [Palestine Liberation Organization]." As previously noted, I had actually said, "I support the programs of the Black Panther Party." This may have been equally distasteful to many potential voters, but they were going for the Jewish vote and needed to back up their claim that I was "the wrong kind of Jew."[21]

The next day, as the votes were being tallied, Andy Shaw, reporting for ABC News, was sitting in my campaign office as we waited for the results. All but one precinct was in. This precinct—known as Imperial Towers—was a twin-tower high-rise along the lakefront with a thousand mostly Jewish and heavily elderly registered voters. It was a stronghold of the regular Democratic machine, but we had worked it hard, and until the letter had hit, we were getting a growing indication of support.

I was ahead by several hundred votes. Andy decided to go on air and proclaim me the winner. We all thought he had it right. This was how, for fifteen minutes, we basked in the belief that we won. Then reality hit. The call came from our volunteer at Imperial Towers. We were crushed. The numbers were huge, and most of them had gone to Axelrod. Our lead was wiped out, and we lost the election by 206 votes.

The campaign had been replete with innuendo, rumors, and lies. My posters had been defaced with black spray paint, swastikas, and hate-filled messages. My campaign workers and volunteers had endured threats and intimidation. My office had been firebombed. Police who witnessed voters being paid off had stood idly by, refusing to take action.

---

21 After the election, my mother met with Rabbi Robert Marx, who was serving as the president of the Chicago Board of Rabbis. Members of the Agudas Achim Congregation objected to the letter. However, nothing came of any of this.

The police union initially endorsed me, then *un*endorsed me after learning I was in favor of requiring that police officers leave their weapon at home when they were off duty. It didn't make sense to me that off-duty officers could go drinking and be allowed to carry their weapons as though it was expected of them to use their police powers while intoxicated.

The vote in nursing homes in the ward was controlled by the machine. Having the support of ownership and management, machine precinct captains had the run of them. Thorazine was doled out in at least one nursing home to residents before they were taken—in wheelchairs—to vote. In the week after the election, Roger Simon, who had a regular column in the *Sun-Times*, wrote about these tactics, attributing them to *my* campaign:

> Thorazine, a powerful drug that makes you feel like you've been hit 40 or 50 times with a padded club, is given to mental outpatients and others who need it to cope with daily life. After a jolt of Thorazine, you'd vote for Monty Hall if someone told you to. Shiller's opponents accused her of gathering together an entire Thorazine bloc, and running them down to the polling places just after they got their daily doses.[22]

A nursing home on Sheridan Road[23], owned by the Pure brothers and controlled by the machine, was the only place I knew for sure to use Thorazine. My response to Simon's column was, "If only that were true, we would have won the election."

Though we lost the aldermanic election, we had successfully put ourselves on the political map, and a target on our activities. We were a threat.

---

22 Roger Simon, "Out to Ax Axelrod, Chicago Classic in Uptown," *Chicago Sun-Times*, April 5, 1979, 4.
23 The Stratford, located at 4131 North Sheridan, was constantly cited and eventually lost its nursing home license. During the time I was an alderman, some twenty years later, Mitch Hamblet bought, rehabbed, renamed, and restructured the building, making it a model of care.

30.

TRANSFORMING CHILD DEVELOPMENT

After the election, we suspended our child development operation and moved our children back in with their parents. It had been just over six years since we had rented our first apartment for CD in 1973. During that time, our children had lived together in apartments that were intended to be organized from their perspective and for their needs, growth, and development. They had always had food, clothing, organized activities, and, above all, safety. Our primary concern had been to create a learning environment that was focused on the tools they would need to learn how to think (not *what* to think) and that would best prepare them for the world that would confront them in the future.

Even before we came to Chicago, Marc and I had Brendan call us by our names. This was just one element of our efforts at shielding him from our enemies and people who might want to do him harm. We thought it best not to advertise who his parents were. In public, we were Helen and Marc. To ensure this habit, we were Helen and Marc in private as well.

Brendan was the oldest of the children in CD, and the ringleader. He turned two in April of 1973. Carol was three months younger, and Robby was barely six months old. Tania was born that May, and Yvonne in August. David came along the following January, and Lisa later that year.[24] Two cadres were always assigned to child development. During these years either Dean Loumos or Joannie Wallace were overall in charge of CD. Coordinating the schedules of the cadre and the activities of the children, they struggled with the parents over policy and over time spent with the children. Some of us spent a lot of time there; others, not so much. My responsibilities in the organization meant I had less time to do CD, which was a constant internal tension for me.

---

24 The parents for each of these children are as follows: Carol and Robby: Lynn Tremelling; Tania and Lisa: Joy and Tom Lindsay; Yvonne: Laurie Odell and Jack Hart; David: Pat Spaulding and Marc Kaplan. Lynn Tremelling also had four older teenage children who lived with her in Chicago: Lance, Robin, Tina, and Cliff.

There was no doubt that our children knew what their parents were up to: they would play a game of being their parents. Invariably, Brendan would imitate the act of writing. I always assumed he was imitating Marc, as I considered myself more a graphic designer than a writer. These predilections would show up later in his development: the morning after the runoff election in 1979, a nearly eight-year-old Brendan woke me up, excited to show me the petition he wrote demanding a recount. He obviously had paid attention and identified several of the ways in which voters and campaign workers were intimidated, votes were improperly cast, or people were denied their right to vote.

In 1976 we had begun chapters of the Intercommunal Survival Committee in Milwaukee, the Brooklyn neighborhood of Greenpoint, and Stockton, California. However, when we engaged in the special election for alderman in 1978, we recalled everyone back to Chicago. We had rented three apartments in a building on Malden. One of them was for child development. By now Carol and Robby no longer lived in Chicago but other children joined our ranks. Troy, who had cerebral palsy, was a few years older. He was joined by his younger sister Michelle. Anton was five when he came with his mom, Jeri, from California. Several of the children were attending public school a few blocks away: Stockton Elementary for Brendan and Anton, and the Stockton Child Parent Center (the "little school"), a block away in another direction, for Tania, Yvonne, and Lisa. As our children grew older, child development was changing. Their personalities were on full display, and their varied needs could be challenging.

Our children went home with their parents the night of the election, and this was the start of a dramatic change in CD. From this point on, our children stayed with their parents most of the time. During and after the election cycle, several cadres became pregnant. We collectively provided for childcare, and when a new crop of children were born over the next several years, we had a form of child development, but there was no longer a full-time apartment or 24/7 collective responsibility for their care.

Tania and Lisa moved with their mom back to New York City for a few years; Troy moved in with Lawrence Zornes and his family; Michelle went with her mom; and Brendan, along with Anton and Yvonne, was attending public school.

I was always supportive of CD, while ambivalent at the same time. I had had very poor role models when it came to parenting and was determined not to be overbearing, overprotective, smothering, or judgmental.

When he was just a few months old, Brendan had begun to crawl. While he still had a soft spot on the crown of his head, he was frustratingly hardheaded in his determination to get from one end to the other of any room. He moved surprisingly quickly, and my greatest fear was that he would go headfirst into the wall, piercing his soft spot in the process. Staying in a playpen for any period of time was not an option; he wanted to be in motion. So, we got him a jolly jumper. Clamping one end to the doorway between our living room and dining room, he would happily jump for hours. Later, when he was old enough to play on the jungle gym at the park, I would stand just a few feet away as he would play to his heart's content. He would attempt impossible moves as I held back every instinct to stop him, while remaining prepared to jump in if he was about to fall and hurt himself. Giving my son room to grow and develop was for me a top priority. Doing so would be the struggle of my life.

The end of child development was a game changer. Marc and I no longer lived together, but for the first time in a while we were both in the same city and as always working together. We agreed that I had the primary relationship with Brendan, but he was getting old enough to spend time with each of us on his own terms. From my perspective, we never had any issues about this between us—although I can't say if that was how Brendan perceived it.

After six years of child development, I was happy to be living in the same apartment with my son. But the transition wasn't easy. Brendan felt anger about the six years he had spent in CD, which I didn't understand, expecting that I could automatically assume an authority he wasn't prepared to accept. This came to a head one day after we had an argument that turned physical. Several hours later, Brendan located the gun we kept in the apartment and waited for me to see him with it. Reflecting on the incident today, he says he wanted me to be afraid of him. I was not scared of him; I was scared *for* him. After I took the gun away from him and hid it, we didn't talk about it again (at least not until I wrote this book), but this marked the beginning of my conscious attempts to make more time to bond.

We also applied the lessons learned to a second generation of movement children. In the early 1980s, we created a leaned-down version of CD, with the children coming home to their parents every weekend.[25] That second generation of movement children appeared to have developed a bond among themselves, without spending every night away from their parents.

However, among this second wave were some that never went to CD or went sparingly but still maintained ties to the other children. This included two boys that had a tragically similar life trajectory: Eddie Lee Ruff and Cody Camacho.[26] Both were born in the early 1980s. Both ended up serving multiple tours in the Iraq War; both suffered from PTSD; and both ultimately committed suicide several years apart. There's a rabbit hole of what ifs, and ultimately these tragic deaths remain a constant reminder that it's impossible to separate the political work we do from the personal lives we lead and from the impact it has on the people we love.

During the next ten years, Brendan was pretty much a latchkey kid. We lived in a six-flat on Malden street. For a time Marc lived in the same building. I never lived alone, but I was rarely home when Brendan arrived after school. There were two tasks we would always do together: weekly trips to the laundromat and grocery shopping. The latter was important as there were many evenings when he made his own dinner. I wanted to make sure I bought food he wanted to cook for himself.

I remembered being dragged to places with my mom as a child, and I didn't want to put Brendan through that. Whenever possible, if he wanted to go somewhere with me, I wanted him to know up front how long we might be gone and what we—and especially he—would likely be doing. I was always glad when he chose to come.

---

25 The parents for each of these children are as follows: Tierra: Paula Hartman and James Ratner; Michelle and Troy: Paula Hartman; Jackson: James Ratner and Anne Toomey; Sara: Ann Cline and George Atkins; Karla: Karen Zaccor and Alan Mills; Rachel: Maureen Grey and Marc Kaplan; Amanda: Mary Ann Majer and Paul Siegel.

26 Eddie Lee was the son of Suzie Ruff and Marc Zalkin—and therefore Brendan's only biological sibling. Cody was the son of Jeri Reed and Ron Camacho, foster-son to Jack Hart, and cousin to Kuumba Lynx founder Jacinda Hall Bullie. Jacinda, whose mom, Sybil Hall, was married to Jack, had a close relationship to our original CD children.

We upgraded our typesetting equipment at Keep Strong Publishing Company. Bobby Rush was now teaching at Daniel Hale Williams University on the West Side. He hooked us up with jobs designing and printing the myriad of forms the university needed. Brendan would sometimes come with me to the West Side campus during this time. This was a majority-Black institution where every policy maker was African American. The fact that this was reflective of an entire continent where Black people were the majority became a conversation between him and me during the long drive to and from the West Side.

. . . .

31.

POLITICAL REACTION
ATTACKS AGAINST THE LUNCH PROGRAM AND THE CLINIC

Beginning in 1975, the Uptown People's Community Service Center operated a free lunch program during the summer months. Funding for the program came from the federal government, providing for the distribution of free lunches on weekdays to schoolchildren by local governmental agencies and nonprofits. It was not our intention to participate in this program. Indeed, as a rule, we stayed away from money provided by governmental bodies. However, we were swayed by the bad quality of food the children were getting. Convinced that we could do better and that the children deserved a meal that was healthy as well as appetizing, we dove in, applying for—and receiving—federal funding.

In the beginning we faced some hurdles placed in our way by local political forces, but with community support, our free lunch program survived and thrived. While the program was geared toward school-age children, it was not against the rules to provide lunches to others. It was, however, against the rules to ask for reimbursement for meals that did not go to school-age children. Many people who lived in the heart of Uptown were poor. Many were food-challenged and spent at least a few days a week without adequate access to nutrition. We weren't about to police how people used the lunch program for survival, so we instead created what was, in essence, a fire wall to ensure that the federal grant funds only were used for lunches served to school-age children.

By 1979 we had lunch programs at virtually every playground in the heart of Uptown and on the Sunnyside Mall—about seven, all told. We had every school-age child sign in each day at each site with their name and age. We then requested reimbursement for only the number of lunches that corresponded to the sign-ins. Everyone else who came for lunch—younger children and adults alike—were not included in the tally. We ate the costs of those lunches, paying for them out of small donations we raised privately.

In the summer of 1979, the *Lerner Press* ran a front-page exposé of our summer lunch program. Les Sussman, their enterprising reporter, joined up with State Representative Billy Marovitz to "expose fraud" in our summer lunch program. Marovitz was from a political family and a golden boy of the North Side Jewish Donkey Club. His uncle was a federal judge and a close friend of Richard J. Daley, and his father was a longtime member of the Chicago Park District. The next day a similar story ran in the *Chicago Tribune*.

My recollection is that they followed a man who lived at the Malden Arms to the Gooseberry Playlot down the street and photographed him receiving and then eating a sandwich from the summer lunch program. Surly in nature and unkempt in appearance, Tony Enderle owned the Malden Arms and was always around. He was also a precinct captain for the machine. If you moved into his building and were on general assistance, social security, or social security disability, you made him your protective payee. And most everyone who lived there was.

The checks came on the first of the month, from which the protective payee took his rent, leaving anywhere from five to twenty-five dollars to each tenant to buy food or other incidentals. The *Tribune* story quoted the manager at the Malden Arms saying she bought lunches for tenants in her building. More than anyone else, she knew how badly they needed this food.

Others were quoted saying the numbers at the lunch program sites were dwindling and that they saw people walking off site with lunches and selling them. All of the stories assumed that all the lunches that did not go to children had been paid for with federal funds. The repeated refrain

The first attempt to shut down our summer lunch program was in 1976. In just two weeks before the program was slated to end for the summer the lunches were cut off by the State Department of Education and Food. Over 300 children and their parents picketed their office in Chicago, marching and chanting for their lunches. By the end of the afternoon the lunches were reinstated.

in both stories was that taxpayers were footing the bill for freeloaders and that the service center was reaping untold thousands for lunches children weren't getting. They saw what they wanted to see: fraud.

In the end, after an extensive investigation, we were cleared of any wrongdoing. The letter we received clearing us a few months later also congratulated us for having one of the best-run programs in the state of Illinois. When the *Lerner Press* finally had to acknowledge that they got the story wrong, they did so at the back of the paper.

By now the clinic had been up and running for a year. Additional funding for a hard-fought-for special black lung program at the clinic was committed, and the future looked bright. But there were stormy days ahead. Tensions that existed between George Dunne, the president of the county board, and Dr. James Haughton were coming to a climax. Dunne was not a fan of the Health and Hospital Governing Commission and wanted it disbanded, with responsibility for the county health system including its hospitals and clinics returned to the county board. He also wanted the new funds coming for black lung to go to County Hospital and not the Uptown clinic.

Locally there were tensions between the Uptown Community Health Services Community Board and the local political machinery. We were the outliers, the young Turks, the Black Panther radicals. The city-run Uptown Health Center was the repository of many of the Forty-Sixth Ward patronage workers. In proving that Uptown was a "critical manpower shortage area" for health resources, we had shown how ineffective the city's health center was. They were embarrassed, and both their reputations and jobs were threatened.

We had battled the machine and the liberal establishment in the election and lost. They all smelled blood, and by 1980 the clinic had become a target. Marion Volini, the alderman of the Forty-Eighth Ward, where the clinic was located, had won a special election in 1978 to fill a vacancy at the same time as the special election I had first run in.[27] Along with North Side liberal alderman Dick Simpson, Volini responded to a request by some of Angela Turley's supporters to fire the community board and create a new one.[28] Cook County Board president George Dunne meanwhile presented a budget to the board to defund the Uptown People's Community Health Center. Since the clinic was a joint effort between the county and federal governments, this would effectively shut it down.

There were tensions as well between the clinic staff and community board. We were perhaps overenthusiastic in our approach to advocacy—although I don't think so, given that we only accompanied patients as advocates at their request. The board was perhaps particularly sensitive to rules and regulations regarding privacy. On top of the usual petty conflicts of agenda that occur in many work situations, tensions were

---

27 Marion Volini's husband was one of the attorneys representing the police in the Hampton/Clark civil trial. I saw him every day during the trial. None of us were surprised that she came after the clinic. However, Marion turned out to be her own person. She was still alderman during Harold Washington's first term as mayor and was part of his coalition of twenty-one. Years later when I was an alderman, we established a respectful working relationship.

28 Angela Turley had also run for alderman of the 46th Ward in February 1979, coming in third.

aggravated by a lack of trust between us (particularly between Paul Siegel, Slim Coleman, and myself, and Quentin Young and Ron Shansky) over real or perceived diverse agendas for the future of the clinic. In any event, we ended up in a legal and political battle that came to an end almost a year later.

The community board of the clinic had taken the county board to court to stop the closure. While the Health and Hospital Governing Commission was funded by the Cook County Board, the clinic's operating contract was with the Health and Hospital Governing Commission and the federal Department of Health, Education, and Welfare. The basis of our lawsuit was that George Dunne and the county board did not have the authority to defund the clinic.

We won the lawsuit, but after that outcome was appealed, the state supreme court ruled that the county board could close the clinic. By then, at the urging of Dunne, the state legislature decommissioned the Health and Governing Hospital Commission, returning all county clinics and hospitals to the direct control of George Dunne and the Cook County Board. Haughton was gone and the black lung funds were headed to County Hospital.

We would now have to turn our attention to forcing accountability from the remaining city-owned and controlled Uptown Health Center. The Chicago Area Black Lung Association would do the same with the black lung program now housed at Cook County Hospital.

. . . .

32.

HOUSING SET ABLAZE FOR PROFIT

In Uptown, fire was such a regular experience that many simply took it for granted. Typically these fires were not mistakes; most often they were instead the logical extension of neglect, left to ignite on their own. Sometimes they were intentionally set. Always someone profited from them. It was a rare situation when the victims of a fire had any control over the situation—other than not living in that building at that time.

Most Uptown buildings had seen little maintenance over the decades. In many, the original electrical wiring from the 1920s or before was still in place, frayed and deteriorating. There were no upgrades, no circuit breakers, and the circuits were designed for one or two lamps, maybe a radio—not TVs, hair dryers, toasters, or multiple uses of lights, radios, and other appliances. Without the benefit of breaker panels, overuse of a wire—especially one already frayed and touching another— would lead to overheating and fire that could spread without warning. Landlords and owners took no action to improve the systems; indeed, they were incentivized not to.

Insurance scams ranked high on the agenda of some of these landlords. For others, a vacant piece of property could be more valuable than the building that had stood on it.

Arson was one of the more visible and violent ways that buildings in Uptown were vacated and cashed in on.

When I first began canvassing in Uptown in 1972, I had been regaled with stories from people who had lived on the block, which lay vacant, waiting for construction of the first Truman College building. The common thread in each was the failure for any formal eviction procedures or notifications. These stories consistently followed one of two narratives. The first was, "I was woken from a deep sleep early one morning by shaking and loud noises. Outside, our front stairs had been demolished by a wrecking ball. We had to move immediately. We were lucky to retrieve our clothes." The other, more chilling narrative was, "It was the middle of the night. I smelled smoke and saw flames lapping at my front door. I gathered up my children and we fled. The fire department was located across the street, but no fire engines showed up for at least twenty minutes. We lost everything."

Throughout the 1970s, devastating fires struck in Uptown on average once every three days. The fire station on Wilson Avenue was one of the busiest in the city. We wouldn't see changes for another decade.

In our own experience, arson had already been the cause of multiple fires: first in 1975 at the Campaign for Community Control office on Lawrence Avenue, then at our apartment on the 4600 block of Kenmore in 1976, followed in November 1978 by the one at our office at 1222 West Wilson, and finally at my campaign office on Cornelia in 1979. No one had been hurt in any of these fires, but in each case, except

Wilson Avenue and the first floor of the building on Cornelia, the buildings had been left uninhabitable.

I don't know whether the fire on Kenmore was targeted or its cause more typical of the fires common in Uptown. I'm sure the fire at the Campaign for Community Control office was arson, and politically motivated; members of the Black Panther Party were staying in the office on Lawrence at the time. The campaign-office fire was started by a Molotov cocktail thrown in through the front window. The fire on Wilson was set by teenager Randy Price in the vacant laundromat located beneath us on the first floor of the building; Randy had previously set crosses on fire on several front yards of buildings where people of color lived.

It was difficult getting the city's attention on out-of-control arson. Because they owned so many buildings with so many fires, Charlie Roberts and a group of suburban businessmen were a target for us.

Charlie Roberts, who we dubbed in *Keep Strong* "slumlord of the month" on more than one occasion, owned multiple buildings in Uptown with a checkered history of safety and fire. One of these was the fire that destroyed the four-story Ellis Hotel in January 1979. Two of the building's seventy-nine residents died in that fire. Many of the remaining residents jumped, and in some cases tossed children, out windows to escape. This was the last of three fires in a week at the Ellis. Fire extinguishers had been removed after the second fire, and a "smudge pot" filled with potentially explosive diesel fuel had been placed in the fourth-floor hallway.

Alderman Ralph Axelrod's ward secretary, Jerry Orbach, was a corporation counsel in housing court. In this capacity, Orbach could have demanded immediate receivership for this building long before it became a candidate for fire. The Ellis Hotel had a history of serious and chronically unaddressed housing violations. It had been in and out of housing court for nine years. We had no doubt the fire could have been avoided. We had no doubt that the city officials who could have acted to avoid this tragedy ignored the problem. And we had no doubt that victims of the fire were just more people considered "disposable"—undeserving of concern or compassion—by the powers that be.

Roberts, along with a group of suburban businessmen, had purchased more than three dozen buildings in Uptown and Edgewater between 1968 and 1976. In an exposé Marc Zalkin printed in *Keep Strong*,[29] he referred to them as the Charlie Roberts Gang. "Roberts and his partners came to Uptown in the late 1960s when the land was cheap, tenants easy to find and redevelopment just a couple of years down the road," Marc wrote. By the end of 1979, seventeen of their buildings had gone up in flames—more than sixteen people dying as a result.

During the summer of 1979, Marc initiated a joint arson investigation between *Keep Strong*, the Better Government Association, and the ABC-TV news magazine *20/20*, following a tip that another Charlie Roberts-owned building, the Parker Arms, was going to burn. But officials from the state's attorney, police department, and fire department were uninterested and uncooperative after they were contacted. Across the street was a three-story building with a vacant studio apartment we were able to rent. The film crew from New York set up their equipment and we were good to go—until they contacted the bomb and arson division of the police department "out of courtesy." We were sure the presence of this film crew would get back to the owners of the court-way building. In any case, nothing happened for the next six or seven days and the crew pulled up stakes and returned to New York. It would be a few weeks, but the Parker Arms would ultimately still go up in flames.

Another Roberts building, a court-way located at 4520–4530 North Malden, went up in flames on December 27, 1979, just after midnight. It was fully occupied when fire swept the building. The building manager, Ray, who had a history of managing buildings consumed by fire, had taken rent and a security deposit from Uptown residents Pat and

---

29 "Murder by Fire," *Keep Strong*, Vol. 4, No. 9 (February 1980), 5.

In our ongoing attempts to get the city's attention, we organized a walking tour with Andy Mooney, then Jane Byrne's commissioner of Neighborhoods (left). Weeks later we demonstrated at HUD's downtown headquarters (right).

Jim Shaw for an apartment in this court-way building. When he failed to get it ready as promised, he convinced them to move into another apartment a mile north on Winthrop, which they did with their two children. Within forty-eight hours, both buildings were in flames. Seven people died in the fire on Malden, and six at Winthrop. Jim Shaw was one of them.

Rosa Maria Robles was one of them as well. Her daughter, Carmen Sandoval, had moved into the Winthrop building a few months before the fires, paying rent to manager John Meyers for a two-bedroom apartment that needed some repairs. Promised that it would take just a few days to get it fixed up, she agreed to temporarily stay in a studio. "But I was there for weeks," she later recalled. "When I complained, he talked real loud to me and said he would put me on the street. When I told him he couldn't just put me on the street, he said he was a sheriff and showed me his badge."

A few days after this verbal altercation, Rosa moved into the Winthrop building as well. Like her daughter, she had to wait for him to fix up her apartment and was "temporarily" in a studio. Although she was restricted to a wheelchair, the studio was on the third floor. They felt they had no other choice. Then Meyers told Carmen he was selling

As ABC's *20/20* exposé neared, Uptown went downtown. Armed with coffins representing those who had died in fires we went to city hall before moving on to HUD offices.

the building.[30] "I said I was going to move, and Mommy said she would move also. Meyers said, 'Don't move.' He told us he had another building." Carmen and her sister moved into 4522 Malden.[31]

"Mommy never moved out of the building on Winthrop," Carmen continued. "She lived without a stove or refrigerator in the little studio. She was living like a dog. We kept telling Meyers that my mother needed heat in the apartment because it was so cold. They couldn't even take a bath because there was no hot water. Meyers said he was going to move Mommy in here (4522 Malden)." But then there was a fire. As Carmen explained:

---

30 As a tenant, it was often difficult to know who actually owned a building you lived in. It was common for someone new to show up to collect rent claiming they were the new owner. Sometimes this was someone buying a building on contract or at least until they could no longer afford to pay the mortgage. Sometimes it was a scam. Sometimes it was a contracted rent collector or junior partner spreading rumors.

31 "Murder by Fire."

The day before the fire [on Winthrop] we had a fire here [on Malden]. The police kept us outside till 3:30 or 4:00 in the morning. . . . My uncle said he tried to save my mother's life. He had my mother on his back. She fell. He couldn't see or breathe because the smoke was so thick. The last thing he heard about Mommy was when she said, "Pito, I'm dying." He looked for her, but he knew she was already dead.

I found the lady that was living across the hall from my mother. She told me that no one could find John Meyers. He had run away with the money and no one could find him. Other people are looking for John, too. One lady had given him $225, and he didn't even give her an apartment. She was sleeping in the hallway. She was very upset, crying and screaming. Meyers had locked up her stuff in the basement. . . . They're all together. I'm telling you. They got insurance.

"When the building has insurance, if it's in bad shape, then the owner sends some people to burn the building so they can get paid," Carmen concluded, summarizing what most of us were thinking.

I don't remember whether anyone ever caught up with John Meyers. I'm sure none of the tenants got their rents back.

The community responded. Tenant patrols were organized for protection. Rallies were organized to demand action by public officials. We organized a walking tour with Andy Mooney, Jane Byrne's commissioner of neighborhoods, through the heart of Uptown, highlighting the impact arson was having and demanding investigations of every fire who profited and how—along with arrests and prosecutions of owners and managers for arson and for the intentional neglect that had led to the fires. But nothing got the attention of the powers that be like the *20–20* exposé that aired in February 1980.

As the feature aired on ABC, Chicago firefighters went on strike. They were demanding that Jane Byrne make good on her promise of a union contract for firefighters. In the seven months since her upset election as mayor, Byrne had backtracked, leading the firefighters union to respond with the strike, which extended to a week, then two. A parallel situation was unfolding with police officers to whom Byrne had also promised a contract during her campaign. She needed to double down to send a message to police as well as firefighters.[32] A week into the firefighters' strike, she began hiring nonunion men (and a few women) who were willing to cross the picket line. Many of them were people of color who would otherwise never have gotten the chance at this job. The striking firefighters were furious, calling them scabs.

The strike lasted for three weeks, exposing the ugly side of the Chicago Fire Department. The service of police officers, firefighters, and public school teachers is important in every community, but in Chicago in 1980, very few people of color held these jobs. They were not simply good-paying jobs; these are jobs where cultural sensitivity—or lack of it—can mean the difference between life and death; success and failure.[33]

In Uptown, the relationship between the community and firefighters was not particularly good. From the point of view of many firemen (I don't remember many women firefighters—if any—in Uptown at the time), they were doing their job, which was a dangerous one. From the point of view of many residents who were victims of fire, it took too long for the fire department to respond to fires, nor was it understood why their doors had to be broken down or their windows busted, or their furniture torn apart. It was hard to believe that all this destruction was necessary to put out a fire. No one ever gave an explanation. The communication was poor and made worse by the lack of respect shown by many firemen.

While the Uptown community had tension with firefighters, we obviously needed them. Concerned the community would be left unprotected during the strike, the Heart of Uptown Coalition organized a fire patrol armed with fire extinguishers, sand, and shovels. For the duration of the strike, our ragtag teams patrolled the streets and alleys of the heart of Uptown for signs of fire. Still, we had some concerns that we lacked the training to deal with some situations, such as if we came across anyone who needed medical attention.

---

32 By the end of Byrne's term, sworn employees of the police and fire departments had contracts.

33 As I write this book, the Chicago Fire Department has yet to reach racial parity in the makeup of its workforce.

In November 1978, it had taken the fire station on Wilson Avenue almost a half hour to respond to the fire set in the abandoned laundromat located under our second-floor office where we produced *Keep Strong*. Our consequent efforts to find common ground with the firefighters working there were unpromising, at least at first. However, someone in the coalition eventually struck a friendship with a paramedic stationed there, and he offered to provide CPR classes to our volunteer fire patrol.

During the winter of 1979–80, I attended these evening training sessions; Brendan, then a few months shy of nine years old, came with me. We had moved our office to this second-floor space in 1976. On the street level was our legal program, a laundromat, a local bar, and a dry cleaner. One third of our second-floor space was dedicated to *Keep Strong* Publishing, one third to Coalition and ISC offices, and the last third to the Fred Hampton Memorial Hall where we held our Country Music Sundays and community meetings.

During one of our evening CPR classes, we were taking a break. I had left the gathering to do some other work. Brendan had left the hall as well, getting some fresh air and apparently deciding to make a quick run across the street to the corner store to get some candy before it closed. It was a few minutes past curfew (Chicago has a 10:30 p.m. curfew for unaccompanied children), but he figured he could get across the street and back before anyone noticed; and after all, his mom was right there.

The hall in which we were meeting was lined with windows along Wilson Avenue. It was a winter night but the room was warm, so pretty much everyone was sitting on the open window sills. In a hurry to return with his candy, Brendan, running across the street, was spotted by a blond-haired female police officer, who cocked her revolver as she pointed her gun at his back. While someone came charging down the hallway to find me, everyone else was shouting to Brendan to stop running. They saw the cocked gun. Thankfully, he heard them and stopped. He was in a patrol car by the time I got downstairs. I joined him to have a very unsatisfactory conversation with the officer and her partner, who lectured me about the curfew before presenting me with a curfew-violation summons. Furious, I nevertheless understood that we had quite literally dodged a bullet.

While the police were patrolling us, our fire patrol patrolled for fires, focusing on alleys. During the course of the two-week strike, the Heart of Uptown Coalition fire patrol put out several garbage and garage fires. While we didn't receive recognition or assistance, we reported every fire we found. Our suspicions of collusion by some striking firefighters were acknowledged when several of them who worked out of the Uptown fire station were charged with setting at least some of those fires.

Ultimately the striking firefighters got their contract, while we continued our campaign against arson for profit, demanding action by the mayor, police, and state's attorney. Uptown was not alone in this endeavor: communities across Chicago faced a similar rise in fires and arson. All of us wanted a comprehensive approach to discourage and end this activity. In response, we got some lip service, with the mayor and state's attorney announcing task forces on arson. Following one of our guiding principles—"Hope for the best, but prepare for the worst"—we organized tenant patrols in buildings that fit the profile for a fire.

After one tenant patrol caught an arsonist hired by the building owner in the act of setting a fire in a court way on Clifton, we finally saw an arrest and conviction of an owner. No one lost their lives in the fire (although many lost their belongings), and the intentionally set fires slowed down dramatically. Still, other tactics—including illegal lockouts, water shutoffs, and failure to correct violations that resulted in buildings being vacated by judges' orders—intensified when it was more advantageous for an owner to get rid of tenants.

· ·

33.

EMPLOYMENT ACTION COALITION

As we entered a new decade and with a year of elections behind me—and any thought of running for public office vanished (or so I thought)—I took an eighteen-month stint to work as the executive director of the Employment Action Coalition.

The Employment Action Coalition was the brainchild of the leaders of the Coalition to Stop the Chicago 21 plan. The architects of the 21 Plan had direct ties to the companies and financial institutions that were the engine behind Chicago's plant closings. Some of these—like the Schwinn factory on Chicago's Northwest Side—were in areas that provided new lucrative opportunities for development. Their close ties at city hall embraced the changes—and, in doing so, failed to assist the people most negatively affected.

A shifting economy, impacted by developments in technology, was changing Chicago's workplaces. Aging equipment, along with an increased cost of living in the city, was a lethal combination for poor and working people. In the ensuing decade, factories moving out of the city and taking their jobs with them would be a real threat. A lack of public policy or political will to find local solutions was evident. Chicago was not prepared—at least when it came to those who would be most affected.

We asked Don Benedict of the Community Renewal Society to house and support this venture, whose purpose was to unite communities affected by plant closures across the city in an effort to impact the city's policies and create relief for the thousands of families already experiencing harm from lost jobs and pensions. A faith-based social justice organization, CRS was founded in Chicago 1882 to address the social, educational, and economic needs of newly arrived immigrants. With ties to the United Church of Christ, CRS embraced the history of the Congregationalists who demonstrated a commitment to racial justice and civil rights. Don welcomed me and the Employment Action Coalition into the CRS family.

Almost ten years earlier, Don had done the same for John McDermott, Lillian Calhoun, and the *Chicago Reporter*, a magazine that focused on racial and economic inequities in Chicago. It was here that I first met Laura Washington, a journalist who would later become editor of the *Reporter*. Their investigative reporting dovetailed seamlessly with the work I was doing—at the Employment Action Coalition and with *All Chicago City News*.

Chicago was in flux. Plants were closing. The public schools were in crisis. Public transit was facing labor unrest and increasing fares. Public housing was in disarray as the questionable and self-serving practices of its board chairman, including years of deferred maintenance,

Plaintiffs in the lawsuit demanding community representation on the city-appointed Economic Development Committee to hold a strategy meeting. Seated from left to right: Bob Lucas representing Kenwood Oakland Community Organization, Jack Hart, sitting in for Slim as representative for the Uptown People's Community Service Center and the Intercommunal Survival Committee, Marion Stamps representing the Tranquility Memorial Community Organization, and Art Vazquez on behalf of the Pilsen Coalition against the 21 Plan. Standing are Susan Rosenblum and Marty Oberman, then alderman of the 43rd Ward.

were taking their toll. Police misconduct was an unspoken and equally unrecognized reality—sending hundreds (or more) of innocent men and women to jail. The war on crime was, in the eyes of its victims, a war on the poor and oppressed communities where its attention was focused.

In all these ways, Chicago was truly "a tale of two cities"—one being the everyday people struggling to survive, the other being the corporate elite and the politicians who paved their own way. Wisconsin Steel, Elgin Watch, Schwinn Bicycle, Bell & Howell, Stewart Warner, and Montgomery Ward were just a few of the companies leaving or threatening to leave. Factories in Chicago were old, many obsolete, and it was more expensive to retool them than to move somewhere else and start fresh in places where labor was cheaper. Technology and competition in the steel industry affected the nearby steel mills, which one by one shut down. The once-dominant printing business shrank quickly as early impacts of technology became evident.

Thousands of jobs were lost—most not to return. Meanwhile, the new jobs, where available, required many in the workforce to be retrained. Who was going to retrain them? The building trades were hard to get into, and to do so one often had to call upon family ties. Trade schools had been segregated for years, and those trained for these jobs tended to keep them in the family.

Chicago was a union town, but the unions often reflected the same contradictions that existed in the city at large. Dynasties had developed, and the retention of power was too often the first motivator—before the interests of the majority of workers—in addressing grievances and during negotiations. However, an independent movement among younger organizers to democratize the unions was gaining strength as the changing economy impacted the landscape in which they were functioning.

Frank Lumpkin at Wisconsin Steel, Rudy Lozano as an organizer for the International Ladies Garment Workers Union organizing the unorganized, and the workers at Schwinn and at Stewart Warner were just some of the "upstarts" who worked hard at redirecting union leadership to be more effective. Those most active in the leadership of this movement were Black and Latino. We covered their various efforts in *Keep Strong*, and they were now part of the Employment Action Coalition joining the unemployed and soon-to-be displaced workers in many of our activities.

The Employment Action Coalition focused on targeting public attention on the public bodies responsible for dealing with the city's growing unemployment. We started with the Chicago City Council and Economic Development Commission. The EDC, created by Mayor Daley in 1975, was responsible for designating federal funds coming to the city for economic development and focused most of its attention on realizing the Chicago 21 Plan.

We held hearings throughout 1980 with workers being displaced or under the threat of losing their jobs. Testimony ranged from complaints about the unrepresentative nature of the EDC, questions about its meetings being closed to the public, questions about programs funded by the EDC that focused on a few well-connected firms while neglecting small firms, and its failure to develop programs for the thousands affected by layoffs and plant closures.

We invited all fifty aldermen. Six responded. Danny Davis, Cliff Kelley, and Lawrence Bloom attended; three others sent representatives. Elgin Watch employed about four hundred people. When the company moved to Florida that year, most of them lost their jobs, highlighting the dynamic that was gripping the city and region. We wanted the city council to investigate the EDC. The aldermen that attended agreed.

Concurrently, community activists and organizers filed a lawsuit in federal court. The plaintiffs were Bob Lucas, filing as an individual and on behalf of the Kenwood Oakland Community Organization; Marion Stamps, individually and on behalf of the Tranquility Memorial Community Organization; Art Vazquez, individually and on behalf of the Pilsen Coalition against the 21 Plan; and Slim Coleman, on behalf of the Uptown People's Community Service Center and the Intercommunal Survival Committee.

The court ruled that the city had violated clear federal requirements for open meetings and representation of all stakeholders on boards and commissions that determined how federal funds would be spent. We consequently successfully reached a consent decree requiring the appointment of six candidates to the EDC's Overall Economic Development Program Committee.

This committee was the group that prepared the city's submission for federal funds for economic development and job training. The consent decree required that going forward, at least 25 percent of the members of this committee were to be racial minorities with equal distribution being given to Latino and Black candidates, and with at least 40 percent female members.

We won the suit, but as soon as the city agreed in court to restructure this commission, rather than make the agreed-upon changes to the committee membership, they instead restructured it out of existence. It seemed that by winning, we had in fact lost. We would now have to take our fight to the political arena.

34.

LASTING LEGACIES
THE UPTOWN PEOPLE'S LAW CENTER
AND BLACK LUNG WORK

They were not my primary focus areas, but the two most indelible legacies in Uptown that continued out of our organizing there in the 1970s were the Chicago Area Black Lung Association and the Uptown People's Law Center.

The Black Lung Association, in conjunction with the UPLC, trained many paralegals from Uptown's impoverished white community who would have huge impacts, including the late Belinda Belcher and Gary Lester. Other folks like Tina Douglass, Antonia Feliciano, Richard Schmidt, and Robert Hodges played important roles in both entities.

The Black Lung Association would eventually fade away (a couple of decades later). The UPLC, as an entity, however, is likely the most enduring legacy of the organizing work in Uptown in the 1970s. And in some ways, its evolution tracks the evolution of thought and activism in Uptown over six different decades. The center was initially headed by ISC members Pat Spaulding and Jack Hart under the guidance of Jim Chapman. Following the 1983 mayoral campaign and Harold Washington's election as mayor, Marc Kaplan replaced Jack as the executive director and Tom Johnson took the legal helm, leaving a few years later to start a law firm with his wife Leslie Jones and several other former Legal Aid attorneys.[34]Alan Mills, who volunteered at the center as a law student, came on as legal director in 1992, becoming the UPLC's executive director a decade later.

The center has always focused on poverty issues such as social security and tenants' rights. But in recent decades, it has become known

---

34 Tom would go on to become one of Chicago's most impactful election code attorneys, responsible for many of the changes in election law and voting we take for granted in Illinois today, and he continued to work black lung cases up until he and Leslie were bludgeoned to death in their home in April 2020.

as the premier firm dealing with larger policy issues concerning the incarcerated. As the chants of "Fuck the Pigs" of the 1960s evolved into thorough scholarly work around police and prison abolition in the twenty-first century, the UPLC evolved as one of the legal forces working to figure out how to collaborate with activists to animate some of the human rights and civil rights legal avenues toward a society free of prisons.

One of the many narratives of the intertwined relationships between the legacies of our organizing in the 1970s involves Monica Cosby. Monica would be one of the young Uptown kids that would work with a cadre of kids in the early 1990s to form various youth programs under an umbrella group called the Uptown Youth Force (to which I shall return later). In the mid-'90s, Monica was charged and convicted of cooperating with her abusive partner to kill his mother. Monica spent two decades in prison, where she stayed in touch with Alan and Belinda from the UPLC and where she became an activist. During this time, Monica's mom was employed at the law center, where she ran the social security disability program. Robbie Hodges, one of the investigators who helped in her defense, was trained at the law center after he himself was released from a stint in the state prison system. (He was also the first person Alan Mills ever visited in prison or jail.)

Upon her release, Monica continued her activism as a board member of Moms United against Violence and Incarceration and as an organizer with the Westside Justice Center—a nonprofit criminal justice and legal services operation started by my son in 2015 that cobbled together many of the lessons of our work from the 1970s and beyond—and undoubtedly some of his own.

PART IV

CHICAGO JOINS THE COUNTRY AT A CROSSROADS

35.

THE NATIONAL PENDULUM SWINGS

The Great Depression of the 1930s brought unheard of hardships and the threat of insurrection and revolution. Unions were at their height of influence and a vehicle for mass action. In spite of cycles of repression, the Communist Party and other left-wing organizations enjoyed a great deal of support. Out of necessity, the government responded, and President Franklin Roosevelt signed executive orders and laws designed to address the dire conditions facing millions of Americans.

While these actions provided enough relief to ward off the threat of revolution, they were imperfect, and their implementation was unequal. Farm laborers and domestic workers were never included in the Social Security and old-age retirement program. At the insistence of Southern states, the national welfare system was limited,[1] and most of the civil rights and housing acts enabling it could, with a little creativity and heavy doses of racism, allow local governments to ensure their control of who got what in their states, allowing for the hegemony of Jim Crow laws.[2]

Even so, they represented a new direction for the country and would impact the political debate for years to come. A notion of government responsibility—including taxing the rich to have the resources to achieve them—would be an acceptable (albeit often challenged)

---

1   Local governments, along with charitable organizations, had previously been the sole options for public assistance, the rules of which were often subjective and elusive. Women who chose to work found themselves under attack for neglecting their children. If they sought public assistance, they were charged with being morally unfit. While the federal funds would now support the states' programs, the legislation creating the welfare system only received enough votes for passage after demands by Southern states forced a compromise that established welfare to be a state-by-state affair administered through state juvenile courts. This ensured that the main beneficiaries in Southern states were white women.

2   Obviously, there were some exceptions to this—primarily when the Supreme Court ruled, as in the *Brown v. Board of Education* ruling, or when presidents took action, bringing in federal troops or the National Guard.

approach to the government's role. The notion that the government had the responsibility to step in when the capitalist economy was inadequate—and in fact failing—for significant numbers of Americans had been a defining one since the New Deal response to the Great Depression of the 1930s. Inherent was the notion of entitlement—an assumption that as human beings we all had the right to expect the protection of our basic human needs.

As an unpopular war waged in Vietnam, the civil rights struggle was expanding. The nonviolent philosophy emblematic of the Southern civil rights movement met the rebellions and demands of the urban north. Although Congress passed the country's first civil rights legislation in eighty years in 1957, increased pressure by the movement to remove Jim Crow and poll taxes for voting led to passage of the Civil Rights Act of 1964 and the Voting Rights Act of 1965. The War on Poverty followed with mounting acknowledgment of severe poverty among both white and Black Americans.

By the end of the 1970s the country was at a crossroads. Federal programs from the Works Progress Administration to the 1960s War on Poverty were gestures to reverse the ills of the poor in America, but by 1970 the pendulum was clearly swinging the other way. As this shift was occurring, we reported on its impact on ordinary people's lives in *Keep Strong* magazine.

Nixon's election in 1968, which signaled this change in direction, would be temporarily disrupted following the scandal of Watergate. But not for long. There were multiple recessions throughout the 1970s, beginning around the time I arrived in Uptown. Dramatic changes in the economic policies of the American central bank and the removal of the gold standard precipitated interest rates to rise to nearly 20 percent, pricing many out of new cars and homes. Unemployment was in the double digits. Oil prices exploded.

Economists like the University of Chicago's Milton Friedman argued that the cause of all these ills was massive budget deficits. Cuts in federal programs, they argued, were a necessity. Public welfare and Social Security were under attack. As unions were being scapegoated, these economists argued union demands for good wages and retirement benefits were bankrupting the country.

The transition from entitlement for basic needs to trickle-down economics had begun, attended by the belief that Americans should "pull themselves up by their bootstraps."

Meanwhile, the world economy was shifting as more Third World countries broke the yoke of colonialism, demanding and winning independence. However, the playing field was not an even one, and the influence of capital (here and abroad) quickly attached financial constraints to most efforts at reclaiming land and infrastructures, limiting these new nations in their efforts to provide for their citizenry. Here and abroad, the demand for privatization of government functions was a common refrain.

This shift from entitlement for basic needs was well underway by the time Ronald Reagan was elected president in 1980. With the energy generated behind the emergence of the "silent majority," Reagan had the wind at his back as he reshaped government. Taxes on the rich went hand in glove with the withdrawal from states of millions of dollars in funds to support those things many of us believed the government should be responsible for: support for public housing, public education, public transit, welfare, Medicare, and Social Security.

Reagan's first two years began what became a steady decline in taxes paid by the wealthy (and an increase in the numbers of poor households paying taxes). As taxes on the rich declined, government institutions designed to ensure housing, education, transit, health, and mental health care to those less fortunate—even mail delivery—all suffered.

Between 1980, the year Ronald Reagan was elected, and 1987, the year Mayor Harold Washington died, the amount of Community Development Block Grant funds allocated to Chicago decreased by $100 million. Other cuts followed. These funds were a big chunk of the money available for critical services in Chicago's low-income neighborhoods.

36.

A LOCAL MOVEMENT IS BORN

In 1979, Jane Byrne surprised Chicago with her unlikely win against the machine's chosen candidate. Many characterized her as the "snow queen," attributing her success to Mayor Michael Bilandic's inept response to the major snowfall in Chicago in the months leading up to the election. And that was certainly a factor—one that had led to increased support for Byrne in the Black and Latino communities where the worst of Bilandic's poor performance had been felt. By running on a platform of reform and promises of independence and responsiveness to Black and other disenfranchised communities, Byrne had gained the advantage.

In the early days of her administration, Byrne appointed West Side activist Nancy Jefferson to the police board and Renault Robinson to the Chicago Housing Authority board. Her choice of Angeline Caruso over Manford Byrd, a popular and highly qualified candidate, for acting superintendent of Chicago's majority–African American school system was disappointing, although her initial appointments to the Chicago Board of Education came close to reflecting the racial makeup of the school system (a Chicago first). After that, her appointments—particularly to the board of education, the Chicago Housing Authority, and the leadership of the police department took a turn. To many, they were dismissive of those who had elected her, exposing a perspective that was truly out of touch and arguably outright racist.

Years of institutional racism and corruption had taken its toll. The Democratic machine was operating in concert with a barely existing Republican Party and the financial and industrial elites who represented the historic movers and shakers. Excluded from this club were those without the power of money or clout—in other words, virtually everyone. The trick, however, was the heightened manipulation of white-skin privilege, the historic isolation of the Black community using publicly sanctioned deed restrictions and other public policies, and the additional virtual invisibility of Latinos and poor whites living outside Chicago's segregated Black communities.

Byrne, as would happen to Harold Washington four years later, was immediately embroiled in a political struggle with the city council old guard she had described as "an evil cabal." But unlike him, she quickly realigned with this cabal as any hopes or expectations that many in Chicago had held for a shift toward fairness, openness, and independence in local government and politics were dashed.

Police misconduct was nothing new in Chicago's poor and minority communities. In 1972 Congressman Ralph Metcalfe broke with Mayor Richard J. Daley over police brutality in the Black community, issuing a report that began with, "The time for action, for police reform, has come." Nine years later, not much had changed. So, when James O'Grady resigned as the superintendent of police immediately following Byrne's upset victory in April 1979, there was hope in the Black community that a Black superintendent might take that job, and an expectation that this would be possible and make a difference. Father George Clements, the Afro-American Patrol League's spiritual advisor, said at the time:

> The first thing the next police superintendent has to understand is that there are all kinds of disorientation and chaos in the Black community. But there is one common theme that can unite it, and that is its hatred for the police. This is a schizophrenic thing. . . . You should know that there's a saying in this neighborhood about that motto "We serve and protect." Here we say what it really means, "We serve whites and we protect whites from Blacks."[3]

First Deputy Superintendent Sam Nolan, a thirty-four-year veteran of the department and one of only a handful of Black police officers in command positions, automatically replaced O'Grady as the acting superintendent. In an eerie echo of when Wilson Frost was unjustifiably passed over as acting mayor, presumably because he was Black, barely three years earlier, Byrne made it clear that she would not hire Sam Nolan as police commissioner, saying she wanted to look outside the city for candidates. She created the Office of Public Safety, appointing Nolan to be its head—a move that was considered by many to be an end-run effort to put to bed any consideration of Nolan for the permanent job of superintendent. When the police board completed their job of sifting

---

3   Afro-American Patrolmen's League archives, Chicago History Museum.

through the applications of nearly a hundred hopefuls for the job, as required, they provided Byrne with three names for her consideration. One was from out of state; two were from Chicago. Two hours later, Byrne appointed Richard Brzeczek—the only one of the three who was white. Brzeczek had been with the department for thirteen years and most recently had been the assistant deputy police superintendent in charge of legal affairs for the superintendent's office.

While receiving praise from his fellow Chicago police officers, the reaction from the Black community was immediate, and included a march on police headquarters led by Reverend Jesse Jackson, who called Brzeczek's appointment "an extension of Mayor Byrne's racist policies."[4]

Meanwhile, Chicago public schools were immersed in chaos. Facing a previously undisclosed financial collapse, Joseph Hannon abruptly resigned as general superintendent the day before Thanksgiving. Two weeks later, Byrne engineered the appointment of Angeline Caruso, a white woman who was the associate superintendent for instructional and public services, over Deputy Superintendent Manford Byrd, a Black man who had been her boss. Byrd was passed over in 1975 for Hannon, who he also had outranked.

In Springfield, the state legislature was crafting a short-term bailout of the schools. However, there was a catch: following the recommendation of Governor Thompson, a School Finance Authority would be created to oversee and control all spending. While the schools got a onetime injection of needed funds to make their payroll, the School Finance Authority would demand huge cuts in service to students, layoffs of teachers and other school staff, and the closure of thirty-five schools.

A month later, as Brzeczek began his new job in Chicago, the state legislature was passing legislation in Springfield to dismantle the existing school board and create a new one to be appointed by Mayor Byrne. The schools were in a financial crisis and under court order to develop a plan for desegregation. In mid-April 1980 Byrne made her appointments. For the first time, the board had a majority of nonwhite members. This realignment, however, would not last long.

---

4 *Chicago Tribune*, January 12, 1980, 4.

The board's first official action was to ignore the mayor's choice and unanimously chose Reverend Ken Smith[5] to be their president. Their second official act was to create the board's committees, including one to immediately act in getting an acceptable desegregation plan before the federal court. The previous board failed to take action, resulting in a loss of significant federal funds to the school system. They chose Joyce Hughes to be its chair. Smith and Hughes, both Black, were chosen unanimously by the full school board.

The previous majority-white board was reluctant to take on desegregation, reflecting the historic stance of Chicago politicians and the consequential segregation of Chicago neighborhoods. Not surprisingly, there was a reaction from the largely segregated "white ethnic" Northwest and Southwest Side communities to Byrne's appointments. They demanded inclusion on the board, and Byrne responded. Less than a year after the new board was constituted, Byrne announced that she was replacing two members—both Black men—with two ethnic white women from the Northwest and Southwest Sides of the city, one of whom was a longtime opponent of school desegregation.

State Senator Harold Washington was critical of Byrne and her treatment of Sam Nolan, Manford Byrd, and Ken Smith. When Congressman Ralph Metcalfe announced he would not seek reelection, Byrne recruited machine stalwart Benny Stewart to succeed him. Harold Washington jumped into the race. Successfully defying Byrne, he won with over 50 percent of the votes cast, besting Stewart and several other candidates.

In the same primary election in 1980, Richard M. Daley (the former mayor's up-and-coming son) won the election for Democratic nominee for Cook County State's Attorney. They both went on to win their respective elections in November.

We had covered all these events in *Keep Strong*. In October 1980, however, we pivoted from the magazine to a citywide newspaper. *All Chicago City News* would be a biweekly, bilingual newspaper with a focus on Chicago's shifting political and economic dynamic. The focus

---

5   Byrne had appointed Tom Ayers, retired ComEd executive, to the
    board with the explicit intention that he be the board's president.
    Ayers's primary residence was in a Chicago suburb, and there were
    charges that he was therefore ineligible to even be on the board. Ayers
    joined the vote for Smith.

was the collective resistance to what we felt to be a national move to diminish victories for racial and social equality, which had been won through great hardship and commitment by millions of people over the preceding fifty years.

As an activist journalist, I not only reported and photographed the demonstrations that ensued, but participated in many as well. As editor, Marc Zalkin wrote in the first introductory issue, "This paper will be produced and distributed by a growing network of grassroots activists from Juneway Terrace in Rogers Park to Trumbull Gardens on the far South Side." The paper, he continued, "would advance and promote the causes of communities across the city struggling for the basic necessities: jobs, housing, health care and quality education." Columns by active organizers from all sides of the city were promised as a central feature, along with a page of useful information dealing with legal, health care, and consumer problems that many Chicago residents faced daily. Jeri Miglietta and I were the education editors. For the next six years, I covered many events, writing articles, taking photos, and contributing to production.

A week after the general election, *ACCN* interviewed Congressman-Elect Harold Washington. In spite of Jane Byrne's best efforts, Richard M. Daley had won his race for Cook County state's attorney. Harold Washington had done the same. *All Chicago City News* asked the congressman-elect: "How do you see Rich Daley's election in relationship to future political power movements in Chicago?"[6]

"I see the Daley ploy as a direct threat to the development of the continuing of independent politics in this city," he replied. "The independent political movement has been going on at a steady, slow pace. It reached its crescendo in this city when Singer led a band of independents that took over the Chicago contingent of the Democratic convention in 1972."[7] He continued: "The independent movement became most visible in 1976 under a person who was not an independent, Metcalfe, who the independents rallied to, Black ones and White ones... Then you had Daley's death and my mayoral campaign of 1977 which was a rebuilding

---

6   *All Chicago City News*, Second Introductory Issue, October 1980, 10.
7   Bill Singer was a North Side independent. After winning election as an alderman in a special election in 1969, he continued to be a thorn in Daley's side, ultimately running against him in 1975.

process." After reciting a series of election victories "under the stripe of the independent movement," he turned to Rich Daley. Referring to Daley's election for state's attorney, he stated:

> Some of the Black independents gave credibility in the Black community to Daley by virtue of their endorsements, which were blind and didn't go into his record at all. I think what has happened is that they have given momentum to Daley who, notwithstanding what anyone says, is going to run for mayor in 1983 and is going to try to take over the Democratic Party. There is nothing in his record that would lead any thinking person to assume that he would do anything other than put together a prototype, a replica, of his daddy's and Cermak's machine, which obviously is not dead but needs only some readjustment in terms of his goals. . . .
>
> It is not a racial fight, it's an independent fight. But since what I have tried to say indicates that the seeds of independence in this city are primarily in the Black community, then it follows that the leadership of that movement should come from there. But it should be a coalition, obviously. . . . It's an awakening, an arousal on the part of Black voters and also a degree of sophistication on the part of Black voters. Our election I think represents that. I would like to think that I had sterling qualities. . . . But even if I have them or didn't have them notwithstanding, *it was the movement in this case clearly, not the man or men or women who were involved.* I think that will continue.[8]

Foreshadowing the future, he concluded:

> My primary responsibility is to continue to develop as best as I can this independent grouping that has been going on in this city for the last 25 years at least. That is a question of organizing locally politically so that people can really have the organization that can affect not just the federal but the state and local governments as well.

---

8 Emphasis added. "The plan, not the man" became a theme for the need for change during the time from the beginning of Harold's campaign for mayor and through the aftermath of his death—the point always being that one person alone does not make change.

Two years later, after an unusually productive first term as congressman, Harold would heed the call to jump into the race for mayor of Chicago, where he would face both Jane Byrne and Rich Daley in the Democratic primary. But first, Chicago would have to face dual crises in its public education and public housing institutions.

· ·

37.

SCHOOLS IN CRISIS

In September 1979—two months before the schools were declared to be in a crisis—*Keep Strong*'s front-page story asked: "CHICAGO SCHOOLS—Can They Serve the Children?" Brendan and Anton were now at Stockton Elementary School, and Jeri and I were both involved in the local school advisory council.[9] The board of education had recently lost over $22 million in federal funds due to its failure to come up with a desegregation plan that was acceptable to the feds. Bilingual education was virtually nonexistent.[10] As 475,000 students (including 32,000 entering kindergarten) were expected to begin a new school year, it seemed appropriate to examine the state of the schools.

We highlighted interviews with parents in the Uptown, Humboldt Park, and Austin communities whose schools provided a cross section of the system. The reading levels in all three showed the same trend. Between the 1975–76 school year and the 1978–79 school year, the average student's reading level fell at least two grades, while spending fell an average of 23 percent per child.

Regardless of the community or school they came from, parents complained that too many teachers did not make an effort to understand the community they were teaching in, and how family culture and dynamics impacted their children's learning behavior.

---

9 Prior to 1989.

10 At the time, English was the second language for nearly 30 percent of Chicago's public school students, the vast majority of whom spoke Spanish at home.

Uptown parent Joann Jacobsen told *Keep Strong* she didn't think the school understood what being poor is. "I think the teachers need to be educated according to the neighborhood they're going to work in. If more of the teachers would try to understand at least why a child has certain emotional problems, it would be better. I think emotional problems are a lot deeper and a lot more serious than measles and chickenpox."

Humboldt Park parent Maria Martinez, mother of four children, told us the schools were failing students with limited English skills. "HEW [The Department of Health, Education, and Welfare] has funds for bilingual special education but they are holding them back until the board of education comes up with a good program. They haven't come up with one yet; it's not a priority for them."

South Austin parent Dorothea Oliver told us:

> I've seen teachers come in, knowing nothing about the community, nothing about the kids and you can't come from Glencoe or Skokie and never have been in the Black community and tell me that 'I feel your child needs so and so.' You don't know what I need, what I'm going through. I also feel this is one way the kids get pushed through the system. By the time a child reaches the ninth grade, he or she is lost.[11]

Echoing our experience at Stockton, parents complained bitterly about subjective and broken disciplinary and special education policies, that too many teachers did not understand or make an effort to understand the community they were teaching in, and how the family dynamics impacted their children's learning behavior. By further failing to inform parents of issues the school identified affecting their children, the result was less education, fewer students in school, and fears for their children's futures.

Chicago's public school system did not have an encouraging record. Segregation had been endemic, along with a growing trend of school closures and cuts in classroom resources that was undermining confidence that students were getting their best chance to learn.

In the mid-1960s, civil rights activists, teachers, and parents had protested the ubiquitous twenty- by thirty-six-foot aluminum mobile units,

---

11 *Keep Strong*, Vol. 4, No. 5 (September 1979). Subsequent quotations in this chapter are all from this issue of *Keep Strong*.

installed primarily in the Black community to relieve overcrowding and dubbed "Willis Wagons," after then school superintendent Benjamin Willis. "Wagons are for loading, not learning," charged Bob Lucas,[12] a founding member of the Congress on Racial Equality (CORE), who, with the Woodlawn Organization, organized a series of one-day boycotts, marches, and pickets against the "Willis Wagons." Their demands were simple: let their children attend nearby white schools with plenty of empty seats while the new schools promised for their children were built.

In 1975, after Hannon was appointed general superintendent of schools, his first act was to announce the layoff of two thousand teachers. Four years later, after cuts and inflation, there was 50 percent less money allocated to classrooms for books and supplies than in 1975. During this same period, the student population decreased by 2.65 percent. Although it was expected that teachers and other staff would decrease as well, the loss disproportionately impacted teachers. Going into the 1979 school year, there were 4.1 percent fewer teachers but only a 1.9 percent decrease in nonteaching administrative employees.

The previous year, the federal Department of Health, Education, and Welfare issued a report rejecting the school board's claim that segregation in Chicago schools was a result of housing patterns. Rather, they concluded it was the result of specific, official actions taken by the board of education over many years:

> In summary, Chicago school officials have intentionally created and maintained a racial discriminatory dual school system. In response to expanding minority school populations, increasingly overcrowded black schools and nearby underutilized white schools, school officials took numerous actions and failed to take many other feasible actions, all of which contributed to creating and maintaining the racial segregation of the district's schools.

The report noted that Jenner School, located in Cabrini Green, was grossly overcrowded, while two white schools just two miles north "had decreased to such an extent that they were combined into a single administrative unit." Yet no effort was made to relieve the overcrowding at Jenner.

---

12 Bob Lucas was later the executive director of the Kenwood Oakland Community Organization and one of the organizers with whom we worked in challenging the Chicago 21 Plan.

When school boundaries were adjusted for Ogden Elementary School in 1961, rather than include students from overcrowded Jenner, located less than a mile away, the boundaries were manipulated to ensure that white students from a third school would be sent to Ogden to increase their enrollment. Similarly, in the Hyde Park community, attendance areas were manipulated so that the newly constructed Kenwood Academy would receive the vast majority of white students in the area and the existing Hyde Park High School would become 98.2 percent Black.

Keeping the schools segregated was costly. Enrollment in public schools had been declining since 1969, and by the beginning of the 1979–80 school year, there were more than a hundred thousand fewer students in the system. And yet, during the same period, the board of education built an additional 110 new buildings, to the tune of over $400 million. Again and again, where they were situated and how the attendance areas were drawn guaranteed the continued segregation of the new schools. The failure to improve the educational activities in the schools was not considered to be one of the causes for this decline. Rather it was an accepted notion that white parents were taking their children out of the Chicago public school system (to private schools and to the suburbs) in order to avoid attendance at school with Black children. While there is no doubt that racism was a factor, had they not been so sure that their children would suffer the same fate of poor instruction and overcrowded classrooms, some of these parents may not have been so quick to move their children and their families elsewhere. The lack of school resources and overcrowding were not considered as additional reasons for their actions—conditions which, if addressed, may have seen a different outcome, and ultimately improvement for all students as well as Chicago's tax base.[13]

HEW's report brought new attention to an old and lingering reality. While Hannon disputed the report's findings, Byrne's transition

---

13 The failed political will to meet Chicago's version of Jim Crow in housing, education, and employment policies is consistent and destructive. When magnet schools were later opened with required racial quotas and lots of resources, white parents were more than happy to send their children there. Maybe if we made sure all schools had the resources needed to fully teach the children attending, we might solve some of these hairier systemic problems.

team embraced them, giving a sense of hope that the status quo at the board of education was on the verge of change. We hoped that our focus on the schools in *Keep Strong* would inform that change.

Then the other shoe dropped: the board of education ran out of money. They did not have enough funds to meet their payroll and to repay $89 million in debt service. For years the board of education had balanced their budget by borrowing short-term notes, in expectation of property tax revenue they expected in the upcoming year.[14] This was pretty much what they were attempting to do again. They tried to sell $124.6 million in short-term notes for the cash they needed immediately. But this time, the banks refused to fund this borrowing, precipitating a major crisis. On the eve of the sale, two of the major bond-rating firms—Moody's and Standard & Poor—dropped the board of education's bond rating, making the loan virtually impossible. The two Chicago-based banks—First National and Continental—led the refusal to fund.

The old-guard Chicago politicians, the Republican governor, bipartisan state legislators, and the finance community placed the blame on "lies" by the school administrators. The response was swift. Superintendent Hannon resigned while simultaneously ordering seventeen hundred layoffs and a budget cut of $70 million.[15] The governor and the state legislature agreed to a one-time bailout, advancing the board $37 million—an amount the schools received monthly from the state for general operating expenses. But this advance was coupled with the creation of a School Oversight Committee drawn from the financial community.

In December, Angeline Caruso became the acting superintendent of schools. Caruso was Byrne's choice, and board president Catherine Rohter embraced the move. In January the state legislature created the School Finance Authority, giving it control over the board of education's

---

14 Ironically, the entire time I was on the Chicago City Council (1987–2011), the city always issued short-term notes (referred to as tax anticipation notes) to cover the property tax to be collected in the future. For instance, 2020 are taxes incurred in 2019, which the county collects each year for the prior year's assessment.

15 The layoffs included five hundred special education positions and two hundred assistant principals. The budget cuts targeted the purchase of equipment, books and supplies, and school closures.

finances. The SFA's board was to be made up of five directors and had the power to issue bonds for school expenses and to approve all Chicago Public Schools budgets. Parents and teachers, however, were skeptical.

The board of education has never received funding directly from the City of Chicago.[16] Rather, about a third of the property tax paid by Chicago property owners goes to the board of education. The board depends on these property taxes, along with federal and state funds, to operate. Historically, there are several ways in which the schools were (and still are) shortchanged. The property taxes that go to the board are based on a percentage of the value of the property as assessed by the Cook County Assessor. Some of the wealthiest property owners are companies that successfully challenge their assessments. This has always been a very political process in Chicago, and they've had the clout to get their assessments lowered well beyond their worth. The result is that those with the most to give have been those who give the least.[17]

In 1979 the board of education was one of the city's largest landlords. In addition to all the school buildings it owned, the board was landlord to several large companies—including Inland Steel Corporation and Continental Bank—who were paying 50 to 67 percent less in rent than they would have had they rented from a private landlord. Why were we losing resources for our children's classrooms while subsidizing these large companies that could afford market rent?

While the federal government hasn't been a big funder of local public schools, along with President Johnson' War on Poverty came funding for poor students at all levels, as well as for bilingual education, students with disabilities, and desegregation of the schools. However, Chicago's failures in the areas of bilingual programming and desegregation

---

16 Part of the financial bailout for the schools was a requirement by the banks that the City of Chicago have skin in the game and an agreement that the banks would lend some of the money the board needed to the City of Chicago, who would then lend that money to the board.

17 The board of education uses a percentage system to determine what it gets from the total property tax collected each year. Therefore, the amount of property taxes the school system gets increases as property assessments go up and decreases if they go down. For many years, if they needed more money, they had the option of increasing their percentage. In the years after the school crisis of 1979, this percentage was capped.

threatened these funds, resulting in them being withheld in 1979 under Hannon's leadership.

The Illinois State Constitution adopted in 1970 gave the state the primary responsibility for education. It reads:

> A fundamental goal of the People of the State is the educational development of all persons to the limits of their capacities. The State shall provide for an efficient system of high quality public educational institutions and services. Education in public schools through the secondary level shall be free. There may be such other free education as the General Assembly provides by law. *The State has the primary responsibility for financing the system of public education.*[18]

However, having the primary responsibility for funding public education has never meant that funding was adequate, and in 1979 the funds coming from the state were limited. What they were willing to do, though, was give the banks the ability to loan money to the school system—and to do so at an interest that would make such lending "worth their while."

In early January, negotiators from the country's three largest bond houses, as well as Continental and First National,[19] emerged from two days of secret meetings in the governor's mansion. They had made an agreement to fund $800 million in notes to the board of education that included an immediate jump in interest rates from 7 percent to 11 percent, and the stipulation that the School Finance Authority would now collect the money directly from taxpayers for them.

The board of education had already paid $187 million in interest to banks in 1980, with another $59 million due by August. The new funding was expected to bring the total interest for the year to nearly $300 million—more than a third of what was being borrowed. The loans had simply become a taxpayer-funded vehicle for the banks to make a windfall. There was little concern for the public interest.

---

18 Emphasis added.

19 Coincidentally, these two local Chicago banks were also significantly invested in South Africa's apartheid government. A decade later, when I introduced legislation strengthening our sanctions against South Africa, they were two of the three banks in Chicago that still had investments in South Africa despite US sanctions.

It was bad enough that those responsible for running the schools for so long placed children at the bottom of the list of priorities for the board. But rather than address the resulting inequities, the powers that be were again blaming the victims, or at best ignoring them, while legislating solutions that served the financial community first. To my recollection, none of the members of the newly constituted School Finance Authority had children in the public schools. It was doubtful that any of them had attended Chicago public schools either. None had experience or knowledge of the schools where minority and working families sent their children. The effects of the failure to provide an education, and with it the tools to engage fully as adults, were not among the priorities being considered.

Parents and teachers were alarmed—although the teachers union soon went along with the legislative action. The hope and expectation they had nurtured for a refocus on the classroom and the education of minority and poorer students was now looking like a pipe dream.

We were incensed. Parents from every corner of the city descended on the January meeting of the board of education. When school board president Catherine Rohter went to take her seat, she found she had been displaced by West Side activist Nancy Jefferson. Parents and teachers from all over Chicago made their voices and concerns heard, demanding: "No more cuts!" "Restore bilingual education!" "Fund the classrooms, not the banks!"

The primary agenda for the meeting was a vote on $44 million of the $60 million in immediate cuts demanded by the banks before they would agree to the loan package that, along with the creation of the School Finance Authority, was the basis of the agreement with the governor to bail out the schools. After removing and arresting some of the demonstrators from the room—with and without force—the board was at an impasse. Saying that the cuts fell too heavily on teachers and not enough on administrators and maintenance staff, half the board members refused to support the package presented by Caruso. With a vote split five to five, the cuts were not approved. The teachers union announced they were going on strike. The banks warned that the bailout was in jeopardy.

Along with the funding package, bailout agreements, and creation of the School Finance Authority, legislation was passed requiring the appointment of a new school board by the end of April. The lame-duck board capitulated, ultimately voting for the immediate $60 million in cuts as well as another $120 million by the beginning of April—all required by the SFA.

In the months before Hannon's resignation, the board of education approved $750,000 to pay two consultants developing the "Chicago Mastery Learning Program."[20] Caruso, who four months later would become the acting superintendent, was the associate superintendent of the Department of Instruction Services and chief cheerleader for this program. While touted as a means to enable students to work individually and progress through reading and math at their own rate, the actual implementation proved to be problematic at best. By the time Ruth Love became school superintendent in March 1981, the program was established as the primary vehicle for classroom instruction and the system's standard for advancement from one grade to the next. From our point of view, the worst had been accomplished.

. . . .

38.

THE MOLLISON BOYCOTT

Our organizing for Chicago's public schools brought me into the orbit of Dorothy Tillman. It would be the start of a long friendship, earmarked

---

20 "Continuous Progress / Mastery Learning" had been initially introduced as a pilot program to be tried at the May School on the city's West Side in 1975. Despite questionable results for the children, the program was projected as the answer to the low reading and math achievement of students in Chicago's inner city and was expanded into most lower-achieving schools—again with questionable results. The newer version, "Chicago Mastery Learning," was touted as an improvement to many of the criticisms the board was receiving from parents and teachers alike. The primary change—besides that it would not be the basis for promotion in every elementary school—was that there would now be workbooks for the students and work guides for the teachers.

by our challenges to the miseducation practices of the Chicago Board of Education and the equally misguided policies of the newly minted Jane Byrne administration—all enhanced by Dorothy's wealth of experience in the civil rights movement.

Born in Montgomery, Alabama, Dorothy had grown up between Montgomery and Pensacola, Florida. In her teens she had joined the Southern Christian Leadership Council (SCLC), becoming a field staff organizer by the time of the Selma to Montgomery marches in 1965. It was in that capacity that she was on the Edmund Pettus Bridge on "Bloody Sunday," when white state troopers brutally attacked the 600-person civil rights demonstration. Later that year, she was one of the advance people who came to Chicago ahead of Dr. Martin Luther King Jr. to prepare for his 1966 move here. While King had hoped to bring his philosophy of nonviolence to the North, it soon became clear that this was easier said than done.

In November 1967 Dorothy and her husband, musician Jimmy Tillman, bought a house in West Englewood—a changing but still majority-white community just west of the historic "Black Belt." There they experienced the same racial animus Dorothy had experienced while marching with King in Chicago at Gage and Marquette Parks. Taking advantage of Chicago's historic racial tensions, real estate–inspired fear campaigns that encouraged whites to sell low—but not to make the same reduction for Black prospective buyers—were common. Although they experienced hostility that included an arson attack against their garage, the Tillmans stayed in their home until they moved to San Francisco two years later, where they would remain for a decade before returning to Chicago in 1979.

After the Tillmans moved to San Francisco, they took up residence in the Alemany Housing Project, a former army barracks. The project housed 177 families with no direct access to public transit or recreation areas for their children. Then pregnant with her first child, Dorothy vowed to change all that. She became the chair of the Alemany Family Cooperative Association in 1970, a platform she used to take action alongside the many families living in the long-neglected project.

After leading a host of Alemany families to the seat of power to demand action by Mayor Joseph Alioto, then a tour of their housing project with the mayor, tenants surrounded a city bus near the entrance to the

Dorothy Tillman and I filed our nominating petitions at the same time for the 1987 election. Among many other things, we had Tom Johnson (standing behind us) in common. He was our attorney then and until his untimely death.

housing project. Following her training with SCLC and Dr. King, this action harmed no one and did no damage to the bus or its driver. The bus was simply not allowed to move until the police arrived, at which point they arrested Dorothy and Reverend Cecil Williams, pastor of Glide Memorial Church. However, the city took no action; it simply continued to make promises that a plan would eventually be developed.

Fed up, Dorothy and a large group of tenants went to the Public Utilities Commission, the agency that controlled bus service. They had done their homework and developed their own plan. With this in hand, they took over the meeting, moved their item to the top of the agenda, substituted their plan for the one that would take months, and demanded a vote, making it clear they had no intention to leave until it was adopted—which it was.

A few years later, the Tillmans moved back to Chicago, renting a three-bedroom apartment in a six-flat located on the 4400 block of South Indiana Avenue, just a few blocks from the Irvin C. Mollison Elementary School. Enrolling the four oldest of her five children in Mollison, Dorothy immediately became engaged in the school and active with the local school council and the parent-teacher association. Children at Mollison appeared to be doing well. But when only thirty of the school's sixty eighth graders graduated in June 1980, it was obvious that something was seriously wrong.

Tillman was fully prepared to utilize everything she learned from her mentors at SCLC, particularly Dr. King and James Bevel, to turn Mollison from what she called a "factory of failure" into a "school of success." Tillman, along with a core group of strong, concerned parents, did their homework over the summer. By the time Mollison reopened for the 1980–81 school year, they were ready. It was time to pass on the knowledge they had gained and to train other parents and prepare to take action. Following a series of meetings and one-on-one interactions with parents, several things were clear: their principal posed a problem; their children's safety was at risk; and their children were falling behind in math and reading.

That December Dorothy Tillman was elected president of the local school council as parents representing two hundred students rallied against the school's apparent failure to educate and to provide safe conditions for students. They prepared to take action in January. Everyone had a role and responsibility. Plans were finalized for freedom schools for the impending boycott. Some parents were responsible for the picket lines, others for communicating with parents and or the media, others for meals, whatever would be needed for a successful boycott.

Dorothy Stevens had been the principal at Mollison since the school opened in Bronzeville in 1962.[21] The school's student population was entirely Black. Stevens was white and near retirement age. Parents were not pleased with her leadership. Stevens, parents charged, was insensitive to their children. She, Tillman said, was dictatorial, condescending, and ineffectual. And then there were her methods of disciplining the children.

Several years later, after entering the political arena and becoming an alderman, Tillman would become known for the many, sometimes exquisite, hats she wore. But in 1981 she prepared for this battle with her hair swathed in a black scarf and a straight back as she stood tall,

---

21 You will not see this name as one of Chicago's seventy-seven community areas. This neighborhood in the heart of Chicago's historic Black Belt is identified as Douglas, after Stephen Douglas, a known segregationist who ran against Lincoln for president in 1860. In the 1930s, the *Chicago Defender* popularized "Bronzeville" as an alternative.

holding her slight figure erect. Alone she was a portrait of strength and determination. Surrounded by a core group of parents carrying the same sense of purpose, it was hard to believe they would fail.

Their initial demands were simple: change the professional leadership at the school, provide an immediate investigation into the low scores, and implement a closed campus for lunch.

At a meeting called in December to discuss school safety and whether to make the school a closed campus, Tillman said that earlier in the school year, "some gangs came over to Mollison and trampled over our kids. . . . The kids ran, and Mrs. Stevens would not open the door. The children were pulling at the door, but it was not opened because it was not yet one o'clock."

Tillman and the local school council felt that sending children home for lunch was disruptive to their education. It interfered with the day; some students didn't make it back for afternoon classes; not all parents were able to be home to provide lunch to their children in the middle of the day; not all parents could afford to have food at home for lunch. All the children at Mollison were eligible for a free lunch, ensuring them a midday meal. The break for lunch would be shortened and be less disruptive to the learning process.

During the meeting, a math teacher reportedly said, "Maybe only one student in the whole school is operating on a sixth-grade level and he's in the eighth grade. Everybody in this school is at least three levels behind in math." This bombshell was the last straw and confirmed Tillman's and other engaged parents' suspicions that the curriculum based on the Continuous Progress / Mastery Learning program was fundamentally flawed.

A form of Mastery Learning (Continuous Progress / Mastery Learning) was originally introduced to the school system in 1975 to a few schools. With Chicago public school students as the guinea pigs, the curriculum was developed by consultants handpicked and protected by Caruso who in 1979 made it the basis for student promotions from one grade to the next. (And in the process providing the two consultants a hefty payday.) They were confident that this was at the heart of their school's decline.

Chicago Mastery Learning required a lot of testing, and testing requires grading. At Mollison it was common for there to be students working in as many as four or five different levels at the same time in a classroom.[22] There was less and less time available to teach plus give the required tests and grade them. Quietly, many teachers whispered their complaints. In any case, most students were not getting tested and therefore not moving forward. But more on this later.

By now *All Chicago City News* was in full swing, and along with Jeri Miglietta, my beat·was education. We covered the events at Mollison closely. Mollison's parents tried to meet with Acting Superintendent Caruso. Caruso was dismissive. Not to be deterred, they went to plan B. Led by Tillman, parents organized a boycott of the school, presented their case to the board of education, and took multiple arrests. Nearly 80 percent of the school's students honored the boycott. The striking parents organized three alternative learning sites and operated a twenty-four-hour hotline for Mollison families. With support from the broader Black community, Alpha Phi Alpha (the first African American inter-collegiate Greek-letter fraternity), supportive educators and volunteer teachers prepared curriculum and taught classes in math, reading, and art. Children received breakfast and lunch as the striking parents continued to press their case at the board of education.

As momentum grew, on February 2, the board of education granted Stevens a leave of absence from Mollison. Caruso, however, refused to reassign her, telling reporters Mollison is "a good school. It's been a tight ship." Meanwhile, Frank Gardner, deputy superintendent of the area in which the school was located, said testing and instruction programs at Mollison were being reorganized as a result of the parents' protests.

Parents, concerned that Caruso's support of Stevens would prevail, continued their protests, making it clear they would not end until the board of education permanently removed Dorothy Stevens. They returned to Mollison, initiating a second week of protests, occupying the principal's office. And there they stayed for three days, until the police came and arrested eight of them for trespassing, leaving behind an "eviction notice" for Stevens.

It was in the course of covering their occupation that I learned about the school's vault. As it turned out, the principal's office had a walk-in vault that was about thirty square feet in size. Presumably, the intended purpose of the vault was to lock up sensitive files, money, financial files,

22 This was also the case in most of the city's public elementary schools.

and in general matters that needed the protection of a lock and key. But there were rumors that children who were sent to the principal's office were often made to sit in this vault, with the threat that doors could be closed and locked if they did not behave. Defensively, staff confirmed that this space had been used as a time-out area, claiming no child had ever been locked in. Confirmation of these rumors was the last straw.

In mid-February, veteran principal Edith Dervin was transferred to Mollison, replacing Stevens. Dervin instituted a closed campus and revamping the school's education policies. For the first time, Mollison had an African American principal who believed all her students had the potential to learn, was aware of their struggles, and had the experience, determination, and connections to revamp the school environment and make it culturally friendly and educationally inviting.

Stevens was assigned to another school, retiring in 1985. Following her retirement and with the support of the principals association, Stevens filed a libel suit against Tillman claiming she was defamed and removed because of her race. Tom Johnson, Tillman's pro bono attorney (as well as mine), argued it had been Steven's performance and not her race that had led to the campaign against her. Only one of the nine potentially defamatory statements on the part of Tillman that went to the jury were determined to be knowingly false. Even so, when asked for the monetary damages she had to pay Stevens, the jury decided it would be the minimum required: one dollar.

....

39.

THE PARENT EQUALIZERS CHALLENGE CHICAGO MASTERY LEARNING

Jeri Miglietta moved to Uptown with the group Marc Zalkin had brought back with him from California to work on my first aldermanic election. She came with her son Anton. For a year, Anton, a year and a half younger than Brendan, joined him at child development. In many ways they grew up as brothers, often together and from time to time living in the same apartment. It was therefore natural that Jeri and I would team up as parent activists. As 1981 unfolded and the events at Mollison school played out, we were facing our own issues at Stockton Elementary School, where Brendan and Anton attended. As we had learned over the preceding years, it was impossible to separate our children's education from the dynamics of the community surrounding their school.

Uptown continued to be impacted by unstable housing conditions. Lead poisoning was a chief concern, affecting children at an alarming rate, and impacting their ability to learn. Often the cause went undetected. This was before any tenant protections existed in Chicago, and the result was devastating to most children living in these conditions.

The impact of all this was evident in the schools. In the early 1980s, neighborhood schools adhered strictly to their corresponding attendance areas—unless, of course, you knew the precinct captain. It was not uncommon for a child's family to move a block or two away only to have to enroll in a different school. The children in my son's class one week were not necessarily there the next. Sometimes a child would transfer two or three times in a year because their family had to move.[23] They might even make it back to their first school by the end of the school year.

This was frustrating for teachers as well, but often they had little if any knowledge of why a child came and went. It was typical that these children would develop learning issues and poor results on their standardized tests. Many of the teachers were from the suburbs, often white, and rarely shared a common life experience with the students they taught. Not aware of the backstory of their students' lives, often parents and their children were blamed for poor achievement. It had so far proven nearly impossible to turn the narrative away from the blame game and toward an approach that respected the children and parents.

But the Mollison parents had given us inspiration. They had challenged assumptions at their school that negatively impacted their children's progress, and they had forced a change. Their demands to turn around the failures of education at Mollison had also put a spotlight on

---

23 Most commonly, these moves were due to fires or conditions that caused the buildings to be uninhabitable. Sometimes it was due to nonpayment of rent. Most often it was a consequence of poverty.

Represented by attorneys Anna Langford and Jim Chapman, Mollison parents filed a lawsuit with a laser focus on removing Chicago Mastery Learning, receiving support from parents in schools throughout Chicago. This would be the seeds for the nascent Parent Equalizers of Chicago.

the Chicago Mastery Learning program. Charging that this program was defective in teaching math and reading—and using their school's testing and failed academic achievement as an example—parents at Mollison had gone a step further, arguing the system should be replaced.

Without the removal of Chicago's version of Mastery Learning, Tillman argued, even the best principal and teachers couldn't "stop the miseducation." Represented by attorneys Anna Langford[24] and Jim Chapman, they filed a lawsuit with a laser focus on removing Chicago Mastery Learning, receiving support from parents in schools throughout Chicago. This would be the seeds for the nascent Parent Equalizers of Chicago.

When Ruth Love replaced Angela Caruso as general superintendent in March 1981, she enthusiastically adopted Continuous Progress/Mastery Learning as her own, at some point renaming it Chicago Mastery

---

24 Anna Langford was a civil rights attorney and the first African American woman elected to the Chicago City Council in 1971. After she was defeated for reelection four years later, she returned to private practice until 1983, when she successfully ran again for alderman, serving until 1991.

Learning. In the process, she explained away common complaints from teachers and parents while tweaking the program to assuage its critics. While there was controversy in the academic community about the pros and cons of this particular pedagogy, as parents, we saw it as a form of "planned failure."

Some teachers liked the structure this program gave them. It literally provided a page-by-page guide to the teacher, removing any requirement that they develop lesson plans. However, those teachers who wanted a more individual approach to their students did not have the opportunity. And those who wanted a focus on reading were dismayed that a by-product of the program was the discouragement of reading books.

The workbooks provided to students were cheap in construction and had many spelling and grammatical errors. The print was sometimes light and broken, making it difficult to read. Many teachers contacted us with their own complaints—mostly that they were bogged down by all the paperwork and struggling with "ridiculous" exercises that their students found difficult to understand. All this, they told us, prevented them from teaching reading, let alone science and math.

Two sets of notebooks were available. One set was for students, and another set was a guide for the teachers. Students were allowed to write in their books in their classroom, but, strangely, were not allowed to take them home. But most disturbing was the cultural and racial insensitivity embedded in their content.

Children in kindergarten classes received one book. Those in first grade through eighth grade received two workbooks. One was titled "Comprehension," and the other "Word Attack Skills." The first program unit in the fourth-grade comprehension workbook was "Message and Content." This lesson, which introduced the fourth-grade student to the Chicago Mastery Learning Reading Program, was blatantly racist.

I looked at this photo and saw a man with an afro, labeled as papa, scowling as he looked toward Orville, a young man also with an afro, who is sitting, eyes closed, in a lounge chair holding a cup with a straw. "Papa" is pushing a lawn mower. None of the three possible answers reflected what my answer would have been to the question "What can we say about Orville now?"

Look at the picture of Orville and Papa Orville ...

...then answer the question below.

Q: What can we say about Orville now?

A:
○ Orville likes to fox-hunt.

○ Orville is a fine, upstanding citizen.

⊗ Orville doesn't help his Dad with the chores.

If you chose the last answer, then right you are! Orville may like to hunt foxes, and he may be an otherwise upstanding citizen, but all that the picture tells us is that he is lazy. Look! He lies around while his poor Dad does all the work!!

The content of the picture is made up of Orville, a lemonade, a lawn chair, some lawn, Orville's Dad, a lawn mower, and a sign.

The message is "Orville doesn't help his Dad with the chores."

Or maybe the message is "Kids don't like to help their parents with the chores."

Got it? Let's see.

Forget the fact that many students in Chicago public schools in the early '80s were being raised by single mothers, or that the fathers they did have most likely didn't have a lawn, lawn mower, or the time or opportunity to cut grass—let alone to hunt foxes. I didn't, and doubted that any of the students taking this quiz did. Many students in Uptown were immigrants from other countries and were not yet US citizens, and most probably would have said they considered themselves upstanding. The idea of Orville being an upstanding citizen is dismissed by the flat statement that this picture only tells us he is lazy, presumably because he appears to be sleeping while his father is working. Is that what the father's scowl meant? Or could he be frowning because Orville is falling asleep with a glass in his hand that likely has liquid in it (as it contains a straw)? Is it really accurate to say "Look! He lies around while his poor Dad does all the work!!"?

A second lesson, also encountered by a fourth grader, was no better. Students were told: "Look at the cartoon below, then complete the sentences.

The student is asked: "What message does the cartoon give us about kids?"

    a. You have to practice to be a kid.

    b. Kids are reckless.

    c. The voting age should be lowered to eleven.

The workbook says the correct answer is "Kids are reckless." After a few more questions, the students have an answer sheet to look at and grade themselves with. On this answer sheet, Chicago Mastery Learning tells us that this is the right answer because "the cartoon makes one kid look reckless to tell us all kids are reckless." Nothing about the obligations of people in society to find common ground or common rules. Nothing about the responsibilities of adults. No critical thinking. Just a blanket lesson: "If you are a 'kid,' you are reckless."

The third lesson was "BIGGER is BETTER, and smaller is worse," and "People who own more are happier"—the "correct" answers to the questions based on the following cartoon:

Question 1 asks, "What is the message here about size?
    a. BIGGER is BETTER, and smaller is worse.
    b. How big something may be is not so important as how
       good it is.
    c. Cadillacs are difficult to park.

Question 2 asks, "What is the message here about people?
    a. All men are created equal.
    b. People who own more are happier.
    c. The things we own are not important.

Even without the scholarship of recent decades, it was obvious that this type of message to children—that if they were smaller or did not own more they were worse off—should not be taught in public schools.

The next page in unit one was the formative test. The instructions warned the student that "if you read the answers BEFORE you take the test, your nose will fall off!" Insulting as this seemed, the answers made even less sense.

Look at the cartoon below, then answer the questions.

1. What message does the cartoon give us about things that belong to us?

    ○ a. Once they're housebroken, sheep are excellent house pets.

    ○ b. It is jolly fun to share our property with others.

    ⊗ c. We must carefully guard our property from theft.

The correct answer is *c*, "We must carefully guard our property from theft."

The teacher's answer sheet explained that *b* is wrong because sharing may be fun for the wolf, but the sheep don't look at all "jolly." For *c* the answer sheet tells our ten-year-old: "Excellent! The picture tells us 'Watch out for thieves. They're everywhere and they're sneaky!' Score one."

From a critical thinking point of view, the concept of a wolf in sheep's clothing can provide a valuable lesson about being aware of your surroundings, and knowing the true reality of people around you. In the picture, the wolf looks like a predator, not necessarily a thief. Taken in its entirety, the lesson here ought to be, "Don't make assumptions."

Beau Jones and Michael Katims the two consultants responsible for Chicago Mastery Learning, argued that the material was developed for students who were behind level and developed to reflect the world realistically. "This is a terrible world," Katims explained during a presentation to the board of education in November 1981. We didn't agree. The terrible things we saw in the world were things we were determined to change, and when it came to the education of Chicago public school children, Chicago Mastery Learning was now our number one target.

In the year after the creation of the School Finance Authority, Jeri and I also worked with the Alliance for Better Schools Coalition (commonly referred to as ABC). ABC was the brainchild of community organizations working with parents in their respective communities (like Nancy Jefferson's Midwest Community Council) and a progressive wing of the Chicago Teachers Union (represented by Paula Baron) who were frustrated by the failure of school policy makers to focus on the classroom. We learned a lot and developed contacts in many schools, but we felt the need to work more closely with parents.

On all things board of education, Jeri and I were partners. We had been going to board meetings since the beginning of the school finance crisis and had developed a network of parents—many of whom were supportive of the Mollison parents and encouraged by them to organize for closed campuses or other changes. Marion Stamps, Nancy Jefferson, Art Vazquez, Rudy Lozano, and virtually everyone we knew engaged in community organizing in Chicago were also engaged in their local schools. All of us agreed that we wanted our children to have an education that taught them their true history and role in society—an education that would give them knowledge of self.[25] Angered by the horribleness in Chicago's version of Mastery Learning, Jeri and I joined Dorothy Tillman and others to form the Parent Equalizers of Chicago.

The concept behind the PEOC was that children, represented by their parents, were the one group that had no formal representation at the table when school policies were developed. The finance community had the School Finance Authority. The mayor and politicians had the school superintendent. The teachers had the teachers' union. The principals had the principals' association. The parent-teacher associations were perceived to be the domain of more privileged parents, while

---

25 Point 5 of the BPP Platform and Program.

parent advisory councils were volunteer organizations that had no power and were not in every school.

The Parent Equalizers were going to balance the scales. Our logo was a scale, similar to the sort that typically represented Lady Justice. On one side of the scale were all the entities with an interest who were at the table. On the other side, balancing them, were the children represented by parents and the PEOC.

Our first order of business was to study Chicago Mastery Learning— its history and contents, how it was supposed to work, and how it was used in the schools. Our second order of business was to hold forums in every school we could get into, so these two activities were seamless. We began in each of our home schools.

We learned that the reason students were falling behind in most classrooms was that they weren't tested on the level on which they had been stuck for months and months. They were not learning new material, and they were essentially in a holding position. Teachers were stressed. Parents were not allowed to help their children at home, in part because of the board's policy that prevented the children's workbooks from leaving the school. Since all of Chicago Mastery Learning was done in workbooks, parents had no way of helping their children. There was essentially no homework for students in the elementary school grades. Magnet schools, however, were exempted from this policy.

We had no pretense of being trained in the pedagogies popular at the time—including Mastery Learning. But we were our children's first educators and had a stake in their development and future. We wanted them to become critical thinkers and expected the schools to help give them the tools to get there.

Within a year, there were Parent Equalizers in nearly three hundred schools. We reviewed the workbooks and elicited the parents' take on their content. Most of the tests we reviewed had ten questions. If a student got eight of them correct, the student would move on to the next skill. It didn't matter if the question they got wrong represented a crucial piece of knowledge without which they really could not be determined to have learned the skill.

We developed a skit that we used in our workshops that addressed this. Using the example of making a pot of coffee, we filled a pot with water. We took the filter and put it in the coffee machine. We then

Within a year, there were Parent Equalizers in nearly three hundred Chicago schools.

plugged in the machine and brewed the coffee. After three minutes, we took the pot and poured our coffee. We broke down the ten steps (representing skills) that would have to be accomplished. We passed because we had ninety points, or 90 percent, correct, but we had hot water—not coffee. The 10 percent we failed was putting the coffee into the filter. The objective was to make hot coffee. The result was hot water. But we passed with 90 percent and were therefore able to move to the next skill. Our concern was not whether the standard was high or low enough; it was whether our children were learning the skills necessary to function and flourish in the real world.

Jeri and I were involved at Stockton Elementary and were on the committee to select a new principal. We were also active in the (powerless) parent advisory council. We heard from other parents about issues they had with the school, problems their kids were having, and their difficulty in understanding what was going on. Many of the parents had not finished high school. Jeri was a GED teacher, so hosting a class for parents was a no brainer. We would adopt a discussion of the school budget to focus on the math they would need to pass. For reading and science, we would use both positive and negative examples from the Chicago Mastery Learning program. The idea gained traction, and Jeri was soon teaching a class down the street from Stockton at the Beacon Street Hull House.

The more we engaged in the Parent Equalizers, the more we learned about problems affecting the learning environments of children. We heard from multiple sources about one fifth-grade classroom where children were often ordered to sit in the "cloakroom," which actually meant sitting on the floor under coats hanging from hooks along the back wall of the classroom. I asked the principal to allow me to tutor five of the children in that class. "I'll work with them in the school, out of the classroom if you'll give me another one to work in. The teacher can pick them. She can send me the kids she puts in the cloakroom." After the fifth-grade teacher jumped at the offer, the principal agreed. I had each child read for me. None of these ten- and eleven-year-olds were reading much above a second-grade level. I looked through their Chicago Mastery workbooks and found nothing that even referred to sounding out letters. There was no phonetics to be found.[26] I was horrified and angry. These kids were just being thrown away.

During the following summer, the teacher who gave me her students to teach died of cancer. I do not know if anyone in the school knew how sick she was. I came to learn that she had continued teaching to retain her medical insurance. I suspect she also may have craved the companionship of the school community and the sense of purpose she may have gotten from remaining there. By all accounts, the issues we were addressing with her were recent, and she had been one of the teachers praised by parents and students alike. For me it was a clear example of the kind of support teachers need to maintain the ability to teach our children with the patience, love, and respect they deserve. They too need patience and respect—and this is often lacking in the context of the school community and the bureaucracy within which they have to function.

Meanwhile, the Parent Equalizers were having an impact. Teachers in a growing number of schools, having now learned about Chicago Mastery Learning, were demanding its removal. We had numerous

---

26 I understand that teaching phonetics was out of favor during the 1980s, and that many educational institutions turned to other systems to teach reading. Most of us had learned to read with phonetics and didn't understand why it wasn't still a tool available to teachers in Chicago's schools.

Parent Equalizers at Stockton Elementary School prepare for the arrival of Schools' Superintendent Ruth Love by informing other parents and students about Chicago Mastery Learning.

objections to the program, but number one was the ability of our children to learn to "read and write in order to be able to function in the year 2000." Charging that the content was racist, violent, disrespectful to the child's relationship to family and community, superficial, and, in many cases, unpleasant to look at (as well as to read), we were confident our number one priority would not be realized through the program.

Students had been back to school for a couple of months in 1982 when we learned that Superintendent Love was planning a visit to Stockton School. This was an opportunity we couldn't miss. A group of us at Stockton worked for weeks mobilizing parents. We prepared large posters demonstrating visually what we considered to be some of the most egregious errors and consequences of Chicago Mastery Learning. Our goal was to line up outside the school as Love entered and engage her in a discussion of our educational picket.

The day before her planned visit, the principal called me to his office. He presented me with a letter notifying me that my son had been selected for a special testing for students interested in attending Whitney Young Academic Academy—one of Chicago's newer magnet high schools. The school had an academic center for seventh and eighth graders. To ensure racial equity, students were selected to attend on the basis of a quota system. But first they had to pass an entrance exam. Brendan was always good at taking tests, so I had no doubt he would do well. But why was he even being considered? He was, after all, in fifth grade. To go to Whitney Young, he would have to skip a grade. We had not talked about this, or the idea of attending school outside the neighborhood. What was up?

Principal Carl Lieberman made it clear he was doing this as a favor to me. Having brought it up immediately after trying to dissuade me from proceeding with the educational picket of Ruth Love, he expected a quid pro quo—"I do this for you and your son; you call off the picket." I told him that I would have to talk to Brendan; that if he in fact decided to go to Whitney Young, he would do so because he was eligible to do so. Thanks but no thanks. No special attention wanted.

Of course, that was my perspective. As it turned out, this had been Brendan's idea all along. He was in fifth grade, and his class would be going to Arai Middle School for the next school year; he had wanted to avoid going there. A school outside the community would likely mean less of my presence. I don't know when he came up with the idea of Whitney Young, but it had apparently been after the regularly scheduled tests were given earlier in the school year. Having missed the deadline, he would need someone with clout in the system to get an exception made for him to get tested. He cleverly figured that the principal would look favorably on helping him out, in part because he assumed that doing so might give him some leverage over me. Brendan made it to the test, did well, and convinced me that skipping a grade was no biggie.[27] We still proceeded with the picket.

It would take the election of Harold Washington to the mayorship, the appointment of a new school board, and a lot of educating both about the Chicago Mastery Learning program before it was finally removed in 1985.[28]

· ·

40.

ANGER AT SCHOOL BOARD APPOINTMENTS OPENS THE FLOODGATES

The terms of the new board of education members appointed in April 1980 were staggered, with three of them being just one year in length. Leon Davis and Michael Scott had every reason to believe that their short time on the board would be extended for at least one full term when their appointments were to expire on April 30, 1981. Jane Byrne, however, had other plans. Just weeks before Ruth Love was scheduled to begin as the new superintendent, Byrne announced she was replacing Davis and Scott with two white women—one of whom had been a longtime opponent to desegregation. The third board member whose term was to expire in April was Mexican American businessman and

---

27 I'm not sure he figured all the consequences of this decision. At the time he was not quite five feet tall, a thin twelve-year-old going to a high school with bigger, older students. Years later, when his own daughter had a choice of skipping her first year of high school, he insisted that she stay put with her age group and do a full four years.

28 It would still be used where teachers desired it as an additional tool, but Chicago Mastery Learning would no longer be the primary teaching curriculum of the schools or a vehicle for student advancement.

Byrne ally Raul Villalobos. He was not removed. Byrne reappointed him before orchestrating his selection to be the next board president.

Rose Mary Janus, a Northwest Side resident, had been a campaign worker for Byrne and attributed that to her selection to the board. She worked as a school aide at the school where she was also the president of the school's education council. Her two teenage children were attending different public high schools.

Betty Bonow, a Southwest Side resident, had been fighting desegregation efforts for twenty some years, arguing that the issue was about maintaining local schools. "If the white people are not reassured that children will be able to attend the school closest to their home, they will pull their kids out," she said. But when her opposition extended to changing attendance areas to maintain the local schools while creating racial diversity, it was apparent that this was really about race.

The nuances of desegregation were important. Not every Black parent wanted their child bused. Like most parents, first on their agenda was their children's education. They wanted their children to have the same access to teaching and resources as students elsewhere in the system. Many preferred those resources be brought to their neighborhood schools. Some were willing to have their children go elsewhere to accomplish their education, but they wanted them safe, respected, and successful.

When the appointments for the new board required by the state legislature were announced the previous year, for the first time the racial parity on the board was reflective of the student body—60 percent Black, 20 percent Latino, and 20 percent white. Byrne's new appointments destroyed that representation. This did not bode well for desegregation efforts and incensed the Black community.

School board appointments had to be approved by the city council. As with all appointments, the appropriate council committee (in this case the Education Committee) held a hearing and vote to send the appointments to the full council for consideration.[29]

---

29 School board appointments were rarely rejected in committee. Committee members were decided every four years at the first city council meeting following municipal elections. Although this was a legislative responsibility, the committees and their makeup were usually determined in consultation with the mayor and with the mayor's support. The only time

In 1980 Allan Streeter was a Democratic precinct captain and city employee in charge of the lead poisoning prevention program in Chicago's Department of Health. In January 1981 he was appointed by Byrne to fill the vacancy of alderman of the Seventeenth Ward, following the resignation of Tyrone McFolling. The Seventeenth Ward[30] Democratic committeeman William Parker, a staunch Byrne ally, recommended him for the job. Streeter was, as one journalist put it, "loyal, hardworking and well liked. He made no waves, rocked no boats."[31] He was assigned to the city council's Education Committee, and when Byrne's appointments came before the committee a few months later, he voted for them. Marion Stamps and Dorothy Tillman were in the council chambers that day. I joined them, along with enough other parents and school advocates to fill the council chambers. Our protests were loud as Streeter voted in support of the appointments of Janus and Bonow. Shouts of "Traitor!" resonated.

In the days that followed, Streeter heard from thousands of constituents demanding he change his vote. And he did. When the vote came before the full city council he voted no, earning the wrath of Byrne and Parker. When a federal judge declared his appointment invalid and ruled that a special election had to be held for the position of Seventeenth Ward alderman, Byrne saw her chance to be rid of this "turncoat." Streeter welcomed the opportunity to take her on, saying at the time, "When a mayor names an alderman it demeans the office because she thinks she can tell him what to do."[32]

Leading up to the election, Byrne threw everything she had at Streeter. On Election Day, all forces loyal to her were in the Seventeenth

---

in modern history that this was not the case was during Harold Washington's first term, when Vrdolyak and Burke organized a coalition of twenty-nine aldermen to oppose Harold at every turn.

30 The Seventeenth Ward would later become famous as the home base for Father Michael Pfleger and St. Sabina Church. It was also the home ward for Terry Peterson, a later alderman who became an ally of the second Mayor Daley and played important roles in various Chicago agencies. The Seventeenth Ward is one of several South Side, Black, middle-class wards (Wards Six, Eight, Nine, Twenty-One, and Thirty-Four) with inconsistent relationships with the machine and with independent Black politics.

31 Vernon Jarrett, editorial, *Chicago Tribune*, May 1, 1981.

32 *Chicago Tribune*, February 10, 1982, 3.

Ward. But so were the forces who had become fed up and were determined to support the courage shown by Streeter in voting his heart and community interests first.

I was a poll watcher during the runoff election that determined the alderman of the Seventeenth Ward. As we were closing the precinct, Bob Shaw, alderman and committeeman of the Ninth Ward, and another staunch Byrne ally entered the polling place.[33] At that moment, one of the election judges had collected all the ballots and was attempting to take them into a back room of the polling place. A *Keystone Cops* scenario ensued as the poll watchers—myself included—chased her around the room. Standing six foot nine, Bob Shaw towered over all of us, as he yelled that we should all sit down, and that she knew what she was doing and had a right to do it. We were screaming, "No she doesn't! Someone call the Board of Elections! Get someone down here!" We finally succeeded in getting her to sit down and turn the ballots over to the other judges to be counted. When the votes were counted, Streeter had overwhelmingly won that precinct and the ward.

· ·

41.

PUBLIC HOUSING IN CRISIS

Anger and frustration with the schools was matched only by that with the Chicago Housing Authority (CHA), and Marion Stamps was in the middle of it.

I don't remember the first time I met Marion, but it was during the 1970s, by which time she was a seasoned community activist on the city's near North Side. Slim Coleman had known Marion since coming to Chicago. During one of the early meetings between Slim and Marion that I joined, while expounding on the failure of the welfare system to

---

33 Shaw's support for Byrne, which he continued through the 1983 primary election for mayor, cost him his aldermanic seat. After apologizing to his community, he successfully campaigned to regain his seat in 1987.

provide a true opportunity for recipients, Marion suggested that a much more effective system would be to ensure that everyone living in America receive a minimum living wage (at the time, she suggested this be $10,000 a year). They would then, she said, not have to struggle to figure out where their next meal or rent money would come from and would consequently have the time and space to truly contribute to their own, their families', and their community's development.

Since coming to Chicago from Jackson, Mississippi in 1962, Marion had lived in Cabrini or subsidized housing in the immediately surrounding area. As founder and director of the Chicago Housing Tenant Organization (CHTO) and the Tranquility Community Organization,[34] Marion was an advocate for Chicago Housing Authority tenants. The organization's day-to-day activities mirrored the Ten-Point Program of the Black Panther Party, with a focus on housing, education, and police (Marion referred to police as "an occupying army"), and always with her focus on the "babies"—their education, their future, and their survival.

Marion had met Fred Hampton and joined the Black Panther Party in 1968. She attributed her activism to knowing and learning from Fred. Marion ran the breakfast program on the North Side, getting up every morning at six o'clock. As she later put it: "Fred Hampton didn't want you to give kids powdered eggs so you had to make sure that you had real eggs, real grits, real everything. But that experience and dealing with those young children at that time of the morning made us all feel better, and the children feel better. We knew that those children went to school first of all, full, and secondly, they had already gained some knowledge before they went into that classroom, so it wasn't going to be as easy to miseducate [them] as it would if they had not come to the program."[35]

Laser-focused on the Black community, Marion brooked no tolerance for anything but respect and self-determination for that community, and especially for Black women. In her view, getting control over the institutions that managed the community's public housing and public education was a necessity. Ending the police occupation of the community

---

34 It was renamed Tranquility Marksman Community Organization after the murder of Ed Marksman in 1981.

35 Marion Stamps, interviewed in *Eyes on the Prize II: America at the Racial Crossroads, 1965–1985* (Boston: Blackside, 1987). Subsequent quotations from Stamps in this chapter are from the same series.

was a clear priority. There were many who called her style "in-your-face activism," a description I'm pretty sure she would have embraced.

As Marion later told the interviewer for the documentary series *Eyes on the Prize II*:

> If you have any idea in terms of how it is to live in a public housing development, in a slave control city like Chicago, then you know your work is cut out for you. Public housing in Chicago has been used as the one political arena that every politician depends on because it's a concentrated area of Black votes. If you take all of the public housing in Chicago and put them together, then we would become the second largest city in the state next to Springfield. . . . My involvement was to rid the community of the slave masters because we were in fact controlled by the Daley machine. . . . We began by educating the residents and the tenants about what their rights were as tenants.

The education of tenants led to collective actions that focused on the federal laws and policies that actually governed public housing. With Marion in leadership, CHTO gained a national reach, ultimately affecting changes in the rules for tenant participation in decision making and establishing the right for tenants to weigh in on the Chicago Housing Authority's vendors and the jobs they created. These were all steps along the way, in Marion's words, to "having the right to set the tone and the standards by which we were going to live in public housing."

This did not necessarily sit well with local politicians.

Appointed by Richard J. Daley, Charles Swibel had been the chairman of the Chicago Housing Authority since 1963, overseeing the deferred maintenance of virtually all CHA properties. Marion was an outspoken critic of Swibel, charging he used the CHA as his personal portfolio to enrich himself rather than provide decent housing to public housing residents. As she put it, "Swibel ran CHA like it was his own private personal plantation, real simple." There was plenty of evidence to back up her claims.[36]

---

36 See *New York Times*, July 9, 1982. According to the *Times*, Swibel had never been convicted of any wrongdoing, though he "was frequently accused of engaging in unsavory deals in the letting of contracts for maintenance and repair of housing agency properties and for banking agency

Taking a page from his sponsor Mayor Daley's playbook, Swibel was known for adjourning commission meetings during the public-comment portion of the meeting when tenants raised anything he didn't want to hear. Nothing had changed after Daley's death and replacement by Michael Bilandic. While campaigning for mayor in 1979, Jane Byrne had promised to remove Swibel if elected. In a blink of an eye, after her election, he became a confidant with her full backing until the day he resigned.

A federally commissioned audit released in March 1982 concluded that the CHA was "a vehicle for patronage" that had been mismanaged for years. According to the *New York Times*, the audit further said, "In every area examined, from finance to maintenance, from administration to outside contracting, from staffing to project management, the C.H.A. was found to be operating in a state of profound confusion and disarray."

In 1982, CHA managed 45,870 apartment units, second only to New York City's public housing authority that owned or leased 170,000 units. Sixty-seven percent of families living in CHA housing received welfare, while in New York, this number hovered at 25 percent.

Some years earlier HUD had announced a rental policy that required rents be set at market rates based on the area median income. In urban areas, this would mean that rent in the public housing units would be higher (sometimes significantly so) than rents in apartments in the area where the public housing units were located. Objecting to this, New York City requested and was granted a waiver. Chicago did not—a failure that would impact the stability of the developments for years to come. At the time, an individual household paid 30 percent of their income for rent. If someone in the family was able to secure a decent-paying, stable job, it was likely that their rent would end up being more than the rents available elsewhere in Chicago. It was a no-brainer that anyone who was gainfully employed would be leaving CHA as soon as they could find another cheaper and better-maintained apartment.

A year before Swibel resigned in 1982, Byrne moved into an apartment at Cabrini, infuriating Marion and many CHA residents. "You're going to bring yourself up into the public housing community and tell us that only you can save our children?" Charging that this was the

---

funds in institutions that he also dealt with in his private real estate ventures."

Calling Jane Byrne's move into Cabrini-Green insulting and a publicity stunt, Marion Stamps makes sure her voice is heard. Marion is standing with other members of CHTO, with Lu Palmer joining them.

Mayor Byrne: "Why are you negotiating in bad faith?"

ultimate disrespect, Marion later explained, "I could not accept that because I understood that if we had allowed these children to believe that their salvation was going to come from the great White hope, then what did that say about me as a mother, as a grandmother, and as a Black woman?"

In Uptown we were having our own problems with Byrne. Immediately after her election, she made a commitment to us that she would settle the Avery lawsuit (the lawsuit we had filed in 1975 charging the city was engaged in a conspiracy with CHA, HUD, and a private developer to destroy an integrated community). Two years had passed when, during federal mediating sessions ordered by the judge hearing the case, an agreement was reached jointly by the Heart of Uptown Coalition, the city's Department of Housing, and the federal HUD. It awaited the signature of the mayor, who had given us every reason to expect her support. It didn't come.

An ABC Network editorial report read by TV executive Peter Desnoes, airing several times during the week of April 13, 1981, captured our hopes and disappointment with Byrne:

> You might recall that last September we were here in Uptown. We told you about how it's been called many things: a human dumping ground, a haven for arsonists, and a promised land of sorts for condominium developers. We told you that there was a feeling by a number of Uptown residents that low- and moderate-income people might be forced out because of the lack of adequate affordable housing.
>
> We told you about the efforts of the Heart of Uptown Coalition, which would involve the direct participation of residents in the growth and development of their community ... and slow down the displacement of lower-income families. The solution grew out of a lawsuit the coalition filed and the consent decree which followed. The settlement would establish a land bank cooperative. Residents of Uptown would purchase shares in the co-op for six dollars. The cooperative would then develop two thousand new or rehabilitated housing units for shareholders. Additionally, specific federal, CHA, and community development funds would be set aside for Uptown. This would further ensure that new or rehabbed housing in the community would

have an equitable racial and economic mix. The plan was unique and showed quite a bit of promise.

Now, however, it may never get off the ground. Mayor Byrne apparently has decided not to sign the consent decree. Coalition members, who demonstrated outside the mayor's Cabrini-Green apartment Monday said that this is a complete reversal of her original posture. The mayor had the chance to demonstrate her commitment to an innovative plan which had the potential to be a model for the city. Unfortunately, it appears now that Uptown, a community that hasn't had many chances, has lost again.

As the editorial noted, the Heart of Uptown Coalition had gone to Cabrini to express our displeasure with Byrne. But we had also been there in support of Cabrini tenants. While Byrne was seemingly enjoying her Cabrini digs, we joined disaffected residents outside the apartment in which she had temporarily taken up residence. Seeing this as a publicity stunt, they chanted "Byrne go home" while demanding she provide them with the support they needed to improve their own living conditions.

· ·

42.

POWER
PEOPLE ORGANIZED FOR WELFARE AND EMPLOYMENT RIGHTS

By the beginning of 1982, opposition to Byrne's reelection was gathering momentum in the Black community, with sentiment in Chicago's other poor and working communities not far behind. Lu and Jorja Palmer formed Chicago Black United Communities (CBUC). Initially engaged in fighting to get asbestos out of schools, they turned their attention to the running of a Black candidate for mayor in 1983. To confront the prevalent cynicism they were encountering in the community ("You can't have a Black mayor in Chicago; you can't beat city hall"),

CBUC coined the slogan "We shall see in '83." Their plan for a Black plebiscite to choose a candidate to run against Byrne was in motion. Meanwhile, political support for Allan Streeter's special election was being mobilized.

When we held our first *All Chicago City News* banquet in a downtown hotel that April, Congressman Harold Washington was our keynote speaker. Jim Chapman introduced Harold, challenging him to make the run for mayor as he did so. Harold began his remarks with a tease. "My mother always told me to come when called," he retorted to Jim. The crowd went wild, but that was all we got; it would still be a while before Harold would "come when called" and announce his run for mayor.

Harold didn't miss the fact that he was speaking to a multiracial crowd of some one thousand people in the ballroom of a downtown hotel. There were activists from every corner of the city. Harold knew many of them from his work in the state legislature and in Congress, and he had worked with the Chicago Area Black Lung Association as he championed their cause for a Black Lung Trust Fund, which he had helped make a reality as a first-term congressman. He had just completed a successful campaign leading the effort to extend the Voting Rights Act of 1965 and protect the gains of the civil rights movement.[37] He had simultaneously been a leader in efforts by the Congressional Black Caucus to present an alternative vision for government, which they had aimed to accomplish by presenting a federal budget that provided an alternative to Reagan's draconian cuts to urban areas. He spoke to every one of us—from the vantage point of a congressman.

---

37 We unfortunately lost many of the protections for voting rights he had helped codify when the Supreme Court struck down key provisions in the Voting Rights Act. While the majority claimed that Barack Obama's election as president proved these restrictions were no longer necessary, Justice Ruth Bader Ginsburg, in her dissent, said the focus of the Voting Rights Act had properly changed from "first-generation barriers to ballot access" to "second-generation barriers" like racial gerrymandering and laws requiring at-large voting in places with a sizable Black minority. She said the law was effective in thwarting such efforts. The law had applied to nine states—Alabama, Alaska, Arizona, Georgia, Louisiana, Mississippi, South Carolina, Texas, and Virginia—and to scores of counties and municipalities in other states, including Brooklyn, Manhattan, and the Bronx.

POWER (People Organized for Welfare and Employment Rights) voter registration drive during summer of 1982. Registration occurred outside employment and welfare offices throughout the city.

Around this time, CBUC held its plebiscite vote on all potential candidates. Harold Washington was the first choice. While he would not yet commit, he declared that anyone running for mayor with a modicum of expectation for success would have to be assured an adequate source of funding and at least fifty thousand newly registered voters. People all over the city took on the challenge.

In the coming years, opportunities to register to vote would open up and become much more accessible, but in the spring of 1982 that wasn't the case. A prospective voter either had to go downtown to the Board of Elections and register, or they could register in a location in their ward during an eight-hour window available thirty days before any given election. This opportunity was rarely publicized, and unless you were a supporter of the machine, you were not likely to be informed or reminded.

Harold's call for fifty thousand new voters was repeated again and again, reverberating throughout the city. Ed Gardner, CEO and founder of SoftSheen Products, committed his money, time, and communications and graphics departments to promote October 5, the voter registration day scheduled to occur before the November national and state elections. "Come Alive October 5" was emblazoned throughout Chicago's Black community.

Our growing coalition was energized by this, but we were on the search for more times and places for people to register. Walter Tunis had been an organizer and advocate on welfare issues in Uptown for almost a decade, spending a lot of time at Welfare offices. Everyone knew Walter. So, in 1982 during a strategy session later that spring, Walter suggested that welfare and unemployment offices would be great places to register people to vote. Most people visiting these offices were there for a long time waiting to be seen. They were clearly not being served well by the powers that be. They were largely unregistered to vote.

This idea, embraced by our coalition partners and their partners throughout Chicago, became POWER—People Organized for Welfare and Employment Rights. The acronym became a clarion call, reflecting the common goal of welfare reform and worker's rights, that all who lived and worked in Chicago should have adequate income to sustain a basic quality of life, as well as the need to strive for *power* if that were to be achieved.

For this plan to work, the Board of Elections had to agree to send voter registrars to all the welfare and unemployment offices—no small feat.

Walter did welfare defense work out of the Uptown People's Law Center, where Tom Johnson was now the staff attorney after having served a stint at the Uptown office of the Legal Assistance Foundation. Engaging Project LEAP and other reform organizations committed to expanding voter participation in Chicago elections, Tom immersed himself in the legality and details of making this idea happen. By the summer, we had the cooperation of the Chicago Board of Elections.

POWER volunteers organized teams to go to each office. Each team had transportation to carry portable tables and chairs that would be set up on the sidewalks outside of the welfare or unemployment office. Deputy registrars joined them. The community organizations had assigned teams responsible for one or more registration sites. This large, single-minded volunteer effort—and the organizational logistics required to carry it out—contributed to the successful overall voter registration drive that resulted in over two hundred thousand new registered voters by October.

However, the impact of these efforts would ultimately extend much further, as we would see during the upcoming municipal elections.

43.

CHICAGO'S FIRST BLACK MAYOR

The November 1982 general election was approaching, and Harold was running for reelection, representing the first congressional district in the US House. A number of prominent figures in Chicago's political scene had thrown their hat in the ring as potential mayoral candidates, but nothing was sticking. Meanwhile, Harold kept his cards close to his chest, as rumors he was considering a run for mayor persisted.

By now, Keep Strong Publishing Company had become Justice Graphics. With an expanded printing capacity at our fingertips, we were prepared to print any materials necessary for a Harold Washington campaign for mayor. Richard M. Daley had already announced that he was running against Byrne. By now it was apparent that if Harold ran, he wouldn't announce until after the November general election. That would give us a limited time to get the required nominating petitions signed. We needed a head start that could also serve as a push, an incentive for him to run, so we printed up thousands of nominating petitions and gave them to anyone in the city—really everyone we could find—who was willing to circulate them at polling places on the November general election day. I suspect others did the same. The effort was a huge success. Two weeks later, Harold announced his run for mayor.[38]

My recollection is that Harold's hesitancy was in part because he loved his job as a US congressman. He needed assurances that this would be a serious campaign with serious financial and grassroots support behind it. With a finance committee committed to raising the necessary funds, 250,000 newly registered voters in the city, and enough signatures already collected to put him on the ballot, he agreed.

---

38 In Illinois, primary elections for state and federal offices are held in March, preceding November general elections. In Chicago, until 1999, the nonpartisan election for alderman and the primary election for mayor, city treasurer, and city clerk were held on the last Tuesday in February. The general election for these three offices was held six weeks later. Any race where an aldermanic candidate did not receive at least 50 percent of the vote had a runoff at this time as well.

He had secured his reelection to Congress, so whatever happened, he would have a job he loved.

Harold announced that he was running in the Democratic primary for mayor on Wednesday, November 10, 1982. The energy was electrifying. The next day, Slim and I joined some one hundred volunteers at a brainstorming session with SoftSheen's graphics division. On the way back to Uptown, I told Slim I had an idea for a logo but wasn't sure how it would play. He told me to go with it.

We had a hand-operated machine to make buttons. By Friday, we were knee deep in buttons bearing the design, which would become the symbol of support for Harold. It had come from a simple idea that had been in my head since co-developing the logo for Cha Cha Jiménez's aldermanic campaign eight years earlier. In my mind's eye, the slogan "Dawning of a new day" above an image of Cha Cha had elicited a vision of a vibrant sunburst. In this campaign I realized that vision with a sunrise emanating from a simple statement: "Mayor Washington for Chicago." At Justice Graphics we were partial to blue, and the buttons reflected this—a throwback to our days producing literature in support of the Black Panther Party.

The design of the button was a collaborative effort with Maureen Grey and James Ratner. While I had a clear vision for the concept, I needed help with the layout. These were the days before computer-generated graphic design, so thin strips of tape would be used to create an image of the sun's rays. This took a more precise and practiced hand than mine. Maureen accomplished the task and, with James Ratner, chose the type style we ended up using. James then printed the buttons.

We distributed the first ten thousand buttons over the weekend. By Monday we were getting demands for more, along with demands for literature. These were the days when door-to-door canvasing was the heart of campaigning, and we knew that doing so without literature about one's candidate was a fool's errand. Few voters outside of the First Congressional District knew Harold Washington. So, along with the buttons, we designed and laid out a walking piece—also in blue and black.[39]

---

39 Coincidentally, or maybe not, later versions of the button would have royal blue and pure white colors, which happened to be the same colors of Harold's (and Huey Newton's and Bobby Seale's) Black fraternity.

On Monday, Harold was not pleased. It wasn't that he objected to the content or design of what we had done; on the contrary. The issue was that he didn't like the colors. While always up for a fight that was brought to him, at his core I knew Harold to be a cautious strategist. The brown and gold colors of his congressional campaign material suited him well. The royal blue now symbolizing his fledgling campaign, not so much—and he would not let me forget it.

After the 1979 marathon of elections, I had sworn I would never run for political office again. I was not fond of the manipulations, superficiality, and cynicism associated with politics. However, we had been involved in every aldermanic campaign in the Forty-Sixth Ward since 1975, and the pressure to run someone was building. Ralph Axelrod chose not to run again, and his ward secretary, former corporation counsel hack Jerry Orbach, was the machine candidate. Charlotte Newfeld, who lived in Lakeview (the southernmost part of the Forty-Sixth Ward) had also announced her run for alderman. She was active in the campaign to prevent nighttime baseball at Wrigley Field. That and her focus on gay rights were the hallmarks of her campaign for alderman. But Charlotte was not making an endorsement in the mayoral race, which was our focus. I refused to run: I wanted to do everything possible to elect Harold. Paul Siegel had worked tirelessly on behalf of coal miners and was well known in Uptown. On this basis, we agreed that Paul would be our aldermanic candidate. While coordinating the ward for Harold Washington, I coordinated Paul's schedule. He endorsed Harold, and we fought for them both.

While I was focused on election work in the Forty-Sixth Ward, cadre from the Intercommunal Survival Committee were on the Northwest Side and the South Side campaigning for Harold. Their primary focus was finding and organizing white voters to support him.

In February, when the primary votes were all counted, Harold Washington had won an upset victory, besting Byrne and Daley—either of whom political pundits had predicted would beat him. He was now the Democratic nominee for mayor of the city of Chicago, where for decades the Democratic nominee had been the presumed winner. This had been the case since 1931 when Anton Cermak, a Democrat, ousted William Hale Thompson, the last Republican to hold the mayor's seat. The mayorship, we expected, was already in hand. However, this election cycle would be different.

Harold's opponent, Bernie Epton, was a moderate Jewish Republican with a history of some support of civil rights. He had run for mayor on the Republican ticket with little hope of winning; he was to be their sacrificial lamb. But now, a seasoned African American legislator with an independent and progressive bent had won the Democratic primary. Here was Epton's moment, his shot at the prize. "When you have almost two-thirds of the Democratic voters losing their candidate," Epton said as he laid out his strategy to go directly after anti-Washington primary voters, "there is a fertile field for my election."[40]

Most politicians are career politicians. Each election is a step forward on that chosen career path. Sometimes advancement comes by winning. At other moments, it is advanced through the mere act of running, regardless of the outcome. In theory one would hope that path would be led by the candidate's ideals, which would be known and transparent to voters. Often it is. But even so, overriding everything most often is personal ambition and the self-interest that accompanies it—too often with a self-imposed disregard to the impact of one's actions. While Epton's strategy may have been politically sound—taking advantage of an unforeseen opportunity—it was racism that made it viable.

Epton played to the angry and racist overtones of the Democratic committeemen defecting to his candidacy. Speaking directly to the ethnic whites who had divided their vote between Daley and Byrne in the primary, Epton's tagline on all his commercials—in print and on air—was "Epton for mayor: before it's too late."

We were jolted—if not surprised. Lawyers, doctors, and educators joined a massive grassroots effort and were drawn to Harold's campaign. Many progressive Jews joined them. The result of the February elections left candidates in fourteen wards short of the 50 percent plus one vote required for election, meaning that, along with the mayoral general election, there would be a runoff for each of them in April. Eight of these were in wards that had gone overwhelmingly for Harold in February. Two were in wards he had won but where one of the candidates in the runoff did not support him, and four were in ones where he had little support.

---

40 Taken from Paul M. Green, "Chicago Election: The Numbers and the Implications," *Illinois Issues*, August 1983, 18.

The Twenty-Second and Twenty-Fifth Wards encompassed most of Pilsen and Little Village, two adjacent communities separated in part by the Cook County Jail. Although the population was largely Mexican, their voting influence had been minimized significantly by the way their boundaries had been drawn to accommodate machine stalwarts Vito Marzullo and Frank Stemberk. Community and labor activists Rudy Lozano and Juan Velazquez ran for aldermen in Twenty-Two and Twenty-Five respectively. Neither received enough votes to force a runoff, though Rudy came within thirty-seven votes in the Twenty-Second; but that didn't dampen their efforts to campaign for Harold in the general election, focusing on winning a margin for him in their home wards as well as broad support for him in all of Chicago's Mexican and Puerto Rican communities. Joined by Art Vazquez on the South Side and Luis Gutiérrez on the North Side, along with a multitude of community-based activists, they played a significant role in bridging the gaps between the Black and Latino communities leading up to the 1983 election. Differences around bilingual education and public housing had to be bridged and resolved. Harold welcomed their perspective on these and other issues, acting quickly to ensure that Latinos had new access to city government after his election.[41]

In the Forty-Sixth Ward, Jerry Orbach faced off with Charlotte Newfeld. Paul came in third, garnering enough votes to prevent an

---

41 Juan Velazquez lost to Vito Marzullo, an old-school machine alderman
   with reputed ties to the Chicago mob. Rudy lost to another machine
   politician, Frank Stemberk, who held a small apartment in the ward but
   actually lived full time with his family in a Chicago suburb. A lawsuit charging violations of the Voting Rights Act and discrimination
   against Black and Brown voters through gerrymandering resulted in
   an order to redraw the maps with Black and Brown majorities to reflect
   the city's population, and then to hold special elections in seven wards,
   including these two. Seeing the writing on the wall, both Marzullo and
   Stemberk resigned. Juan Soliz (Twenty-Fifth Ward) and Jesús "Chuy"
   García (Twenty-Second Ward), with Harold's endorsement, handily
   defeated their handpicked machine-connected successors. On the North
   Side, a runoff in the Twenty-Sixth Ward would decide control of the
   city council. In what looked like a tight race, Luis Gutiérrez bested his
   machine-supported opponent and gave Harold the twenty-five votes he
   needed to wrest control from the two Eddies (Burke and Vrdolyak).

Harold Washington, Juan Velazquez, and Rudy Lozano, 1983.

outright win by Orbach. Harold subsequently endorsed Charlotte, and so did we: we were confident she would be the better ally for him in the city council, and it looked more and more like this was going to be important. While Harold was immersed in his election and those of his supporters still facing runoffs, Ed Vrdolyak, the Cook County Democratic Party chairman, was hard at work shoring up a majority of aldermen-elect and aldermen in runoffs to follow his lead as he campaigned tirelessly for the Republican mayoral candidate.

Many in Chicago had been surprised when Harold had beaten Byrne and Daley in the primary. Symbolically, he was to be Chicago's first Black mayor. But Harold was so much more than that. He was a progressive legislator who was both a product of Chicago's notorious Democratic machine and independent of it. He had roots in the justice movements steeped in the Black community and the independent movements of the white liberal community. He was experienced, eloquent, and a tried and tested politician. He functioned at the highest levels of power while relating to any person in the urban ghetto of his upbringing. His back was straight and his heart open. His mind was clear and focused, miles ahead of his time. But in many ways, Harold's candidacy was an unexpected path and unique to the times that produced it.

Harold promised to cut off the machine patronage army—a promise that spoke to both the white liberal looking for good government and the Black working person looking for an opportunity. Promising that the only demand to be made on city employees would be for "a full day's work for a full day's pay," and not one to do political work, Harold repeatedly promised reforms. The machine, with Vrdolyak as lead henchman, was concerned. But the weapon Vrdolyak used in speeches to Democratic Party workers around the city, as he campaigned for Epton, was race. In runoff wards like the Forty-Sixth, where the aldermanic vote was likely to be close, he played the race card again and again.

On April 12, 1983, Harold won the mayoral election. The streets erupted in celebration as supporters of the city's first Black mayor danced into the night.

I joined a good ten thousand fellow campaign workers and supporters at Donnelly Hall (now an extension of McCormick Place) that evening as we anxiously awaited for Harold to arrive and declare victory. This, we thought, was the moment of a lasting victory. We had done it. A "man of the people" would ascend to the fifth floor of city hall and command respect, responsibility, and power. And as naive as that may seem in hindsight, we had every reason to believe that once elected, Harold would have the mayoral power to bring the city together, redirect its resources to be responsive to everyone, and open the door to talent previously not considered.[42]

Unfortunately, the vitriolic rhetoric of the Epton campaign was just the beginning of a five-year racially tinged and motivated campaign to undermine the reforms at the top of Harold's agenda.

---

42 Equally apparent in hindsight is the similarity of those times to the resistance Barack Obama would face two decades later upon his presidential election.

PART V

1983-1987: THE WASHINGTON YEARS

44.

"COUNCIL WARS"

Harold Washington loved politics and being a politician. Besides enjoying a good fight—he was once a boxer—he saw the possibilities it entailed. Politics was a means to good policy, and he enjoyed that journey immensely.

Harold hated the characterization of "council wars." He particularly disliked the popularization of the city council as a comedic act.[1] The division in the city council was organized by two aldermen (and supported by twenty-nine) and on full display at the first council meeting over which the new mayor presided. When they found that they could not dissuade him from reforms that threatened their hegemony, they challenged his ability to get anything done—and then blamed him for the resulting inaction.

This was serious business to Harold. It essentialized the institutional racism and institutional corruption that had caused many of the ills facing most Chicagoans. It was his mission to address these twin institutional roadblocks. He could, and would, go toe to toe with anyone in his path. Harold became mayor to a city that just a year earlier he had described as "two cities." With the assistance of many talented people, his mayoralty was about making a new narrative for Chicago: one city acknowledging its vast diversity with a "hammer of fairness" and problem solving whose benefits would apply to everyone.

When he took over the reins of city government in April 1983, he described Chicago's fiscal problems as "both enormous and complicated." Spending was out of control, resulting in a shortfall of at least $100 million, while the school and transit systems were projected to have deficits of $200 million.

The "financial crisis at hand" would take front and center. In his inaugural address, the new mayor minced no words as he declared a freeze

---

1   The phrase "council wars" had been popularized by Chicago comic Aaron
    Freeman, who developed a skit by the same name that quickly become
    popular. Harold disliked its overly simplistic analysis of the struggle
    reshaping Chicago's political landscape.

on all city hiring and raises; the layoffs of several hundred city employees hired for political consideration during the election cycle; and a promise to cut executive salaries starting in the mayor's office. Speaking to his signature call for fairness and his commitment to reform, Mayor Washington was clear about the partnerships he intended to bring to city government. As he put it in his address:

> When it finally comes down to basic issues, I'm only going to be successful if you are involved. . . . The real challenge is in the neighborhoods, as I've said for the past several months. I'm asking the people in the neighborhoods, all of the neighborhoods, to take a direct role in the planning, development and city housekeeping so that our city becomes a finer place in which to live.
>
> I'm calling for more leadership and more personal involvement in what goes on. We know the strength of the grassroots leadership because our election was based on it. We want this powerful infrastructure to grow because the success of tomorrow's city depends upon it, and the world and country look for an example as to how we can find the way out. Information must flow freely from the administration to the people and back again. The city's books will be open to the public because we don't have a chance to institute fiscal reforms unless we all know the hard facts."

Then came his vision:

> I am optimistic about our future. I'm optimistic not just because I have a positive view of life, and I do, but because there is so much about this city that promises achievement.
>
> We are a multi-ethnic, multi-racial, multi-language city and that is not a source to negate but really a source of pride, because it adds stability and strength to a metropolitan city as large as ours. . . . Racial fears and divisiveness have hurt us in the past. But I believe that this is a situation that will and must be overcome. . . .
>
> Most of our problems can be solved. Some of them will take brains, some of them will take patience, and all of them will have to be wrestled like an alligator in the swamp.

But there is a fine new spirit that seems to be taking root. I call it the spirit of renewal. It's like the spring coming here after a long winter. This renewal. It refreshes us and gives us new faith that we can go on. . . .

We have a clear vision of what our people can become, and that vision goes beyond mere economic wealth, although that is a part of our hopes and expectations. In our ethnic and racial diversity, we are all brothers and sisters in a quest for greatness. Our creativity and energy are unequaled by any city anywhere in the world. We will not rest until the renewal of our city is done.

Today I want to tell you how proud I am to be your mayor. There have been 41 mayors before me and when I was growing up in this city and attending its public schools it never dawned upon me nor did I dream that the flame would pass my way. But it has. And that flame, like the buck, will stop here. And we won't quench it, we'll brighten it. We'll add oil and make it brighter and brighter and brighter.

It makes me humble, but it also makes me glad. I hope someday to be remembered by history as the mayor who cared about people and who was, above all, fair. A mayor who helped, who really helped, heal our wounds and stood the watch while the city and its people answered the greatest challenge in more than a century. Who saw that city renewed.

Mayor Washington was good to his word, but there would be a backlash by those unmoved by it. At his first city council meeting, his council opposition roared. If they expected him to flounder, however, they were quickly disabused of that notion. Holding firm, he began what would be a four-year game of political cat and mouse. Always the consummate politician, he took his case directly to the people and the households who would be hurt by the obstruction of the so-called Vrdolyak Twenty-Nine.

The "council wars" that ensued were about power and control, the maintenance of the status quo. Enhanced by racism, they were driven by a fear of change. For the next three years, the Vrdolyak Twenty-Nine prevented the approval of Washington appointees to boards and commissions, slowed down the implementation of new initiatives to improve

The "Council Wars" that followed Harold Washington's 1983 election were about power and control: the maintenance of the status quo. No matter how hard they tried, Ed Burke and Ed Vrdolyak and the coalition of twenty-nine that they led were not able to grind the city to a halt as they intended. With hands raised, Burke is on the left, alderman of the 14th Ward, under federal indictment as this is being written. Vrdolyak, then alderman of the 10th Ward (in front of him), who made a big deal of Harold Washington's late tax filings, was sentenced in 2019 to eighteen months on a tax evasion conviction. He previously served an eighteen-month sentence for another income tax evasion charge.

people's lives, and impeded innovative efforts to improve the city's fiscal health. However, they were unable to grind the city to a halt as they intended. The team Harold put together to lead the city was talented and diverse. More women had leadership roles than ever before. New commissions, mostly established through executive order, broadened access to city government for the Latino, Asian, and African immigrant communities as well as the Black community.[2] The Human Rights Commis-

---

2 A member of Harold Washington's transition team, Rudy Lozano was expected to lead the new Latino Commission when he was murdered in June 1983. While the shooter was arrested and charged, many questions remained—primarily the answer to who was behind his murder, and their motive. The Commission for Justice for Rudy Lozano (of which I was a member) unfortunately was never able to get a satisfactory answer. "Was Rudy's success in unifying Blacks and Hispanics for political reform,

sion was given teeth. Community organizations were asked to broaden their partnerships with the city. Infrastructure improvements—repairs to vaulted sidewalks, sewer updates, water main replacement, and street resurfacing—were newly available in many of Chicago's communities. Despite the dark clouds of the Vrdolyak Twenty-Nine, Harold Washington's new dawn was spreading light.

· ·

45.

"VOTE WITH PURPOSE"
THE 1984 PRIMARIES

On the eve of the Illinois presidential primary, in March 1984, party nominations for state representatives, state senators, congressmen, delegates for each of the presidential candidates, and the election of ward committeemen were all in play. Mayor Harold Washington saw the election as an opportunity to galvanize and expand his base of support at home while influencing the direction of the Democratic Party nationally. He decided to run in Chicago's congressional districts for president as "a favorite son." By doing so, he would have a voice at the convention to be held in Oakland, California, in June 1984.

At the top of his priorities was a federal agenda for urban America. I would have a front-row seat—at the convention and in the first of Mayor Washington's "Vote with Purpose" campaigns that would be a mainstay of every election for the next three years.

---

which posed a challenge to the entrenched machine power, the motive in his assassination? Were the threats from specific individuals before and during Rudy's campaign connected with his death? Why have these individuals never been questioned about the threats made on Rudy's life and the lives of his family? Did Rudy's fight against the exploitation of undocumented workers cause the employers to see him as a danger to their operation? We still do not know who killed Rudy Lozano. We may know who pulled the trigger." Commission for Justice for Rudy Lozano, *Rudy Lozano: A Son of the People* (1983).

Interest in the Democratic primary was exceeded only by the municipal elections the year before. As candidates began collecting signatures on their nominating petitions, Harold announced the formation of his Political Education Project. Joe Gardner and Mercedes Mallette would be its codirectors. I was on staff. Attorneys Bob Anderson and Robert Jenkins provided legal assistance.

By the end of the year, 239 candidates had filed for spots on the ballot for committeeman in each of the city's fifty wards. Many others were filing to run as state representatives and senators. David Cantor, a longtime Washington supporter and Independent Voters of Illinois member from Hyde Park, was quoted in the press proclaiming, "Mayor Washington's Political Education Project will give legal support to anyone that needs it." We were inundated with requests—way more than two attorneys could handle. The dynamic around these elections was electrified by the political battle in city hall. Harold's supporters were energized. In the end, nearly fifty attorneys volunteered to assist.

Petitions for Harold's "favorite son" delegates were filed in all of the five of Chicago's congressional districts. They were challenged only in the Fifth Congressional District, by Ed Burke's cronies. Since the district included precincts in the city and in the county, it was heard before Cook County clerk Stanley Kusper, an inveterate machine loyalist. With Alderman Vito Marzullo as his sponsor, Richard J. Daley chose Kusper for this position.

Tom Johnson, who knew more about election law than most, agreed to take on this challenge if I agreed to assist with the preparation work. Most of the signatures on the petitions, Burke's associates had argued, were fraudulent. At first glance, it seemed it would take a miracle to turn this around. But getting on the ballot in this district was a priority for Harold—and therefore for us all. First, we charged Stanley Kusper with a conflict of interest. We thought we were tilting at windmills, so were surprised when he recused himself. But we still needed to prove the signatures on the petitions were valid.

To gather the proof we needed, we took to the streets, armed with affidavits and a notary. Ultimately, a sufficient number of voters whose signatures were challenged swore that they were registered to vote and that their signature was genuine. Against all odds, the Fifth

Congressional District slate was restored to the ballot. We had used the law, politics, and community organizing, and won.

Once all the challengers were complete and the ballot for the March primary set, we were tasked with coordinating the mayor's "Vote with Purpose" campaign. Harold had made endorsements for all races, and he wanted to make sure that every voter had a Vote with Purpose palm card to take with them to vote.

With all his endorsements locked down and sample "Vote with Purpose" ballots designed, there were 156 different versions. We needed to find a way to mail each registered voter their correct sample ballot. In 1984, the only computer printouts available were labels of registered voters by zip code. The Chicago Board of Elections had a "key book" that contained all of the districts for every address in the city. Camping out at the mail house for a week while cross-checking each address against the key book, the labels were attached to the correct palm card for that address before going to the post office, where the postal workers union made sure their members got them delivered before Election Day.

This would become the dry run as the first of many "Vote with Purpose" mailings for the next four years.

46.

POLICE MISCONDUCT AND THE HEGEMONY OF THE FOP

In Uptown in the 1970s, an FBI informant used his special relationship with local law enforcement as a cover for the "juice operation" he operated, through which he ensnared many young people into his web of burglaries and petty crimes. With promises of cash rewards, he enticed cash-strapped adolescent boys to do his bidding. Beginning with petty crimes, these teens were sent out on more lucrative burglaries as they grew older. Once committed, they were kept in line through threats of violence; if they attempted to leave, they got a severe beatdown—message sent.

The stories of unwarranted and inappropriate activity by the police in Uptown were constant; in fact, they were a part of the experience of virtually every family I interacted with from the moment I stepped foot in the community in 1972. So it did not surprise me when three thousand mostly poor and white Uptown residents joined us in October of that year for the Rally to End Police Brutality and Establish Community Control headlined by Bobby Rush, minister of defense of the Illinois Chapter of the Black Panther Party.

In the years that followed, the stories of beatings in the basement of the Chicago Transit Authority station at Wilson and Broadway were topped only by the stories of young people driven to Lake Michigan with threats of being thrown in, or taken to areas of the city controlled by rivals and left to fend for themselves in hostile territory. From the perspective of the police involved, there may have been a rationale, but for the abused these were clearly hostile acts (or threats) of violence by men wearing uniforms and guns that gave them life-and-death control over their victims that usually ended in harm, incarceration, or both.

In retrospect, it is not surprising that the heart of Uptown was one of the hunting grounds for mass killers John Wayne Gacy and Larry Eyler. Nor that the only defense against the disappearance of our children came from within the community and with community action. After all, the police did not take complaints from Uptown residents seriously; the people living here provided their fodder, not their respect. They did little to investigate these disappearances.

Throughout the '70s and early '80s, my experience matched those of many women I knew. We were often propositioned by men in cars—including men in police cruisers—while walking in Uptown. I had become used to the catcalls of construction workers when as a teenager I had spent my summers in New York City, but this was a whole new and much more intimidating experience. The whispered stories of police cars parked on the Sunnyside Mall with police officers having sex with women inside were too numerous to be discounted.

In 1983, a known federal agent was working for the Forty-Sixth Ward alderman, and simultaneously providing support for a neo-Nazi gang operating in Uptown—with assistance from the police.

The Town Hall police station (Twenty-Third District) was located in the Forty-Sixth Ward at the corner of Halsted and Addison. The heart of Uptown was divided between this police station and the Twentieth District station located on Foster Avenue.[3] People living in the court-way building located behind the Town Hall station complained often of screaming coming from inside.[4] I heard these complaints when I canvassed the area for Cha Cha Jiménez's campaign for alderman in 1975 and during my campaigns in 1978 and 1979. The screams were as consistent in their occurrence as the official denials of them. The tenants who lived there moved often.

We knew who the worst players among the police in Uptown were, and we were confident that, if pursued, these were some of the police with the most instances of complaints from the Office of Professional Standards. We also had evidence that a handful of police in Uptown were involved in the dissemination of Nazi literature.

In *Keep Strong* magazine and then *All Chicago City News*, our citywide coverage was filled with stories detailing issues with police conduct. From the West to the North to the South Side of Chicago, police shootings of civilians went before the Office of Professional Standards only to be thrown out, ignored, or ruled not sustained (meaning the officer was exonerated) again and again. Witnesses we talked to were rarely called before these decisions were made. The office had, in fact, been the product of the 1972–73 fight for community control of policing. Its creation was supposed to be a victory. But, as these dire circumstances amply illustrated, it was not.

Before the 1980s, Chicago police officers had never had a contract. Instead they had unsigned handshake agreements, or "sweetheart deals," during the twenty-one years Richard J. Daley was mayor. However, Jane Byrne changed all that.

During her campaign for mayor, Byrne had floated the idea of replacing the civil service status of police officers (and the historic

---

3   With the turn of the century thirty years later came a rebuilding of many Chicago police stations, including both of these. Town Hall was replaced with a newly constructed station in 2010. The Town Hall building was preserved and became part of a senior affordable housing complex targeted for the LGBT community. Over time the boundaries of the police districts have changed. The new building that replaced Town Hall became the Nineteenth District.

4   This court-way building was torn down and replaced with the parking lot for the new police station that replaced Town Hall.

handshake agreement) with a collective bargaining contract for police and firefighters. At the time, there were multiple groups that represented police officers and to whom they paid dues. In return, these groups, or "lodges," became their advocates within the department. These various police unions generally broke down along race and ethnic lines.

One of these was the Afro-American Patrolmen's League, formed in 1968 to battle racial discrimination inside the police force and in the community. With officers Renault Robinson and Frank Lee at his side, and joined by Father George Clements and State Senator Richard M. Newhouse, Edward "Buzz" Palmer[5] read the fledgling organization's official proclamation to a crowd of curious bystanders and the media on the sidewalk outside the AAPL's new offices on Sixty-Third Street:

> We are going to elevate the Black policeman in the Black community to the same image status enjoyed by the white policeman in the white community—that is, a protector of the citizenry, and not a brutal oppressor. We find it impossible to operate within the framework of existing police associations because they support. . . the shooting of looters. We will no longer permit ourselves to be relegated to the role of brutal pawns in a chess game affecting the Black community in which we serve. Donning the blue uniform has not changed us. On the contrary, it has sharpened our perception of our responsibility as Black males in a society seemingly unresponsive to the needs of Black people.

These were volatile times. When riots had broken out on the city's West Side two years earlier, the trigger had been the shutoff of fire hydrants during a heat wave—when few if any residents had air conditioning or access to pools. Then, just six months earlier, Martin Luther King Jr. had been killed. The rioting had been met with state-sponsored violence that had heightened the poor relations between the police and the Black community. It was then that Mayor Daley had issued a "shoot to kill" order that would become infamous. Allegations of police brutality were rampant, while city leaders demonized the "looters" (or protesters). Additional resources to address the inequalities experienced in

---

5 Buzz would serve as AAPL president until he left the police force a year later.

the Black community were nonexistent. Then, just months later, police beat and bludgeoned demonstrators on national TV during the protest against the war in Vietnam at the Democratic Convention.

By 1969, Renault was the AAPL president, and Howard Saffold their executive director. In December, when Fred Hampton and Mark Clark were murdered by police officers, they responded by protecting the surviving Panther leadership. After leaving the police force a year later, Buzz Palmer had become head of security for Malcolm X College,[6] where he, Renault, and other AAPL members had often picked up extra security work on their days off. In that capacity, they had come in contact with many Black Panthers who attended the school. Fred Hampton and Renault consequently had found occasion to meet and engage in numerous conversations, and Renault had not considered him dangerous.[7]

On the morning after the murder, Renault toured Fred's Monroe Street apartment, where he observed that "if it was a shootout, it was a decidedly one-sided shootout."[8]

By now, Renault and other AAPL members were receiving death threats and either indifference or retribution from the police brass. At the same time, AAPL membership continued to grow. They provided a security detail for Reverend Jesse Jackson while he challenged the construction industry to hire more Blacks on construction sites—and were reprimanded. In 1972, Congressman Ralph Metcalfe split with Daley over the treatment of two Black health professionals at the hands of white Chicago policemen. Around that time Renault and State Representative Harold Washington got together on a bill for a Police Review Board.[9] In 1973 Renault and other members of the AAPL participated in the Black Panther–sponsored citywide Conference to End Police Brutality and Establish Community Control. Their activities were beginning to receive attention. After they filed a discrimination lawsuit against the

---

6 Originally named Crane College, it was renamed to Malcolm X College after a prolonged struggle led in part by activist and attorney Stan Willis.

7 See Robert McClory, *The Man Who Beat Clout City* (Athens, OH: Swallow Press, 1977), 63.

8 McClory, *Clout City*, 62.

9 The bill didn't go far, but it stirred a reaction from Mayor Daley. See Dempsey Travis, *An Autobiography of Black Politics* (New York: Urban Research Institute, 1987).

police department and city, they were noticed—and disciplined by the command structure, while being harassed, threatened, brutalized, and even arrested by white police officers. For a time, since there were no grounds to fire him, Renault was transferred to police headquarters, where his assignment was to watch the alley behind the building.

The AAPL leadership fought for the hiring of Black officers and for promotions to the rank of sergeant, lieutenant, and captain of working Black officers. While Chicago, then almost 40 percent Black and 14 percent Latino, had over ten thousand police at the time, barely one-fifth of them were Black. Police treatment of citizens in Black and Latino communities differed dramatically from in the rest of the city. The AAPL filed a lawsuit charging the city and the Chicago Police Department with discrimination and successfully filed a court order to require the additional hiring of Black, Latino, and women officers to the force. The Fraternal Order of Police (FOP) fought them every step of the way, joining the city and the department in opposing these changes.

Given this sordid context, when Byrne gave the green light to a single union to represent police officers in negotiating a contract, AAPL and the other ethnic unions were concerned. They feared a contract negotiated by a union who saw their fiduciary responsibility to their members (primarily white ones) would undermine the police department as a vehicle for public safety for all Chicago's citizens.

John Dineen, the president of the Chicago chapter of the Fraternal Order of Police, was also the president of the national FOP. The membership of the FOP, nationally as well as locally, was almost entirely white. Not surprisingly, the leadership saw their interests from that perspective as well—and were very effective in protecting them. In both capacities, Dineen had the FOP argue against the AAPL's federal lawsuit, insisting again and again that discrimination was not an issue in the city and certainly not a concern in the police department. In spite of these protests, Judge Prentice Marshall decided in AAPL's favor, ordering the city and police department to increase the number of Black, Latino, and women officers on the Chicago police force.

Byrne determined that an election would be held to determine who would represent all non-ranked police officers in contract negotiations. Again, at the time there were nearly a dozen different unions, each representing some type of ethnic or cultural group. In the first round, the two highest vote-getters were the FOP and "no union." A runoff was held. Byrne appeared to be supportive of a failed effort by the Teamsters to represent the police officers, but in the end she might as well have said, "I support anyone but the AAPL, and by extension a 'no union' vote."

Leading up to the runoff election, the AAPL attempted to get some assurances that the FOP—expected to handily win over the "no union" option—would honor their concerns and withdraw their objections to the federal court's mandate to hire and promote more Black, Latino, and women officers. Their concerns went ignored.

The first contract was finalized in the summer of 1981. Byrne agreed that the FOP would be the sole negotiator for all police officers, who would be required to pay dues to the FOP—even if they chose not to be members. To further cement the FOP's hegemony, the section on discrimination took on odd turn. In an ironic twist—given the concerns of the AAPL—this clause protected the existing workforce against discrimination, essentially locking in the status quo of a police force that was demographically out of sync with the population of the city. Rather than speak to the lack of Black, Latino, or female officers on the police force, the contract protected the existing status of the overwhelmingly white officers.[10]

In the decade following the FOP's ascendancy as the sole union, most of the other police organizations would die. Under the leadership of Pat Hill, the AAPL would hold on for thirty more years. But with each passing year, its influence would only wane as the power structure of the Chicago Police Department targeted AAPL leadership, and Black cops forced to pay dues to the FOP saw little reason to also join the AAPL. During the forty years following the "labor reform" that brought collective bargaining to Chicago police, the city (and the department) would become more diverse, less segregated, and more

---

10 In the first contract, the language of Section 10.2, "Non-discrimination" read: "In the application of the terms and conditions of this Agreement, the Employer shall not discriminate against officers, and employment-related decisions will be based on qualifications and predicted performance in a given position without regard to race, color, sex, religion, or national origin of the officer nor shall the Employer discriminate against officers as a result of membership in the Lodge." Age and sexual orientation were added in later years.

progressive; meanwhile, the FOP rank and file would continue to move more toward a culture of white supremacy, reflected in its election of John Catanzara as its head in 2020.

One day in the summer of 1982, I went to the old police headquarters at Eleventh and State. I was there to provide bail for Marion Stamps, members of Tranquility Memorial Community Center, Dorothy Tillman, and a few members of the Intercommunal Survival Committee who had been arrested during demonstrations against Byrne's Chicago Fest. The protests had been initiated by Lu Palmer and Jesse Jackson as the Black community, enraged by Byrne's appointments to the Chicago Housing Authority on the heels of her appointments to the school board, reached a boiling point. As I approached the side entrance to the station, I glanced inside a parked squad car. In plain sight, written across the console between the two front seats, were the words "White Avengers."

During Harold's first term, we had had our share of run-ins with the police in Uptown. But activity in Uptown was an echo of problems with police misconduct, torture, and murder of people of color elsewhere in Chicago. Gang activity was endemic at Cabrini, and much of Marion's attention was involved in negotiating treaties—an echo of the activities Fred Hampton had engaged in a decade earlier and that were a particular target of the FBI's COINTELPRO. The Chicago police looked down upon these efforts, leading to Marion's insistence that the police "are not here to serve but to police us" and that they were no more than an occupying force in the Black community.

Jon Burge was a commander on the South Side of Chicago who was already renowned (although not yet acknowledged) for beating false confessions out of arrestees and sending them to jail for years—and sometimes to death row. Meanwhile, an investigation of Burge, among other allegations of police brutality, was underway by students of Ed Marxman, a professor at the University of Illinois's Jane Addams School of Social Work. He was very close to Marion, and these investigations were ongoing when he was murdered in 1981.

Now that Harold was mayor, we thought maybe we would get some relief. Harold had successfully moved the Office of Professional Standards out of the central headquarters of the police department, then located it at Eleventh and State, so that civilians did not have to go to the very police they were asking to be investigated with complaints of police misconduct. But the times were not yet ripe for accountability. Harold was clear. "I do not control the police department," he told me during one of several conversations on this topic. "Not yet," he said after clarifying that a shift in culture would require a process of change. At first, I did not understand this.

One of his assistant corporation counsels who worked on police misconduct was equally clear on the limitations for accountability: they were constrained by the police contract, if not by tradition and the renowned "blue wall of silence." We had a list of officers who were engaged in a host of questionable activities. Some we knew to be passing out Nazi literature. Others were suspected of sexual assault, drug trafficking, and possession of stolen weapons. A few were known for their brutality. But the time for getting relief was not yet ripe. To our frustration, the union contract required *all* complainants to be known before an investigation could be initiated. But many with complaints were afraid of retaliation if they gave their name, and even then the contract created a long and complicated process, making it difficult to hold officers accountable for their actions. Other provisions limited access to an officer's file to one year. Since most investigations by the Office of Professional Standards didn't begin until well after this window of time, these files could not be used to determine an ongoing pattern of misconduct. It was no surprise that most allegations received a determination of "not sustained."

Over the next two and a half decades, there would be some minor changes, but most significant was the increase in successful civil rights claims against the city. But more on that later.

47.

A VORTEX OF WHITE SUPREMACISTS AND FEDERAL AGENTS

These days, when I hear some liberals fret about the coziness between white supremacist street organizations and law enforcement, I look back at Uptown during the 1970s and '80s and just laugh.

In Uptown, our goal was to organize those we worked with to take on the challenge of social justice and effectuate change. Everything we did was designed to educate and inform. What is the source of a problem? Who is the policy maker? What is the best demand we can make, in this place, at this moment in time, to get a desired result and move our interests forward?

That doesn't mean to say there weren't tensions. It was both our expectation to always challenge racism, and our hope to build a more just world. And we understood that the fight for social justice is a protracted struggle requiring a long-term perspective.

At the core, always, was the color line. Often, we challenged racism directly. We had no choice.

This is where Kevin Zornes comes in. When I met his father, Lawrence, he was a street preacher in Uptown. Intentionally an "anti-racialist," he had a hearing impairment that was congenital and a deep Southern accent. He had joined other ex–coal miners in the mid-1970s to found the Chicago Area Black Lung Association. In this capacity, he worked with Congressman Harold Washington to grow support for and pass the legislation that created the Black Lung Trust Fund.

Lawrence had seven children, of whom Kevin was one. Kevin had inherited his father's hearing defect and, like his father, had a very deep Southern accent. The two combined to confound many of his teachers, who defaulted to the assumption that he was unteachable. At the age of seventeen, he had not learned to read.

In Chicago, it was common for small groups of young people (most often male) to form gangs on a block-by-block and/or neighborhood basis. In Uptown in the '70s and early '80s, there were the Kenmore Boys and the Wilson Boys, among others.

Jerry Orbach had been elected alderman of the Forty-Sixth Ward in the same election that had brought Harold Washington to the fifth floor of city hall as Chicago's first Black mayor. Tom Mosher had become Orbach's chief of staff. By all accounts prone to erratic behavior, Mosher was known to the activists who, almost twenty years earlier, had come to Uptown to organize JOIN. A protégé of business magnate Clement Stone, he had grown up in Uptown. This was the same egotistical and disruptive man who had joined me and twenty-eight other students on our SDS-sponsored trip to Cuba in 1968, and subsequently outed himself as an informant when he testified in front of a Senate Subcommittee on Intelligence. Following Mosher's return to Uptown after Harold was elected in 1983, I became aware of his presence there when I noticed him sitting in a car outside my home, watching my front door. His stalking was a little unsettling.

Mosher organized the White Rebels, pulling membership from teenagers involved in the Kenmore Boys, the Wilson Boys, and the Uptown Rebels. I had first known him as an agent provocateur on a federal payroll, and it seemed he most likely still was. Among Mosher's recruits was Randy Price, who in late 1978 was responsible for setting fire to the building on Wilson Avenue that was the home of the Heart of Uptown Coalition and housed *Keep Strong* magazine, the Uptown Community Service Center, and the Fred Hampton Memorial Hall; and later for at least one burning cross, à la Ku Klux Klan. Randy had been a student at the Shimer College outpost we ran in the 1970s. "He was a reasonable student, didn't cause problems, and he tried," George Atkins told me one day, as we reflected on some of our wins and losses.

Orbach joined Ed Vrdolyak's opposition to Harold Washington as one of twenty-nine aldermen determined to make sure that Harold could not affect any of the promised changes on which he was elected. Racial animus became their favorite tactic, and in Uptown, Mosher was dispatched and well suited to do their dirty work, while Orbach feigned ignorance.[11]

---

11 Mosher's efforts seemed to focus on two groups that were inclined toward racial animus and violence—the Rebels and the Gaylords. At the very least, his position as Orbach's chief of staff gave them cover. At its worst

Kevin Zornes was fearful when he came to a family friend, and ultimately his father, in the early months of 1985. For some time, he had been one of many who under the banner of the White Rebels were meeting in a basement on Magnolia with people who identified with the Nazi Party and the Klan. At some point, he had signed an *x* on a Nazi Party membership form. He said he wanted none of it; that he had just wanted to be accepted by his friends and had not known what the paper was. He had been told, however, that if he quit he would die.

Rattled and fearful, he brought his dilemma to Paul Siegel. He didn't want to be associated with the Nazi Party. He felt this affiliation was an affront to his parents and everything they stood for. Paul encouraged Kevin to share this with his parents, and, together with Lawrence and his mother, Dolly, Kevin made his decision to quit.

Days later, Kevin was dead by a gunshot wound under his left ear, administered by Jerry Shields in the building managed by his mother. Shields, who associated with Randy Price, was a juvenile and spent some time in jail for this murder. Shields's defense was that Kevin had killed himself in a game of Russian Roulette.

Lawrence Zornes requested to have his son's wake at the Uptown Community Service Center in the Fred Hampton Memorial Hall. The family wanted to be able to greet people who were coming to give condolences. It was also his hope and expectation that whoever was leading this racially hate-filled organizing would show their faces. He wanted to know who they were.[12] We knew that Tom Mosher was behind organizing these youth. But who was providing their hate-filled political education?

To accommodate the family, another room was set up for them to greet their visitors. One of these visitors was Harold Washington, who wanted to express his condolences to Lawrence on the loss of his son.

A few months later, on June 14, 1985, in the midst of a contentious city council meeting during the debate over the federally funded Community Development Block Grant budget in a move intended to derail

---

interpretation—and our belief—he tried to manipulate them to incite racist violence. He was likely aware of the Rebels' connection to the Donald Black faction of the Klan and the Nazi literature they were peddling.

12 As it turned out, members of a right-wing group from Michigan did come and were followed, allowing us to determine the group that was involved.

action and defer a vote, Ed Vrdolyak charged that Mayor Washington had gone to a Nazi funeral conducted by Slim Coleman—"a Nazi funeral director." Slim, who was in the press box on the side of city council Chambers, jumped the rail as all hell broke loose.

Vrdolyak was peddling the notion that whatever Kevin was doing he shouldn't have been doing, and he got what he deserved. We sharply contested this narrative, standing behind our conviction that Kevin was a young person struggling with who he was and made a choice to reject hatred and was killed for it. His family, in any case, deserved our respect and condolences. White youth in Uptown needed to know they could take a different direction and would be received by a welcoming community if they did so.

Vrdolyak and Burke (who backed him up) were making left-wing statements for a right-wing program: the aim of the Vrdolyak Twenty-Nine and their "council wars" was to stop the Black mayor and his challenge to the dying (but still breathing) Democratic machine, by any means possible. Meanwhile, Orbach, who had earlier led the charge that I was "the wrong kind of Jew," wore his Jewish identity on his sleeve, while under the protection and with the prestige of his office, white supremacist organizing was going on under his nose.

Outraged by this turn of events, Jim Chapman, representing the Zornes family as their attorney, demanded an apology—which they never got—from Vrdolyak. He then went a step further taking his case to the Anti-Defamation League. In a packet sent to the ADL, Jim enclosed "the hate literature the Neo-Nazi group, which apparently is operating in Chicago generally but concentrating in Uptown, circulated following the wake for Kevin Zornes." He explained, "Immediately after Vrdolyak's attack upon the floor of the Council, members of this group were seen distributing this and related literature on the streets of Uptown. In other words, while no one else would give any credibility to this Neo-Nazi group, Vrdolyak in fact did and now has emboldened it."

Jim arranged a meeting between Marc Kaplan, myself, and two people from the ADL where we laid out the relationship between Orbach, the Rebels, and Nazis. We gave them names of people connected to Orbach and Mosher, shared what we knew from our own observations, and asked them if they would be willing to investigate further. We hoped for their acknowledgment and exposure of what was, to us,

(Left to Right) Jim Chapman, Lawrence Zornes, and Dolly Zornes demanding an apology from Vrdolyak.

an obvious connection between the overtly white supremacist organizing and the Vrdolyak Twenty-Nine, including the Jewish alderman whose district included Uptown—Jerry Orbach.

The ADL, however, refused to make a public statement, or even to voice concern to Alderman Orbach for the activities in which his chief of staff was engaged. The inaction of the League was summed up in an interoffice memorandum that concluded, in part, "The situation is not as bad as it could or might be."

48.

THE PLAYING FIELD CHANGES

Despite the attempts by the council majority to obstruct the new mayor at every turn, the city council passed 94 percent of mayoral initiatives between 1983 and 1986. Harold had several tools at his disposal: he went directly to the people in any ward where the alderman was opposing an initiative that, if passed, would address their concerns; he negotiated and cajoled, having some success here and there in peeling away the opposition; he could threaten a veto, which his opposition did not have the votes to overturn; and he could issue executive orders.

By the end of 1985, the city's finances had been stabilized, and the face of Chicago government had changed. Blacks, Latinos, Asians, and Native Americans were now an integral part of city government, joining their white counterparts as department heads and appointees to multiple boards and commissions. Women in leadership roles expanded dramatically and included major city departments for the first time as the city saw its first Commission on Women's Affairs. The Commission on Latino Affairs was expanded and empowered. An executive order ensured a minimum level of minority- and women-owned businesses' participation in city contracts. A working relationship was established with the business community. Neighborhoods were prioritized. New funds to repair streets and sidewalks in every ward were approved. Private and local funds were leveraged against a growing decline of federal funds for housing, leading to new housing for low- and moderate-income Chicagoans. Health was prioritized, and already improvements in infant mortality were noticeable. A new community-based (non-police-driven) anti-gang initiative was already showing positive results, with a decrease in the incidence of murders and violent crime. Corruption in several city departments was unveiled and acted on. Freedom-of-information policies were implemented, shining a light on city government where there had been none before.

But opposition politics did not wane. While the media focused on attacks designed to create confusion, rather than on the content of the changes in city government, the Vrdolyak Twenty-Nine continued to

Thirty-nine percent of top-level positions were held by women in the Washington administration compared with twelve percent in the previous administration. Here the women literally had his back.

hold up confirmation of Harold's nominees to some of the most impactful boards. The changes in leadership his base was crying for in the Chicago Park District, the Chicago Board of Education, the Chicago Transit Authority, and the Chicago Housing Authority were all being held hostage.

According to the 1980 census, the city population was 39.5 percent Black, 14 percent Latino, and 43.2 percent white, with other races at 3.2 percent.[13] In spite of this diversity, during Jane Byrne's tenure as mayor, the majority of aldermen had approved a map that drew ward boundaries in such a way as to retain majority-white populations in the vast majority of city wards. Black, Latino, and white independents decried the maps, charging that they were gerrymandered and unfair. A lawsuit charging discrimination was filed.

The US District Court found the city guilty of gerrymandering the boundaries to exclude minorities and ordered a new map be drawn, leading to special elections in seven wards in March 1986, three years into Harold's term. This was the election that first made Luis Gutiérrez, Jesús

---

13 According to HUD, by 2000 the population was 31.3 percent white, 36.4 percent Black, 26 percent Hispanic, and 6.3 percent other races.

"Chuy" García, and others aldermen. The Rainbow Coalition, whose presence was still felt in 1983, was reaffirmed as Black, white, and Latino activists from around the city showed up in support of the Black and Latino candidates pledged to support Harold. When the results were in, there were twenty-five aldermen voting with Harold and twenty-five against. Finally, as the tie breaker, Harold had the votes to get his appointees approved—among the most notable being appointments to the Chicago Park District Board, historically one of the most segregated and biased institutions in the city. However, the true test would come in the regularly scheduled municipal elections the following year.

. . . .

49.

THE 1987 ELECTIONS

In 1985 Harold had asked me to be his photographer on a trip he was making to Israel and Rome. While I had often been in the mayor's face taking pictures for *All Chicago City News*, I wasn't a great photographer. I could frame a picture, but this was 1985, long before the advent of digital photography. Film was developed in a darkroom, and how you set the camera made a great difference. Lighting, the quality of negatives, and all manner of details, today fixed almost as if by magic, were determined by one's skills with a camera. Mine were not great. I got by by taking a lot of photos, relying on my eye for graphic arts, and a hope and a prayer.

Over time it became obvious that Harold had not asked me on his trip for my photography skills. Rather, he was courting me to run for alderman of the Forty-Sixth Ward. Getting me to do so would be a hard sell, and he did so masterfully. Orbach, then the Forty-Sixth Ward's alderman, had joined the Vrdolyak Twenty-Nine and was firmly ensconced in Harold's opposition.

Uptown made up about half of the Forty-Sixth Ward, and that's where our base was. We still had some infrastructure from earlier elections in Lakeview. Following the conclusion of my marathon three elections of '78–79, we had learned a lot about how the machine manipulated the voting apparatus, which we estimated had cost us about twenty-five hundred votes in the 1979 runoff. I had sworn to never run for political office again. But in 1986, in spite of this determination, I couldn't deny that it was possible to beat the current alderman. And I had many reasons to want to. With the realization that I could be the twenty-sixth vote for Harold Washington's agenda, and in doing so could end the dominance of the old guard in their obstruction of change in Chicago, I embraced the challenge.

Not only was Jerry Orbach part of the Vrdolyak Twenty-Nine, but he put his full support behind the gentrification of the heart of Uptown, embracing every effort to force out people of low and moderate incomes. As an assistant corporation counsel, Orbach was assigned to the housing court prosecuting building code violations. The slumlords who owned and operated rental units in the heart of Uptown had been well protected by the machine for years—a tradition that continued with Orbach. When he was in a position to make their buildings safe, Orbach did not do so. If we were to create decent, safe, and affordable housing to replace the slums many people were living in, we would need the full support of the mayor and the alderman.

But by now, defeating Orbach was personal. He wore being Jewish on his sleeve like it was a trophy while his chief of staff played footsie with Klan and Nazi organizers, an association that had led, in part, to the murder of Kevin Zornes. In 1985, shortly after Kevin's death, Brendan's friend Rob Faulkner had tracked me down. He wanted to talk to me about Brendan. Brendan had been acting distant and moody, but he wasn't speaking to me about it. I was concerned.

Rob was also concerned. "There's something you need to know. The guy who killed Kevin Zornes threatened Brendan," he told me. The Sunnyside Mall, then still a barren two-block slab of concrete, was contested territory. Brendan's affront was that the kids he hung out with were not just white but Black, Latino, and Asian. At gunpoint, Jerry Shields had threatened him to stay off the mall, along with his friends.

Brendan's spring break from school was around the corner. I used whatever credit I had on my sole credit card, rented a Winnebago, and whisked Brendan off to a ten-day East Coast road trip. When we returned, he recruited Marc Kaplan (who was known as "coach") to show him how to lift weights and to work out with him. His next move was to sign up, along with Jason Yolich and Ricky Spurgeon, to play football at Wells Park and win the "Mum" Bowl, played at Soldier Field.

The Park District football season began shortly after he spent most of July in Florida with Mike and Susan Klonsky. "We were there for Tropical Storm Bob," Susan would later recall. "While stuck indoors, Mike taught the kids poker and blackjack. I believe Slim called to ask if we could take Brendan because some white gang—maybe some sort of skinheads—were after him."

Brendan and I were about the same height when we spent the first ten days of April on the road, just days before his fourteenth birthday. That summer he played a season of football and bulked up, and he had grown taller. By September he was closing in on six feet. It would be a few years before he reached his full height of six feet four inches, but this, it turned out, was enough to keep the bullies at bay.[14]

The machine captain of this precinct was Jerry Orbach's brother, a supervisor in Chicago's Department of Health. While Orbach himself lived three quarters of a mile south, he had many relatives living at 4250 North Marine Drive, and they worked the precinct hard. Truth was not a factor as it became clear that their strategy was lies and misinformation based in racial fears, just as it had been in 1978 and 1979.

In February 1987, challenged by former mayor Jane Byrne, Harold Washington won the Democratic primary, and in a three-way race, I received 38 percent of the vote to Jerry Orbach's 40 percent. While I faced a runoff, Harold faced a three-way race against Don Haider, the Republican nominee, and Ed Vrdolyak, who was on the ballot as an independent.

Harold bested Byrne in the Forty-Sixth Ward, but by just nine hundred votes. The contested issues going into the general election in April were supporting Harold in the city council, provision of a ward service office responsive to everyone in the ward (regardless of their political affiliation), and development without displacement.

The Jesus People USA, a Christian intentional community in Uptown, represented a voting block of 250 people. While our paths often crossed, they were close to Orbach and had given him their full support

---

14 To this day he insists he was never intimidated. Intimidated or not, it appeared to me that he was taking the offense.

in the primary. They operated a soup kitchen, provided shelter in their building for homeless people, and were also part of the coalition with the Organization of the NorthEast (ONE), who were behind an effort to pass an anti-displacement ordinance. We should have been natural allies.

In the week leading up to Election Day, ONE sponsored a forum for the two Uptown wards where runoffs were scheduled. It was held at Truman College, where the lecture hall was filled to capacity. Denny Cadieux and the rest of Jesus People leadership were among those in attendance. Run like a typical Alinsky-style meeting, the forum was set up to ask each of us a series of questions that required a yes or no answer. A ONE representative held the mic before each of us in succession as we gave our answers. On most questions, the answers were strikingly similar, leaving little room to make distinctions between the candidates or to discern what we actually might do once in office.

When they got to the question on housing and displacement, I had had enough. I don't remember the actual question, but I know that I found it to be meaningless. Everyone at the podium would have had no problem giving a yes answer, yet I knew there was no one else on that podium who would actually support any real effort to address the need for low-cost housing in Uptown, let alone the rest of the city. I was the first respondent to their milquetoast question. Seizing the moment, I grabbed the mic, restating the question as I thought it should be asked, then answered the question I had now posed. I then challenged the crowd to demand an answer to my question from each of the remaining candidates. And they did. Orbach could not bring himself to say yes, as he refused to veer from the original yes-or-no question.

On Saturday, three days before the election, Cadieux told George Atkins that the Jesus People would be voting for me. It would soon become apparent that while we had our differences, we had many common interests. I would have won the election without their support, but what it did provide was enough of a cushion to ensure I did not have to face a recount.

When the results came back, Harold had been reelected. Vrdolyak had overshadowed the Republican candidate, who received less than 5 percent of the vote. Clearly this election had been a referendum on the council wars. In spite of a decisive win, Harold was displeased with the results of the election, and particularly that Vrdolyak had received 42 percent of the vote. It was hard not to believe that so many of these voters had supported Vrdolyak on the basis of race. We would continue to talk about this during each of the meetings I had with the mayor during the following seven months. It was disheartening and hurt his heart.

PART VI

ALDERMANIC YEARS:

FROM MAKING THE MAJORITY TO BEING THE MINORITY VOICE

50.

TRANSITION TO THE ROLE OF GOVERNING

With my election on April 7, 1987, Harold Washington was guaranteed a twenty-six-vote majority in the city council. He assured me he would now have a comfortable majority of forty on most matters, and he did, but he wasn't going to let any grass grow. Rules of procedure for the new city council and its committees—along with their respective chairs, vice chairs, and members—had to be agreed to and voted on. While the ceremonial inauguration was scheduled for early May, Aldermen Tim Evans, Larry Bloom, and Eugene Sawyer called a special meeting in April to get this done and establish the new playing field.

In Uptown, we had our own statement to make with a swearing-in ceremony in the front lobby of Truman College. This was where the college's opening ceremony had been held more than a decade earlier. There were ongoing demands to guarantee that those most affected by the construction of the college would be welcome here. With Jim Chapman symbolically swearing me in as the alderman of the Forty-Sixth Ward, it seemed like the perfect place to celebrate this victory that was energized by the choices made so long ago for the development of Truman College.

On May 4, the official inauguration day, after a celebratory second swearing-in at the band shell in Grant Park, we all returned to city hall. Following the mayor's reception on the fifth floor, we headed to the second floor, where I chose my office. This involved confirming furniture and office equipment—an IBM electric typewriter, telephones, and a fax machine—and collecting what was possible from offices vacated by departing aldermen—coffee machines, office supplies, file cabinets, and anything else that was lying around and not yet claimed. I also arranged for the office to be swept for electronic listening devices, or "bugs." The sweep revealed that the phones were in fact bugged. The office I was moving into had been the office of Alderman Percy Hutchinson. He had been indicted for insurance fraud, and the bugs could have been a remnant of his occupancy. Still, I had become used to my phone being electronically monitored, and I decided to assume the worst: that they were there for me.

There was a lot of schmoozing and politicking going on with lots of handshakes, a few hugs. After securing my office, I moved toward the lobby of the second floor. A fellow alderman who was one of the original twenty-one aldermanic allies of Mayor Washington pulled me toward him, put his arms around my shoulder, bent down, and whispered in my ear, "Now that you're here, it's time to go along to get along."

He might as well have said, "Make no waves"—a disposition that was not really in my nature. I wasn't elected to "make no waves"; I was elected to fight for a just and fair city where all voices are heard, where development could occur without displacement, and institutional racism and institutional corruption would be challenged and addressed. I grabbed George Atkins, my acting chief of staff,[1] and headed for the elevators, telling him, "We're going back to Uptown and only coming back here for council meetings and committee meetings. We're going to put together the best service office possible. We'll figure out how things work and don't work for real people, and let that be our guide." There were several legislative initiatives I was committed to pursue, and I had to set up a functional ward service office. We'd have to learn to walk down two paths at once. This would be easier said than done, but my inner stubborn streak was up for the challenge.

The next day, I met the mayor. I thought a lot about my agenda items. We had spent the last fifteen years fighting the Daley machine and the false reformism of Jane Byrne. But what was it in particular that we were fighting? The political status quo in Chicago was a defender of a system that was responsive to those with money, influence, and power. The consequence was that the needs of the many were rarely prioritized, and were often left unmet. After all, Uptown was not the only community that faced high infant mortality, inadequate housing, schools lacking resources, the loss of good paying jobs, high unemployment, and crumbling sewers, streets, and sidewalks. Harold brought with him an era of hope and expectation that this would be turned around. He asked (and cajoled) activists to join him and bring innovative ideas and programs to the table, and they did.

---

1 George served in the role of chief of staff for a few months. He would be in and out of my office as my political partner for the next twenty-four years.

Harold had deep support in the Black community and broad support elsewhere, creating an umbrella and making room for anyone who cared to join. But this was an inherently difficult task. Not everyone would completely agree on which problem to tackle, which solution to pursue, or even that there was a problem to begin with. And not everyone wanted to be part of that umbrella. And while Harold's opposition had been knocked down a peg by his reelection and newly established control of the city council, it remained fierce.

Bringing about a new way of thinking about politics in Chicago would be a process and require long-term effort. From day one, problem number one was how to maintain the power of the mayor's office while a determined opposition wanted to stop us in our tracks. We would have to build a ship while already at sea, whether we liked it or not.

As an alderman, I now had a responsibility to be responsive to the people who had worked so hard to elect me. Most were volunteers who had their own reasons for their support. They wanted Harold Washington to have a reliable ally in the Forty-Sixth Ward. Or they wanted to have an alderman committed to finding a way to do development without displacement. Or they wanted an alderman who would sweat the small stuff and make sure that the ward got its fair share of city resources. Or maybe some just wanted an alderman who would give them a voice. Some were hoping for an opportunity for a job, some for a way to serve.

Others wanted to get their streets cleaned, their street lights working, enhanced access to basic health care at the Uptown Health Center, or improvements in the parks where they and their children played, or at the local office of the Department of Human Services where they might go for employment, housing, or emergency food assistance.

As always, top of my agenda was housing, and particularly the issue of development without displacement. In his first term, Harold had professionalized the Department of Housing by bringing on staff who had respect for the need for low- and moderate-income housing, enough experience to know the ins and outs of federal laws and resources, and the creativity to expand the department's universe. As housing commissioner, Brenda Gaines turned Jane Byrne's abysmal record in affordable housing creation on its head. Under Byrne, the city had paid for more than it got when it came to the little housing it created; in the first term of the Washington administration, by contrast, three dollars from private sources were leveraged for every dollar spent by the city. Meanwhile, Washington's administration took advantage of changes in the federal tax code leading to the creation of the Chicago Equity Fund and the low-income housing tax credit—both tools for affordable-housing creation that, in the short term, would be fairly successful.

My agenda for that first meeting with Harold as an alderman was bookended by housing issues: bailing out the Chicago Housing Authority and preventing the potential loss of ten thousand units of HUD-financed low- and moderate-income housing. In between was a list of job openings in various city departments and my take on what it would require to get the best hire for these positions, as well as a request for his support of a youth employment initiative (which he backed wholeheartedly).

A special council meeting was called for later in the week to consider a bailout of the Chicago Housing Authority. By court order, the CHA was finally building low-rise scattered site housing, but reimbursement by HUD was slow, and the program was facing bankruptcy.

Attorney Alex Polikoff filed a lawsuit on behalf of CHA resident Dorothy Gatreaux in 1966 charging the housing agency with discrimination. In 1969, federal judge Richard Austin agreed, ordering the CHA to build seven hundred units of low-density, low-rise public housing in white areas and to stop all other construction of low-income housing until this was accomplished. However well-intentioned, this "corrective action" spelled doom for the future of Chicago's already-troubled public housing. Local aldermen objected to any proposed public housing in their ward—even if it was a building for just one or two families, or if half the units went to current local, low-income residents. Land was purchased and lay fallow because the city blocked their use for public housing, while money was spent on lawyers instead of housing.

The unintended consequence of the consent decree had been to increase the racial polarization in the city, leaving it with a dearth of affordable units.

The CHA was already in turmoil in its efforts to oversee housing that had become substandard and dangerous. In addition to managing housing units, the CHA was responsible for the maintenance of internal roads, sewers, garbage collection, and public safety on the typically large campuses where the existing high-rise housing developments were built. Deferred maintenance cursed the authority for decades. Until Harold was elected, it had been a crisis lacking a political will to find a solution.

For years we had covered many stories in *Keep Strong* and *All Chicago City News* about the conditions at CHA developments. Although there had been a slight reprisal of HUD and its attention to the plight of public housing authorities during Jimmy Carter's one term as president, the withdrawal of resources by HUD and a policy of planned failure of public housing had been a reality since the 1960s. Consequently, coupled with the self-serving management of the authority during the time Charles Swibel was at the helm, CHA was facing dire times.

I was keenly aware of all of this. From where I stood, HUD should have been supportive of any effort to build scattered-site public housing in Chicago. They were shrugging off their financial responsibility, and Chicago was coming to the rescue. By making a loan to CHA, weren't we doing HUD's work for them? Wasn't this a slippery slope? Torn, I went to talk to Harold about my vote.

We spoke about government and the notion that it has a responsibility to provide for those for whom the economic or political or social systems are not working. We discussed how political support for funding the basic services necessary to provide such a "security blanket" was waning. We talked about the recent history of the CHA, and the one hundred and some people living in subpar conditions in units that were irreplaceable and in high demand. We talked about some of the problems, and about what it would take to implement solutions. And we talked about how none of that would mean anything if we didn't first stabilize the scattered-site program.

It turned out to be less about a vote than it was creating the space to build the ship while at sea. The vote was expected to be close, and my vote could very well make the difference. Harold reminded me that we were playing the hand we had been dealt; that the problems of the CHA were "herculean" and that we needed to take the long view. For now, we had to give it a chance to survive.[2]

---

2   To ensure another day for CHA to turn things around, or at least have the chance to, I voted yes. Three months later, federal judge Richard Austin doubled down, appointing the Habitat Company as receiver for the scattered-site program.

4848 N Winthrop was a 300-unit, HUD-owned building in Uptown. It had been a victim of deferred maintenance for years. During the summer of 1987, several aldermen and state legislators held a press conference there demanding action from HUD here and in buildings with similar issues throughout the city.

The other bookend to our meeting was the discussion surrounding the potential loss of ten thousand units of high-rise housing, built in Chicago fifteen to twenty years earlier by private developers with low-interest loans provided by HUD. It is noteworthy that about 40 percent of these units were located in and around Uptown. These buildings had forty-year mortgages, but a little-known clause allowed the owners of the properties to prepay them after twenty years. This would be a hard blow to a city already facing a severe affordable-housing crisis. And Chicago was not alone in this dilemma; indeed, cities across the country were in the same boat, and the day before our meeting, a report in the *Chicago Tribune* had highlighted the problem. Harold was the cochair of the US Conference of Mayors' Housing Committee, and I wanted to confirm it would be on their agenda.

51.

THE INOUYE RESOLUTION

The next three months would be a whirlwind of activity, with the city council meeting twelve times before our summer break in August. Setting up a ward office and responding to the onslaught of service requests, which ranged from basic survival needs to city services, would require a major learning process. Finding a balance between business at city hall and business in the ward was a top priority and easier said than done.

During city council meetings, ordinances and resolutions introduced by aldermen were read off by the city clerk so they could be referred to a committee for future consideration. It was common for an alderman to request that the rules be suspended to hear a resolution on the spot. Beginning with my first city council meeting, Harold aided me whenever I stood to speak by giving me prompts. If I rose to be acknowledged during the call of the wards, he would say "Alderman Shiller, are you rising to suspend the rules for the immediate consideration of your resolution?" I would say yes. He would then ask if I'd like the clerk to read the resolution. Finally, he would ask if I would like the resolution added to the omnibus,[3] and again I would say yes.

The old guard, true to form, having lost their majority on the city council, looked toward the state legislature to challenge Harold's administration. In late May, Harold asked me to introduce a resolution in city council urging the Illinois General Assembly to stop the passage of various House bills from usurping the city's right to self-government. I wrote the resolution, got seven of my colleagues to sign on as cosponsors, and submitted it. My intention was to request that the rules be suspended for immediate consideration (and a vote) during the part of the meeting where items introduced by members of the city council were read by the city clerk and referred to a committee for consideration.

Harold's appointees to the Office of Intergovernmental Affairs were Jackie Grimshaw as director and Tim Wright as her deputy. I knew them both, having worked with them on elections and policy issues in the years

---

3   All non-controversial city council items were sent to the "omnibus" for a vote to be held at the end of the meeting.

before my election. At the appropriate time during the call of the wards, I rose to speak. Harold recognized me, and while the clerk was reading the resolution, Tim was suddenly by my side, while Jackie was by Harold's side. I can't say what Jackie said to Harold. Whatever it was changed his mind about going forward with the resolution. Tim meanwhile was telling me I shouldn't have introduced a resolution without Intergovernmental Affairs vetting it first. I was furious—and probably totally overreacted. After all, Harold had asked me to do this! In retrospect, I'm pretty sure I was just a cog (a willing one at that) in a series of moves Harold was making to navigate the efforts being made by the remnants of Chicago's political machine to undermine his authority. And most likely Jackie had additional information that informed Harold's change of plans.

But retrospect was not to come for some time, and I needed to be taken seriously. I bided my time and two months later saw my opportunity. Harold had been elected congressman in 1980, in which office he served until he was elected mayor of Chicago in April 1983. I knew he was fond of Senator Daniel Inouye (a Democrat from Hawaii). Inouye was the cochair of the Senate select committee investigating the Iran–Contra affair. This was the same committee that was investigating the sale of guns and drugs by the CIA in Central America. Lieutenant Colonel Ollie North had just completed his testimony on the affair on July 14, and Senator Inouye had had a lot to say.

The city council was meeting the next day. I hastily wrote up a resolution supporting Inouye, got to city council early the next morning, and began gathering signatures of support from my colleagues. The resolution applauded Senator Inouye, in part for his "point that members of the military are required to carry out all *lawful* orders and required, as we demanded in Nuremburg, to disobey *unlawful* orders." We also praised him for his opposition to aid to the Contras and his "refusal to be intimidated or silenced."

This time I would get a cross section of support. Aldermen Roman Pucinski and Eugene Schulter were stalwart members of the Vrdolyak Twenty-Nine. In 1987 Chicago's Polish population was second only to that of Warsaw. Roman was their alderman. He had been alderman of the Forty-First Ward since 1973 and a congressman for fourteen years before that. He had served in the air force in World War II and with Senator Inuouye when they were both US congressmen.

Roman was surprised when I approached his desk. With a fatherly smile, he politely agreed to read my resolution. Telling me how much he liked the senator, he asked me for my pen and signed. I gathered another eleven signatures, but I was running out of time. I had to turn the resolution in so it could be considered, but I wanted at least one more supporter from the former opposition block. I turned to Schulter, my seatmate, showed him Pucinski's signature, and asked for his as well. Hesitantly, he obliged, and I was good to go.

As the clerk got to the Forty-Sixth Ward during the call of the wards, I was prepared. I hadn't told the mayor or Intergovernmental Affairs about the resolution or my intention to have it passed that day. The resolution simply called for the mayor and city council to send Inouye a congratulatory telegram for his remarks at the close of Ollie North's testimony. But I was pretty sure that if he heard the resolution and the names of those who had joined me as sponsors, Harold would appreciate it. Again, at the appropriate time, I stood up and asked to be recognized. Surprised and with a quizzical expression, the mayor did so. Jackie and Tim—bless their hearts—sprang into motion. I requested that the rules be suspended for an immediate consideration of the resolution, that the clerk read it aloud first, including the sponsors, and—somewhat cheekily—requested that the mayor listen while he did so. Jackie was at his side, but as he listened, a smile slowly appeared on his face, turning by the end of the resolution into a grin. Following a brief statement of support by Alderman Pucinski, the resolution was sent to the omnibus.

I had previously scheduled a meeting with the mayor for later that afternoon. Since becoming an alderman, I had grown a newfound respect for the value of time. My meetings with the mayor were well organized. I always had my list prepared, calculated to take no more than ten minutes to get through. Harold greeted me warmly that afternoon. He evidently appreciated my inclusion of aldermen from "the other side of the aisle" on my resolution. After several minutes of reminiscing about Senator Inouye, I finally had to remind him that I had a few things I needed to talk to him about. With a sigh, we moved on. My list was a combination of practical ward matters—from sewers to housing issues to night games at Wrigley Field to items affecting citywide policies.

At the time of my election, three months earlier, we had had two major sewer collapses on each end of the ward. Our goal was to finish

Top: In July 1987, Harold accompanied me on a housing tour of Uptown culminating in a rally where we were greeted with a standing ovation and lots of signs demanding affordable housing (bottom).

the reconstruction of these vital lifelines as soon as possible, and by now there had been a good deal of progress. However, I wanted to be able to inform my constituents of what to look for, and what to ask for if they had further issues with basement flooding. For years, the sewer department had been run as part of the patronage system. Before Harold's administration, getting information about anything sewer-related had been like breaking through the seals of a confidential memo. Things were changing, but I wanted to help that along by bringing the sewer department out to the community to explain directly to the people affected what was going on with their sewers: Did they have sufficient capacity? What was their condition? Were there new techniques that could help them with problems they might be facing?

Wrigley Field was located on the boundary of the Forty-Sixth Ward, and my constituents were split over whether to allow the Cubs to install lights so that night games could be scheduled. This had been an important topic during the campaign. In spite of legitimate concerns, it seemed inevitable that lights would be approved. Nevertheless, this was an opportunity for Harold to affirm his support for neighborhood protections.

My conversation with Harold about housing was also important, given that displacement was such a big issue in the ward. Harold was from the heart of the "Black Belt," on the city's South Side. It was going through a serious process of abandonment. He wanted to understand how it could be that any development could be bad. This was a conversation we had during most of our meetings that led to his commitment to work with me on solutions to the displacement that so many people were facing in developing communities throughout the city—especially in Uptown. While we worked on developing owner-occupied affordable housing in Uptown, we needed a citywide affordable-housing agenda. A tenants' bill of rights, along with other tenant protections, had passed during his first term, and these needed to be protected.

As our conversation progressed, I was quickly getting through my list. Then I noticed him shaking his head. "What?" I asked. "Is something wrong?" "No," he responded. "It's just that your questions are unlike any I get from any other alderman." This inevitably led to a conversation about the nature of politics. I disdained politics and considered the level of opportunism that usually accompanied career politicians to be an anathema. He, on the other hand, loved being a politician and relished it as a challenge.

52.

AVERY LAWSUIT SETTLEMENT ENTANGLED IN HAROLD'S LAST DAYS

By 1987, negotiations in the Avery suit had progressed to the point of agreement with the city. As an alderman, I was looking for opportunities to rehabilitate existing housing and create new housing that would be safe, affordable, and household-size appropriate for the people who had lived there before.

I was excited to be the vice chair of the City Council Committee on Housing, and I was looking forward to the introduction and debate of the legislation I had committed to introducing to address displacement and gentrification. In the '60s and '70s, Uptown had seen its share of arson for profit, salmonella poisoning, unsuitable living conditions, and little if any security on the part of unscrupulous landlords. The promise of the '80s was that there would be relief.

I was engaged in multiple conversations with developers and housing advocates. In addition to flushing out new ideas for creating housing, we focused on stabilizing existing housing stock so that it would be safe and affordable. Our immediate goal was the stabilization of the housing market in the heart of Uptown, while creating political will in the city to change housing policies to prioritize affordability, access, and quality. It was to be a never-ending battle.

During the prior four years, a young developer arrived on the scene with a notion of transforming the Uptown community by creating a series of smaller historic districts. Buena Park Historic District was Randy Langer's first effort to redefine the heart of Uptown in real estate–friendly terms with the hope of gentrifying the area.[4] With the help of Alderman Orbach, this was quickly accomplished. Then came Sheridan Park—the area immediately to the north. Essentially this constituted a huge chunk

---

4   The Buena Park Historic District bordered the Graceland Cemetery, where several famous industrialists are buried, and included most of the area between Montrose and Irving Park Road from the cemetery to Lake Michigan.

of the heart of Uptown. By redefining these neighborhoods, many living in the heart of Uptown (where poor and working families lived and struggled) felt they were intentionally targeted for displacement.

Langer's father was a well-heeled realtor in the Lincoln Park and Lakeview communities to the south of Uptown. He had deep pockets and a reputation for racial discrimination in the operation of his rental units. By 1987, Randy Langer had been buying up buildings with twelve to eighteen units of three- and four-bedroom apartments for several years. He evicted the tenants, rehabbed them, tripled (and sometimes quadrupled) the rent, and left them vacant when no one was prepared to pay the asking price. There were buildings sprinkled through the heart of Uptown in which no one had lived for years. His intent was not hidden. Using his dad's deep pockets, he had held the land until he had changed who lived on it.

If he couldn't rehab a building, he would buy it and tear it down—again, removing housing that was previously home to some of the large families living in the heart of Uptown. With the new historic district designations, his long-term plan was clear: take control of the land, make it seem like a different place by calling the area where this land was located anything but "Uptown," and make a killing.

Following Orbach's election as alderman in 1983, Langer had had a good friend in the city council. Anything Randy wanted, he got. In addition to the new historic-district designations, this included a zoning change for a large lot located at the corner of Magnolia and Wilson. My first act as alderman was to stop this zoning change, as it had not yet passed the full city council.

Randy Langer hired Phil Krone, a political operative, to engage in a media campaign designed to discredit and ridicule me. He launched a full court press, charging that I was a development blocker and had only the basest of motives. Meanwhile he engaged in good old-fashioned Chicago machine politics to block my efforts to turn seventeen vacant land parcels in the heart of Uptown into owner-occupied three-flats.

Once the media attack against me began, colleagues I counted on as allies to address Chicago's housing crisis started falling away, while the mayor questioned the need to control development. He was from the South Side, the home of the historic Black Belt and communities that faced extraordinary divestment during his lifetime. Again, he asked:

"How can any development be bad?" I described conditions in Uptown—which rang familiar to him—and put them in the context of the north lakefront. We were sandwiched between single-family homes on the west and new lakefront high-rises to the east. Poor people would not be welcome for long, especially those who lived in some of the few integrated, racially and economically diverse census tracts in the city. That this was about the different places our communities fell on the cycle of speculation that was Chicago's real estate marketplace ultimately made sense to him.[5]

He promised the full attention of Housing Commissioner Brenda Gaines[6] to my legislative agenda at the beginning of the new year. And he pledged his full support for my proposal to have the city use its tax-reactivation agreement with the Cook County Board to acquire seventeen vacant lots in Uptown that were tax delinquent. These lots would then be available for one dollar each for the construction of a three-flat residential building on each. The buildings would be sold to first-time homeowners, and applicants with a history of living and/or working in the community would get priority. The expectation was that working families would be able to afford to buy because rent from the two additional apartments would help cover mortgage and maintenance costs.

At Langer's direction and on his dime, lobbyist Phil Krone went to work. By November everything was in place for the lots to be transferred to the City of Chicago. At the last minute, however, following intensive lobbying by Krone on Langer's behalf, the Cook County Board Finance Committee (chaired by John Stroger) deferred action on the tax reactivation for these lots.

Harold had assured me that all was a go. But suddenly Uptown had become a piece of the negotiations for the Democratic Party's dream ticket. George Dunne was then the president of both the Cook County

---

5 The cycle of speculation is the movement from investment to divestment, then to speculation, reinvestment, and gentrification, and ultimately back to divestment (although depending on the economy, clearly this step could be jumped altogether, cycling the cost of housing higher and higher without any concern or consideration of the needs for shelter for those with fewer resources).

6 Brenda Gaines came to the city from HUD with extensive experience in creating affordable housing. She was Harold's first housing commissioner. In January 1988 it was expected that she would become the mayor's chief of staff.

Board and the Cook County Democratic Party. This was the fall of 1987, and the Democratic Party was preparing its slate for the primary elections to be held in March 1988. There was talk of a "dream ticket" agreement between Harold Washington and George Dunne. These Uptown lots became a bargaining chip.

During what would turn out to be Harold's last city council meeting, he called me up to the podium along with Rob Mier, his point person for Wrigley Field negotiations. First, he told me to be patient, that he was working on getting Dunne to complete the tax-reactivation transfer. He would follow up with me himself. Then he turned to Mier and told him to meet with me before our next scheduled city council meeting about Wrigley Field. "She has a list of protections that I want to make sure you include."

November 24, 1987, was my fortieth birthday. Just before going to bed, I received a call at home from Harold wishing me a happy birthday. "Can you meet me at eleven tomorrow morning?" he asked. "I have worked things out with Dunne."

On November 25, on my way upstairs to the fifth floor, Rob jumped in the elevator with me, worried that we hadn't yet discussed the Wrigley Field negotiations and that I was on my way to meet with the mayor. I assured him that our plan to meet that Friday was still on, and that I was meeting with Harold about housing, not lights at Wrigley Field. Relieved and reassured, he left me to enter the mayor's office, two minutes late for my 11:00 a.m. appointment.

As I entered the main entrance to the mayor's office on the fifth floor of city hall, all hell seemed to break loose. Delores Woods, Harold's personal secretary, came running out to the front desk, grabbed the phone, spoke into it frantically, and ran back to her office. The sergeant stationed at the front desk asked me to take a seat, as commotion outside the door caused me to turn my head and see Department of Health doctors Linda Murray and David Marder and a paramedic running toward the side entrance to the mayor's inner office with a stretcher. Moments later, Alderman Dick Mell came smashing through the front door, which had been closed moments earlier by Ernie Barefield, Harold's chief of staff, who came out to tell me the mayor had collapsed. Mell, a proud member of the Vrdolyak Twenty-Nine, was gleeful, almost giddy, as he accosted Ernie and demanded to know if the mayor was alive or dead. Hours before Harold was pronounced dead, this would be the first shot fired in the foray to determine the next mayor of Chicago.

. . . .

53.

AFTERMATH AND EFFECT OF HAROLD'S DEATH

Following the announcement of Harold Washington's death, political chaos reigned. Thanksgiving, the next day, was a somber holiday. His body lay in state in the lobby of city hall all weekend as over a million people passed by to say their final goodbyes. The core of Harold's supporters rallied at the University of Illinois Pavilion—a symbolic location, for it was there that Harold's fledgling campaign had gained respectability in 1983, when the sixteen-thousand-seat pavilion had been filled to capacity for a campaign rally on Dr. Martin Luther King's birthday. Again, the pavilion would be filled, but the atmosphere this time around was one of sadness, loss, and anger. Politicians of all stripes were putting their ducks in a row as his funeral was planned for that Monday. The next day the city council would choose his successor.

Upon Harold's death, David Orr, alderman of the Forty-Ninth ward, became the acting mayor. Elected by the city council in April 1987 to be the vice mayor, he would remain in that position as a caretaker until the full city council met on December 1 "for the sole and only purpose of electing an acting mayor of the city of Chicago."

The coalition that had elected Harold Washington mayor was torn asunder in the days following his death. The top two likely candidates to succeed him were Eugene Sawyer and Tim Evans, alderman of the Sixth and Fourth Wards respectively. Evans was the Finance Committee chair and Harold's floor leader. Sawyer, president pro tem of the city council, had supported Harold in his 1977 campaign for mayor and been the first ward committeeman to back Harold's run in 1983.

The white aldermen formerly in the block of twenty-nine did not have the numbers alone to pick one of their own to succeed Harold. But there had always been tension in the broad umbrella that constituted Harold's coalition. The old guard successfully went to work picking off votes. The only way they could succeed was by having a candidate who had been part of that coalition. Sawyer reluctantly became that candidate. Those of us supporting Evans felt that this was a mistake—that the majority of aldermen supporting Sawyer were looking for a place-holder for Rich Daley, who they really wanted, until the special election for mayor that would be held in 1989.

Tens of thousands of people showed up to city hall on December 1 to observe the council's actions. The meeting went on for hours, interrupted on occasion by recesses to allow for backroom dealing and lobbying. This was a battle over the future direction of the city, in which it was clear to many of us that the effort to choose Sawyer was an attempt by the old guard to break the Washington coalition. Indeed, their intent was to turn back the clock on Harold's reforms and return to machine-style politics. To others, it was an effort to keep the mayor's seat Black. Sawyer, they said, could and would do that while keeping the old guard at bay. Early on December 2, he was elected acting mayor.

The next year and a half were chaotic. Feelings were raw. The city's budget needed passage. Harold had proposed a structural change in how the property tax was calculated to allow what he had expected to be a fairer and more consistent capture of these funds. The new majority in the city council immediately killed it.

Meanwhile, he had also offered a reorganization of several departments. His department reorganization remained in the budget that was passed, though it arguably lacked the support or political will needed to ensure the affected infrastructure departments would have what they needed to properly do their jobs.[7]

7　There is an argument that this lack of attention to detail led to a crisis in 1972, when repair work on a bridge over the Chicago River caused a breach, flooding downtown basements, telecommunications facilities, and Chicago's underground pedway with an estimated 250 million gallons of water. It took weeks to recover from the incident, which cost about $2 billion in 1992 dollars.

This was also the beginning of the 1988 political season. The Illinois presidential primary was coming up in March. While Jesse Jackson's second campaign for president would have some visibility in Chicago, there was no "Vote with Purpose" campaign mailing that year. Harold's coalition was being torn asunder. Sawyer was in a tough position (although as far as many of us were concerned, he had put himself there), and despite a number of efforts to continue some of what Mayor Washington had started, he was in the end pretty much a caretaker.

The deal that had elected him acting mayor appeared to come with an agreement to stop an Avery settlement, as well as our proposed tax reactivation proposal and creation of new housing in the Forty-Sixth ward. Sawyer had enough aldermen on his team to stop the vote that toppled this effort, but he declined to do so. After all, how better to send a message to the aldermen (that included me) who had voted for Tim Evans to be the mayor over him?

Chicago's two baseball teams—their rivalries, their successes, their failures—are the stuff that dreams and heartbreaks are made of. Wrigley Field, home of the Cubs, stood across the street from the Forty-Sixth Ward boundary, but it was physically in the Forty-Fourth Ward.[8] Because the ballpark, one of the oldest in the nation, did not have lights, the Cubs could not play night games at home. With the ballpark located on a single square block surrounded by single-family homes, two-flats, and court-way buildings, neighbors were skeptical. Thousands of fans walking through their neighborhood on game days already meant loud noise, litter, drunkenness, parking chaos, and traffic congestion. They had known about the ballpark when they moved there and were okay with the status quo. But the thought of additional security concerns as well after dark drove some of them into fits of hysteria. By 1987, a campaign against the addition of lights at Wrigley Field had reached a climax.

Early in his mayoralty Harold had asked Bobby Rush, alderman of the Second Ward, as chair of the Committee on Energy, Environment Protection, and Public Utilities, to convene all the stakeholders to determine the best way forward. Rush had done so, establishing a task force that included local businesses, block clubs and neighborhood

---

8   When ward boundaries changed after the 1990 census, people living in the Forty-Seventh Ward would also be impacted during home games.

organizations, and the Cubs. I had joined Alderman Bernie Hansen and other elected officials on this task force following my election in 1987.

No mayor wanted to lose this iconic baseball team, and the Cubs were threatening to leave if they couldn't get lights. The community became polarized on the issue. Nevertheless, Rush had made a great deal of progress sorting through the pros and cons and the impacts of lights on the community. By the time I arrived, there had been enough ideas and suggestions to know a myriad of ways to protect the community. I brought these to Harold, whose response was to tell Rob Mier to include my list in any ordinance to be presented before the council.

Sawyer had been acting mayor for three months when the Cubs got their long-sought-after wish. An ordinance authorizing night games at Wrigley Field passed in February 1988. While most of the neighborhood protections were rejected and excluded from the ordinance, the political pressure to provide relief remained. Permit parking, additional cleanup after each game, neighborhood security, additional parking, and remote parking were successfully negotiated before every baseball season while I was alderman.

Citywide, people were divided. Many were angry at the turn of events, setting the stage for a series of elections where Richard M. Daley successfully faced Black political figures who had been part of Mayor Washington's coalition.[9] I supported them all.

---

9   Mayor Eugene Sawyer and Alderman Tim Evans in 1989; Alderman Danny K. Davis and Judge R. Eugene Pincham in 1991; Joseph E. Gardner, commissioner of the Metropolitan Water Reclamation District and my boss (along with Mercedes Mallette) at Mayor Washington's Political Education Project (PEP) a decade earlier, in 1995; and Congressman Bobby L. Rush, former BPP leader, in 1999.

54.

A TENT CITY

In March 1980, Jane Byrne, who had then been mayor for just under a year, had been under pressure by demands from residents and the Heart of Uptown Coalition to respond to the crisis of incessant residential fires, capped by the firefighters' strike. In response, Byrne had urged the Chicago Housing Authority to purchase property in Uptown—but not before exacting a political price. With the race between Richard M. Daley and Ed Burke for the Democratic spot on the ballot for Cook County state's attorney, Byrne had offered to have the CHA buy land for housing in Uptown in exchange for some number of signatures on petitions for one of the men running. We viewed elections as survival programs, and we didn't have a horse in the state's attorney race—both candidates were the same as far as we were concerned. So we had said sure.

CHA had subsequently purchased three adjacent vacant fifty-foot lots on the 4400 block of Malden to build scattered-site housing. The lots, which had previously been the home of at least eighteen large families living in three six-flats, happened to be next door to where I lived.

At the time, the CHA's scattered-site program had been in receivership, meaning the Habitat Company, as the receiver, had been tasked with the responsibility of getting scattered-site housing built. On Malden they had put up a fancy wrought iron fence and let the land sit for years.

In October 1988, just as the weather was turning, a coalition of affordable housing organizations and activists, including the Chicago-Gary Area Union for the Homeless, the Forty-Sixth Ward Fair Share Organization, and the Jesus People USA, organized a "tent city" on this land, demanding action. From their perspective, this was an ideal location for such a project. It was public land. It was designated to provide housing for low-income people. It was safe because it could be secured. The fence had a gate, and the homeless people staying there brought a lock and chain with them, giving them the ability to control access.

For six days and nights, up to seventy-five men and women and a handful of children stayed in homemade tents and shanties, forming their own community and protecting each other. The majority of them went to work during the day (most often as day laborers), while the school-age children went to school. For the most part, they were homeless because they couldn't afford a month's rent. It was not uncommon for someone to stay several nights a week at the Wilson Men's Club, or some other hotel that rented rooms by the night, and the rest of the week on the street.

It was early October, and the nights were cool, but they were able to recycle wood by scouring alleys during the day for furniture and tree limbs that had been discarded. They were able to keep warm by burning these items in metal drums they had found and brought to the site. Tents and wood structures were erected to provide shelter. The tent city received water from the tenants on the first floor of the adjacent building, and food from the Jesus People and friendly neighborhood restaurants. They provided their own security so they felt safe, and held impromptu meetings and musical "jam sessions" with their supporters.

The media came to tell their story. In response many people stopped by, bringing food, blankets, and clothing. Many neighborhood residents came and showed their support as well. Some of my neighbors across the street, however, were not happy. After a few days, their complaints to me, to CHA, and to the receiver began to mount.

One person told me, "Don't I have the right to be able to go outside and not see people camped out in front of my house?" They were not pleased with my response that "the rights of people to have decent, safe, affordable housing trumped the small amount of discomfort that came from having to see the homeless literally from their front window." After all, everyone staying at tent city would have preferred to be housed in a warm and safe apartment.

Five days into their stay—and after two major rainstorms—I received notice from Habitat point person Phil Hickman that the tent city residents would be evicted the next day. Everyone got together to decide what to do. The Jesus People, who lived nearby and often provided shelter to homeless people, agreed to take the remaining food and clothing that had been donated for safekeeping. Representatives were then chosen to join me the next day and refuse to leave, challenging Habitat to have us arrested for trespassing. The charges, we hoped, would lead to a jury trial where we could put the city's low-income housing crisis before the court, along with its denial and neglect of its homeless population.

Top: Tent City, 4445 N Malden, October 1989. Bottom: From right to left: John Trott, Vinnie Strickland, David Scondras, and me, being escorted by police to a police van. (Jeri Miglietta was with us but not shown in photo.)

That evening I attended a meeting convened by gay and lesbian community leaders decrying a series of hate crimes in Lakeview. I bumped into David Scondras. Our paths had crossed before and I knew David, an openly gay alderman from Boston, to be an unapologetic advocate for affordable housing. We spoke briefly about the evening's agenda, and I shared with him my intentions to take a stand the following day when it was time for the eviction. He offered to join us.

In the morning he joined me, Jeri Miglietta (representing the Forty-Sixth Ward Fair Share Organization), John Trott (representing the Jesus People), and Vinnie Strickland (representing the Coalition for the Homeless). The first thing that morning, all the food and everyone's belongings were packed up and moved. At the designated time, a phalanx of police, decked out in dress uniform, walked down the street until they got to the gate at the front of the property, where they cut the lock and entered. Phil Hickman read an order for everyone to leave or face arrest for trespassing. After a few brief statements, the four of us remained, and we were carted away by two separate paddy wagons—one for the women and one for the men.

We never got our trial: all the charges were ultimately dropped. A few years later, seventeen families moved into their new scattered-site townhomes on the lot.

. . . .

55.

HUMAN RIGHTS LEGISLATION

As campaigns ramped up for the 1989 special mayoral election, demands for a gay-rights ordinance were ramping up as well. The first gay-rights ordinance had been introduced to the city council in 1973, but it had not made it to a vote until 1986. Although championed by Harold Washington, in an emotional council session, it had failed to pass. At the time, I had been involved in lobbying members of the council who I had known and worked with on many issues over the years, and had shared the deep disappointment felt in the LGBT community.

In December 1988 the Human Rights Ordinance, rebranded in name and in fact, passed the city council. The city of Chicago's municipal code now rejected discrimination in housing and employment based on sexual orientation, "source of income," age, disability, parental status, and military discharge status, as well as race, color, sex, religion, national origin, ancestry, and marital status, which were previously protected.

Forty-Fourth Ward alderman Bernie Hansen represented "Boystown," the part of the city where predominately gay businesses flourished. He had been part of the Vrdolyak Twenty-Nine and a supporter of Eugene Sawyer to succeed Washington as the mayor. He would lobby his side of the aisle as I lobbied mine. But the credit for passage must go to years of struggle and the four activists—Laurie Dittman, Art Johnston, Rick Garcia, and Jon-Henri Damski, dubbed "the gang of four"—who had provided the leadership to get the ordinance passed.

While these efforts had scored a success, a lot of work was left to be done. The city remained divided on gay rights, and the ordinance had managed to pass by broadening its content, thereby bringing enough aldermen on board. Getting their constituents on board would take more time. For now, this was seen as a wink to a constituency that was primarily white. It would also be some time before there would be widespread acknowledgment of the rights of gay people of color, and even longer for the transgender community.

AIDS complicated things. The crisis was alive and well in Chicago, and it was hitting the gay community hard. Fear and misinformation were everywhere. It was still assumed that this was a "gay disease" that was transmitted through any physical contact, leading many to treat anyone with the disease as a leper. Those who had been infected through the use of needles or from a medically required blood transfusion were treated no differently.

I lived on a street where a cul-de-sac had been created to allow for the construction of the Sunnyside Mall around the time I had moved to Chicago. In 1985, on the other side of the cul-de-sac was a single-family home on temporary loan to a grassroots effort to provide hospice for people living with AIDS. Their presence was kept quiet, as this was early in the crisis, and people with AIDS faced a great deal of discrimination based on a combination of homophobia and racism, further fueled by fear of the disease. I had come across them while canvassing, and visited often. The nonprofit Chicago House grew from this effort and would eventually expand their operation to include affordable housing for families with a member living with AIDS, as well as multiple support services.

56.

MAKING DEMOCRACY WORK

I had been an alderman for barely a year. We had a ward service office to organize and a housing agenda to fight for. School reform and Harold Washington's anti-gang initiative were critical cornerstones to addressing institutional racism. This was the time to build the infrastructure necessary for any of these objectives to be realized.

During my first run for alderman in the '70s, again and again, people living along the lakefront had asked me if I could deliver city services. "If you're elected, will our streetlights stay on? Will we continue to have adequate bus service? Will the potholes get repaired?" These inquiries stayed with me. In my gut I knew that I would only be able to win a second term if I had a ward office that was accessible to everyone and that solved problems. While many people just wanted to keep the minimum of what they had, I was sure they were not getting what they should. In the heart of Uptown there were few expectations because little had been done for so long.

There were hundreds of abandoned cars in every community of the ward that had been sitting on our streets for months. The majority of these were in Uptown. They took up parking spaces and provided shelter to rats and wild animals. Animal control had not been seen in Uptown for who knows how long. Packs of feral cats and dogs were common. Rat holes were obvious in our parkways. Street lighting was inconsistent, and only the rare alley had any lighting at all. Streets that had been recently resurfaced already had cuts in them for utility work or water service.

My first order of business was to change all that. Initially with the support of the Washington administration, our new Streets and Sanitation ward superintendent Sammy DeSosa hit the ground running. But in the first seven months of my first term, I had quickly learned how connected everything was. The summer proved an opportunity for Randy Langer and his media guru, Phil Krone, to blast me daily. My best defense, I had already discovered, was to take my case directly to the people. We organized forums with city department heads on every subject we got inquiries about. Starting with sewers (each end of the ward was recovering from major sewer collapses), Teresa Sagun, the department's chief engineer, provided the details on their condition in our ward and what to expect from the department. Police superintendent Fred Rice, Police Board member Nancy Jefferson, Park District board members Dr. Margaret Burroughs and Sylvia Herrera, and Chicago Transit Authority board member Natalia Delgado all joined us giving many ward residents their first opportunity to speak directly with the people whose actions directly affected their lives.

One of my first legislative acts had been to put a hold on a zoning request that my predecessor had tried to rush through before the election results were known. There had been a prominent vacant lot at the corner of Wilson and Magnolia in the heart of Uptown. Years before, it had housed an apartment building with retail on the ground floor. Langer wanted the zoning increased so he could build a market-rate high-rise apartment building.

Langer had already purchased many of the corner apartment buildings in "Sheridan Park," leaving them vacant until he could get much higher rents. And he had been behind a rebranding of a chunk of the heart of Uptown for the sole purpose of expanding the real estate value, in an effort to move poor and working people out of the neighborhood. It was apparent that when it came to forging a path that would lead to development without displacement, Langer would be a major obstacle.

In the heart of Uptown, this was about who got to decide the future of our community. It would not be enough to stop the zoning change; we needed a process that would be a model for input. Thus, the Forty-Sixth Ward zone committees were born.

I was wary of what was known in liberal circles on the North Side as "representative democracy." I appreciated the effort that was based on a notion of representative government—something Dick Simpson had experimented with when he was alderman of the Forty-Fourth Ward in the '70s. However, I had concerns. I wanted to go beyond the volunteer effort of a few who were recruited to represent their neighbors in zoning and land-use decisions. I wanted a structure to engage community volunteers to be vehicles through which more people would gain a voice.

Breaking the ward into five sectors, we invited anyone who was interested in serving to apply. Each sector would have a zone committee of five people. I was looking for volunteers who were willing and able (and

With Dr. Margaret Burroughs (Park District Board).

who had the time) to do three things: first, to look at a given proposal from a broader perspective than just their own, taking into account how the breadth of people in their boundary area would be affected; second, to participate in a process that engaged people through surveys, forums, or other activities of the committee's creation to ensure the greatest input; and third, to make a decision that incorporated the first two. My goal was to follow the lead of each committee. I expected we might not always agree, but I hoped and expected that there could ultimately be consensus.

The zone committees were among the most energizing initiatives of my first term. I interviewed over 150 people who were interested in participating. I made no distinction if someone supported me or not; I was only interested in their ability to accomplish the three things I needed them to do. Once the zoning committees were filled, we went to work, beginning with a ward-wide meeting of all their members. I wanted everyone to be on the same page, with the same knowledge of the zoning laws as well as my three requirements.

The committees were convened as needed. Most of the proposals they needed to address were fairly straightforward and could be addressed with a survey and/or community meeting.

Top: With Nancy Jefferson (Police Board). Bottom: With Marc Kaplan, Paul Siegel, and Jeri Miglietta during a tour of forty-six ward parks with Park District Board member Sylvia Herrera.

Just prior to the elections in 1986, Orbach had managed to get funding approved for a library in the southern end of Uptown. I didn't question the need for this library—just his chosen location for it. He favored a fairly small lot that would only allow for a five-thousand-square-foot building. That seemed like a lost opportunity and a mistake. I convened the zone committee for that area to find an alternative location that would be supported by its neighbors. Their first choice was the Palacio Theater, where we had held our rally supporting the farmworkers some thirteen years earlier. By now it had long been shuttered and was not in very good condition, but it still held some promise. However, it didn't work out, and we ultimately chose the location where the library stands today, at Sheridan and Buena—a twelve-thousand-square-foot property on which we could build a library of adequate size to provide space for adults and children, a computer lab, a conference room, and a large community meeting space, as well as necessary office spaces.

All public buildings constructed in the city are required to have some public art. I wanted the selection of the art for this library to be done through the zone committee. It was important that the artist chosen had some link to the community. My recommendation of Robin Whitespear, a master at macramé, came from the zone committee and was ultimately approved by the city. I knew and respected Robin, and was certain his art would be a great addition to the library. When we first met Robin in 1972, he had been an alcoholic often found in the gutter. Marc Zalkin had befriended him and spent a lot of time sitting on the curb of whatever street he found Robin at. When Robin later became sober, he created amazing macramé pieces. Also an actor, he became deeply committed to working with fellow alcoholics as they transitioned their lives into productive pursuits. I was overjoyed by his choice and rewarded by the artwork he created for the Uptown Library.

Many of the proposals that the zone committees were asked to consider were pretty straightforward, as the selection of the library's location had been. Others, not so much. The Chicago Transit Authority's elevated red line ran adjacent to abandoned railroad tracks in a two-block stretch between Irving Park and Montrose. There was housing to the east of the CTA rail line, and the wall of the historic Graceland Cemetery was to the west of the abandoned tracks. An area the approximate width of a city street lay between the two sets of tracks. Anyone who parked behind their homes, as well as garbage trucks servicing the homes east of the tracks, used the space under the

CTA tracks as an alley. However, there was no drainage under these tracks. East of the CTA tracks and midway between Montrose and Irving Park at Buena, there was a playground that had been in serious disarray for years. Dumping had become a common occurrence in the area between the two tracks, including of building materials from construction sites. Recently there had been a rash of violent deaths there as well—all women.

This had been a campaign issue during the election. The priorities for my supporters were improvements to the playground and alley. The development of a park for the area between the two tracks was a higher priority for those who tended to be supportive of my opponent. I was deeply concerned about the trend of women being found dead there. This was not well known and didn't seem to be being treated too seriously—another example of disrespect toward women that I would take on.

I reached out to the Park District as well as the water and sewer departments about the needed improvements. While it was clear that the Park District had responsibility for the play lot and its condition, I was hoping to interest them in the passive park. I was not getting a lot of positive feedback, as we were talking big bucks that weren't in anyone's budget. Then I got a call from the Chicago Cubs. They were looking to expand parking for Wrigley Field and wanted to do so in the area being explored for the passive park.

This was not the first request for that land that my office had gotten, so the zone committee was familiar with the area and the complex set of issues that came with it. They had already rejected a proposal by the Department of Streets and Sanitation to use this area as a temporary site for storing abandoned cars. (That was a no-brainer.) Now they were called on to look at the new request. I saw an opportunity to get everything we wanted if we could limit how much area the Cubs actually got, while getting them to ante up on a good portion of the costs for everything else.

The passive park had been named Challenger Park by one of its original supporters. I put him on the zone committee, where he passionately protected space to realize his dream that had been inspired in part by the tragic explosion of the space shuttle *Challenger*. Christa McAuliffe, who died in the accident, would have been the first teacher in space, drawing additional attention to the shuttle's takeoff and consequent explosion. He had wanted to honor her and the rest of the crew that had perished.

The zone committee in this area, led by Romelle Moore Robinson, took on this task with remarkable enthusiasm. They insisted on holding a series of hearings in the community with representatives from the CTA, the Park District, all of the city departments affected, and the president of the Chicago Cubs, Don Grenesko, present at them all. Grenesko hadn't been known to make many public appearances, which outside of the ballpark had been rare.

Meanwhile they surveyed the community, getting input on each of the issues that needed addressing and the particular impediments we might encounter. If we were able to find a way to put a sewer and water drainage under the L tracks, was the CTA on board for making this an actual alley under their tracks? Would the people living adjacent to the L tracks continue to have access to parking? What would be included in a new play lot? How would the area be illuminated at night? What would be done with the crumbling wall that protected the cemetery and was owned by them? Could the Cubs just get access to a portion of the area they coveted and allow for alternative activities when the ball team was not playing at home? Could we still have space for Challenger Park, and if so, what would that look like and who would maintain it?

This was obviously important to the Cubs, and with this agreement to negotiate and to attend the hearings, the rest of the city agencies and departments came along for the ride. I doubt anyone thought we would be able to craft a solution that would address all of the concerns on the table, but the zone committee came through. This was an opportunity to craft a comprehensive solution to a complex set of issues, including some conflict, controversy, and divergent priorities and it was realized successfully. In the end, the Cubs agreed to pay 60 percent of the costs of the entire project in return for receiving control over the southern 40 percent of the area between the L tracks and the cemetery wall. They agreed as well to allow for community use of this area when the ball team was not playing at home.[10] The CTA gave approval for the alley

---

10 The nature of this use would change over time. Initially they allowed for basketball and soccer to be programmed in this space by the Park District's Gill Park Field House. Years later it became available for

and worked out agreements for access by all of the residential properties to the east of the tracks. The Park District agreed to the rehabilitation of the play lot and the development and future maintenance of Challenger Park on the remaining 60 percent of the area between the L tracks and the cemetery wall. Ultimately the cemetery agreed to properly maintain their fence that was near collapse.

A little farther north, another zone committee was charged with the task of determining the future of the Sunnyside Mall. Should it stay a mall, or should we return it to a street? Should we build a new play lot on Magnolia, around the block from the mall, where there had been a play lot that was abandoned years ago? I lived a half block from the mall on the street that had been cul-de-sacced to make way for it. Personally, I was in favor of returning the mall to a street and creating more parking, but I kept my opinion to myself. It was up to the zone committee to create a community process and come to a conclusion. I was there to be a resource and negotiate for the resources to effect their vision. They conducted a community survey, distributing surveys among all the households on the blocks immediately surrounding the mall and potential new play lot. Just over one hundred surveys were received.

The night the zone committee met to receive them at the Uptown Hull House, located on Beacon Street just down the street from the mall, a group of community residents joined us to hear the results. I had expected a large number of people would want to have the mall returned to parking, but I had no idea what anyone actually thought; I was determined to leave this up to the zone committee so that my own feelings would not influence the outcome.

I was not surprised that everyone who came to observe was suspicious of the outcome before it was read. On one hand, those from my base were sure the others whom they knew as gentrifiers were going to have their way. On the other, those who were largely middle class and not particularly fond of me were sure my base of supporters were going to have theirs. All together an equally divided group of maybe twenty to thirty people formed a circle around me. As a representative from the zone committee handed me the results to read out loud, they leaned in, as if getting ready for a fight. All but four of the respondents had chosen

---

community residents to receive permits allowing them to park overnight. That was its status when I left the city council.

Top: Summer youth workers in 1989 cleaned up an empty lot that was around the corner from the mall and owned by the city. Their sign says "No Drugs! No Violence! Respect Zone. Bottom: Pickets outside Truman College on a day Mayor Richard M. Daley was expected: "Mr. Mayor—transfer our lot."

to keep the mall. All the air seemed to leave the room. Ready to pounce, everyone checked themselves, taking a moment to digest what they had heard and then sighing with relief, if not disbelief.

It would take me winning the 1991 election, and some not so sub-tle community action, to get the desired result: a new expanded play lot on Magnolia along with the greening of the mall. Each became a community design project. Condos, scattered-site housing, market-rate housing, and some still-affordable privately owned housing all faced the mall. Teachers at the local school (a few of whom lived in the area), their students, families from the scattered sites, and a handful of condo owners participated in a multiyear attempt to connect them all in a joint project in the community where they all lived.

In the westernmost area of the ward, the zone committee was charged with addressing a request to make a quarter-mile stretch of Grace Street one way, going westbound. The street was used as an alternative route for many people going to Wrigley Field for home games and was relatively narrow; while cars were parked on both sides, two cars could barely pass one another. Making it one-way would make one lane of traffic more manageable. They felt having the flow of traffic be westbound would minimize the impact of traffic on this residential street.

The zone committee decided to conduct a postcard survey. Prepaid postcards along with a fact sheet were dropped at every apartment and house in a two-block area surrounding the potentially affected blocks. The surveys were returned with the majority of respondents agreeing to the change. The street was then made one-way westbound, and all hell broke loose. I asked the zone committee to convene a community meeting to give everyone another opportunity to voice their concerns. More than a hundred people showed up at a neighborhood church. With people talking over one another, it was difficult at times to hear what anyone was saying. Emotions were high when an elderly man who had been relatively quiet spoke out saying, "Just turn the damn street one-way eastbound." The room got suddenly quiet before person after person suggested that would probably work for them. Lesson learned—majority input, informed by an array of experiences and coupled with common sense, would go further toward a true solution than just a majority sentiment.

In some zones, there was little for the committees to do. I experimented with having the zone committees weigh in on loading zones or handicapped parking requests, but over time the meetings were becoming perfunctory, and the amount of time interviewing people to sit on a committee that didn't always have something to meet about didn't seem to be very productive.

By my third term, I established a ward-wide zone committee. Their responsibility was to help me get at the truth of the matter, sort out the stakeholders and who was most affected, identify potential solutions, and give me the best possible information to make a decision. I learned a lot about process from the early practice of the zone committees. Going forward, this community process would do a great to deal to inform my approach to a wide variety of issues.

. . . .

57.

DOMESTIC VIOLENCE

Women, alone and scared, in emergency rooms bruised and beaten; women who suffer at home with internal and external bruises fearful of further violence, afraid to go out to local school council meetings or block and community activities—women—fearful, afraid, alone, in hiding. A terrible waste of human potential. A serious attack against the respect and self-respect of the core of over one-quarter of our households.[11]

My personal experience is that most women, regardless of race, ethnicity, income level, or nation of origin, experience sexual or domestic violence in their lifetime. We struggled with domestic violence in the Intercommunal Survival Committee, and while we committed unhesitatingly to ending it, as a group we were conflicted about how best to address it. Public policy regarding rape, sexual assault against minors, and domestic violence was a joke. DNA was just beginning to be considered legitimate evidence by the courts, and even when rape kits were taken, they were rarely analyzed. False rape charges, especially against

---

11 Preface to my statement calling for the creation of a subcommittee on domestic violence to the City Council Committee on Human Rights and Consumer Protection in June 1989.

March opposing violence against women.

Black men, were expected by many in the Black community—situations in which the falsely accused could rarely be exonerated without the tool of DNA evidence, too often sending the innocent to jail while leaving serial rapists on the street.

I was determined to raise the level of respect for women in Chicago and energize a response that contained a path to empowerment for women (and others who were victims), as well as support for that path. If we could start with the violence in the home and turn that around, perhaps that would contribute to a sea change on how we addressed sexual assault and rape.

In 1990, new police statistics showed a dramatic increase in domestic violence, with 97 percent of victims being women. Richard M. Daley had by then won the special election for mayor, leading to the reorganization of city council committees and my successful effort to create a subcommittee on domestic violence—the only one while I was alderman to include members of the public. I had modeled it after my recollection of David Orr's development of the Landlord and Tenant Ordinance during Harold Washington's first term.

I was pretty sure that most aldermen would not participate in the subcommittee; indeed, there had been audible snickers from some of my colleagues when I first suggested it. To make sure it would be effective and have a life of its own, I therefore invited all the domestic violence activists in the city to participate. Because many of the issues intersected with policing at one time or another (not the least of which was domestic violence within police families), I requested the police department participate in the subcommittee. In time, Sergeant Sue Kelly would become a strong advocate for solutions to the problems faced by the mostly women experiencing domestic violence.

Through the subcommittee, voids in service became clear. Ideas for how the city could address these gaps were myriad. One such area of concern was that women who were victims of domestic violence with orders of protection against their abusers needed a safe place for court-ordered visitation between their abuser and their children to take place. I proposed funding such a program using Community Development Block Grant funds but that request was rebuffed. In November 1990, I continued to lobby and raise the issue throughout the budget hearings, taking every opportunity with numerous commissioners, including the budget director, Health and Human Services commissioners, the corporation counsel, and finally the police superintendent.

On the last day of two weeks of budget hearings, as the very last department came to the council floor, I girded my energy to take a last shot at getting answers from Police Superintendent LeRoy Martin. As Martin took his seat next to the chairman of the Budget Committee, a good eight or nine bulky white, uniformed officers sat next to and behind him, chatting and socializing among themselves and Budget Committee staff.

I was bone-tired and frustrated. The chairman repeatedly limited my time for questions and generally gave me a hard time. We were almost done; this was to be the last hearing, and for me it was one of the most important. I had many questions to ask, and I knew I had to be quick if I was to get through all my concerns. I went through my routine questions as all the officers sitting behind Martin chatted away, sometimes so loudly that it was hard to hear his answer. It was rude and distracting, but I kept going. I asked about police accountability, response to hate crimes, domestic violence calls, the homeless.

Suddenly, it just became too much. Out of nowhere and way beyond my control, I burst into tears. The room became silent. I couldn't speak for a few moments as I worked hard to compose myself. As I was doing so, I noticed the chairman and his chief of staff having a brief conversation. Meanwhile, a couple of the remaining aldermen, visibly unsure of what to do, came to their microphones, expressing concern and apologies. The chief of staff made his way around the council chambers where I was sitting in my regular seat on the opposite side of the room, knelt down beside me, and asked if a grant for supervised visitation for domestic violence victims of a couple hundred thousand dollars would be acceptable. My most embarrassing moment had become the biggest material impact I would have during that budget season.

For ten years, the subcommittee would meet regularly, focusing attention on domestic violence and raising the level of respect for women. During that time, the city and the county's court system response to domestic violence improved some. Voids in service were identified—including domestic violence in communities of color and in gay and lesbian communities—and the city was challenged to respond to them. After Bill Clinton became president, he championed grants providing block grants for local police departments including funds to address domestic violence. The city grabbed this opportunity to hire a domestic violence coordinator, hiring one of the more vocal advocates and establishing a section within the police department (later moving to the health department).

After community policing expanded to all twenty-five police districts in the mid-1990s, standing committees were established in each district. I proposed having a committee on domestic violence. With the police superintendent refusing to take a position, district by district, most of the commanders rejected the idea.

An early 1990s ordinance to protect the location of domestic violence shelters would take more than a decade to pass, until which time, domestic violence shelters would remain targets of the purveyors of violence. If their partner left them to seek safe harbor in a shelter whose address was publicly attainable, sometimes the shelter would become a target.

To receive public funds, a domestic violence shelter needed to be "legal," meaning it had to be licensed by the city. Under Chicago's zoning code, all domestic violence shelters were considered a special use, requiring them to receive approval from the city's Zoning Board of Appeals before getting a license to operate. In doing so, their location became part of the public record. The only alternative for some shelters was to be underground, making it difficult to raise the funds necessary to operate. I wanted this changed.

My greatest opposition came from the majority of aldermen who considered domestic violence shelters to be no different from homeless shelters—which were anathema to most of my colleagues. Finally, with the passage of an ordinance in September 2004, homes providing shelter to less than fifteen victims of domestic violence no longer had to provide their address—a partial victory.

. . . .

58.

CHELSEA HOUSE BECOMES FRIENDLY TOWERS

In the first decades of the twentieth century, Uptown had been known, in part, for its high-end senior housing. The Lawrence House and Chelsea House provided studio units, three meals a day, and other assistance to elderly people. By the 1960s the neglect of building conditions, by then endemic in Uptown, had become status quo in these former "jewels." By the late 1980s the Chelsea House housed mostly seniors on fixed incomes who had few, if any, choices in conditions that were becoming dangerous to their health.

The seniors living there deserved heat, running water, and the three meals a day they were promised. When they were not getting these, the ward committeeman had gone to court and won an emergency order to remove everyone from the building. Its residents were to be sent to the basement of a public school several miles south. There was no plan for how long they would be there or where they would go after.

When my office got the call that this was happening, we immediately went to the building and basically took over the main office. We moved all the seniors to warm apartments, refusing to let anyone move them without their consent. We went to court and requested a receiver in place of the removal order. Liz Caldwell, my staff assistant, and I moved in. For a week we slept in the office (which wasn't heated) and arranged for meals (breakfast from Ann Sather, lunch from McDonald's, dinner from Leona's).[12] We met with each of the tenants and their families to figure out the best alternative—whether to stay, move to another apartment with better heat and plumbing, or move somewhere else.

Then we went hunting for a longer-term solution. The building needed a new owner who was serious about improving the conditions, so that it could continue to be available as housing for those still living there. The Jesus People USA were interested. JPUSA had a collective lifestyle with a leading body of elders. They were evangelists who had developed what we perceived as a close relationship with the machine, evidenced by their seemingly loyal gift of two-hundred-plus votes for machine candidates in local elections. We had developed a mutual dislike.

However, this had changed following the forum at Truman College that had preceded my runoff election in 1987. While we had what appeared to be some significant fundamental differences—most notably on abortion and a woman's right to choose what happens with her body—we found we had a great deal of common ground. They shared our growing concern for the displacement occurring in Uptown. They had a news magazine, which, I was surprised to learn, was progressive and open-minded in its interaction with the evangelical community. Their commitment to serving the poor was genuine, and they practiced what they preached. We could work with each other.

They were looking for a building to purchase where their entire community could live in one place. The seniors remaining at Chelsea needed adequate housing. JPUSA needed a new home. JPUSA was pretty sure

---

12 Ann Sather and Leona's were local restaurants located in Lakeview. I had met their respective owners during the many meetings dedicated to working out the details for lights at Wrigley Field. Tom Tunney, who would later become the alderman of the Forty-Fourth Ward, had opened the second floor of Ann Sather's, known particularly for its cinnamon buns, to the community as the AIDS crisis raged in the 1980s. Leona's, a family business started by their grandmother as a pizzeria, was in 1989 in the hands of Sam and Leon Toia, who were known to support many community efforts.

they could accomplish both goals. They made an offer and were accepted as the future owner. With the receiver, they immediately went to work restoring heat to the building and getting the kitchen operational so the seniors could once again receive their three meals a day. Within a year they had closed on the purchase, making the top three floors exclusively affordable housing for seniors. They developed their own senior support program, providing assistance for health, recreation, employment, legal, and other services unique to their new senior community. They built a separate dining area for the exclusive use of the seniors and moved their own families into the rest of the building, which became known as Friendly Towers.

. . . .

59.

THE WINDING PATH TO THE AVERY SETTLEMENT
SAVING UNITS ONE BY ONE

During the first city council meeting after we buried Harold and chose his successor, my tax reactivation proposal had been killed by the new majority in the city council.[13] A settlement agreement in the Avery case was close, and this tax-reaction proposal was the first of many steps toward realizing our goal of creating the replacement housing for the units that had been lost when Truman College was built. This initiative was equally dead in the water. But my fight for an affordable housing policy for Chicago was not.

---

13 City council rules allow for any two aldermen to defer any matter until the next city council meeting, at which time a majority of aldermen would have to agree to take the matter up again. Up until this point, I am unfamiliar with any instance that an item that had been deferred in this manner was brought to a vote by the city council when the intention and effect was to defeat it.

Following the refusal of the city council to support a request to the county board to transfer these nineteen lots to the city for redevelopment for affordable owner-occupied three-flats, Randy Langer bought the majority of them for the price of their back taxes from the county.

In 1989 he approached me about selling the lots to the Chicago Housing Authority for scattered-site public housing. In a compromise that was applauded by some and decried by others, Langer agreed to sell six properties to Habitat (one of which would be swapped with a lot owned by the city for the development of a play lot.) In return, he acquired the city-owned lot he had coveted since I had refused his zoning change request at my first city council meeting. The agreement for one of these lots on the 4400 block of Clifton was to build a housing complex for senior citizens. This was the location of the courtway building that had been abandoned after the landlord set fire to it and was subsequently successfully prosecuted for arson. The rest of the lots, located on six different blocks were to have a total of eighty-seven scattered-site apartments built on them. As it turned out, CHA would later reject Habitat's intention to build senior housing on Clifton, claiming it was too close to the Chicago Transit Authority tracks. Instead, this lot would become home to the managers of scattered-site housing on the city's North Side.

Ironically, having attacked me for demanding low-income housing, Langer's greed prevented the development of owner-occupied three-flats that were replaced with low-income public housing. Later, when the information became available about the details of his agreements with the CHA, it became apparent why Langer had made this proposal. The receiver of the scattered-site program was required by the federal Department of Housing and Urban Development and the City of Chicago to pay "market rate" for the land—significantly more than the sum of the back taxes Langer had paid to get ownership just over a year earlier. In the end, he netted nearly a quarter million dollars and got his coveted lot. Uptown got eighty-seven low-income units.

As this was playing out, Access Living, an activist organization of people with physical disabilities, was looking to address the housing crisis for their members and others they represented. People with disabilities face many challenges in finding appropriate housing. With an idea of creating cooperative housing for a community of both the disabled and able-bodied, Access Living held classes for potential participants in a co-op housing initiative. They formed a development corporation, called KOSOH,[14] and approached me to support such a project in Uptown. I was delighted and expressed excitement about the opportunity.

KOSOH's intention was to build community, and they were already working with many of the individuals and families who hoped to move into the housing they planned to create. The Avery plaintiffs, meanwhile, wanted to preserve and expand the community by ensuring that housing was available to families living in Uptown who continued to face displacement.

The Avery negotiations had continued after Harold's death, but hopes of a settlement having a broader impact on city policy were gone. By 1989, a settlement was reached with the city and HUD that amounted to $100,000 for low-cost housing in the heart of Uptown. KOSOH identified the vacant building at 927 West Wilson as the one they would buy and rehab. Their goal: "to create housing for the disabled and non-disabled people, from various income levels, with access features for people with a multitude of disabilities." The Avery plaintiffs agreed that the settlement funds should go toward that rehab.

None of us had expertise in the actual development or management of housing. However, we had a lot of experience studying people's needs and the many barriers to meeting those needs. We were idealistic in our goals, and unrealistic in what it would take to realize them, but we were undeterred by any of that—until we were.

As the rehab progressed, there was a shortfall of funds during construction, and corners were cut. The initial rehab missed issues with the first-floor plumbing, rendering multiple apartments uninhabitable. A fire (the result of arson) in the freight elevator created chaos and suspicion. Substance abuse was an issue.

There were many fingers pointed, but the real culprit was lack of experience and resources coupled with a dose of idealism. All of us who

---

14 KOSOH was an acronym made up of the first name of the five people at Access Living who formed this new development corporation to realize their vision. While I don't recall who all of these founders were, I do know that two of them were Ora Schub and Susan Nussbaum; two extraordinary women, each talented in their own right, and fierce advocates for people living with disabilities.

were involved, at one point or another, made mistakes. Building community takes a lot of work. You have to start with where people are at, establish your commonality, and build trust. This takes time, a lot of effort, and resources.

KOSOH pulled out after a few years. When their development partner, Chicago Equity Fund, went bankrupt, the building was up for grabs, along with two others, totaling seventy-seven units of affordable housing that had been under CEF ownership. Dan Burke and Tony Fusco had been attorneys with Legal Assistance working out of the Uptown office before establishing the Chicago Community Development Corporation. In 1989 they purchased and rehabbed 850 West Eastwood—a HUD-mortgaged high-rise—and kept it affordable. After some cajoling, they agreed to take over the three CEF buildings and preserve them as low-income housing.

Building after building in Uptown was turning condo. Over the next decade and a half, a corresponding divide between the people moving into these condos and renters—particularly those in subsidized apartments—would become evident. Not so surely, but quickly, the economic divide was deepening (accompanied by a growing racial divide). The housing stock was becoming bifurcated—high-income condos and low-income subsidized units, with little in between. A stable, healthy community needs the opportunity for people and families to grow in place. We needed more affordable housing with more options—including individual and tenant ownership.

Developers often asked to meet with me, usually because they needed some assistance from the city—approval for a zoning change or an ordinance allowing them to use an alley for access to their parking or for a special use. Whatever the case, it was an opportunity. Every meeting with a developer included at least fifteen minutes of my picking their brains about ways to make the housing they were building or rehabbing more affordable.

I had done this since my first month in office. The idea for the owner-occupied three-flats on city-owned land came from conversations with developer Elzie Higginbottom. It was a good example of my vision for building community and was directed at ensuring that young people who had grown up in Uptown, many of whom would be the first in their families to go to college, would have access to a place they could afford.

A number of them were by now teachers and artists—still deeply concerned with serving their community and giving back.

While this earlier plan may have died with Harold Washington, its concept was never far from my thoughts as I struggled against the powerful dynamic of Chicago's manipulated housing market to find a path to development without displacement for people to have homes that they could afford and still provide for food, health care, and all the necessities of life.

There were a number of developers who accepted my challenge to dig into their own experience and come up with ideas. A new citywide program for affordable condominiums grew out of this. The idea was to have a percentage of condos in any given building or development to be sold below market value to eligible first-time home buyers whose household income did not exceed 80 percent of the median income. To be eligible, the potential buyer had to attend an eight-week course in homeownership and secure a mortgage. To ensure that families with moderate incomes could participate, I insisted that the condos being made available were at least two-bedroom apartments and that their sale price did not exceed $140,000.

Additionally, I sought a commitment from the city that these home buyers would be able to assess our various programs that provided them with down payment assistance. This led to discussions with the Department of Housing and ultimately a series of ordinances that allowed me to proceed in the ward and ultimately create a citywide program.

Eighty-eight condos became available in the Forty-Sixth Ward through this program. Prospective owners participated in a lottery that we held in the lobby at Truman College.

As my goal was to create an opportunity for homeownership for people who would not otherwise have that opportunity, the sale price was important. While I was able to hold the line on increasing the price in the Forty-Sixth Ward (as well as the minimum unit size), the influence of the real estate market prevailed in the amended citywide ordinances: in the end, the allowance on the sale price was pegged to a household earning 120 percent of median income. Moreover, the median income used by the city in all these calculations came from the Metropolitan Area Statistics—a figure that was at the time significantly higher than the actual median income in many communities in the city, and generally higher than in the city as a whole.

The impact of the economic downturn that began in 2008 would result in massive foreclosures throughout Chicago, and the citywide Chicago Partnership for Affordable Neighborhoods (CPAN) program would not escape its reach. In the Forty-Sixth Ward, however, for the most part, the new condo owners were able to weather the storm largely because their mortgages were manageable. One exception was where the developer did an end run around me, getting approval from downtown to sell one-bedroom apartments with a higher sale price—resulting in at least one foreclosure.[15]

. . . .

60.

JOINING THE FIGHT AGAINST APARTHEID

In 1976 I had been asked to publish *Zimbabwe News* by Eddison Zvobgo, a visiting professor at Wheaton College who represented the Zimbabwe African National Union in the United States. He would later be one of the negotiators for ZANU at Lancaster, helping set the terms of independence of Zimbabwe, before becoming a minister in the new Zimbabwe government.

Eddison had been familiar with *Keep Strong* magazine and knew me as the managing editor and reporter for the magazine, as I had interviewed him for a story or two. He had wanted a publication that he would write, and for which he would provide all the graphics, while we would handle typesetting, layout, and printing arrangements. Eddison would take care of transport to Mozambique, where the ZANU fighters were camped.

In the end, we produced two issues of *Zimbabwe News*. While typesetting, copy-editing the text (along with Eddison), and designing the layout, I was exposed to and educated about the anti-colonial struggles

---

15 There were some other unforeseen impacts of the economic downturn that affected the new home buyers indirectly and were caused by developer mistakes, financial issues, or bank policies that made it difficult for CPAN owners to refinance and take advantage of falling mortgage rates.

in southern Africa. The intrigue he described between the southern Africa Frontline States and their many liberation movements and organizations was striking. *Zimbabwe News* reported on the repressive actions taken by the Rhodesian government (which were decried by the United Nations), as well as the progress of and conflicts within the liberation struggle to end colonial rule. After the Lancaster Agreement was reached, I was anxious to visit the fledgling independent country.

When the opportunity to attend a conference of reporters in Harare, Zimbabwe, in November 1989, was offered to me and Slim, I jumped at the chance. This was a trip that would not only bring us to the region, but ultimately lead the Chicago City Council to strengthen our sanctions against South Africa at a critical moment: at that time, the apartheid government was struggling to maintain power while arguing that sanctions should be lifted because Nelson Mandela had been released.[16]

Zimbabwe was then nearing year ten of independence.[17] One of the concessions in the Lancaster Agreement had been a moratorium on land reform for ten years following independence. This was a big deal, as over 90 percent of the people were Black Africans, while the vast majority of the land was owned by white landowners mostly of English descent who were often absentee landlords or farmers. Expectation for the long-anticipated redistribution of land was high. Meanwhile, a focus on education through university was giving a growing number of Zimbabweans access for the first time.

Before leaving Chicago, Slim and I checked in with Prexy Nesbitt, who was active in the anti-apartheid movement in Chicago, nationally and internationally. Prexy had known Eduardo Mondlane, president of the Mozambican Liberation Front (FRELIMO), during the

---

16 Nelson Mandela was released in January 1990. Based on his release, the South African government immediately lobbied the US government for removal of sanctions imposed on the apartheid government.

17 During a three-month period in 1979, the British government convened a conference at the Lancaster House in London that resulted in agreement on an Independence Constitution, pre-independence arrangements, and the terms of cease-fire. Besides the British government, the parties represented were the Patriotic Front members, Zimbabwe African Peoples Union (ZAPU), and Zimbabwe African National Union (ZANU), along with the Rhodesian government, setting the stage for an independent Zimbabwe following elections in 1980.

time Mondlane had lived in Chicago, attending the same church. For a while, after Mozambique achieved independence in 1975, Prexy had been a consultant for the government. He arranged for us to take a side trip to Mozambique before returning home.

In Zimbabwe we heard stories from before independence of Black soldiers being recruited as mercenaries by the Rhodesian military to attack white settlers and blame these attacks on the liberation fighters. There were now reports of fresh attacks of the same nature attributed to the South African Defence Force.

In Mozambique we came face to face with the war waged by the South African Defence Force to undermine the independent government that had been established there in 1975. FRELIMO had successfully forced the Portuguese colonial government to relinquish power. Led by Mondlane until his assassination by Portuguese secret police, and his successor, Samora Machel, FRELIMO brought health care, local control, and peace to the areas they controlled during their struggle for independence.

There was no doubt that the South African apartheid government felt threatened by the growing territory on and near their borders that was being transformed from governed colonies to independent Black-controlled countries bent on turning around decades of manipulation, economic ruin (for the majority native peoples), and deep racial divides. Their lands had been stolen, and their country's riches of gold, diamonds, and other minerals ripped from the earth had barely paid for the subsistence of those who they had employed to do so.

Mozambique's independence was a blow to South Africa, whose government and military were poised to use any means necessary to stop the model and the promise that Samora Machel's FRELIMO government provided. Machel died in a plane crash in 1986 when a false beacon, which many claim was sent by the South African military, sent his plane into the mountains between Mozambique and South Africa.

In Mozambique we were regaled with stories of brutality. Mercenaries from the Mozambican National Resistance (RENAMO), funded by the South African Defence Force, would surround a village and round up everyone there. Any grown men still there would be executed on the spot. The male children would be separated, and everyone else told to return to their homes, which were for the most part grass huts. The male children would be given torches of fire and forced to light the cottages. After those inside had died, they would be told, "You are now a soldier with RENAMO. You killed your family. If you try to leave or go to the authorities, you will be tried for murder."

Land mines were everywhere. We visited one hospital where we found women, elderly men, and children recovering as best they could from loss of limbs.

I was shocked by the destructive impact of South African apartheid on the region and the lives of people living there and their right to determine their own destiny and form their own governments without interference. I came home determined to explore what we could do from here.

In 1984, Randall Robinson, head of the US-based advocacy organization TransAfrica, had announced the beginning of the "Free South Africa Movement." Actions against investments in South Africa by pension funds and university endowments became commonplace in Chicago, often accompanied by arrests for trespassing and/or civil disorder, and led by campus-based student and other organizations, including the American Committee on Africa and the Coalition for Illinois Divestment from South Africa. Every Thursday, protesters, sometimes numbering in the hundreds, gathered outside 444 North Michigan Avenue; the thirty-first-floor offices of the South African Consulate were their target. While most protesters remained on the street, informing passersby and encouraging them to join in speaking out against apartheid, a smaller group often attempted to get an audience with the South African Consulate, looking for a commitment to end apartheid and sitting in while they waited for a response that was often answered with an arrest for trespassing. During a five-month period beginning in December 1984, at least eighteen people were arrested during these protests.[18]

---

18 A flyer from the Free South Africa Movement Defense Committee identified these eighteen protesters as Congressman Gus Savage, State Senator Richard Newhouse, Jackie Jackson (representing PUSH and the Rainbow Coalition), Addie Wyatt (retired VP of the Amalgamated Meat Cutters), Steve Cullen (international VP of AFSCME), Alderman Allan Streeter, Heather Booth (national co-chair of Citizen Action), Paul Booth (international area director of AFSCME), Reverend Ralph Henley (of Discipleship Missionary Baptist Church), Larry Hildis (Northwestern University student), Eric Hudson (Chicago public high school student), Robert Lucas (director of Kenwood Oakland Community Organization),

Eight of these protesters, arrested during two different demonstrations, requested a jury trial for their trespassing charges, which proceeded to trial in May 1985. Using the trial as a forum on apartheid, attorneys Stan Willis, Lew Myers, and Tim Wright adopted a necessity defense—in essence, they argued their clients had no choice but to trespass in order to express their beliefs.[19]

Two days of testimony included statements by South African activists Albie Sachs[20] and Dennis Brutus, Senator Paul Simon, Congressman Charles Hayes, and Prexy Nesbitt, describing the harm of apartheid and why it was necessary for the defendants to act as they did—violating a local misdemeanor to uphold international condemnation of apartheid. During jury selection, most potential jurors of color were eliminated, leaving a mostly white jury who deliberated for two days before acquitting all defendants on the basis of the International Human Rights Law of Necessity, affirming that the defendants' demonstration opposing apartheid was necessary to correct a greater harm.

In 1986 the city council passed Chicago's first anti-apartheid ordinance, restricting some city resources to companies doing business with South Africa. Supported by Mayor Harold Washington, this legislation, introduced by Alderman Danny Davis and others, languished in committee for thirteen months before its passage. Concurrently, Congress passed the Comprehensive Anti-Apartheid Act of 1986, imposing sanctions against South Africa. First introduced in 1972, it was vetoed in 1986 by President Reagan, whose veto was overridden.

Edward "Buzz" Palmer (president of the Black Press Institute), Jane Ramsey (director of the Jewish Council on Urban Affairs), Reverend Orlando Redekopp (of Church of the Brethren), Mark Rogovin (director of the Chicago Peace Museum), Thomas Savage (representing the Second Congressional District), and Reverend Ron Shupp (of Clergy and Laity Concerned). If memory serves, there were likely more arrestees not mentioned on this flyer during this time.

19 On trial were Streeter, Cullen, Ramsey, Lucas, Palmer, Redekopp, Booth, and Savage.

20 Following the end of the apartheid government in South Africa, Albie Sachs would be one of the founders of South Africa's new Supreme Court. In 1988, while he was living in exile in Mozambique, he was the target of a car bombing by South African security agents. He lost an arm and sight in one eye.

Although I was in South Africa after Nelson Mandela was released from prison and had the opportunity to attend a rally for the end of apartheid and the formation of a constitutional convention based on one person one vote which he spoke at, I did not have the honor of meeting him until he came to Chicago in 1994. Photo by Antonio Dickey.

Meanwhile in Illinois, there were ongoing demands to require public pension funds to divest from all holdings in South Africa. However, legislation in Springfield stalled, and pension funds were not included in the Chicago ordinance or the congressional law.

In January 1990, following decades of mass demonstrations, international pressure, and economic sanctions, Nelson Mandela was released from prison. However, no changes were made to apartheid. That same month, I began meeting with local anti-apartheid activists. They had a national network and understood much better than I the financial implications of sanctions and their impacts on the South African economy. My primary asks: How do we best send a message to maintain US sanctions until South Africa ends apartheid, what are the weaknesses in US sanctions, and how should we amend Chicago's ordinance to best address this?

At that point in time, there were still three Chicago banks with investments in South Africa. The local activists' answer was to force their divestment. If we found a way to do this and it passed, it was the

During a 1991 trip to South Africa, I attended a million-strong demonstration in Johannesburg demanding the end of apartheid and a new constitution based on the principle of one person, one vote.

belief that the Port of Oakland would follow, and likely other municipalities as well. With Mandela now free, the South African apartheid
government argued that international sanctions should be lifted. There
were indications that the president and Congress might be leaning that
way. Taking a stand now and keeping the pressure on until apartheid
was in fact rejected and dismantled was more important than ever.
Strengthening—not lifting—sanctions would be our contribution with
the greatest material impact.

Seventeen drafts later—amid growing public interest in Mandela
and his cause following his historic visit to the United States (which
didn't bring him to Chicago but did bring him to nearby Detroit), and
after successful organizing which gained the support of two of the three
banks—we passed an ordinance that had the agreement of the two banks
to divest within six months, as well as the restriction of the third from
serving as a municipal depository for the city unless they did so as well.

Over the course of the previous six months, I had spent hours and
hours explaining the ordinance and its many changes (through all its
drafts—mine and the administration's) and educating reporters on the
conditions on the ground in South Africa (and the entire southern Africa region) and why this was important and relevant to us in Chicago,
and appropriate for the city council to act on. Consequently, we had an
informed press on this ordinance.

Usually, the process for passage of an ordinance begins with its introduction at a council meeting, where it gets sent to a committee to
be heard. In this instance, the ordinance was assigned to the Finance
Committee chaired by Ed Burke. To get before the full city council for
a vote, an ordinance has to pass out of committee. When it is on the
agenda of a committee, members of the public have an opportunity to
request to be heard on the matter—an opportunity they do not have
once it goes before the full city council.

When what we thought was the final compromise ordinance came
before the Finance Committee, we had already redrafted the ordinance
seventeen times to garner the support to get it passed. The administration aldermen (particularly Burke and Pat Huels) presented an ordinance
of their own as a substitute. It had great language in it. The problem was
that this language was all in the "wherefores" and "whereases," and even
in the definitions, but it was nowhere to be found in the meat of the

ordinance, which described the teeth for action and enforcement. It was in fact a paper tiger—all show, no power.

It didn't take much to expose this. My demand was that they take their definitions and back them up with actual requirements for divestment and consequences for failure to act. Under public scrutiny, they agreed, and we ended up with a compromise ordinance, which the brain trust of activists felt confident accomplished our goals.

So back to the Finance Committee we went for what was scheduled to be the committee vote to send the ordinance to the full city council. At the last minute, during the committee hearing, Alderman Burke demanded a language change. Without it, he said, he would not proceed with the vote.

I had no idea what that change would mean—or even what he meant by it. But it was clear Burke thought this was a poison pill that would kill the ordinance. There was a group of aldermen who were my natural allies opposed to the compromise, and it was clear he was playing one of his games, hoping to get me to back down so he would have an excuse to kill the whole thing. I called a time-out. He gave me five minutes.

I rushed to the back of chambers and got on the phone to New York with the one person in the brain trust who was an expert on the international finance aspect of sanctions and read her Burke's language. My question: Would this subvert the ordinance and change the underlying material impact we were after? Her response was an emphatic no. What a relief. I rushed back into chambers, took my seat, and said, "Mr. Chairman, I accept your language and am ready to proceed." Burke is famous for becoming flushed in the face when he is agitated. By the time he took the vote, his face was a rosy pink.

The apartheid government fell, and a democratic government was formed in 1994.

61.

TRIPLING AIDS FUNDING

From the early 1980s well into the 1990s, any mention of HIV or AIDS sent shock waves. Fear of this mysterious deadly virus for which there was no apparent cure easily escalated into a frenzy, swirling with anger, hate, and recriminations. Although HIV can only be transmitted through bodily fluids, fear grabbed hold of the collective imagination—ignorance prevailed, as did the belief that any human touch or breath could cause someone to be infected.

The most likely ways for the disease to be transmitted are through sex, sharing of needles (by drug users, but also through mishaps in the hospital or by first responders), and blood transfusions.

Ryan White was a thirteen-year-old hemophiliac who contracted AIDS from a routine blood transfusion he received in an Indiana hospital in 1984. Amid professed fears he could infect his classmates, Ryan was barred from attending school. With the support of his family and armed with factual information about the virus he carried, he fought for the right to attend school and was ultimately successful.

While Ryan fought for his own human rights, the gay community organized as well. Their demands focused on gay rights, as well as funding for HIV/AIDS treatment and education.

In 1990 Congress passed the Ryan White Act. Finally, some federal grant funding was available to cities, counties, states, and local community-based organizations to provide a comprehensive system for HIV primary medical care, essential support services, and medications for people living with HIV to improve health outcomes and reduce transmission among hard-to-reach populations. Many, however, felt these resources were not enough and that local cities, counties, and states needed to have skin in the game.

After the passage of the Human Rights Ordinance in December 1988, the AIDS crisis received new focus. Health as well as human rights were high priorities. The AIDS Coalition to Unleash Power (ACT UP), a grassroots political group focused on fighting the disease, had been formed in New York City in March 1987. By the end of the year, there were local chapters in many US cities, including Chicago, where a relatively small but dedicated group of activists were laser-focused on demanding the city take action. However, more often than not they were dismissed by the powers that be as being too radical and "crazy."

They got my attention. I appreciated their courage, passion, and creativity while demanding to be heard, and I felt their frustration and agreed with their message. Disappointed in November 1991 by the city council's failure to increase funding to address the growing AIDS crisis in Chicago's 1992 budget, I jumped at the chance to do something about it.

In December Kit Duffy invited me to dinner at Jeff McCourt's house. Kit had been Harold Washington's liaison to the LGBT community and a longtime friend, going back to the early days of the Chicago Area Black Lung Association, where she volunteered. Jeff McCourt, the editor and publisher of *Windy City Times*,[21] was planning an editorial on Chicago's failing response to the AIDS crisis. The paper had been publishing political cartoons by Danny Sotomayor since Sotomayor and others had formed ACT UP in Chicago. It was time to up the ante.

At that point in time, 4,526 cases had been reported to the board of health with the number growing daily. While Chicago had received nearly $13 million from the Ryan White Act and other governmental funds, the city's contribution of $1.07 million had not increased since 1989—the year the Human Rights Ordinance went into effect, followed by Richard M. Daley's election as mayor.

We were joined by Lori Cannon and Pepe Peña, along with Jon-Henri Damski, Laurie Dittman, Rick Garcia, and Art Johnston (known as the gang of four, referring to their leadership passing the human rights legislation). They laid out a strategy to increase the city's funding. I enthusiastically agreed to be their champion on the council.

Having rewritten my original anti-apartheid ordinance at least seventeen times before arriving at language that could pass the council in 1990, I proposed that we do a resolution, get as many additional sponsors as possible, call for hearings, and force the administration to triple the city's spending. No matter what suggestions I might make for where the money would come from, they would most likely find another, so

---

21 Although *Windy City* cofounder Tracy Baim was not at this meeting, she would play a big role going forward through her coverage in *Outlines*.

let them write the actual appropriation ordinance. We would use the resolution to organize and build support.

The AIDS Advisory Council, composed of over one hundred community leaders and health and social service providers, had previously completed an AIDS Strategic Plan. We had a media outlet, activists passionate and ready to go, and a blueprint for what needed to be done. What we needed now was the money necessary for that plan to be implemented and the political will to do so. Tripling Chicago's commitment would go a long way to making that a reality.

In January, the resolution was introduced. It had twenty-eight sponsors. At the time I told the press, "I'm not going to say where the funds should come from, except to say that it should not be taken away from other health needs."

Mayor Daley held a press conference after every city council meeting. At the press conference that day, when asked about my resolution and raising the city's spending on HIV/AIDS, he said, "Over my dead body." Danny Sotomayor was in the hospital fighting his last stand with AIDS, but ACT UP was alive and well.

Hearings were held, and activists testified. Echoing the sentiment of many, Steve Wakefield, director of Test Positive Aware Network, testified, "In other cities, AIDS has been declared an emergency and the local government has responded appropriately. That hasn't happened here." ACT UP hurled challenges to increase the funding (usually through banners they would unfold before the mayor almost daily). Aldermen received irate calls from their constituents demanding action.

In late April 1992, I took a call from Pat Huels, the mayor's city council floor leader. "Can Ed Burke and I sign on to your AIDS-spending ordinance?" he asked. "Sure," I responded. "As soon as you write the ordinance." Which they did. "This will be done with the clear understanding that we will . . . come up with $2.5 million," Burke told the *Chicago Tribune* later that same day. "It will be in the form of an ordinance and will result in the identification and appropriation of $2.5 million for the battle against AIDS."[22]

---

22 The personnel costs of additional staff dedicated to the AIDS crisis added to the $2.5 million, resulting in a near tripling of spending by the city on its public health response to AIDS.

Fifteen years later, I was inducted into the Chicago Gay and Lesbian Hall of Fame. With Mayor Daley officiating we were surrounded on the stage by a quartet of stalwart Washington supporters. The irony escaped no one. From left to right: Kit Duffy, myself, Daley, Brenetta Howell Barrett, Connie Howard, and Bennett Johnson.

On the same day, Daley announced the creation of a new position within the Chicago Department of Health to coordinate all AIDS activities for the city. He appointed Judith Johns, former executive director of Howard Brown Memorial Clinic and one of the advocates to increase AIDS spending by the city, to lead this effort. Also that day, Cook County Board president Richard Phelan announced a new initiative to coordinate AIDS services between the county's hospitals.[23]

The campaign—a combined effort of community, political, legislative, and media action—had successfully established a responsibility on the part of Chicago's local government that went beyond the initial demand for tripling our spending on AIDS. We had a strategic plan and now commitments (complete with staff) from the county and the city to meet an important aspect of that plan—the coordination of services throughout communities in the Chicago metropolitan area.

23 Including Cook County, Oak Forest, and Provident Hospitals, Cook County Jail, and eight neighborhood clinics (Bethel Wholistic Health Center, Circle Family Care, Erie Family Health Center, KOMED Health Center, Lawndale Christian Health Center, New City Health Center, Chicago Health Outreach, and Winfield/Moody Health Center).

62

MY 1991 REELECTION CAMPAIGN

As I completed my third year in office, I had to decide if I would run for reelection. I had come to the job in large measure because Harold Washington had asked me to do so. My dislike of politics had not changed, and I still viewed it as a necessary evil I would have to contend with if I continued as an alderman. But did I want to? I had to decide.

It had taken the first two years for me to learn the job. These had been tumultuous years. In that short span, Chicago had had four mayors,[24] and with each I'd had to learn to navigate new waters. I'd had my fair share of fights with developers and gone toe to toe with them. It felt like some progress was being made—two steps forward, one step backward. I had even passed some major legislation and impacted city priorities on fighting HIV/AIDS and domestic violence. But there was so much more to do. Little had been accomplished at this juncture that could come close to having an institutional impact on any of the concerns that had brought me to political office in the first place. In the back of my mind, Harold's oft-repeated counsel rang like a battle cry: "It will take twenty years to have an impact on institutional racism and institutional corruption."

By 1990, the Washington coalition was fracturing. Was I up for another four years? Since his death, political pundits had been calling me a one-term alderman who had won on Harold's coattails. Without him, they said, I didn't stand a chance. However, what I lacked in self-confidence I made up for in stubbornness. Once again, I was in.

In Chicago, the bulk of a city council member's job is acting as a glorified city services clerk. Because of how the Democratic machine had built itself around rationing garbage pickup, street cleanings, and other city services as political rewards through its selected aldermen, most communities were accustomed to aldermen being their primary point of contact for government services. It took two to three years of

---

24 Harold Washington (April 29, 1983–November 25, 1987), David Orr (November 25, 1987–December 2, 1987), Eugene Sawyer (December 2, 1987–April 24, 1989), and Richard M. Daley (April 24, 1989–May 16, 2011).

my first term for us to get a handle on navigating all of the city, state, and federal bureaucracies; to understand how to truly provide services. This was especially true because services in the heart of my ward had been traditionally neglected.

Two years into my first term, we hired a Youngstown, Ohio, transplant who had come to Uptown in the mid-1980s. I had met Denice Davis when she'd attended a forum for potential candidates interested in running in the city's first election for representation on the newly formed local school councils. Denice would end up being my longest-serving staffer, working with me until my retirement—albeit with a few breaks.[25]

While Denice would eventually hold the position delegated by most of my colleagues to their chief of staff, her strength was in her knowledge of and compassion for the survival needs of our constituents. She recognized the invisibility of these needs and was passionate about addressing them. So as far as I was concerned, she was my "chief of survival."[26] If someone's survival was at risk, she would make sure it was on my radar. She was passionate about the youth of Uptown and determined to be their advocate, while she was relentless in challenging them to be accountable. Early on she regularly updated our comprehensive list of affordable housing opportunities in the ward while responding to the daily deluge of requests for city services. Over the years, Denice transformed the service office to be far more inclusive than any previous or comparable ward service office—doing things like providing special days for the homeless, people returning from prisons, and other individuals to access comprehensive services (for instance, getting ID cards), or bringing the city's largest food bank into the ward monthly for mass distribution to the poor and elderly. But all that would transpire in the years to come, after we had gained the confidence of incumbency and won reelection.

Denice, and all my staff that first term, learned the ins and outs of providing city services from David Ochal—a fast-talking, hardworking city employee who had started as staff for the machine, then was part

---

25 In the early 1990s, Denice took a fifteen-month hiatus to join Bobby Rush's congressional staff, shortly after he left the city council.

26 Meaning she was concerned with the day-to-day survival needs of our constituents.

of Harold Washington's administration, then helped train me and the rest of our staff on providing city services, before eventually becoming a longtime cog in the Daley administration.

For me, the primary role of my ward office was to be the "bureaucracy buster" for our constituents. Learning how to provide access to good city services in that first term was vital to the overall mission of re-centering the government to provide for those that had been traditionally neglected, but it was also simply a required part of the job.

The 1991 election was the closest I would come to losing any of my five reelection campaigns. Bernie Hansen and I shared ward boundaries. As alderman of the Forty-Fourth Ward, he represented most of Lakeview and all of Wrigley Field. He was running Mike Quigley, his chief of staff, against me. He had the support of Mayor Richard M. Daley and the full machine, including the army of some three hundred patronage workers who descended on the ward every weekend for the two months leading up to the election.[27] Efforts by Hansen and Daley raised several hundred thousand dollars for Quigley's campaign.

Although the campaign was free from some of the obvious and vicious lies of previous ones, it was nevertheless a bare-knuckles political fight focused on housing, development, police brutality, and other survival issues. With their disproportionate resources, and efforts to label me a socialist who hated the police and wanted to keep Uptown a ghetto, the machine thought they would glide to victory.

When the votes were counted on February 24, 1991, Mike Quigley was in the lead by a slim margin. Victor Samar, a third candidate in the race, had received enough votes to force a runoff. Election night was somber. Incumbents forced into a runoff do not usually win. And now, every machine alderman in the city could focus on my race. The press and political pundits wrote us off.

---

27 Among the ward organizations that sent city workers in were Forty-Seventh Ward Park District Workers from the Ed Kelly machine; Forty-Eighth Ward Water Department workers from the Volini/Osterman organization; Nineteenth Ward Sheriff's Department employees from the Sheehan and Hynes families; Thirty-Third Forestry Department workers from the Mell Organization; of course a bunch of Eleventh Ward streets and sanitation workers from the Daley Organization; and even some suited-up Law Department lawyers knocking on Uptown doors on any given Saturday.

Political cartoon printed in *All Chicago City News* for which I received some criticism. At the time it seemed to me to be pretty accurate.

George Atkins, back to run my campaign, analyzed the data and saw that unlike previous elections, we had not maximized our support in Uptown. Several of our comrades from the Intercommunal Survival Committee who had been so vital in the multiple elections in the 1970s and '80s rededicated themselves to a six-week campaign sprint. They recognized the importance of keeping the Forty-Sixth Ward as a model of how to govern from the perspective of those who had the least power and were most impacted.

With a rededicated set of former ISC cadre and a reenergized group of volunteers, we focused the runoff message on two issues: development without displacement in Uptown, and having a universally praised ward service office for the entire ward. Even in such hyper-local races, the maxim "All politics is local" remains true. As such, the voters were moved not so much by our victories in the city council as they were by our assurance to operate in a fair and just way in the ward and to stick to our commitment to keeping Uptown economically and racially diverse. Their campaign called me a "crazy radical"; our response was to point out that those things they considered crazy and radical must have been why the ward had such an effective service office and system for making local decisions on zoning.

At a debate about a week before Election Day, held at St. Mary of the Lake School (in the part of the heart of Uptown that had been most gentrified), Quigley took a question and used it to bring out about half a dozen recent copies of *All Chicago City News*. I had not been affiliated with the paper for several years, but Brendan was now the managing editor, and that was the connection. The articles that Quigley derided talked about police brutality, economic justice, and racial justice. It was his attempt to show that I was an out-of-step far-left radical. But halfway through the presentation, even though he was on home court, you could see he realized that maybe this was not the most effective tactic. My response was to ignore the show and continue to harp on the need to govern from the perspective of those most impacted—and how that philosophy resulted in tangible improvements for everyone in the ward such as new sewers and protections for residents when Wrigley Field got lights. I told the voters that I was always going to fight for affordable housing; some may have never agreed with me, but at least they knew that with me they were going to always have a fighter to advocate for their access to services.

My campaign rallied, winning the runoff election by nearly 8 percentage points after having been behind by a couple of votes in the primary. That we won, after having almost lost the primary, while sticking to our political principles on the defining issues, and with the entire citywide machine throwing everything they had at us, would make every other election after that easy, if not almost perfunctory.

On May 9, 1991, during the first city council meeting following our inauguration ceremony, I approached the podium where the mayor sat as he chaired the meeting. This took him by surprise; Rich Daley and I rarely talked, and when we did, he was outwardly on edge—sometimes giggling, always seeming nervous. He had worked hard to defeat me. He took a moment to approach and extended his hand to me. As we shook hands, I congratulated him on his win. Visibly surprised, he reciprocated. Unable to help myself, I added, "It was a pleasure beating you, Mr. Mayor," before receiving a nervous smile, leaving the podium, and returning to my seat.

The election had placed a strain on many people working in the Forty-Sixth Ward who were trying to maintain a relationship with both me and the mayor and his allies. Dave Ochal, who by then had been my chief of staff for a couple of years, was creative and masterful at getting things done. His talents were recognized by the close-knit advisors with whom Daley had surrounded himself. They had been solicitous during the campaign, dividing his loyalties. When it was over, Dave had accepted their offer of a high-level job at the Department of Streets and Sanitation. We worked hard at not burning that bridge.

When our Streets and Sanitation ward superintendent subsequently announced his retirement, I knew I needed his replacement to be someone who would work hard, be thorough, and not be intimidated by the political thorns that accompanied the job. I asked Art Johnston if he had any suggestions. My instinct was that he might, and if so, that it might be someone the mayor couldn't say no to. Art sent me the résumé of Don Nowotny, an openly gay man who had the skills to do the job, was smart, serious about working, and apparently not worried about the potential political pressure cooker he might be walking into—at least not initially. Daley had courted the gay community during the election and couldn't say no to an outwardly gay candidate who was supported by one of the city's leading gay activists. Nowotny was in.

63.

UPTOWN YOUTH FORCE

We saw our future in our children and the youth of our community. We viewed our children as citizens of intercommunalism—the inherent interconnection between all human communities regardless of their race, ethnicity, or nation. Our challenge was twofold: to give them the tools they would need, and then to let them fly.

Correspondingly, our organizing in Uptown was informed by the needs of our youth—their health, physical development and well-being, and their ability to learn how to think (rather than *what* to think). The Heart of Uptown Coalition had established a child safety network and developed a host of recreational and educational activities. Understanding that many youth in Uptown faced great challenges, we wanted them to have the best shot at reaching their full potential. We were involved in the schools. We stressed recreation, fighting for access to public facilities: basketball at Truman College, gymnastics and swimming at Gill Park, softball at Clarendon Park. Whenever possible we paired these activities with reading, writing, or math instruction.

The racial tensions that were often just below the surface in Uptown did not escape the youth. Our activities were designed to lead them to work through these, learn of their commonality, and create the opportunity for them to coexist and reject racism. For those who were the object of racial attacks or other bias, our goal was to give support as we challenged the powers that be to open new paths for them to walk down.

Since the election of Harold Washington, we'd had access to summer jobs and, through our various programs, had hired young people between the ages of fourteen and eighteen to work on any of a number of projects. Our focus was work that needed doing and activities that enhanced problem-solving skills and interaction between groups of kids who would otherwise have nothing to do with each other. They participated in community cleanups. They worked on the summer lunch program. They visited pregnant mothers to let them know about available nutrition programs for them and their growing families.

Two years into my first term as alderman, the Heart of Uptown Coalition's summer program included a multiracial group—including Black, Latino, Vietnamese, and white students—who were assigned to work at the Black Ensemble Theater. Their job was to write and produce a musical play. Jackie Taylor, the theater's founder and director, and Jimmy Tillman, its musical director, joined Jeri Miglietta and Sean Griffin, an actor Jeri had recruited, in designing the summer project. This was a paying job, and the kids were expected to act accordingly. Jackie worked with them on writing the story, while Jimmy worked with them on writing the songs for their musical. Sean worked with them on acting techniques designed to break down their defenses. Everyone worked with them on their attitudes. Difficult discussions about drugs, sex, and racism were had. Tensions around these topics challenged their focus, and it seemed like a miracle when the summer program culminated with their production of *Uptown Sounds*, a musical play they wrote and performed about a teenage girl who overdoses on drugs.[28] One student became an ensemble member of the Black Ensemble Theater. At least one didn't survive the summer.

In summer 1991 a group of our kids—the sons and daughters of the Intercommunal Survival Committee and of the Heart of Uptown Coalition—came to the adults in their lives and said, "It's our turn now. We're going to run the summer and recreation programs." They had grown up together through our many programs, bonding through sports—as participants and as observers—as well as their choice of friends. By now many of them were out of high school. Some were in four-year colleges or on their way there, with academic or sports scholarships helping pay their ways. Others were at Truman College, where they found themselves as engaged in activities focused on the direction and funding for the City Colleges as they were on their studies. All of them had spent their summers playing softball and basketball games initiated by the Heart of Uptown Coalition.

Calling themselves the Uptown Youth Force, they were successful in expanding the summer softball league, demanding greater access to the softball fields at Clarendon Park, and organizing a football team. They

---

28 Local filmmakers Denice DeClue and Bob Schneiger followed them throughout the summer and later produced a film that was shown on WTTW, Chicago's public TV station.

also began a newspaper, *The Voice of the Next Generation*. *The Next Generation* would be the predecessor to the *Chi-Town Lowdown*, distributed citywide for a couple of years in the mid-1990s. Also during this time, poets and youth activists taught writing and arts through what would later become the spoken word and hip-hop-focused Kuumba Lynx. While all of this was occurring, Anton Miglietta and Jason Yolich started a morning student tutoring program at Stockton School called Rise and Shine. It was the beginning of what would become known as Youth on Youth, which would focus on youth-led programming, on their education, and on their future. It would lead to the training of more than fifty young progressive teachers and the transformation of Arai Middle School into the Uplift Community High School. But more of that later.

. . . .

64.

NAVIGATING THE POLICE

Throughout my tenure as alderman, I had a tension-filled relationship with the local police districts.[29] My demands for accountability and community control had not gone unnoticed. During my 1978–79 campaigns, I had called for a regulation to require officers to leave their guns at home if they intended to engage in drinking. Early in my first term as alderman, I had requested the investigation of two vice cops after rumors alleged their involvement in drug dealing on their beat. To say the least, this was not well received.

As a freshman alderman I had tested my ability to observe police officers at work. I had been rebuffed any time I stopped to observe

---

29 The Forty-Sixth Ward was entirely in the Twenty-Third Police District, commonly referred to as the Town Hall District, when I first was elected in 1987. After the 1990 remap of city wards, the Forty-Sixth Ward's boundary changes moved the ward north, adding some blocks that were in the Twentieth District (formerly known as the Summerdale District). Both districts were notorious in their own ways.

interactions on the street between officers and constituents—especially if the constituents were the poor of Uptown and/or people of color. "I don't care if you're an alderman. Move on. You have no business here." These were the most common refrains.

During the mayoralty of Richard J. Daley, police superintendents had retained a Red Squad within the police department that intentionally spied on Chicagoans. Its net had been expansive, including pretty much anyone who disagreed with the mayor or challenged him in any way. Concurrently, the police department had run a beat representative program where community reps appointed by local police district commanders had worked to "enhance" community relations with the police.

Before a federal lawsuit exposed and forced the dismantling of the Red Squad in the mid-1970s, the two had been indistinguishable. Both the beat representative program and the Red Squad had been creatures of the machine and political in nature, serving to maintain a good relationship between the police and a relatively small segment of the community; as a rule, poor people and people of color were not included, with the exception of those with a special relation to or sponsor from the machine. Violence and complaints of police misconduct, along with forced confessions (in place of substantive and effective detective work), had been the norm.

The Daley administration's response to gangs and gang violence had been "shoot to kill" and "lock them up." This stood in stark contrast to the approach favored and demonstrated by Fred Hampton and Cha Cha Jiménez in 1968 and 1969, which had striven to change the gang dynamic, bringing those involved into a positive collective interaction to make change and away from their individualistic reaction to the challenges of surviving in a hostile environment. This, they had argued, was the more effective path to fighting crime. It had been handily dismissed and demonized by police and the FBI.

With its existence now exposed, the primary change that occurred after the Red Squad was dismantled had been a nascent movement to find new solutions. With the beat rep program no longer in play, and with the election of Harold Washington, community-driven efforts to explore new approaches had become possible.

During Mayor Washington's first term, we brought Police Superintendent Fred Rice to meet with a roomful of community people concerned about their safety—many of whom wanted help from the police but feared misconduct. A first for us, the meeting had left us hopeful that it might be possible to change the historic dynamics.

Leroy O'Shield, the commander of the Austin District on the West Side, had begun a partnership with the local City College. They created a science-based project focused on aviation. The idea was to create a positive and welcoming environment for teenagers in the police district as a means to find common ground, build mutual respect, and change attitudes in which those involved had become stuck. Meanwhile, the city was funding innovative programs in various communities to address gang involvement and violence. These came with an assumption that given the chance and support, the futures of many Black, Brown, and poor white youth, whose paths seemed destined to lead them into the criminal justice system, could be turned around.[30]

All of these initiatives met resistance from many police officers, and always from the Fraternal Order of Police. Indeed, following Harold's untimely death, these initiatives were doomed. In their place, again and again members of the city council introduced small-fix ordinances that were designed to "crack down on crime" but that in reality cracked down on youth (particularly youth of color). Crackdowns on curfew violations as well as requirements for officers to write up cards on all interactions with young people on the street led to superficial assumptions that had drastic effects. Rather than encouraging teens to stay in school, to succeed where they had failed before, the alternative schools many attended were targeted for harassment and demonized.

We were struggling with this reality in Uptown, where tension between local police and young people was a constant dynamic. Relations were not much better with many adults in the community—at least those who had been around for some time. There was little trust that a police presence would turn out well for them or their loved ones. This was not a phenomenon limited to the heart of Uptown, but the status quo in all of Chicago's Black, Brown, poor, and working communities. It was also a dynamic reflected in the local politics of the Forty-Sixth Ward. My political opposition increasingly tied my efforts at improving

---

30 I do not think that it is coincidence that four of the six years with the
   lowest murder rates in Chicago between 1970 and 2005 occurred while
   Harold Washington was mayor.

Marion Stamps joins a broad coalition of Black leadership to announce a city-wide gang truce circa late 1980s to early 1990s.

affordability to crime (even as the years passed, and crime decreased), while aiming to achieve "law and order" by enhancing gentrification. This tension increased, becoming more and more polarizing as the ward became more and more gentrified.

By the end of my second term, talk of improving police–community relations was finding a new focus—community policing. Five of Chicago's twenty-five police districts were engaged in a community policing pilot program. But this time, their version of community policing did not include engagement with young people (outside of the various historic junior officer programs, or visits by "officer friendly" to elementary and middle schools). Although the districts covering the Forty-Sixth Ward were not included in this pilot, the potential for its expansion provided a focal point to meet with the commander of the Twenty-Third District about the tension that existed in Uptown and an opportunity to find some common ground. I took full advantage, holding monthly meetings with Commander Clisham (and every commander after him).

Several "drug corners" attracted many from outside the community to drive by and make purchases. Just a few blocks off Lake Shore Drive, these corners were convenient and had the appearance of being a safer place to buy drugs than the city's South or West Sides. Surely drugs were bought by locals as well, but the many luxury cars passing through for a quick stop and rapid turn back toward Lake Shore Drive convinced those who noticed that this was the engine behind the drug (as well as prostitution) trade on these corners and in much of Uptown.

Lillian Malachi lived in a court-way building near the corner of Agatite and Hazel, a known open-air drug market. Beverly Washington, Kanzella Hatley, and Beverly Ross lived on the corner. These four Black women were determined to make a difference. Their experience was that when the police did come, the dealers disbursed. The usual result (and complaint) was that anyone else around, especially young people, would be racially profiled and harassed—often leading to arrests for disorderly conduct.

Finding that unacceptable, they brainstormed their options. During the summer of 1994, in response, on many nights around 9:00 p.m. they took whatever chair they had handy and went outside to the corner, where they sat, played music, sometimes danced in the street, chatted, and caught up with their neighbors. By creating a noticeable presence, they closed down all trade while they were there.

That September, things came to a head when police shot and killed a Latino teen. The shooting, which happened a block from the corner of Hazel and Agatite, was ruled a justifiable homicide. The officers involved said the teen was selling drugs from the roof of a building when he began shooting at officers on the street below, who fired back. The police had apparently been called by tenants in the building who heard people on their roof, suspecting trouble. For several hours, helicopters circled the area, while the streets for several blocks in each direction were cordoned off.[31]

Young people, many of whom were sons and daughters of activists with the Heart of Uptown Coalition, knew the teen who was shot. They were hurt, and they were angry. While there were those who dismissed the event as being just another casualty of an unacceptable illegal drug trade, these teens and many of their parents, grandparents, and friends

---

31 The *Tribune* reported, "Area residents said they remembered him as a gang member who was friendly with neighbors, but who hung out with a bad crowd and sometimes hopped onto the roofs of passing cars for a ride." *Chicago Tribune*, September 28, 1994.

didn't trust the official account and demanded to know why he had to die for allegedly selling drugs.

We had just begun circulating nominating petitions for the upcoming aldermanic elections, scheduled for February 1995. The primary potential opposition candidate circulating petitions was a former vice cop who was now an attorney representing police (he would later become a defense attorney and a judge). Tensions were rising on all sides, with politics taking its turn as well. The temperature had to be turned down.

I asked the commander to come to a community meeting. The auditorium at Arai Middle School was a kiva—a sunken hall surrounded by a theater-inspired seating arrangement where attendees approached from above. This location assured the participation of the entire community—adults and young people alike, including both those who were 100 percent behind the police actions (many of whom had a bone to pick with me), and those who wanted a more nuanced approach.

Commander Clisham wore a hearing aid and couldn't make much out without it. The meeting was likely to get volatile, and my objective was to let everyone speak, rant, rave, whatever—just get their anger out (and hopefully out of their system)—while we would just listen, making every effort not to respond defensively. The last thing I wanted was to put more gasoline on the fire, and defensive responses by either of us would do just that. I explained this to him and asked him to turn off his hearing aid and appear to be listening. Without the benefit of the silence I expected he would enjoy, I promised to do the same.

The 1995 reelection campaign revolved around "crime and violence," which were really proxies for my opposition's argument that our housing policies were creating the crime. They usually never said outright that we were keeping too many Black and Brown teenagers in the community, but the arguments were clear. By the mid-1990s I was one of just a few opposition voices in the city council, but the elections always revolved around opposing visions for the future of Uptown.

Somehow we got through that meeting and the upcoming election. Soon after, Commander Clisham retired, and Joe DeLopez became our new commander. I asked for monthly meetings, to which he agreed. After the new city council was inaugurated along with Mayor Richard M. Daley, who was beginning his second full term, it was announced that the police department would begin a citywide community policing program called Chicago Alternative Policing Strategy (CAPS). Community members were chosen by the local police commander to convene monthly meetings in each of the city's 279 police beats.

It had been my hope that these meetings might afford an opportunity to find common ground for beat officers and community residents finding themselves on all sides of the divide—between those who felt protected by the police and those who desired their protection but had little expectation of receiving it. If the true intent of the CAPS program was to do problem solving, trust would have to be established. Finding common ground was to be a first step.

We never got there.

It's important to stress how in the 1990s, the concept of CAPS followed two decades of fighting for "community policing," and how there was so much hope that CAPS would actually make a difference. Over time, however, it became clear CAPS would neither reduce violence nor improve community and police relations. The monthly beat meetings became echo chambers for venting anger, frustration, and easy scapegoats. We had to look for other solutions. There were several nonprofit groups that had experience in gang intervention in the city. Whenever possible, I had them work with youth in Uptown, BUILD and Ceasefire being the most effective. With some assistance from Commander De-Lopez, we were able to sponsor midnight basketball at Truman College.

In retrospect, however, the most effective anti-violence work was the youth recreation and education programming done by the sons and daughters of the community.

As with most things in life, it often takes twenty years or more to truly learn whether something was a good idea—whether it accomplished the desired goals, and if not, to have the experience to know why not, and change direction. We embraced Leroy O'Shield's strategy in the Austin District. It was fresh and innovative, and assumed the best of young people on the West Side. But try as O'Shield might, many of the majority white officers (and some of the Black officers as well) in that district resisted it. The mid-1990s version of community policing would fare no better and in fact created more alienation between sectors of the community and the police in many of Chicago's twenty-five police districts.

The police department was, and still is, dominated by a culture embedded in white supremacy—reflective of the dominant culture in our country. In retrospect, it was a fool's errand to think we could effectively address this bigger dynamic without addressing the driving force of the power structure that embraced it. Attempting to change one police station at a time was not going to lead to systemic change. As long as the dominant culture of individual police remained steeped in white supremacy (regardless of the race of the cops), community-related programming at police stations (as opposed to schools or parks) would be nothing more than public relations and indoctrination.

The corollary to Harold's constant refrain of "It takes twenty to thirty years to effect institutional change" was another ISC maxim: it would take twenty to thirty years to see what things we did right and what we did wrong. While some of the things we did twenty, thirty, forty, and fifty years ago seem like obvious failures now, they did not at the time. And vice versa. The real point is that if we had not taken action, not done the things that made sense at the time, and not followed the natural path where the movement and the people brought us, we would not have been able to look back thirty years later to see what went wrong. There are undoubtedly things that leaders and movement activists are doing today that they will look back at and cringe about in thirty years. But if they don't do them they will never know. There is nothing inconsistent about being moored to principles of justice, fairness, and equity, while being flexible about the paths and solutions to obtaining those principles. In fact, history has shown that it's required.

. . . .

65.

HEAT WAVE

On a Friday afternoon in the summer of 1995, Chicagoans were enduring the third day in a row of extreme weather, with temperatures in the upper nineties. Heading into the weekend, we'd heard on the news that there was no end in sight, and that we should expect temperatures up to one hundred degrees for the next several days. I called the Department of Human Services to get the hours and locations of cooling centers over the weekend so I could post them for my constituents. The response I got was that there were no plans for any cooling centers.

Given that I suspected people without air conditioning were already experiencing a life-threatening situation, I was horrified at the response. I took note that I would be seeing Mayor Daley at a public event the next day. The Jane Addams Senior Caucus was holding a meeting and rally at St. Luke's Church, on Belmont Avenue in the Forty-Fourth Ward, and the mayor had committed to come. The event was standing room only as a crowd of over five hundred packed into the church sanctuary to hear the mayor's response to their demand for support for affordable housing for seniors. The caucus had settled on a location in the Forty-Sixth Ward that once housed the Palacio Theater, and they wanted his commitment to work with me to get it done.

As the meeting proceeded, so did the first reports of people in the city dying from the extreme heat. Everyone was anxious to wrap up the meeting—so that the seniors could get home and out of the heat, and the city officials could get moving on addressing the emergency. By noon the mayor had agreed to the demand for senior housing, and the meeting was breaking up. I approached the mayor, explaining to him that I was concerned that the blueprint for dealing with heat waves was being ignored and that at a minimum cooling centers should be opened immediately.

Mayor Daley and I were not on the best of terms. Symbolically to many in city government, as the one consistent vote against his budget, the position of the mayor's palace guard and commissioners was to avoid me at all costs. In spite of their evasion, I had learned to be effective in service delivery. I had studied the city budget in great detail, as much to know what was available to my constituents in each department as to ensure a public discussion during our annual budget hearings. Obviously this was a double-edged sword. But, armed with the knowledge of what was actually budgeted, and by working directly and respectfully with the people in each department who actually did the work (while protecting them by keeping our exchanges private), I was able to get a lot done. But this was bigger than all that. There had to be action and direction by the mayor. This was way more important than the political advantages to be brought by exposing the city's failures. People were literally dropping like flies.

By Monday morning I was meeting with Tim Degnan (head of Intergovernmental Affairs and political operative for the mayor), Pat Huels (aldermanic floor leader and alderman of the mayor's home ward), and George Atkins (back as my chief of staff). A decade earlier, during the summer of 1984, the city had experienced a similar, albeit shorter, heat wave. Following an outbreak of deaths due to the excessive temperatures smothering the city, Harold Washington's health department had sprung immediately into action. One outcome was the heat emergency plan that they had intended as a blueprint for all future heat emergencies.

I suggested to Huels and Degnan that they dig up those heat wave procedures, giving them a list of fifteen things that could and should be done immediately to save lives and alleviate some of the pain people throughout the city were experiencing. They did not seem to be taking me very seriously. I knew they were only there because the mayor told them to be, and that all were fearful of the media deluge I could potentially create.

At that moment I was much more concerned about the people dying. Hundreds had already died from heat-related causes, and some of the deceased had lived in my ward. All were people with few resources living in difficult housing situations or homeless, and few if any had access to cool air and therefore any relief. Their bodies simply couldn't take the heat, and the threat the continuing extreme conditions posed to children and the elderly was undeniable. The death toll would ultimately reach 739.

The city had to take this emergency seriously. Multiple departments had the expertise, resources, and mandate to respond. Wellness checks of senior citizens living alone as well as adults living in single room occupancy hotels would be a good first start.

Opening cooling centers 24/7 throughout the city until temperatures dipped below ninety degrees was a no brainer. If locations weren't available, Chicago Transit Authority buses should be available and stationed with their air conditioning on near locations where the largest number of deaths were occurring. We had successfully implemented this approach for victims of fires in my ward a few years earlier, as a place for people to wait while the firefighters did their job and the Red Cross helped explore options. Why not do the same now to cool people off?

Fire hydrants were a common source of cooling for children. However, playing in hydrants was dangerous and frowned upon: not only were children often blind to passing motorists, but there was a constant fear that the loss of water pressure would make it impossible to fight any fires that might occur. I suggested placing sprinkler caps on fire hydrants and recruiting adults to supervise their opening so children could get cooled off safely. Where public pools were available, they obviously needed to be opened, and their hours expanded.

These were among the fifteen or so suggestions I demanded the city implement by the end of the week. I promised I would not go to the media unless they failed to do so.

On Friday morning, Degnan found me to let me know all my suggestions were implemented. With a somewhat cynical smile, he grinned and said, "So you won't be going to the press?"

I did not. Knowing and believing that my word was my bond was an important element in my ability to successfully navigate the political waters. But I did receive some pushback from some of my close friends and supporters who felt I should have taken the opportunity to blast the mayor and his administration for being callous and unresponsive. In the end, I chose a material impact (in this case ending the deaths) over political expediency.

· ·

66.

STEADYING THE COURSE AS AFFORDABLE HOUSING HITS A DRY SPELL

Marina Carrott was appointed housing commissioner by Mayor Richard M. Daley in 1992. She would spend the next five years doing her best to make sure that no affordable housing initiatives saw the light of day in Uptown. My staff and I knew every rental building in the ward, kept track of their rental policies, identified any potential rent subsidies (along with vacancies) and made that information available to anyone looking

Demonstrations for affordable housing were common, often focusing on preserving abandoned buildings and vacant lots for affordable housing. Showing the need and making the demand again and again helped to create the sea that would eventually break the logjam allowing a modicum of new housing. This, however, came too late for many. The Cambodian community had been prominent in Uptown until the buildings they lived in again and again were slated for condo conversions. While Kompha Seth, director of the Cambodian Association is pictured below participating in a march for affordability, by my third term the Cambodian community had little presence here.

for an apartment they could afford. By my second term, the numbers of people coming to my ward office for that list had grown exponentially, and I was anxious to stabilize the housing market for all who lived in the ward. In spite of city hall's intransigence, it was time for some concrete action toward assuring development without displacement.

Following Harold Washington's death, the legislation I'd introduced in my first term had gone nowhere. I had initially hoped to get some support from the acting mayor, Eugene Sawyer, but quickly realized that was not to be. If we were going to impact city policy, it was going to be through community and legal action. As an alderman, if I couldn't yet affect legislation, I would do my best to win over building owners and developers one by one.

Lakefront SRO (single-room occupancy) units had been formed during the years of the Washington administration in response to the growing needs of homeless people to find housing. They had received strong support from the administration as they developed a supportive housing model in their first rehab of the Harold Washington Apartments. They were breaking ground, addressing a specific need, and were able to garner broad support. The Harold Washington Apartments were in the Forty-Eighth Ward,[32] and Lakefront SRO had the support of the alderman who had voted for Sawyer and was a close ally of Mayor Daley. In the course of the next several years, as they purchased three additional buildings in the Forty-Sixth Ward, they did not lose this support and were consequently a rare exception to Carrott's obstruction.

Most of the long-term affordability could be found in the HUD-financed high-rises built during the late 1960s and early '70s. Each of these had a different mix of subsidized units. A few were 100 percent subsidized with Section 8 certificates.[33] Most had a mix of Section 8 rents and what was considered moderate rents.[34] Originally built with

---

32 It was redistricted into the Forty-Sixth Ward after the 2000 census.

33 Tenants living in these units would pay 30 percent of their income as rent. HUD would pay the difference between the market rent on the apartment and the rent the tenant paid.

34 In return for a low-interest loan from HUD, the developers of these buildings had agreed to rent the apartments that did not have Section 8s attached to them at a below-market rent agreed to by HUD. These rents would be reviewed annually or at the request of the building ownership and tended to be only slightly less than the market rate.

low-interest loans at a time when mortgage rates were double digit, the developers that built them had not maintained them very well. Deferred maintenance and poor management came to a head when, in 1979, tenants at 810 West Grace successfully worked out an agreement with HUD to transform their building into a co-op.

In 1986 the owner of 833 West Buena, located across the street from a row of mansions in the southern end of Uptown, announced he would take advantage of a previously unknown prepayment clause. The Heart of Uptown Coalition took this as a warning shot. If a HUD-mortgaged building in Chicago could terminate its commitment to affordable housing twenty years earlier than originally promised, how many more HUD-mortgaged building owners would do the same?

In response, we joined the Organization of the Northeast (ONE) in taking on the fight to keep these units affordable. Mobilizing tenants and other supporters of affordable housing, ONE brought Boston congressman Barney Frank, a committed advocate for affordable housing, to a rally to bring attention to this impending loss.

Between 1966 and 1991, hundreds of thousands of units of housing had been built in every state of the union. While most of these in Chicago were in buildings that were considered housing for families, quite a few nationally were in buildings dedicated to senior citizens. A hue and cry exploded nationwide as tenants realized the potential loss of their housing.

Confronting the issue head-on was Congressman Frank as he led the charge in Washington for a solution. He successfully appealed to Republican and Democratic congressmen who had these HUD-mortgaged high-rises in their districts—many of them housing senior citizens, a reliable voting block for most incumbents.

During the following five years, multiple acts of Congress passed and were enacted to encourage the preservation of these buildings' affordability. This encouragement came in the form of renewed and additional subsidies and financial packages to the current owners, the opportunity for tenants to gain ownership, and a requirement that all buildings that stay in the program have tenant elections for an advisory board for the building.

There were just over four thousand of these units in the Forty-Sixth Ward, each of them unique and facing its own challenges. Their preservation would be a priority.

HUD regulations and federal law required all HUD-mortgaged buildings to have tenant associations elected by the majority of tenants. Tenants organized in every building to make sure they had a say, ensuring they had a path to preserve their housing. Each of the buildings in the ward had a creative and innovative solution. Some were co-ops or tenant-owned; some were public-private partnerships; some were owned by nonprofits. In the end, the breadth of creativity in Uptown created models for the country as a whole; and, it could be argued, the existence of these high-rises and their remarkably diverse immigrant populations ensured most of the remaining economic and racial diversity in Uptown.

The first building in the country to prepay their mortgage was 833 West Buena. The last to take advantage of the incentives to preserve affordability would be 707 West Waveland. The deadline to apply for the preservation financing approved by Congress was closing in, and the tenants at 707 West Waveland were unengaged. It was unclear what would happen to their building, and I was concerned, while they seemed unaware. The character of this building was unique among the HUD-financed buildings I was familiar with. In most buildings, there tended to be a significant number of people who were refugees from one world conflict or another. However, the majority of people living here had been born in Chicago, with a minority from several African nations. Most of the people I knew who lived here had been young professionals working in state government jobs, so I was surprised that they appeared to be unaware of the potential loss of their homes.

The meeting space was in the bike room of their building. Large enough to comfortably hold up to thirty or so people, with a constant hum from the building's mechanicals and very poor acoustics, the bike room was filled to capacity as I shouted above the din to get everyone's attention. My goal was to challenge them to take command of their housing situation, put together a core group, organize the rest of the building tenants, and make a proposal. And they did. Barely meeting the deadline, a core group of tenants led by Cynthia Stewart did the work to get majority support in the building and found a development team they could work with. They submitted their application just under the deadline.

During Marina Carrott's tenure, the preservation of HUD-financed buildings was pretty much the only affordable housing development in the Forty-Sixth Ward that she couldn't block. But that didn't stop some from at least getting started. There were many others who shared my concerns. The Jane Addams Senior Caucus had by then been active in Lakeview for years. Lakeview had been through a rash of condo conversions in buildings where seniors had previously lived comfortably and with rents they could afford. Now they were finding fewer and fewer places they could afford. They went about doing something about it.

Ruth Shriman, their founder, had provided inspiration and a no-nonsense, can-do spirit that would be carried on by Mary Burns and others following her death in 1994. The caucus "went to school" with student architects at the University of Illinois at Chicago who were assigned to work with the seniors to design their future senior-only building. They looked for potential properties that would accommodate the housing they envisioned. They organized support for their effort, leading to the meeting I had attended at St. Luke's Church in the middle of the city's 1995 heat wave. It was there that Mayor Daley, faced with hundreds of seniors, was asked by Mary if he would agree to support the city's sale to them, for one dollar, of the land where the former Palacio Theater sat. He said yes.

It would take another four-plus years from that day for this new housing to reach completion, and it would not be an easy road. The site of the former Palacio Theater was located in Buena Park on the southern end of the heart of Uptown, and had received designation as a historic district when Jerry Orbach was alderman in 1984. At the time, we had been concerned that this was a realtor-favored move, designed in part as a marketing tool that would result in the rapid gentrification of the neighborhood. We had not been wrong on that account. The core of my opponents who were committed to seeing "not one more unit of low-income housing" in the Forty-Sixth Ward took immediate aim at this housing.

While Buena Park Neighbors and Sheridan Park Neighbors mobilized opposition to the housing being proposed by the Jane Addams Caucus, Mary Burns and her steering committee of committed caucus members kept focused on designing their building, getting it financed, and protecting the political support they had earned.

The first tenants moved into the Ruth Shriman House (named in honor of the person who had inspired the project in the first place) in January 1999 to apartments with full kitchens and large bedrooms. Buena Park Neighbors, who had charged that the senior housing would be a blight on the community, create crime, and bring down their property values, never apologized to Mary and the other tenant leaders. They did, however, ask if they could hold their monthly meetings in the building's well-equipped and sizable meeting room.

This would be the second time since I had become alderman that a proposal for affordable housing for and by a particular group of people was rehabbed or constructed at the initiative of a not-for-profit. In both cases, the not-for-profit would initially own the property with a non-profit partner. In the case of KOSOH, it had been the Chicago Equity Fund. In this case, it was the Interfaith Housing Development Corporation. In both developments, multiple layers of financing followed by a patchwork of subsidies would be used to accomplish the goal of providing housing affordable to people with fixed incomes that ranged from very low to fairly moderate.

Following construction, both buildings experienced problems. In the KOSOH housing, the plumbing took years to correct. At Ruth Shriman, attempts to solve a problem with the facade of the building, which allowed a mysterious appearance of water inside apartments after a heavy rain, were elusive. Finally, additional facade work corrected the problem, although I hear there is still the occasional complaint.

Management of affordable housing is a difficult task. We have a market-driven economy where the highest and "best" use reigns. Any notion to provide affordable housing is an outlier, posing a challenge to this status quo, just as any notion of rent control is anathema. Property taxes are an important source of income for the Chicago and Cook County governments, as well as the board of education and several smaller taxing bodies, but they are a serious drain on the finances of affordable housing.

Buildings housing lower-income tenants and receiving less income than market-rate housing paid the same property taxes, and these taxes increased as the community became more and more gentrified.[35] The buildings developed by KOSOH and Jane Addams Senior Caucus were

---

35 Over time, some avenues for relief have been created, but they have been limited in their reach and duration.

challenged from the beginning. While their issues varied, they required more expertise than could be provided by the two not-for-profits, or by their supporters (including myself).

The Jane Addams Senior Caucus, as Access Living had done a few years earlier, was committed to more than the bricks and mortar. They were a grassroots effort led by seniors to provide opportunities to take collective action together. Members of their housing committee intended to live in the housing they were designing, and they had every intention of creating an environment that would enhance community.

. . . .

67.

"IS BURKE IN JAIL YET?"

Following my run for alderman in the special election in mid-1978 and the campaign's continuation in the 1979 election cycle, Marc Zalkin had taken over most of my duties as managing editor of *Keep Strong*. He had begun with a series of investigative reports that would start with the so-called Donkey Club's move from the West Side to the Forty-Sixth and Forty-Eighth Wards and arson for profit in Uptown. As we began publishing *All Chicago City News* in 1980, Marc was uncovering connections between Alderman Ed Burke's voting record in city council and clients of his law firm, who were affected by city council action. Smelling a rat, he wrote about it in the paper.

Marc was diagnosed with multiple sclerosis in 1980—although in retrospect he had shown symptoms as early as 1970, when we were living in Racine. The trigger was probably the time he had spent the summer before working in a forge lifting fifty- to one-hundred-pound pieces of iron in upward of one-hundred-degree temperatures, five days a week for a good eight weeks. Two years after his diagnosis, Marc spent the coldest months of the winter of 1982–83 as part of Harold Washington's advance team during his successful primary run for mayor of Chicago. Leading into the election, Marc was using a cane to steady his step. By its end, he was using a wheelchair.

Harold liked the speeches Marc wrote, and after his election Marc was hired as an assistant press secretary, a position he held until Daley was elected and cleaned out the holdovers. For the next eight and a half years, MS ravaged Marc's body, but he managed to continue to organize any number of ability rights groups and activities. For the most part, he needed health care assistance 24/7. He had become good friends with Linda, a nurse who coordinated his health resources to fit his needs and who was his best advocate on all health-related matters.

In the spring of 1996, Marc was admitted to the ICU at Northwestern Hospital. We were married but separated, and Marc was on my insurance. Early in the day, I got a call from the hospital asking me to come as soon as possible. I was concerned—this was the ICU after all—and arranged for Brendan to come home that same day from Washington, DC, where he was attending Howard University, before heading to the hospital.

Marc had pneumonia in one lung and had been put on 100 percent oxygen. When I arrived, he was not really aware of anything going on around him and incapable of agreeing to or denying any treatment. The staff at the ICU seemed frantic. They pulled me aside immediately. They wanted to give Marc a tracheotomy, and Linda had refused on Marc's behalf. "He had made it clear he wanted no life-sustaining tubes, ever," she said.

The staff figured out that Marc was on his spouse's insurance and that his spouse was an alderman, and an outspoken one at that. Hospitals are dependent on the city for many things. They were anxious for my approval. A trach, they promised, was just temporary, but without it he would not be able to continue to breathe and would die.

I asked when they thought it would get to that point. "Anytime in the next twelve hours," they said. I asked them for an hour to confer with family and friends. I talked with Linda and then left the hospital to meet up with George and Brendan, who had by now arrived from DC. Brendan was Marc's closest adult family, and any decisions had to include him. Because I didn't want the burden to fall on him, I recruited George (the one person close to us both) so that we would make any decision that might be required together.

The docs swore that the trach was not a permanent tube and that it could be removed as soon as Marc recovered from pneumonia, at which point he would breathe on his own. We agreed that I would stay in the ICU overnight, or until such time as the doctors felt it was a now-or-never situation. We agreed that at that point I would consent to the tracheotomy. With a show of relief, they let me stay, roaming back and forth between Marc's cubbyhole in the ICU and the ICU waiting room, where I was otherwise camped out. At 6:00 a.m. they told me he was barely breathing. Moments later, they gave him a tracheotomy.

Thirty days later, Marc was moved to a patient room in the hospital. For the first time in a month, he was not receiving 100 percent oxygen and was aware of his surroundings. When he first woke up in the regular hospital room, I was standing by his bed. He took one look at me and said, "What are you doing here?" Then, without skipping a beat, he said, "Is Burke in jail yet?"

After returning from California to coordinate the field operation during my three aldermanic elections in 1978 and 1979, Marc had organized several grassroots campaigns on the Northwest and Southwest Sides of Chicago. Most notable was the Family Advantage, which focused on retaining bus service on South California Avenue and relief from high gas and electric bills. Zeroing in on Peoples Gas, an ordinance before the city council was designed to pressure the state legislature and the Illinois Commerce Commission to rein in Peoples Gas and lower rates that many were having difficulty paying.

While purporting to be supportive, Alderman Ed Burke was instrumental in preventing the ordinance from passage. Marc was livid. This kind of double dealing was unacceptable. Marc suspected that while claiming to support efforts demanded by his constituents to rein in Peoples Gas with one hand, Burke's law firm was representing Peoples Gas with the other.

After Harold Washington's election as mayor, Marc had many opportunities to see Burke's political duplicity firsthand. Mayor Washington's opposition might as well have been called the Vrdolyak/Burke Twenty-Nine; the two were peas in a pod, opportunistically deploying a cynical and racist playbook to retain power. As an assistant press secretary, Marc often wrote remarks for the mayor. He did his own research and had a front-row seat.

Three years following his stint in the ICU, after a difficult struggle with an aggressive form of MS, Marc died in early 1998. When I returned to my first city council meeting after burying Marc, Ed Burke presented me with a death resolution honoring Marc's life. Asking me if it would be okay to introduce this to the full city council for a vote, I could only imagine Marc turning over in his grave. However, I then thought of his mother and how proud she would be to have such a resolution. I could have written one myself, but I decided instead to tell Burke Marc's story—the one I just related. If, after that, he still wanted to present his resolution, that would be fine with me. He smiled and said sure, and I let him know Marc thought he belonged in jail. When I was done, he nodded his head as his face turned a bright red, and proceeded to introduce and request passage of the resolution.

Two weeks later, I received parchment copies of the resolution, along with a letter from Ed Burke. It was a formal letter, personalized with a note that read, "Helen, I'm certain Marc would appreciate the irony. Ed."

. . . .

68.

MY THIRD TERM
FROM TWENTIETH-CENTURY ACTIVISM TO TWENTY-FIRST-CENTURY GOVERNANCE

My first term was primarily defined by the collective trauma of Harold Washington's death and the incessant hope that the coalition and vision that had driven his campaign would still be ascendant. Whether it was Tim Evans's campaign for mayor or that of Danny Davis, Joe Gardner, or others, we kept hoping for the leader that would pull it together. Alliances that included Dorothy Tillman, Bobby Rush, Luis Gutiérrez, Jesús "Chuy" García, John Steele, Ray Figueroa, and others afforded some victories as the machine regrouped.

Similarly, my second term had significant, albeit finite, victories both in the council and in the ward as I and my office remained grounded and tied to organizers and activists who were still active and effective locally and citywide.

By the time I was elected to my third term in 1995, my commitment to a career as an elected official—something I never planned or desired—had become clear, and most of that grounding and backup had dissipated. Danny, Bobby, and Luis were all now in Congress. Chuy was in Springfield. Tim Evans and Ray Figueroa were judges. Daley, the son, had completely consolidated power.

There's a narrative that for years I was the lone voice against Daley and what remained of the machine. This, of course, was never true. But when people tell that story, they are talking about the years from 1995 to 1999, when I cast the sole vote against the city budget. And sometimes it felt like they were right.

In the ward, almost all the community institutions we had created in the 1970s had faded away. Justice Graphics, which continued publishing newspapers that impacted the citywide dialogue and provided context for my work, closed in 1998. While the Uptown People's Law Center would survive, the Uptown Learning Center, the Chicago Area Black Lung Association, the Uptown Community Service Center, and the Heart of Uptown Coalition had all faded away in the mid-1990s. Slim Coleman moved to organize in West Town.

My staff in the first two terms had mostly consisted of older folks with the history and context of our earlier struggles and included Sandra White, whose mother was a plaintiff in the Avery lawsuit. Beginning in my third term, my staff, aside from Denice Davis, was younger and included Lily Rodriguez, whose eighth-grade class I had taught at Arai, and Keri Krupp, who had interned at the Law Center during her senior year at Northwestern. When Keri left the following year to begin graduate school, Tania Lindsay—Joy and Tom Lindsay's daughter who had lived with Brendan in child development for the first six years of her life—took her place. Later Eric Butler, fresh from a stint as a board member with Voice of the People, would come on board. These were a solid group of people committed to social change and serving the people. But they weren't the 24/7 cadre I had grown to rely on. They had lives.

The fading away of our community institutions left me untethered. My young staff were committed to social change and embraced the challenge to be bureaucracy busters in service of our constituents. But our ward was divided, and gentrification was outpacing any attempts to stem the tide. This dynamic had a life of its own that brought with it a mean spirit that weighed heavily on all of us. Construction was beginning on the affordable senior housing that had been championed by the Jane Addams Senior Caucus. The persistent opposition it met was venomous, antagonistic, and specifically targeted Tania as she represented me at several meetings. Beat meetings for the Chicago Alternative Policing Strategy program were also increasingly antagonistic.

In retrospect, I was impatient with the inexperience of my staff—expecting more from them than was fair. I failed to realize the extent of the pressure they were under (most often on my behalf). My attention was divided. I enrolled in a master's degree program at DePaul University's School for New Learning in September 1997. Designed for working students and with an emphasis on critical thinking, this program provided numerous opportunities to take a critical look at all aspects of my work and history, and would prove invaluable—but in these first few months it was no doubt a distraction. In November, I turned fifty. Tensions with my mother over my brother's abuse so many years earlier had come to a head. I was frustrated by the changes in the ward. In retrospect, I was sending mixed messages and increasingly short with my staff. They revolted, staging a walkout just days before the new year.

While faced with the unplanned reorganization of my staff and the beginning of a decade-long process to realize the Wilson Yard development, Justice Graphics was selling the building where my office was located. Paris Dance (a popular lesbian bar and dancehall), with whom we had shared a parking lot, closed and was bought by the same developer purchasing our space. After ten years, we had to move.

We received our first email address from the city in January 1998, just as Maggie Marystone came on board. In her early twenties, Maggie was relatively new to Chicago, having been raised in Springfield, Illinois. Denice DeClue, a supporter and Uptown resident, had recommended Maggie after she worked with her on a film project. Maggie had even less experience than Lily, Keri, and Tania when they first came to work for me. But she was smart, quick, curious, and absorbed everything around her like a sponge. She quickly became our in-house techie, learning everything she could as the city set up the first websites for each alderman.

The next nine months saw Marc die from complications of MS, the birth of my granddaughter Justice, and the marriage of her parents, while I cobbled together a staff and began what would be a decade-long process to realize the Wilson Yard development and the prospects of another election—if I was to run for a fourth term.

The next generation was in full gear with their work. In 1997, Youth on Youth was thriving. Dozens of the present and former participants were in school to become teachers. And there were many community institutions that had existed before us that were marching on. The revolution we had envisioned thirty years earlier had not happened. In its place was a revolution in technology that I didn't quite understand. My skills, relationships, and impact now were firmly planted in my understanding of city government, of its budget, and of how to impact city policy. But I needed to come to peace with leaving the structures and grounding of the 1970s and '80s that had guided so much of my work in the past and find that grounding in the work of the next generation and other leaders in the community.

I also had to relearn an important lesson: to choose humility over the prestige of power. Indeed, such power is elusive and self-serving at best. There were simply things I could not control. The retrenchment of power in the machine and right-wing forces was out of my control. But I could continue to hold them accountable and provide fodder to activists through the budget hearing process. There were only so many things I could do in Uptown to ensure that those most affected had a say, but I would keep doing them. I would focus on the things I could impact and be intentional about connecting with the people in the community doing the work.

I had learned important lessons: do no harm—remember that every action, every law passed, every policy implemented has unintended consequences, and that sometimes these consequences outweigh the benefits of whatever the original goal was. Define public policy from the perspective of those most affected. Use the benefit of a positive material impact for those with the fewest resources to evaluate positions on legislative decision making.

These realizations would fuel my work for three more terms.

69.

HOMELESS TASK FORCE

When I had first arrived in Chicago, Uptown had a legacy of social services. While the Intercommunal Survival Committee and later the Heart of Uptown Coalition interacted with them, our focus was to create programs in the community by and with the people most affected. We were focused on "survival pending revolution" and organizing for the change we sought. However, people often turned to existing private and public institutions and social service agencies for help and assistance. There were times when we found these programs lacking or disrespectful, and we were not shy about saying so. Sometimes (like with the lunch program during the 1970s) we started our own—to do it right. Sometimes we acted as advocates. But when the machine-aligned Uptown Chicago Commission[36] demanded they move out of Uptown, we were the ally of any services that brought relief to the day-to-day struggle to survive that so many people faced.

When I became alderman, I had a mantra that my staff and I were "bureaucracy busters," meaning our job was to advocate for our constituents with the bureaucracies of government, break through their roadblocks, and get results—especially when we were told that our requests were not possible. To be effective, the social services that served people in need required more collaboration and coordination. Some of the agencies were already attempting to do this. I supported and strove to enhance these efforts.

By 1998 there were a growing number of homeless people in the city, particularly in the Forty-Sixth Ward, while there were insufficient resources available to address the cause of this increase, let alone respond to people's immediate needs. For the most part this was a

---

36 Started in 1954, the UCC was a civic organization aligned with local financial, insurance, and hospital interests and reflected the interests of the regular Democratic Party and the political machinery of Richard J. Daley. During the 1980s, its leadership changed, as did its membership, focusing on people moving into the new condos and influenced heavily by real estate interests whose bread and butter was gentrification.

population of people better left invisible. Many homeless people had begun to camp out in Lincoln Park, on the east end of the ward. Complaints to the Park District forced them to to move to an area between Lake Shore Drive and Clarendon Avenue, and in the process many people lost the few belongings they had, in a further destabilization of their already-fragile existence. Homeless shelters were struggling to provide adequate assistance such as food, shelter, employment assistance, health care, and safe daytime activities, but not everyone had (or wanted) access to these services.

The Department of Human Services and the police department were the city agencies most involved, as were Thorek Hospital and Weiss Memorial Hospital (the two hospitals in the ward.) I met monthly with Joe DeLopez, who was now the commander of the Twenty-Third District and was in near-constant touch with Carmelo Vargas, who was in charge of emergency services for DHS. I was frustrated with and angered by the mean-spirited demands to remove the homeless from sight—even when they were doing no one harm. I was hungry for some seriously effective problem solving.

DeLopez and Vargas agreed to join me in organizing a tour of all the homeless providers. The idea was to put all the policy makers together (from the city and from each of the agencies) and do some brainstorming. By now Evelyn Diaz had joined my staff, following her graduation from the master's program at the University of Chicago's Harris School of Social Work. I had met her while making a presentation to one of her classes earlier in the year. Evelyn would eventually become a very accomplished administrator for the Daley administration, then for Rahm Emanuel; later she would become the president of the Heartland Alliance. She was extremely talented, and I was lucky to have her on my staff, even briefly. This was a perfect project for her.

We requested the bus used by the mayor for ward tours and contacted all the agencies. With their schedules in hand, we designed a series of three tours—one for each of the three shifts the police worked. DeLopez committed his sergeant to joining me on all three shifts. He would come himself during the day. Vargas committed to all shifts, additionally assigning staff who were in charge of responding to homeless services during each. Each of the service providers agreed to have someone with us on the bus during each shift. They notified their staff at every site we would visit of when and why we were coming. With feedback from each site, they also worked with us to make sure our visit was expected by their clients and that their privacy was respected.

Evelyn managed to get everyone where and when they were supposed to be, whether on the bus or at their program. Policy makers from each of the places we visited joined us on the bus as we talked policy and resources with the police and DHS staff on board, affording a new set of relationships and lines of communication that would prove helpful in the future. But the most innovative outcome was action taken by DeLopez. He would soon after ask for two officers to volunteer to work as a homeless team. When on duty, they were assigned to respond to calls related to the homeless.

These two officers took to their new assignment quickly, interacting directly with the homeless people they encountered. They learned their stories, their trials and tribulations, and came to see them as alive and breathing, full human beings with real needs that were not being met. Increasingly, when they were called on to attend beat meetings when homelessness was on the agenda, they were caught in the divisive polarization along class and race lines that I had come to expect, but that most officers were usually spared. This unit, however, lasted only as long as DeLopez was commander, and it was disbanded when he was promoted a few years later to a position at the central headquarters.

. . . .

70.

BUDGETS
A SYMBOLIC AND TRUE BATTLEGROUND

The Chicago City Council is required by state law to pass a balanced budget each year by December 31. Historically, during my time in Chicago until Harold Washington became mayor, there was little public discussion of the budget. The mayor released a budget in November, and action was taken swiftly by the city council Finance Committee. Most discussion occurred behind closed doors—and usually only with trusted allies of the machine.

Shortly after his election in 1983, Harold issued an executive order that aimed to allow for more discussion by requiring the release of the budget by October 15. Public hearings were held in communities throughout the city before the aldermen met in a newly formed Budget Committee, where every department head appeared to present their priorities for the following year and answer the questions posed to them by aldermen. Almost as important—perhaps in part because now there were fewer secrets—the government was opening up. With the city's 1984 budget (the first one presented by the Washington administration), funds for community organizations to be partners in carrying out programs in health, job training, recreation, education, day care, and gang intervention more than tripled.

During my time as alderman, I served under three mayors[37] and several Budget Committee chairs. That first year, I went to every hearing, quickly realizing that I had a lot to learn. If I was to realize my goal of impacting public policy from the perspective of those most affected, while incurring the least negative collateral impacts, I needed to follow the money. If I was to achieve my secondary goal of establishing an effective full-service ward office, I needed to establish relationships with every department—with those who made the policies as well as those primarily responsible for carrying them out. Understanding the budget would be the foundation of these efforts.

By the time Richard M. Daley was elected mayor, I had a better understanding of how things worked and of the city's operations. But now I encountered a roadblock when it came to the budget: the word was out to department heads and city workers—I was a persona non grata. Because I was not a member of the Budget Committee, I was only able to ask questions after all members present had asked theirs first. A time limit of ten minutes was placed on all first-round questioning. Unfortunately, few aldermen attended most hearings, and after the first round, no committee member had any questions to ask; as a result, there was no second round. Often just one other alderman besides the chair was present, unless we were hearing from the Department of

---

37 Four if you count David Orr, who served in an acting capacity for six days following Harold Washington's death.

Streets and Sanitation, any of the infrastructure departments, or the police department.

My response was to be prepared and to persist. Each September, I studied previous budgets for each department and formulated questions for every department head, sending them letters with my questions in advance of receiving the mayor's proposed budget. This gave them plenty of time to prepare answers prior to their department's scheduled appearance before the city council Budget Committee. It would be more than a decade before I received a response to most of these letters, but I didn't let that stop me. I made the best use of my ten-minute rounds of questioning. In that public forum, before interested citizens who would come to hear the testimony as well as the members of the media who came each day, I asked my questions, got some response, and pressed on—often with follow-up questions—hounding each commissioner and Intergovernmental Affairs for the answers.

These budget hearings afforded me an opportunity to get a lot of work done while learning where to find the resources we might need in the ward. From the time Daley became mayor in 1989 until I voted yes on a budget in 2000, as long as I could be counted on to keep quiet about who was responsive to any issue that needed resolving, I could count on getting most of the outstanding service requests from my office completed by the date of the budget hearing for most departments. I would prepare a list of outstanding potholes, sewer collapses, trees that needed trimming, streetlights and alley lights that were out, streets to be resurfaced, or sidewalks and curbs to be replaced—whatever—at least a month before budget hearings were to begin. Few department heads wanted to have me complain in this particular public forum about them or their departments, but they also did not want me to thank them publicly for getting the work done. The mayor was known to listen to the hearings from his fifth-floor office, and they were playing it safe.

Having an impact on police misconduct, affordable housing, and human services—all of great importance to my constituency—was another matter altogether.

For many years Daniel Alvarez was the commissioner of the Department of Human Services. Of Puerto Rican descent and fluent in English and Spanish, he developed an extremely thick accent (making it difficult to understand what he was saying) whenever he didn't want to answer a question—which included most of those I posed to him. I had to work around him.

Under Mayor Daley's control, the Department of Health began to divest itself of its clinics. The Illinois State Constitution gives Cook County the primary responsibility for indigent health care in our region. During the 1960s, at the height of his father's power and the power of the Democratic machine, there had been several federal initiatives that could bring capital dollars and operating expenses for health clinics run by local governments. Old man Daley, never one to pass up an opportunity to enhance his patronage army, had grabbed the opportunity, resulting in nineteen city-run health centers, of which the Uptown Health Center was one.[38]

By the 1990s things were changing. The patronage system of the past was technically illegal. Fewer federal funds were available to the city's clinics, forcing the city budget to take over their funding. Privatization of city services was gaining momentum. Preservation of the city's commitment to its health centers—which provided basic health and mental health services to otherwise-underserved communities—became a priority. The first of these privatizations was the closure, in 1991, of the Chicago Addiction Treatment Center, the only city-run residential treatment center for alcohol and drug abuse.[39]

I was vehemently opposed. So were the many people who had struggled with addiction and alcoholism whose lives had been changed by the center. With the crack epidemic in full swing, it was not the time for the city to have less, rather than more, skin in the game. Arguing that two hundred more patients a year could be served (at about $600 less per patient) by ending the city's program and funding two nonprofits, the younger Mayor Daley's proposal passed in a twenty-eight-to-nineteen vote. The eighteen aldermen I joined in a no vote all represented majority-Black and -Latino wards. This would just be the beginning of

---

38 Not to be confused with the Uptown People's Community Health Center, which we started and operated in conjunction with the Cook County Health and Hospital Governing Commission and HEW from 1978–1980.

39 I never thought it was a coincidence that the closing of the city's only public addiction treatment center was followed by the three years with the city's highest murder rates (1992–94) in history.

Alderman Danny Davis and Jesús "Chuy" García speak to the press at a demonstration in city hall against the closing of the Chicago Addiction Treatment Center. This was the beginning of the elimination of mental health and addiction recovery services in Chicago. I suspect there is a correlation between the failure to have these services available to those who can't afford them on their own and the increased level of violence we seem to be experiencing today.

a divestment by the city in direct health and mental health services that would leave many communities woefully underserved.[40]

Each budget season, I went toe to toe with whoever was commissioner of health. I won some battles while losing others, but we managed to maintain funding for the Uptown Health Center, arguing the city should be doing the same in all clinics and that any closures of city clinics should be transfers to the county health system to preserve the public health infrastructure—keeping a ray of hope alive that this movement toward divestment (privatization) could be turned around, or at least held at bay.

Getting information on anything related to the police was problematic; there were dead ends at every turn. This was not just a problem

---

40 In 1989 when Richard M. Daley became mayor, the city had nineteen mental health clinics. By the time he left office, there were just twelve. In 2012, a year after becoming mayor and as Chicago was faced with rising rates of gun violence, Rahm Emanuel closed six of the city's twelve remaining mental health clinics while turning down revenue, resulting in many people being turned away by those that remained operational.

in the 1990s but also throughout my time in city council. The Budget Office and comptroller held the details of the payouts from the Judgment Fund, which included payments for settlements of police misconduct cases, as well as attorney's fees, both to defendants' attorneys and, increasingly, to outside counsel. The Law Department, the Office of Professional Standards,[41] the police board, and the police department brushed off most questions that veered toward any discussion of accountability. It was simple from their point of view: police officers deserve our respect; they have hard jobs, and anyone accusing them of misconduct is likely a criminal falsely accusing them.

And then there was affordable housing. From 1992 to 1997, when Marina Carrott was the city's housing commissioner, she did her best to shut down any new or rehabilitated affordable housing for poor and working families. Citywide she accomplished little when it came to growing low-cost housing truly available to those in the most need. Taking credit for the tax reactivation program—the same program that would have financed some of our housing plans in Uptown before Harold died—she used it in a manner that enhanced gentrification rather than alleviating it. In several communities designated for its use, local residents viewed this as a means to push poor people out of the city.

I was not the only one concerned. I was joined by community-based development corporations, local developers committed to affordable housing, and local groups fighting the gentrification hitting their communities, as well as local groups and many church groups in communities who were tired of the disinvestment they had faced for years without getting any help or meaningful response. Due to their diligence, there were two exceptions where Carrott's reticence was evaded. Through the Low-Income Housing Trust Fund, a brainchild of the Washington administration, a record number of housing units were subsidized and made affordable to very low-income renters living in private housing;

---

41 OPS became the Independent Police Review Authority (IPRA) in 2007, in part in response to scandals involving OPS including during the time when it was administered by Lori Lightfoot and in part in response to a lawsuit brought by Craig Futterman that revealed that OPS almost never disciplined any police officers. IPRA became the Civilian Office of Police Accountability (COPA) in 2016, largely in response to the cover-up of Laquan McDonald's murder.

and the Chicago Housing Authority's scattered-site program had finally ramped up, becoming increasingly productive.

Julia Stasch replaced Marina Carrott in mid-1997. She had experience financing affordable housing and was aware of the conditions in which many of Chicago's challenged communities lived. My question was, would anything change? In the next year, she convened a collaborative process that included affordable-housing developers, architects, local community groups, and advocates. She invited all fifty aldermen to attend. I was one of four who did. I didn't expect much, but I looked forward to having my say and maybe picking up a few allies to move the city forward on addressing our housing crisis.

As it turned out, this collaboration was a game changer for me, resulting in a four-year housing plan that I could get behind. The department's new mission statement became: "Our mission is to advance the City of Chicago's goals for strengthening the city by developing, revitalizing and stabilizing neighborhoods. We will do this by providing diverse housing opportunities within comprehensive community development strategies." I was still concerned that "revitalization" could easily be used as a code word for gentrification and displacement, but the plan included quarterly reports to the City Council Housing Committee, and stable communities had always been a goal, so this looked like an opportunity to get real attention and resources on the street.

When we opened the Uptown Library in 1993, I sat on a platform with Mayor Daley for the first time. He was visibly nervous, which he showed by giggling. The press conference announcing the affordable housing ordinance was held at the Uptown Library in 1998. As was the usual course of these kinds of press conferences, the city hall press corps would be set up in front of a podium arranged for the mayor to speak from. Surrounding him would be a cross section of individuals who were involved in the process and were supportive of the proposed legislation. It would be the first of Mayor Richard M. Daley's press conferences that I attended.

The mayor made his remarks, as did a handful of representatives from various parts of the city and the affordable-housing community. Then the mayor asked for questions. The first was for me. I was not scheduled to speak, and I'm pretty sure I was considered to be a loose cannon by the mayor and his press secretary, but he had said questions would be answered and they were all looking at me, so I went up toward the mayor, who, again with a stifled giggle, signaled for me to approach the podium. "Why the change of heart?" Bill Cameron, a reporter with WLS radio asked. My response was to emphasize the potential made possible by having a codified plan for affordable housing.

During the 1999 budget process a few months later, budget director Paul Vallas, along with the top two people at Intergovernmental Affairs, was anxious for my support. The tense relationship I had with the mayor had softened some. Several of his department heads seemed less concerned about working with me on any number of projects. Paul Vallas had been working with me to get an intergovernmental agreement between the Park District, the Chicago Public Schools, and the City of Chicago to provide after-school supervision and access to the gym and swimming pool at Arai Middle School. I was appreciative of these changes, but I was still not getting answers to my questions. I voted no.

In 1999, while considering the city budget for 2000, all of my questions were answered for the first time. Vallas made good on the intergovernmental agreement, even though he had failed to get me to vote yes on the last budget. The Budget Office agreed to a citywide amnesty program for outstanding tickets, which was important to me in my quest for a more affordable city. By now I was asking a good five hundred questions in total. Getting them all answered had become a kind of symbolic litmus test. For many years I had been the sole "no" vote. It seemed like an appropriate time to mix it up. I voted yes.

In the next decade, I focused on shining the light on the city's history of covering up police misconduct. The costs were steadily rising each year, slowly overwhelming the city's finances. If we couldn't change it, maybe we could at least bring it out into the open.

The heart of making democracy work is having the knowledge to do so. By the time I left the city council, aldermanic attendance grew to an average of forty at each hearing. Department heads began preparing their budget presentations, including the questions they knew would be coming their way, leading them to pay much more attention to their own budgets as well as the concerns of aldermen.

The more aldermen asked questions and got answers, the more time and opportunity the public had to learn how the city operated.

Two weeks of hearings became all-day affairs open to the public to listen and witness how the city worked and planned to improve—or not—in the year to come. At the public hearing held each year before the final vote on the budget, where anyone interested in doing so could come and speak in city council chambers and voice their concerns for the budget, many were pleasantly surprised to see aldermanic attendance grow as well.

. . . .

71.

THE WAR ON TERROR

Two years later, as I was preparing for the mayor's presentation of the 2002 budget, the twin towers in New York City came down and the Pentagon was hit with a plane. Three weeks later, George W. Bush bombed Afghanistan in retaliation, and ground forces followed soon after. Six weeks later, the USA PATRIOT Act was rushed through Congress, granting the federal government unprecedented powers to access private records, conduct secret searches, detain citizens and noncitizens alike, and deport noncitizens.

In the tumult, the presentation of the mayor's 2002 budget recommendations was delayed three weeks. While the city budget that year did not dramatically change, the heightening of tensions, the attack against civil liberties, and the Bush administration's determination to extend the war to Iraq had long-standing effects.

The consolidation of intelligence agencies in Washington, the creation of the Department of Homeland Security, and the passage of the PATRIOT Act, had domino effects in Chicago, leading to the expansion of the Office of Emergency Communications (formerly responsible only for the 911 and 311 systems), the purchase of more and more paramilitary equipment for use by the Chicago Police Department (with federal funds available just for that purpose), and heightened activity by federal intelligence agencies in Chicago. Paranoia toward Muslims escalated.

The left was energized. Anti-war sentiment combined with PA-
TRIOT Act excesses, contributing to a growth in hate crimes. All
this came to a crescendo in October 2002 when Congress passed a
resolution authorizing the use of military force against Iraq. Chicago
was one of the first cities to act. Concerned that this resolution was a
forerunner to an invasion of Iraq (a country not directly involved in the
9/11 attacks), a rally was hastily called at the Federal Building, which
a relatively unknown Barack Obama was the highest-ranking official
to attend.

As expected, the Bush administration bombed and invaded Iraq in
March 2003. Demonstrations against the war broke out spontaneously,
for a time becoming a common occurrence on university campuses and
on the streets of most US cities.

The city council responded as well. A resolution I cosponsored in
mid-2002 calling for the repeal of the PATRIOT Act led to numerous
hearings and the support of Chicago's congressional delegation. Excessive use of the law, we made clear, had led to civil liberty violations
as well as mass roundups and deportations. Here legally or not, if you
were of Muslim or Hispanic descent you could be a target. This was
soon followed by resolutions against the use of military force in Iraq,
based in part on the fact that evidence of weapons of mass destruction
was unreliable (and we now know largely manufactured). Local governments in cities across the country were doing the same. On the streets
people were demonstrating; meanwhile, in mosques, churches, and syn-
agogues, congregations sought a path to unity.

Following the first of many rallies and demonstrations held in
front of the Federal Building in downtown Chicago, ten thousand
plus demonstrators took to the streets, making their way to nearby
Lake Shore Drive where they turned northbound, taking over a good
quarter mile of the well-traveled parkway at the height of rush hour.
As the demonstrators left the drive, they were corralled by a police cordon, forcing them to an area where they were trapped, before police in
riot gear began mass arrests. Nearly 550 people were arrested, including some bystanders who were caught in the police cordon. Charges
against 192 of them were never filed because the police didn't know
who had arrested them.[42] PATRIOT Act, meet opposition to the war

---

42 *Chicago Tribune*, March 25, 2003.

in Iraq. Protesters were back the next day, and returned for many days and months after that.

· ·

72.

UNFINISHED SCHOOL REFORM
UPLIFT, RENAISSANCE 2010, AND CHARTER SCHOOLS GAIN A FOOTHOLD

All eighth-grade students in Illinois are required to pass a test on the US Constitution to graduate and proceed to high school. During my first two terms, the Chicago Board of Education invited elected officials each January to teach this course in one school in their ward. I accepted the invitation, choosing Arai Middle School. The majority of students at Arai were African American and Latino. Some were from India, Pakistan, Vietnam, and other Southeast Asian and African countries. A small number were white. All the students lived in the heart of Uptown and had previously attended the four neighborhood elementary schools. I would meet with their social studies class once a week through the end of their second semester.

My goal was to give these thirteen- and fourteen-year-olds an understanding that the Constitution was a dynamic document that underwent many changes due to the struggles and sacrifices of many activists during the life of the country. To understand the changes over the years and what it had taken to make them, these students would need to know that at the founding of the country, only white male property owners were considered full citizens with the right to vote and that African slaves were considered to be three-fifths of a person. Then we reviewed the changes that were made, with a focus on the things that most affected them—emancipation of the enslaved, women's suffrage, and civil rights.

With the first classroom I taught, after covering this material, our attention turned to matters the students were concerned about. We settled on one that I could bring to the city council: the poor quality and choice of school lunches. They took a field trip to city hall to attend the committee hearing when their resolution appeared on the agenda and testified to its merit, giving examples from their own lives, before the resolution was passed on to the full city council and adopted.[43] I brought them in to see government in action, and a few years later Lily Rodriguez, one of the students who had taken leadership in preparing the resolution, came to work at my ward service office before leaving to attend college.

I was scheduled to begin teaching again in January 1990. Having just returned from my trip to Zimbabwe and Mozambique two months earlier, I had South African apartheid on my mind. Nelson Mandela's release from prison had just been announced. It was all over the news. Out of curiosity I asked the class of thirty some students, most of whom were Black and Latino, but among them one lone white and four South Asian and Vietnamese students, "Who knows who Nelson Mandela is?" Only the South Asian and Vietnamese students raised their hands. I asked them what they knew about Africa. One student declared, "There are animals there." Another said, "It's a big country." I asked if they knew where slaves had come from. I got mostly blank faces and a few hesitant nods to Africa.

Their social studies teacher was popular and one of the school's few African American male teachers. He was more than happy to accommodate my request to see a copy of the social studies book he was using. He made it clear to me that the principal of the school required him to teach from books and materials chosen and approved by the school's curriculum committee and that he was not a part of the committee. I thanked him for sharing and took the book home. Reading through it that week before returning for our next class session, I was alarmed to find the word "slavery" only once in this text on modern world history. It was contained in the sole mention of the "African slave trade."

I'm not sure what I expected. Part of me was not surprised. All of me was incensed. I immediately brought my findings to the local school council. I thought they would want to know. I knew change would not come unless it came from them.

---

43 The resolution may not have had a huge impact at the time, but it would later inform my efforts to redo the lunchroom and challenge the food contract Chicago Public Schools had with their vendor at Arai and Uplift.

In 1988 the Illinois state legislature had passed the Chicago School Reform Act, creating local councils for all Chicago public schools. Many schools had had councils or parent-teacher associations prior to this. None of these bodies, however, had any legal authority to impact the goings-on at local schools. With this new law, that changed. The principal and two teachers would be joined by six parents, two community members, and, in high schools, a student representative. The teacher reps would be elected by the teachers at the school. The parent reps were chosen by the parents of children attending the school. The community members were chosen by anyone living within its attendance boundaries. This body had the power to review budgets as well as the school's academic progress, and to select a principal when there was a vacancy.

The Heart of Uptown Coalition was active in the elections for parent and community representatives. Their slates had won and were determined to change the culture at Arai from one of "planned failure" to one of success and accomplishment. Curriculum was one of several targets.

I brought a slideshow about apartheid in to the class and used it to compare its history to the shifts tracked by the US Constitution. The students found many similarities to the antiquated policies of the South African government in the US Constitution as it had originally been passed and saw the changes that had occurred in the interim. We explored where they felt their rights needed further protection and how they might be able to effect those changes.

Led by the school's librarian, the response from the teachers was immediate, aggressive, and deafening. They charged I was politicizing the class and demanded that I stop. On the other hand, as parents were informed of the dispute by the local school council, they were as upset as I had been. This was not to have an easy or a quick resolution.

Since forming in 1991, the Uptown Youth Force had continued to organize their Youth on Youth program, and one by one its founders were choosing to become teachers. In 1993, the second year of the program at Arai saw twelve college students, working with eighteen high school students, teaching about twenty-five sixth and seventh graders. This original group of twelve included Brendan, John and Jason Yolich, David "Tone" Taylor, Steve Laslo, Anton Miglietta, Chor and B Ng, Lisa Roberts, Brandon Moody, and Jacinda Hall (Bullie). They were joined the next year by Julio Villegas, Michilla Johnson (Blaise), Jay

"Googie" Yolich, and Jaquanda Saulter-Villegas. Of the original twelve, eight ended up working at Uplift Community High School at some point in time as well as several others who later worked at Youth on Youth.[44] In the next decade, a good fifty new teachers from Youth on Youth were teaching in Chicago public schools.

The early years at Arai would not be easy, however. There was resistance from the principal and the teaching and custodial staff from the beginning. But the local school council was on their side and provided crucial support. After presenting their Youth on Youth proposal at a board of education meeting, they were told, "You can do your program, but first you must have an Arai teacher agree to volunteer as your supervisor." This would be hard going. Some of Youth on Youth's most vocal college students had gone to Arai. Their teachers were still there. Few if any had positive views of the students they had taught and were for the most part disdainful of this effort's qualifications or worth. At the last minute, a teacher was found, but it seemed like every day there were new obstacles—almost all bureaucratic and manufactured by the principal.

In addition to its Olympic-sized swimming pool, Arai had a gym well situated for basketball practice and games. They were housed within a separate building adjacent to Arai's main building. Although the two buildings were connected by a second-story enclosed bridge, the gym and swimming pool also had a separate ground-level entrance, which could therefore be utilized during hours the school would otherwise be closed. In 1995 I would get funds and an agreement between the board of education and the Chicago Park District to open these facilities to the community every day after school and on Saturdays, and to fund lifeguards and recreation staff.

In the meantime, Youth on Youth struggled constantly, and ultimately successfully, to gain access to these facilities every afternoon of summer school. They would teach academic classes in the morning and swim and play basketball in the afternoon. They would grow the program, reaching as many as three hundred students who came because they wanted to—not because they were required to attend summer school. They would, in their mind's eye, transform the education experience at Arai for their younger brothers and sisters. Six years into the

---

44 Michilla would work in my aldermanic office some fifteen years later, while John worked a short internship with me as well.

program, when given the opportunity, they moved to Truman College. They had not given up on their commitment to transform Arai, but they would take a multiyear hiatus from its campus.

When Dr. Phoebe Helm became the president of Truman College, she moved to change the tone at Truman and its relationship to the community. A year into her presidency, in 1997, she offered the college and its facilities to Youth on Youth. They would have access to the school's pool, gym, and classrooms in a much friendlier, much less bureaucratic environment.

While many of a growing number of college student Youth on Youth participants followed up with their education and teacher certifications, Phoebe transformed Truman College. When she arrived at Truman, thirty-two thousand students attended the college. They were from 140 countries and they spoke forty different languages. Two-thirds were enrolled in English as a second language or GED classes preparing students who did not graduate from high school to take the test that, if passed, would provide them with a general equivalency diploma. Few continued on to one or more of the credit classes that were in theory the mainstay of the City College's two-year academic programs. Changing this dynamic would be her first priority.

To get there, she reached out to local elected officials representing all eight of the wards on the North Side, from which Truman drew most of its students. At the same time, she contacted and met with as many principals and counselors at each of the high schools in the same geographic boundaries—many of whom had no relationship to the college and rarely if ever offered it as an alternative to graduating seniors or saw it as a resource for their middle and high school students. With a particular emphasis on Senn and Lake View—the two high schools closest to the college and where the students living closest to the college attended, she set about changing that relationship as she challenged the prevailing culture of complacency. This effort resulted in the resignation or retirement of many of the mostly white faculty, many of whom had been at Truman since it first opened in 1976 and were nearing retirement age. She brought on Marguerite Boyd and Michael Scopes to round out her academic leadership team.[45]

---

45 During Phoebe Helm's tenure (and that of Marguerite Boyd, who succeeded her for another five years before retiring herself), the nascent

Meanwhile, a core group of the original Youth Force organizers participated in "Teachers for Chicago," completing the master's courses necessary to become certified to teach in the city. Some of them ended up in Uptown schools. Three of them (Chor Ng, Karen Zaccor, and John Yolich) would spearhead an effort to teach together at Arai Middle School, leading to the genesis of Uplift Community High School in 2006.

Chor's family had immigrated to the United States from Hong Kong, landing in Uptown where his family settled. He had attended public school outside of Uptown but, along with his brother B, was with the Youth Force crew and cemented these friendships while at the University of Illinois at Urbana–Champaign.

Karen (a member of the Intercommunal Survival Committee) had been typesetting at Justice Graphics for a decade when she decided she needed a change. Her daughter Karla was on the verge of her teenage years and ready to enter Arai when Karen went back to school. She became certified to teach math, her passion.

John was the oldest of five brothers. Jason and Jay (or "Googie," as he was affectionately known) had joined him at Youth on Youth.[46] Their mother, Sharon, was raised in Bridgeport—at the time, a community not welcoming of anyone of color. With five Black children, Uptown was the obvious alternative. When she wasn't attending her sons' football games, working at any number of sub-minimum-wage jobs, or at church, Sharon was volunteering with the Heart of Uptown Coalition.

John had had a difficult path getting through the schools in Uptown. The teachers at Arai had labeled him "uneducable." At Senn

---

nursing program already at the school would become a national model as well as a pathway for the future for students previously enrolled in GED and ESL classes, graduating as many as one hundred nurses each year by the time she retired in 2004. Truman's day care center would blossom into a full-fledged child development curriculum center and career pathway. A bridge program with several four-year colleges—most notably with DePaul University—created a new reality and a sixteen-year path for many whose family had no previous college graduates in their family history.

46 Jason became a Park District instructor and sometimes public school liaison between the Uptown schools and the Park District. Googie became a teacher at Prologue, an alternative school that had started in Uptown during the 1970s. Their two younger brothers would work at Youth on Youth as youth workers throughout their teenage years.

High School, the gym teacher had required uniforms that John knew his mother couldn't afford. The gym teacher didn't want to hear it, so John skipped gym. Finally, the school sent a notice to Sharon that her son was being suspended. No one had reached out to her at any time before, even though this had been going on for months. Sharon was beside herself. In passing, she mentioned this to Jeri, who immediately grabbed Sharon by the hand and drove her and John to Senn, where Jeri confronted the principal, demanding John be returned to school, assistance with the gym-uniform issues, and an apology. John was astounded. "No one had ever stood up to anyone like that before for me or my family." Jeri's message was clear: "That's what we do. You can learn to do it too. Go back to school!"

One of John's teachers when he was a senior at Senn saw his potential and assisted him in getting a baseball scholarship to go to Talladega College, Alabama's oldest private historically Black college. John would become the best teacher whose class I ever set foot in.

In 1998 Chor was teaching at Arai. John and Karen were at Stockton. From time to time, John would invite me to read to his third graders. He was friends with many of his students' parents—they had grown up together—and he took their children's development personally. He believed that each one of them could succeed and was troubled to see them undergo the same dismissive labeling he had experienced as a child. One student in particular who had been labeled by everyone at the school as incorrigible was in his classroom the first year he taught. John worked closely with him and with the special education teacher assigned to work with the students in his class. The child improved dramatically. The next year, in a classroom with a teacher whose only expectation of him was failure, that child reverted to his previous behavior.

John's spirit was shattered by this, and he was determined to do something about it. But what? He wanted a chance to have students for more than one year, matriculating with them from one year to the next. The best way to do this was at the middle school where teachers taught subjects rather than grades. Karen and John taught in different classrooms but shared their experiences, giving each other support. Bringing me into these conversations, they brainstormed solutions to the frustrations they both felt. An idea was born.

Paul Vallas had been the city's budget director before becoming the CEO of the Chicago Public Schools in 1995. When he was budget director, we had found some common ground, and he had helped me secure funding to open up the gym and swimming pool at Arai Middle School to the community. Bringing him this new idea, I asked if he would fund four teaching positions at Arai for an experiment—one each for history, science, math, and English.

I explained to him the idea of having a team of teachers who would teach sixth graders in each of these subjects and move with them to the seventh and then eighth grades. The goal was to ultimately have three sets of teachers so that each year the entering sixth graders would be able to have the same teachers throughout their middle school attendance. Vallas went for it but would fund only three slots. Chor would teach science, Karen would teach math, and John would teach social studies. They would all teach English, working out the curriculum jointly so that each unit would reflect the work each teacher was doing at the same time in their focus area.

The principal was not enthusiastic about this idea, but hesitantly embraced the newcomers because they brought badly needed teachers to the school. Teachers at the school would be a much harder nut to crack. There were many issues. For one, they resented being upstaged by these youngsters, among whom was a student some of them had previously taught and remembered as being unteachable. Karen, Chor, and John worked hard, and their dedication was evident. Some of the teachers took it as a challenge.

The three newly assigned teachers developed their own curriculum. By the time their first class of sixth graders reached their eighth-grade graduation, the trio had developed a model program that was beginning to receive recognition outside the school. Many of the city's public schools were doing poorly, with an unacceptable number of students failing. Schools were being put on probation. The increase in reading and math scores of the students in John's, Chor's, and Karen's classes had raised the average for Arai as a whole and had become the reason for Arai staying off the probation list. Some teachers were threatened by this and seemed to feel these upstarts were not worthy of support.

The group was in touch with educators elsewhere and were finding many who were trying to similarly impact how their students were learning. Their goal from the beginning had been to have an impact on the education in both the elementary schools and the high schools to which their students progressed. Phoebe Helm and Marguerite Boyd at Truman College (president and vice president respectively) championed their cause.

In 2001 Arne Duncan was appointed CEO of the Chicago Public Schools. He was a basketball player who often played pickup games at Margate Park in Uptown. John and Jason Yolich, David Taylor, and other future Uplift staff often played with him. David Pickens had a short stint as Arai's assistant principal in the early 2000s before becoming an assistant to Arne and responsible for Intergovernmental Affairs.

As the team at Arai was starting back at sixth grade with a new batch of students, a new idea was percolating among the Youth on Youth leadership. Now that they had their own certified teachers to supervise the program and access to the gym and swimming pool, they had returned to holding the Youth on Youth program at Arai in the summers. Everyone was invested in what was happening there, and excited about the possibilities. "How," they asked, "can we turn Arai into a seventh-to-twelfth-grade school with a focus on social justice and critical thinking?" With the backing of the local school council, I set up a meeting for them with Pickens. He knew them and heard them out.

Meanwhile, another idea was percolating at the board of education and in the mayor's office. Created in 2004 and touted by Daley as the vehicle to create one hundred new schools in six years to replace existing ones that were failing, Renaissance 2010 was immediately controversial. I don't know whose brainchild Renaissance 2010 was, but what became evident was that it was a pet project of for-profit education companies and that proponents of charter schools who had made sure the committee within the board bureaucracy tasked with its implementation were staunch supporters of charter schools and biased against local neighborhood public schools.

The two very divergent ideas were thrust together in our own personal battle royal when David Pickens told us that we could get our seventh-to-twelfth-grade school if we did so through the umbrella of Renaissance 2010. We (these teachers, their cohort of friends, fellow teachers and activists, the local school council, and myself) agreed as long as this new school would be at Arai, would be a public school with public school teachers who were members of the teachers union, and would begin in the sixth grade with cohort teams of teachers who would follow their class from sixth through twelfth grade. We thought we had an agreement that they could do all this and that the ninth grade would be added in year three, when the current sixth graders would be ready to enter ninth grade, with a new year being added each year after. Naming their new school Uplift, the teaching team prepared their proposal.

None of us were prepared for the ensuing events. Very quickly the initial indication that this was the plan, and that Renaissance 2010 was the avenue to achieve it, took a turn. It was suddenly announced that the Renaissance 2010 committee would be appointing a transitional advisory committee (TAC). They, we were told, would consider all proposals for a new high school for the Arai campus. We were in disbelief. The community was proposing a completely different plan: a middle school that gradually and organically developed into a high school. Proposals began coming in—all from charter high schools. We had our work cut out for us.

The initial board-appointed TAC was controversial. I was included as the alderman, but most of the proposed appointees were not familiar with the neighborhood where the school was located and unknown to local education activists. One appointee was on the board of directors of one of the charter schools we would be evaluating for selection. This was not acceptable. The Arai Local School Council had been elected and included parents and community representatives. Not about to sit still and have their school and its future hijacked, they demanded representation. Shalonda Peterson, Rita Ezell, and Marc Kaplan, all local school council members, were added to the TAC.

Meanwhile, it was becoming obvious that the Uplift proposal was at a disadvantage. The request for proposals from Renaissance 2010 had put an emphasis on the high school grades. This was not what they had bargained for. The core group of Uplift teachers had expected to transition to a high school. Chor was in the process of receiving the certificate that would allow him to become the principal. They had assumed he would have it by the time they expanded their middle school to ninth grade. Suddenly, if they were to get the approval to proceed, they were going to have to start immediately with a ninth grade and a principal with the certification to lead a high school. What to do?

A quick search resulted in the choice of a high school social worker with a principal's certification and experience as an assistant principal, who promised a shared commitment to develop a social justice–themed high school.

Before making its final choice, the TAC agreed that all of the TAC's members would as a group visit classrooms taught by teachers at Uplift and the two competing charter high schools. At each of the charters, we sat in on tenth-grade honors English classes. At Arai, we sat in on each of the three teachers' seventh-grade classes. We took a vote that evening. The result was nearly unanimous for the Uplift team.[47] They had won out on pure grit and an honest display of their effectiveness in the classroom.

But this was not yet a done deal. Arne Duncan was going to have to bless the TAC's choice, and he was leaning toward either one of the charter schools. From the few conversations I had with him, as well as my best effort at translating David Pickens's very careful efforts to give me guidance, it was apparent that we would first need the mayor's blessing if we were to have any hope of getting Arne's. Two days after the TAC vote, I spotted Arne at a city council meeting. Seeing him there, milling about in the chambers behind the council chambers, I knew it was now or never. I grabbed the mayor during one of his breaks and described the actions of the TAC and a brief history of Youth on Youth. I might have thrown in something about my son and that these were his friends. (I knew the mayor's wife had on several occasions told mutual acquaintances that she respected me for not opportunistically attacking their son when he had gotten into trouble in Michigan a few years earlier, so I thought I'd take the sympathy shot.) Then I asked if I could tell Arne that Uplift had his support. Arne was not pleased. He hemmed and hawed until I asked him if we should talk to the mayor together. "No, no. Not necessary," he said as he agreed to sign off on the selection. Uplift would be just one of two public high schools chosen that year by Renaissance 2010. They would receive little if any of the financial support that had been promised.

Arai's student body was dramatically declining, and the school was more than three-quarters underutilized. It seemed to us a no-brainer

---

47 The only dissenting vote came from the woman who sat on the board of directors of a competing proposal.

that the school could be closed down as it was currently constituted and reopened as a new school and program. "Not so fast," we were told, as the other shoe dropped. The seventh-grade students currently enrolled in Arai, we were told, would have a choice to stay at Arai with the Youth on Youth team and be part of the new Uplift Community High School, stay at Arai with the remaining Arai teachers, or choose to return to their feeder school. All four feeder schools, we were informed, would return to being kindergarten through eighth grade. Emblematic of an internal bias against this upstart group—almost entirely minority at that—were the ongoing barriers they would have to navigate, which would impact the time they could dedicate to their core concern—recruiting students from Uptown and providing them with the best-possible education, not only to ensure they would graduate high school but to prepare them for, and nurture them through, whatever postsecondary education they chose to pursue.

In my experience, while individual teachers in most Chicago public schools were dedicated and motivated by compassion toward their students, these characteristics were rarely encouraged by the system in which they worked. As magnet schools with selective enrollment were developed in the '70s, '80s, and '90s, Chicago's best teachers—especially minority teachers and particularly Black male ones—were highly sought after, being recruited to leave the neighborhood schools they more than likely had started in. Schools with high numbers of Black students were thirsting for a modicum of their teaching staff to reflect the racial makeup of their students—if only to challenge the notion that a professional career was out of their reach, let alone to have a better chance of having a teaching body with an experiential awareness of the challenges facing their student body. Uplift was no different in this regard.

Despite all these challenges, they would persevere. Every student in the first high school graduating class at Uplift was accepted into a postsecondary program or continued their education as members of the US armed forces. Collectively, that graduating class received over a million dollars in scholarships. Having achieved this milestone and having done so early, however, had little effect on the continuing onslaught of criticism and interference from the school's bureaucracy. These teachers would continue to have difficulty recruiting Uptown students as sixth-through eighth-grade teachers in the feeder schools closed ranks. These teachers had been in competition for students since day one of Uplift, making it a heavy lift to get their cooperation and collaboration when their eighth-grade students were choosing their high schools. The layer of administrators on the North Side that served as a buffer between the local schools and downtown administrators were used to dealing with mostly white, older, more seasoned principals, assistant principals, and school disciplinarians. All of these positions at Uplift were held by minorities. Their inexperience made them vulnerable and defensive when it came to the overt racism that victimized them.

Uplift has had and continues to have some remarkable teachers. However long it continues to survive, what is most evident is that with leadership that is innovative, flexible, collaborative, and most importantly supportive of its teachers, every teacher can successfully teach, and every student can learn.

. . . .

73.

THE 2003 CAMPAIGN AND A POLITICAL COMPROMISE

Politics and governance is often about compromise. This is true even when (or maybe especially when) the purpose of politics and governance is an attempt to take power from the powerful so that the people can exercise it themselves. In politics, there are two adages that apply. The cynic says that "politics make strange bedfellows." The realist says that "there are no permanent enemies or allies, just permanent interests." Fred Hampton had phrased it a little differently: "Politics is nothing but war without bloodshed, and war is nothing but politics with bloodshed." He also said that "if you dare to struggle, you dare to win. If you don't dare to struggle, you don't deserve to win."

Throughout my career as aldermen, I had many allies that would likely have surprised my activist self. In most cases I was able to move these allies in their thinking and action. Ultimately, however, the alliances were about gaining victories—whether political or related to governance. And, in all honesty, there were times where I was moved to make decisions that were not the purest or most principled. I was, after all, playing the game of politics—even though that was never my objective.

There were dozens of political allies with whom I did not always agree but who were essential to either political or governance wins. State Senator Sara Feigenholtz was my fundraiser before becoming state representative. Her origins were from the Forty-Fourth Ward, but she had also been a fundraiser for David Orr, leading her from being a potential antagonist in 1991 to a friend by 1993. Bridget Gainer had been a go-to in the Daley administration before winning her seat as Cook County commissioner with the help of the Forty-Sixth Ward political operation. Larry McKeon, the first openly gay state representative, was a key ally in Springfield. After I beat Mike Quigley in the 1991 election, Mike became an uneasy ally as he rode up the political ladder to become congressman. The two candidates from the 1995 election would later become judges,[48] in part with help from my son and a former staffer. In the mid-1990s, a young state legislator, Jan Schakowsky, ran for the recently vacated congressional seat once held by the longtime congressman Sidney Yates, and I endorsed and worked for her opponent, J. B. Pritzker (who would become governor twenty years after losing that congressional race, while Jan has proven to be an effective and progressive mainstay in Congress). The fight between Tim Evans and Eugene Sawyer following Harold's death had been a classic fight over power versus vision, as had been my respective endorsements of Evans, Danny Davis, Joe Gardner, and Bobby Rush for mayor between 1989 and 1999.

Perhaps the hardest political decision I made was the decision in 2003 to endorse Richard M. Daley for mayor. Much of the reporting at the time attributed the decision to some type of deal that included his support for Wilson Yard. The truth is, of course, far more complex than that. There were political calculations, governing calculations, and in fact some actual respect for Daley and a large number of his staff.

The political background was that my political right hand, George Atkins, was diagnosed with cancer in 2001. Leading up to the 2003 election, we were unsure what his status would be. My son Brendan ended up

---

48 Robert Kuzas and Lindsey Huge. Huge was knocked off the ballot, leaving me with my first head-up election guaranteed to end without a runoff.

managing my 2003 campaign while he was in his final year of law school. This would be the only campaign he ran where George was not by his side throughout, exposing political vulnerabilities. Indeed, George had always coordinated my campaign activities and field operations. While Jim Chapman had been my finance chair in my early election campaigns, since 1991, Sam Toia had assumed this responsibility. George and Sam had been in regular talks with the Daley political folks since the 1999 election, simply because they feared some political vulnerabilities.[49]

And the governance reality was this: in the Daley administration's rush and desire to get a unanimous vote on their budget, they had given me almost everything I had asked for in 1999 and 2000. I had by then managed to take advantage of budget season to get resources and innovative programs into my ward without the requirement of my vote. So at the time, all that I was really asking for was information, for transparency; indeed, I had spent a decade battling for such answers. And when they realized that that was all they had to provide to get their desired budget vote from me, they started providing it. In addition, however, the administration's agency heads and executive staff were simply more responsive in Daley's later years than their counterparts had been in his first few terms.

And yes, it was important that I continue to have the autonomy to continue to fight for affordable housing, reforms in the police department,

---

49 Ironically, it was also during this period of time that I rejected political overtures from young, up-and-coming State Senator Barack Obama. My second cousin once removed (from my mother's side), Harriet Trop, and her husband, law professor Bob Bennett, had a small gathering for a dinner that occurred near or around Passover in 2000. In addition to the hosts were me and my son, his wife, Brenda; my granddaughters Britteney and Justice, who had just turned two and my grandson Ricky; along with Michelle and Barack Obama and their oldest daughter, Malia, who was around Justice's age. A month earlier, Obama had run against Congressman Bobby Rush in the Democratic primary. At the dinner, the state senator, with that race in his rearview mirror and most likely already contemplating his 2004 run for Senate, turned on the charm and made political small talk. But when the 2004 election came around, George Atkins had a lucrative contract with an opponent to Obama. So, out of loyalty to George, I ignored the entreaties of Obama and many progressive allies and stayed loyal to George by not endorsing in that Senate primary race. (I would later endorse him and work hard in that general election and in his later campaigns for president.)

and other services for the Uptown community. Once I endorsed Daley in 2003, the administration treated me just as they treated all of the other aldermen by allowing for aldermanic prerogative—which is essentially local democracy at work.

Moreover, I feel that I actually moved Daley (a point to which I shall return). Although he undoubtedly moved me too.

Looking back at my endorsement now, or even looking forward to it from the 1980s, it is easy to criticize. But at the time, given the political and governing dynamics, it made sense. The 2003 election ended up being the easiest campaign we ran, simply because the opposition did not have the money or resources of the machine backing them. With Daley out of the equation, the entire race was focused on maintaining a diverse ward. The result was that I won almost 60 percent of the vote in a gentrifying ward. At the same time, I retained the leeway to continue the work on Wilson Yard and other vital projects in the ward.

· ·

74.

WILSON YARD

Urban renewal always loomed large in my experience in Chicago. Many promises had gone unfulfilled, from the designation of a block filled with housing in the heart of Uptown to be removed and replaced with a City College (with the argument that the people whose homes were about to be removed needed access to a new City College), to the middle school built across the street according to the same argument, to the board of health–run clinic being built a half mile away. And I knew that ours was not the only community with this experience.

When I became alderman in 1987 and finally had an opportunity to have some impact on development policy in Chicago, I was interested in finding examples of developments in US cities where people for whom they were touted ultimately remained in the community and benefited. I joined the US League of Cities and went to every workshop on development. Again and again I asked for examples where

people successfully had gotten to enjoy the fruits of developments intended for them. Again and again I received only empty looks. No
examples were forthcoming.

The Chicago Transit Authority L station at Wilson Avenue in Uptown was located on the edge of a five-acre plot of land that included
carpenter and other repair shops used by the CTA to repair tracks along
the North Side leg of the CTA's red line. Above ground level on the
raised rail line was a bus barn that had been used to repair train cars
since the turn of the twentieth century. By 1996 most of the work had
been transferred farther north to the Howard station, but in the process
of moving the work, many chemicals and supplies had been left behind.
The occasional homeless person would sleep there overnight, but the
building was virtually abandoned.

At the time I lived four blocks due west of the bus barn. The lot
directly behind my third-floor apartment was vacant, and I could see
all the way to the L tracks from my back porch. I awakened early one
morning in October 1996 to the site of huge flames and loud sirens. The
bus barn would burn for hours—fueled by a host of chemicals, dried tie
rods, and other supplies. There were suspicions that at least one homeless man had been sleeping there at the time, but the fire had burned so
hot that little evidence could be found to confirm or deny their veracity.

Though the ground-level carpenter shops continued to do some minor repairs, it was evident that the five-acre site presented a new opportunity for development in Uptown. Here, I thought, it would be possible
to engage the community in a process focusing on the needs of the community, identify the resources that would help meet those needs, and
ensure that people living here now and engaged in the design would be
able to benefit from it once it was complete.

The executive director of Upcorp, a community development group
recently formed by the Uptown Chamber of Commerce, had gone to
LaSalle Bank asking for support for an architectural charette around
potential uses of this five-acre CTA site. I was concerned. Historically
people had become very cynical about planning. Any maps designating
potential ideas for this site that did not come from a community process
would easily be considered with a jaundiced eye and dismissed by most
in the community as a predetermined plan from which they would not,
and could not, benefit.

We would need a process that was as inclusive and broad as possible. I went to Kristin Faust, the head of community programs for LaSalle Bank and the person Upcorp had been talking to. Kristin understood my concerns immediately. Together we brought in Upcorp and the city's Department of Planning and began organizing a process we hoped would do the trick. Kristin agreed to send invitations to an inaugural event to all ten thousand registered voters in the precincts that surrounded the Wilson Yard.

To ensure that everyone would have a voice, we first had to ensure that we had a common language. We agreed that this first meeting would do just that. We would take the concept of a design charrette (usually used by small groups of architects), enlarge it to allow for the participation of many, and create a program that explored the possibilities for development on this site. David Hunt, until recently the director of the Chicago Rehab Network, was now engaged in a project of storytelling as a way to create community and common language. He was recruited to lead us through our first step in this process.

On a sunny Saturday in early July 1998, 250 community residents gathered at 10:00 a.m. in the cafeteria of Truman College. For meetings like these, the college would usually set up chairs in a theater-like setting. Not on this day. Circular tables seating up to eight people provided the only place for attendees to sit. There were no reserved seats. The result was a cross section of community members at each table. In a community with as many points of view as ours, this was an important staging for a discussion about development.

By then, I had been the alderman of the Forty-Sixth Ward for eleven years. The earlier struggles over the construction of Truman College echoed as a backdrop to any development plans for the community, which was divided. On the one hand, there were those still pining for housing affordable for those who had been displaced in the thirty years since plans for a new City College had first been disclosed. On the other, there were those who had more recently moved to the community with hopes of buying cheap and growing their nest egg and future wealth.

The internet was just entering our lives in a significant way. We had received an email account through the city that January and were using it more and more to communicate with our constituents. This new phenomenon changed the dynamic quickly and significantly. While communication would prove to be faster, much of it would be more superficial, more reactionary, and less helpful. Throughout the course of the next nine years as we developed and implemented a plan for the Wilson Yard, the internet would prove to be a useful tool for sharing information and receiving input, while it also functioned as a vehicle to create confusion and dissension.

On this day in July 1998, I was pulling double duty. I was in charge of my three-month-old granddaughter while her parents were out of the country on their honeymoon. With Justice strapped across my body, I opened the meeting, explaining our purpose and describing the process we were beginning that day.

The city had agreed to fund a consulting team to do a community-wide survey translated into Spanish, Vietnamese, Cambodian, Korean, Russian, and Urdu—the languages besides English most commonly spoken in Uptown. They were also to conduct interviews with community leaders and hold a series of focus groups with participation from all segments of the community. We wanted everyone to participate in any and all activities, and I explained how they might do so. Then I turned the meeting over to David Hunt.

David had worked with many community-based not-for-profit developers as the executive director of the Chicago Rehab Network and was well aware of the many ways in which the discussion of development—especially affordable and low-cost housing—could become quickly polarized. Drawing on his experience using storytelling as a vehicle to overcome preconceptions, his facilitation helped to engender deeper communication—especially between people who had scarcely interacted before. He began by asking for volunteers to tell their story. Why were they there? What was their interest? This began a conversation, but clearly this was going to be a difficult nut to crack. Most people who had come that day were looking to be told what was coming, and most expected to be angry and disappointed by what they heard.

When David moved to the second part of his presentation, many in attendance didn't know what to make of it. He presented a scenario of building a twelve-unit building and asked those seated around each table to discuss and then answer a series of questions. The response was deafening: "Where is the master plan for us to review?" "What does a twelve-flat have to do with anything?"

Respecting our goal of reaching some common language to proceed with, David explained he had presented a scenario that would allow for a discussion of development terms while using an example that in and of itself would not be controversial—largely because no one really believed that was what would ultimately be the heart of any design for Wilson Yard. Not everyone was satisfied with this explanation, but no one was going to ignore the process to come.

That summer, the city's consultants working with Upcorp conducted nearly a hundred interviews with "community leaders" and multiple focus groups. Several thousand completed surveys were returned. Two additional workshops were scheduled for the fall. To ensure the maximum participation, one was an evening session and the other a Saturday session, again at Truman College.

Knowing there would be differences, we built in a process that included minority opinions.

The room was set up with tables that sat up to ten people. Once again, there were no assigned seats, and most tables included people with divergent views. Every table was given a large map of the Wilson Yard, along with multicolored markers. They were tasked with collectively drawing their ideas of what the development on this land should look like. With the completion of these drawings, everyone at that table was asked to sign as supporters or dissenters of the final product. Each team would then present their map in detail. First, the majority team would explain what they had in mind. Then, the dissenters would explain their alternative views.

That winter and spring, after compiling the input from the two design charrettes, as well as from surveys, focus groups, and interviews, the consultants finalized their preliminary report on the community's ideas. They found that the broadest support expressed was for a big-box store such as Target and low-cost housing. Movie theaters, with significantly more support than any other option, ranked a distant third. Even so, controversy continued.

With the city council and mayoral election coming up in February 1999, a grassroots effort succeeded in placing a referendum on the ballot in eleven Uptown precincts. Asked if they agreed that the city, state,

One table at one of two workshops held in the fall of 1998. Each table was given a map to work with and present both the majority and minority proposals that was later reported to all the other tables. Hundreds of community residents came to one of the two sessions held providing their visions for the future of Wilson Yard.

and federal governments should use every available means and resource to protect existing affordable housing, as well as use every opportunity and resource to create new low-cost housing in our community, 76.5 percent of the people voting in the eleven precincts voted yes.

I wasn't much of a fan of tax increment financing (TIF) districts,[50] and I had been pretty vocal on the subject. The primary use of these special property tax–funded districts in Chicago had been downtown, where well-heeled institutions and developers sought to use them to gain access to taxpayer funds at the expense of the city's neighborhoods.

---

50 A TIF district is a geographic location where financing can be used for up to the twenty-three-year life of the TIF. Monies generated can be used to fund needed public improvements such as repairs to infrastructure, beautification projects, and incentives to attract new businesses and retain existing ones, or help them expand. Authorized by state law, TIFs are controversial because they interfere with the distribution of a portion of property taxes collected on the properties in their boundaries that would otherwise go to other taxing bodies. This is most impactful on schools where half of the property taxes collected in Chicago go to the Chicago Board of Education. The assumption is that after twenty-three years, the TIF funded activities would enhance the value of properties more than if the TIF hadn't existed and thereby be more of a benefit to all the taxing bodies.

However, it was becoming apparent that funding from a TIF district was now the primary funding source for most city-supported development. Even if it was a tool that up to now had been used in questionable ways, I decided to seize the opportunity to fashion it anew. It was equally apparent that having access to TIF funding made affordable housing development a top priority for the Illinois Housing Development Authority—the conduit for many federal and all state funds for such projects.

I was first approached by the CTA and the city's Department of Planning to consider using TIF at Wilson Yard in 1998. I surprised them when I agreed. After Ron Johnson (representing the Department of Planning) had pulled himself up out of the chair that had toppled over with his surprise, I added, "As long as at least 30 percent of TIF-generated funds go to affordable housing, and a majority of the rest go to public schools and other public entities in any TIF created in the Forty-Sixth." Bottom line established. Because the city had few tools for the creation or rehabilitation of housing affordable to poor and working families, TIFs were the primary one we could access, and I was willing to take a stab at using them.

So it was that a TIF district, developed for Wilson Yard as a tool to encourage new private development, was set in motion. It would include the five-acre Wilson Yard site but would be much larger, giving us an opportunity to preserve existing affordable housing and improve the Broadway shopping corridor. The overall goal of the Wilson Yard TIF was to create a cohesive and vibrant mixed-use community. That provided stability to small businesses and residents threatened by rising rents.

In June 2000, we were back at Truman College. Nearly two hundred people showed up that morning for a brainstorming session on the future redevelopment of the yard and the area immediately surrounding it. In the afternoon, each table shared their ideas with the entire gathering. Community residents and local business owners were joined by numerous resource people from the private and public sector. The charrette consisted of eighteen tables, each of which discussed one of ten topics—including architecture, mixed-income housing, new and existing low-cost housing, retail development, job training, business opportunities, development of a multicultural center, and light manufacturing possibilities.

This brainstorming charrette was planned by a group that included the city's Department of Planning, the Chicago Transit Authority, Truman College, Upcorp, Uptown Chamber of Commerce, Uptown Chicago Commission, Organization of the NorthEast, and COURAJ (Community of Residents for Affordability and Justice.) Each organization, representing the full gamut of demands—from a development plan characterized by all low-income housing, to one comprised of retail only with no low-income housing—had mobilized their members to sign up to attend the session and to identify which table they were interested in sitting at. Truman College provided laptops, assigning students to be scribes at each table. The notes they took were edited for clarity and posted on my city website.

As legislation to create the TIF was drafted, these groups continued their involvement. Joined later by the Broadway Merchants, Jane Addams Senior Caucus, and representatives from surrounding block clubs actively involved in their respective zone committees, they became the Wilson Yard Task Force. Through that body, they would help guide and shape the community process and input into the Wilson Yard TIF District, as well as the development plans for the old Wilson Yard (now expanded to include frontage along Broadway).

In August a community meeting was held to review the legal process to create a TIF, and to present a draft Wilson Yard TIF study for review. This draft study had been distributed for residents before the meeting for their comments. A review of the comments received indicated a consensus on many points; and where there was disagreement, there was nothing that required mutual exclusion—or at least that was my view at the time. I likened the process to a table with a "virtual basket." Everything in the basket stayed. Until we had a developer on board who could take the full breadth of possibilities under consideration and bring back a feasible proposal for getting as many of them done as possible, we weren't going to take anything out of the basket. We could add but not subtract.

In spite of a deep divide over how much housing would end up on the Wilson Yard site and how affordable it would be, the committee appeared to be in agreement that every effort should be made to maximize the increment, which would be used for infrastructure improvements, land acquisition, and other eligible activities designated to generate a dynamic retail center, to create as well as preserve an array of affordable housing units, and to provide capital improvements to two area public schools. Still, I would need additional expertise on TIFs to fully grasp all our options and how to best maximize the use of a TIF.

We were back at Truman in September 2000 for the first mandated TIF meeting. More than five hundred residents attended and provided comments on the proposal. Before getting to the city council for approval of the new TIF district in February 2001, there would be three more meetings open to the public where additional comments could be brought.

With a TIF district established, it was time to pick a developer. A request for qualifications (RFQ) was drafted with the "virtual basket" of possible components in mind, including the diverse ideas submitted by the community. Interested developers were invited to submit their credentials. The development group headed by Peter Holsten was selected in August 2002. He would hire David Reifman as his TIF attorney, rounding out his team.

Reifman, along with his best friend David Marder and Marder's sister Phyllis, had just been beginning their careers in 1987 when they first volunteered in my successful aldermanic bid. As a team, they had done amazing precinct work. We had remained friends. They were young, progressive, and seemingly unstoppable. Reifman was just beginning his career at the law firm of Rudnick & Wolfe.[51] As he gained legal experience, he had volunteered on each of my successive campaigns. By the year 2000, he was an expert in TIFs and more than willing and able to help me out. For more than a decade he had worked with his firm's major real estate clients, successfully using TIF districts to their advantage. Here was an opportunity to take the same structure and apply new content. I had no doubt that if we put front and center the needs of those who had been most adversely affected by the earlier urban renewal and more recent gentrification of Uptown, we would end up with an overall development that not only served them but the broader community at large. I'm pretty sure Reifman looked at this as an opportunity to give back. He knew my focus and that I needed him to help me take advantage of the TIF legislation, rules, and regulations in the pursuit of maximum affordability, fairness to any person or business displaced,

---

51 Now DLA Piper, the law firm has gone through several mergers since 1987.

and employment opportunities. His knowledge of TIF rules and regulations, his contacts at Target, and his relationships with leading staff in the mayor's office would be put to good use.[52]

Peter Holsten's selection as the master developer was good news. I had first met Peter when he bought the Norman Hotel on Wilson Avenue, shortly after my 1987 election. With a low-interest loan from the LaSalle Bank as part of their commitment to support affordable housing, he had done so without any other public assistance. Since that early foray into the world of affordable housing, it seemed like this had become a calling for him.

Peter had put in offers for the building before the election, but the building's owners, the Fromme brothers, had refused to sell. They owned other properties in Chicago, including a court-way in the southern end of the ward in Lakeview, all of which were in poor condition. Most of the apartments at the Norman Hotel were sleeping rooms or studios without stoves. Many people used hot plates, which strained the building's very old and compromised electrical system, resulting in most of the nearly one hundred fires responded to by the fire department in the last year.

The Frommes had a close relationship with the regular Democratic machine, routinely offering their tenants a free dinner if they allowed a precinct worker to "assist" them in voting. The day after I was elected alderman, they called Peter with an agreement to buy the building. Peter told me that when he came to inspect the building, there were multiple holes in the walls of the Frommes' first-floor office. Apparently, after hearing the results of the election, they had taken out their frustration and anger on the walls using their fists.

Peter's first order of business was to improve each apartment, starting with those that still had fire damage—much of which had been caused by faulty wiring and the use of hot plates. He concurrently explored what it would take to provide a safe cooking space in each apartment and

---

52 After winning his election, and after I had left the city council, Mayor Rahm Emanuel asked David Reifman to join his administration as his commissioner of planning. David became a loyal member of Rahm's team. He had good intentions. He told me he saw this as an opportunity to redirect resources from downtown to Chicago's underserved communities; this was a goal never reached.

especially in the sleeping rooms—a project we successfully worked on together as it required city approval. By the year 2002, Peter had worked through numerous difficult building situations in privately owned housing, not-for-profit-owned housing, and with the Chicago Housing Authority. He had worked through most problems that are common to both the development and management of housing designed for lower-income Chicagoans. I knew I could count on him to push each of the community priorities to its max and was glad to have him on board.

The Wilson Yard development required a complicated orchestration of many pieces. There were three owners of the properties that lay between Broadway and the Wilson Yard. On the north end of the Broadway frontage was a vacant lot. On the south end was a one-story terracotta-clad building that some argued had historic value. In between was an Aldi food store that was due for a remake. Target expressed an interest but was not sure about putting a movie theater above their store, although they agreed to consider it. Aldi was open to an offer by Holsten to relocate to the vacant lot north of its current location.

We had been in talks with the CTA about a new station at the red line's Wilson stop, and they were open to an entrance down the block by the two stores. The business community, however, was concerned about parking. They had needed a catalyst to create a critical mass on Broadway for decades and were open to a Target, as most did not feel that this would compete with them but rather draw more people in to the area who might also shop with them. The key would be making it as easy for someone driving by to park their car and come into their stores as it would be to park in the Target parking lot.

Jobs were important as well. A Target meant a good three hundred new job opportunities, and, in the meantime, constructing the housing, Aldis, and ultimately Target would employ hundreds. We wanted some or all those jobs to go to community residents. The City College was developing an apprenticeship program for carpenters, and we wanted an agreement for Uptown residents to get into this program so they would be ready to be hired for the minimum number of thirteen carpenter slots required by the TIF regulations when construction began.

With some demanding that the entire site be used to construct housing affordable to poor and working households, and others demanding only retail, or a combination of retail and market-rate housing in the form of condos and artist housing, it was likely that we would get something that would satisfy neither but would include much of what each wanted. As expected, the criticisms came from my left and my right.

It would take another six years, multiple public hearings, and a lawsuit before the TIF notes were sold, permits acquired, and construction begun.[53] The movie theaters couldn't make the finances work and dropped out. Target, however, was still on board, and Aldis agreed to move to a new store built for them just north of their old one. On-street parking was preserved for existing small businesses; all the retail tenants displaced received assistance in moving and securing a new location; more than the minimum of thirteen mostly young men went through the City College program and were hired as carpenters; and, of the three hundred people initially hired by Target, 80 percent lived within two miles of the store. Campus parks were built for Stewart and Arai Schools.[54] And there were 178 units of newly constructed housing, affordable to people living with incomes ranging from 15 percent to 60 percent of the median income.[55]

---

53 Through all of this, it was a high priority to ensure that students learned about process, inclusion, and development without displacement. Hal Baron, Katy Hogan, Lu Palmer, and others at the Associated Colleges of the Midwest brought their students to Uptown annually to learn about our initiatives. And David Schneider, my staff assistant for a time, made the Wilson Yard development and process the center of a study at Northwestern, where he was a student.

54 After I retired from the city council, my successor supported the closing of Stewart School and its sale to a developer, who transformed the school into market-rate condos. At Arai, which had by now become Uplift High School, we had passed an ordinance to provide TIF funds to acquire adjacent vacant land for the development of a science class on urban growing and botany. In his first year, my successor nixed the plan.

55 One building, designated for people over sixty-two years of age, had ninety-eight one-bedroom apartments. A second building (often referred to by Holsten as the "family building") had a mix of one-, two-, and three-bedroom apartments. When housing is financed with tax credits, as these buildings were, the financing assumes that the rents will be geared toward households earning just under the cap of 60 percent of the median income. This was not going to work for me. I spent a lot of time and effort, along with Holsten and

In the middle of all this, a big-box ordinance came before the city council. Walmart had been exposed for business practices that were unfair to their employees and predatory toward small businesses that fell within their orbit. Many people in Chicago were working two, even three jobs to make ends meet because they were working for one of many national food and retail chains that paid the national minimum wage. Organizing for living wages had heightened. As demands mounted for city council action, Alderman Ed Burke proposed an ordinance he could support. Dubbed the Big Box Ordinance, any store with a square footage of more than ninety thousand would be required to pay a living wage of $9.25 an hour (to be incrementally increased annually based on the cost-of-living index). The choice of that square footage was cynical, given that no stores in Burke's ward would be affected; rather, the ordinance would apply only to a Walmart, Target, Home Depot, or Menards. The smaller national chain stores that paid minimum wage, like McDonald's and Burger King, were not affected.

I feel strongly that everyone should have a minimum income above the poverty line. Having to work three jobs and still not getting to that threshold makes for absent parents and latchkey kids. Therefore, any requirement or incentive to improve wages was good in my book. When the ordinance came up for a vote in July 2006, I didn't vote. It passed, and the mayor vetoed it. Now what? Target was a key component in creating a critical mass of economic activity for the Broadway corridor. They were threatening to pull out of Chicago, as were other big-box stores that might come to Wilson Yard. They insisted that the majority of their employees already met the threshold in the ordinance. The starting employees still did not. And I agreed with the supporters that the big boxes were probably bluffing. In at least some parts of the city, even with the ordinance, they would come. It was just too economically profitable for them not to. But in some areas of the city where it had been historically harder to create economic development, this would not be the case.

The overwhelming consensus behind the thrust to pass Chicago's Big Box Ordinance was to prevent big boxes with bad labor records from coming into Chicago, taking over the market, and pushing out

his team, to find additional subsidies so that a much larger swath of those in need would be able to benefit from this housing.

smaller shops with good labor records. The ordinance had three stated goals: ensure service industry workers in Chicago earn a living wage; ensure service workers, including those that work substantial part-time jobs, have health insurance for themselves and their families; and protect union employees at union shops (primarily in several of the supermarket chains) from the predatory practices of big boxes (and most particularly Walmart).

Unfortunately, it seemed to me, this was one of those instances where the ordinance didn't meet the hype: the employers of the vast majority of low-wage service employees working in Chicago remained unaffected and untouched by this ordinance. Because the city mandated a benefits package without making it incentive-based, it was likely to be preempted by federal law and therefore unlikely to be enforced. Two months later, before voting, with a very heavy heart, to uphold the mayor's veto, I expressed agreement with my friends and allies: even if this was not perfect legislation, it might help workers, and there was no guarantee that something better would come in the future. I concurred with them that the passage of the ordinance would be a political victory for those fighting for labor rights. My problem, however, was that such a victory would be illusionary. As I said:

> It is not enough that this law might send a message across the city and nation that we are trying to protect workers. This city and this city council should be about passing non-arbitrary, enforceable legislation that does actually protect workers. . . . This city council has demonstrated a willingness to protect the city's low-wage workers. Let's do so in a manner that really helps them—all of them.

It would be another two years before all legislation required to advance the development plan for Wilson Yard was passed. As the country faced an economic crisis, the final piece—selling the TIF notes to fund the project—was in jeopardy. Private lenders were required to finance initial construction costs not eligible for TIF funding. Target was set to buy its store, but not until construction was complete. The private lenders were uneasy. The economy was on the brink of collapse, and they couldn't see how Holsten would be able to meet their requirement that the portions allotted to housing and small retail would each reach at least an 80 percent occupancy within two years of completion. But I knew he would. We had been taking pre-applications for the housing, and more than two thousand people had already asked to be notified as soon as they could apply to live there. Miraculously in October—literally days before the world markets crashed, leading to the great recession of 2008 and 2009, the notes were sold, lessening the other lenders' anxieties. Within a few months of completion, the housing had 95 percent occupancy. The 80 percent threshold for renting the smaller retail was met within a year.

. . . .

75.

DECIDING ON ONE LAST TERM—AND MY LIST

The survival programs are not per se reformist. Survival programs are not revolutionary in themselves. Survival programs are a means and a tool by which to organize and unify the people for that future liberation which must come about. How do we get there? By the power of the people. And how does power of the people occur? The power of the people is manifested in whether or not the people control the institutions that affect their lives and make those institutions serve their basic desires and needs. Presently they are not controlled by the people. How do we make those institutions serve our desires and needs? . . . We turn them around.
—Bobby Seale, 1973[56]

It was September of 2006 and time to begin circulating petitions if I was going to run for reelection the following February. I was not inclined to do so. The ward had changed dramatically—in part the outcome of a double-edged sword that greeted me once I successfully fought for

---

56 Audiotape in the archives of the author; my emphasis.

resources to improve the quality of life for people living in the Forty-Sixth Ward. We had prioritized development without displacement,
but had seen limited success. There had been significant development—
including housing for poor and working families—but not enough to
stem the tide of gentrification and widespread displacement.

In the twenty years since my first election, the city's economy had
changed dramatically, but basic issues facing many of the people living
here had not. Public schools were still not receiving resources required
to ensure a proper education for all children. Reform was elusive and ineffective. Police misconduct was barely acknowledged as a reality in the
lives of many Chicagoans—especially youth of color. While violence
was down, the perception of it being up framed the ill-fated policies that
were costing the city more than $50 million a year in civil suits, while
the unfortunate tradition of coercing false confessions and emphasizing
harsh penalties for nonviolent crimes continued.

My old friend George Atkins and I sat down to discuss what to
do. "Are you tired of governing, or is this about concern that you might
lose?" he asked me. I was not worried about winning. (I was, however,
concerned about having the energy to do so.) The bigger issue for me
was that I was not inclined to walk away from Wilson Yard when we
were so close to making it a reality. In addition, I had a list of projects I
felt I shouldn't abandon. "Okay," George said. "Make your list. You run
and I'll manage the campaign. After the election, you work on your list,
and I'll manage your staff and ward office."

On that list, along with Wilson Yard, was ensuring the future of
the Black Ensemble Theater, Kuumba Lynx, Uplift Community High
School, Jesus People USA and Cornerstone Community Outreach,
Voice of the People, the People's Music School, completion of the expansion of Truman College (on its existing footprint), and the expansion of my pilot recycling program for citywide use. Most of these had
grassroots origins. All had benefited from my support and advocacy. My
goal for my last term would be to see them through and give them as
much room to grow and root their futures as possible.

The Black Ensemble Theater had been started in the late '70s by
Jackie Taylor, who had grown up in Cabrini-Green, becoming an ac-
tress and landing a part in the movie *Cooley High*. She had been offered a
contract with a major Hollywood studio but declined when they refused

to guarantee her parts other than those in Black exploitation movies. Determined to a life committed to the eradication of racism, Jackie had returned to Chicago, moved to Uptown, and founded the theater according to that explicit mission. For the next thirty years she would grow its programming, focusing on music and drama to challenge the foundations of racism, in part by bringing people into a cultural space to do so. In the process, they outgrew their space in the basement of the Uptown Beacon Street Jane Addams Center. I had hoped the Black Ensemble Theater would stay in Uptown and was overjoyed when Jackie decided it would.

I considered it my job to be their booster. A year earlier, I had introduced Jackie to Alan Bell after meeting him while we both served on the Uplift TAC committee. A constituent living in Lakeview, he had interacted with my ward office concerning some city service issue, but we hadn't personally crossed paths. Our TAC meetings were intense, and I quickly grew to appreciate his input. He seemed ready for another community project, and, as I'd hoped, he and the Black Ensemble Theater turned out to be a match. Now it was up to me to make sure Jackie and the theater could access funds from the Clark Street TIF that was located in the Forty-Sixth and Forty-Seventh Wards.

Kuumba Lynx was a creation of three dynamic women. Jacinda Hall Bullie, a daughter of the Intercommunal Survival Committee, was joined by Jaquanda Saulter-Villegas and Leyda "Lady Sol" Garcia a decade earlier, "promoting hip-hop as a tool to resist systemic violence where Black and Brown youth can reimagine and demonstrate a more just world." With their office and programs located at Clarendon Park, they needed assurances of a permanent home and ongoing advocacy with the city's Department of Cultural Affairs while they continued to build an independent source of financial support.

Uplift was experiencing racism from within the bowels of the Chicago Public Schools bureaucracy. They needed moral and political support in service of a buffer to give them the space to grow and establish their school.

The Jesus People had come a long way from their early days in Uptown. After moving into the Chelsea House and transforming it into Friendly Towers, they had purchased, rehabbed, and retooled two former industrial buildings on Clifton Street into a model for providing services to people who are homeless. They were providing a full-service housing experience to three hundred seniors at Friendly Towers. Subsequently forming Cornerstone Community Outreach, they had also purchased an apartment building where families who were homeless could rent an affordable unit in Uptown. Covering many bases, CCO provided short- and long-term shelter, daily meals, clothing, day care, connections to basic health care, jobs, and security to women with children, single men, and women and families.

The Jesus People had one more project to complete. They had owned the building on the south side of Wilson, across the street from Friendly Towers, since before I was elected alderman twenty years earlier. This was where they produced their magazine *Cornerstone* and where they hoped to be able to worship once it was rehabbed. They had finally secured the financing, but it was slow going. I wanted to make sure they went through the permitting process while I was still an alderman. (They would get their permits and finish their rehab several years later, opening what has become the very popular Everybody's Coffee shop, and making the "Alley" where they worship on Sundays a popular community venue for meetings and events.)

The People's Music School was the brainchild and life work of Rita Simo. Born in the Dominican Republic in 1934, she was a former nun and a concert pianist whose life passion was classical music. The mission of the People's Music School was to provide free classical music education to all. For many years, they had gone without a permanent home. During my second term, however, I had helped them acquire a small city-owned lot in Uptown for one dollar. Since then, on a first-come-first-serve basis, new students had an opportunity to sign up for free classes and learn how to play an instrument of their choice while taking lessons in music theory. On that one day in September, parents would line up hoping to get an open slot. One year, I stood on that line with my granddaughter Britteney. After a wait of several hours, we just made it, scoring the last spot. Ultimately, Britteney chafed at Rita's style of teaching (Rita was serious about her music theory classes; Britteney not so much) and it didn't last long. But Rita never tired of telling the story of how I had stayed in line along with everyone else. In the years to come, the demand for attendance grew to the point that parents would start standing in line overnight. While I didn't have a specific reason for adding the People's Music School to my list, Rita was constantly expanding her reach. You never knew.

Earlier in 2006, the Chicago Equity Fund had gone bankrupt, putting the survival of seventy-seven units of affordable housing in jeopardy. Dan Burke and Tony Fusco had agreed to have their company, Chicago Community Development Corporation, take them over and keep them affordable, avoiding the displacement of the existing tenants. Following on the heels of that disclosure was news that the tax credits on another 150 units owned and operated by Sheldon Baskin, with Voice of the People as the nonprofit partner, were expiring, and that Baskin was considering selling them for condominiums. I was appalled. Following a few weeks of cajoling and arm-twisting, I was able to secure an agreement with Baskin to sell the buildings to CCDC. But they were going to need TIF funds to realize the exchange, along with ongoing preservation of the units as affordable to the existing tenants. I couldn't walk away from this potential loss of housing.

During all the back-and-forth debating about affordability in Uptown, the hyperbole was winning out. While the "not in my backyard" crowd was persistently proclaiming low-income housing was running rampant in Uptown, the actual fact of the matter was that in the Uptown community area, just 18.2 percent of the housing units were subsidized. These units had to be preserved, and that wasn't going to happen without the political will to make it happen. I couldn't walk away from this challenge any more than I could walk away from Wilson Yard.

Before Marguerite Boyd succeeded Phoebe Helm as president of Truman College a few years earlier, they had begun to look at restructuring the school to better facilitate a host of educational initiatives. They settled on a plan to consolidate the administration and student services in one location. Parking for the college was an ongoing issue and irritant to the surrounding residential community. By constructing a new building on existing college-owned property that up until now was being used exclusively for surface parking and incorporating it into a street-level administration building with a multilayer parking lot, they could solve both problems. The bulk of the funding would be through the City Colleges and state capital development bonds secured by Illinois House member Larry McKeon. I acquired a relatively small amount of TIF funds as well, and I wanted to make sure whatever access to construction jobs we succeeded in realizing for community residents at Wilson Yard would carry over to the construction of this building as well.

Marguerite would retire a year or two later, leaving the final design input from the college in the hands of Lynne Walker, the new acting president, for a short while before Mayor Daley appointed Cheryl Hyman in 2010 to replace City College chancellor Wayne Watson following his retirement. Hyman had grown up in public housing on Chicago's West Side, attended a city college on the far South Side, and was a vice president at Commonwealth Edison when she was selected for this post by Daley. Under the banner of reform, Hyman embarked almost immediately on a "reinvention" of the college system. I was not a fan. Historically, each of the seven colleges in the City College system was structured to be autonomous, with a president who had the mandate, responsibility, and authority to grow its programs and was accountable to the community they served. With this new reinvention, that autonomy was the first thing to go. Going forward, presidents would be accountable to the central office. As a result, programs developed in schools by presidents responding to their particular community needs and dynamics would be randomly moved from one school to another.

Lynne Walker had been caught in this shuffle. By the time she had gotten up to speed on the new building, she was a lame-duck president with much less control than either of her predecessors. By the time I completed my last term, the new building was close to completion. In spite of the recession following the economic downturn of 2008, construction had proceeded. Those who had gotten jobs at Wilson Yard were able to continue their apprenticeship at the Truman College site. Plans to expand the nursing program and initiate a tech-oriented program at Truman, however, were not so fortunate.

During my first and second terms, I, along with well-intentioned and passionate volunteers, had supported numerous volunteer pilot programs allowing my constituents to recycle some of their garbage. In 1995 a citywide program known as the Blue Bag Recycling program was instituted. Residents living in buildings with fewer than six apartments had their waste picked up by city trucks and personnel.

Residents were asked to place their recyclables in blue bags that were then thrown in with the rest of the trash. The intent was to separate the blue bags from the rest of the garbage after they were collected. However, the program never reached its goal of reducing waste by 25 percent. The program ended in 2003, and the bags were replaced with blue carts.

Both programs neglected to address recycling in the rest of Chicago, where buildings with more than five units were required to hire private scavenger companies to pick up and dispose of their garbage. The only attempt to even encourage recycling in the significant and large array of Chicago's multi-unit buildings came from the affidavit condominium associations, who had to sign a form saying recycling was provided for in their building when they applied for the annual rebate of seventy-five dollars per unit to which they were entitled.[57]

Active in a neighborhood block club, Rae Mindock and I were at odds for most of my first four terms before we found some common ground. During her participation in the Wilson Yard Task Force, we discovered a joint interest in solving the city's reticence when it came to recycling.[58] With her taking the lead, we designed a pilot program in the Forty-Sixth Ward. The objective was to work with all our high-rises—affordable housing, market-rate rental buildings, and condominium buildings alike—and develop a game plan for recycling. The next step was to take what we had learned and implement it citywide. I would need some more time to do that. In conjunction with the city's Department of Environment, we would develop a tool kit that could be

---

57 The Forty-Sixth Ward had more high-rises than any other ward when my predecessor proposed an ordinance authorizing this rebate. He successfully argued that since homeowners in single-family homes didn't have to pay for garbage collection since it was done by city crews, in the name of fairness, the owners of condominiums in multi-unit buildings should get a rebate. Beginning in 2012 this rebate began a multiyear phase-out. Since 2018, owners of all buildings from which the city crews pick up recycling must pay the city $7.50 a month for each unit in their building.

58 Rae was also interested in zoning as a vehicle for the preservation of the historic elements of Uptown's housing stock. The tools necessary to address her concerns looked like they might double as vehicles to achieve development without displacement, leading to several joint zoning projects.

used as a guide by managers of high-rises and other multi-unit buildings in the city to develop their own custom strategy for recycling.

. . . .

76.

MISSED OPPORTUNITIES
AFFORDABLE HOUSING AND POLICING

As I began my sixth and last term in May 2007, a housing foreclosure crisis was foreshadowing the economic downturn that would worsen as the year continued. In September 2008, Lehman Brothers went bankrupt, precipitating an international financial crisis. A month later, the city council received the mayor's budget recommendations for 2009. Chicago's unemployment rate had increased throughout the year and was now hovering at 8 percent overall, but was as high as 25 percent in the city's Black and Latino communities—a fifteen-year high. Foreclosures were devastating many in the city but were felt the hardest on the city's South and West Sides.

Revenue fell below expected levels for the year as grants from the state, Chicago's share of sales taxes, and the real estate transaction tax revenues collectively declined by just over $100 million. Meanwhile, the 2008 winter months saw an unusual amount of snow and bad weather, dramatically increasing expenses. The city faced an unexpected deficit for the current year and an even larger one for 2009. Privatization of the city's parking meters was the mayor's solution. To head the initiative, he picked his chief financial officer, Paul Volpe, who would later serve a short stint as his chief of staff.

Existing meters in the city were old, and many were malfunctioning. A recurrent scandal for the city involved the collection of money from these meters. Once done by city workers, this job had been privatized early in Rich Daley's administration. The consequence was little accountability, many complaints, and increased demands from aldermen to replace and modernize the meters in their respective business districts. Meters were important to local businesses in neighborhoods where parking was tight; they needed some turnover to ensure parking for their customers. At twenty-five cents an hour, they were affordable enough. When the majority of meters on a block malfunctioned, cars didn't move and the businesses complained. The demand was often for new "pay and display" meters. Very much in demand, they were also expensive.

Frustration with this state of affairs, coupled with concern over how best to address the deepening financial crisis's effect on the city's already-fragile finances, opened the door to a parking meter deal.

To close the city's budget gaps for the current fiscal year as well as the next, the mayor, in his budget address, asked for support for an agreement to lease the city's parking meters. "To be honest," he said, "if we don't reach this agreement, we may be forced to raise revenue in some other way," implying that a property tax increase (anathema to most elected officials) would be the next move.

The agreement remained unconcluded when the scheduled vote on the budget arrived in mid-November, but the city council was assured that it would be before us for a vote before the end of the year. We were promised we would have plenty of time to review the terms (at least that's a commitment I received directly from Paul Volpe) and plenty of time to fill our budget gaps by the end of the year, so we would be in compliance with state law to pass a balanced budget.

With the budget process over for the time being and Wilson Yard funded at last, I finally had a minute to breathe. I had been going nonstop since that meeting with George two years earlier when I had committed to this term. I needed a break and prepared to visit friends in California. Just as I was leaving city hall, Volpe asked me for a few minutes to update me on the parking meter deal. His briefing was, indeed, brief. He gave me the broad strokes but glossed over many of the details, and I had a number of questions. What provisions were in place for aldermen to have the ability to advise and consent to meter locations? The parking rates were being increased too much too quickly; where was the wiggle room? Could these be further negotiated? Would people without credit cards be able to use cash with the new payboxes? Why wasn't there a cap on how much revenue the company got annually before a profit-sharing agreement (which didn't exist) kicked in? He assured me the contract would come before the city council after I returned and that he would get me answers before then.

A few days after arriving in California, I received a phone call from a Chicago reporter. He had called to tell me that a group called "Fix Wilson Yard" had filed a lawsuit against Wilson Yard and were asking the judge for a temporary restraining order to stop construction. He wanted a comment. He then asked me if I knew that a special meeting of the city council was scheduled for a day or two later to vote on the parking meter lease. (I had not checked my email and therefore had not seen the notice.)

It was a seventy-five-year agreement that would pay the city a little over $1.1 billion. Clearly the city needed the money, but there were too many questions, and the agreement left too much wiggle room for the vendor but none for the city. The turnaround was too quick. I was sure Volpe had just been giving me lip service; this was clearly a done deal. I had to decide if I would go home to vote. If I did, I would have to vote no. But whether I voted no or didn't make it back for the vote, the outcome would be the same. The mayor would not have called a special meeting unless he had the votes. I stayed in California.

This turned out to be a terrible deal for the city. While we now have new pay-and-display meters and a guarantee that they will be maintained and upgraded as necessary, we gave up autonomy to decide the cost of parking and the flexibility to change where the meters are located and even the times that they operate. Worst of all, it will end up costing us much more than we got for it. So, a part of me has always wondered: Could I have made a difference, and should I have come back for the vote and tried?

After returning to Chicago, I continued a conversation that was started shortly after the conclusion of the 2007 municipal elections with a citywide coalition of unions and housing advocates. The groups had been meeting with aldermen in their respective communities for going on two years. Their effort was well organized and impactful, raising hope of enhancing housing opportunities for poor and working families all over the city. The large number of foreclosures, increasing unemployment, and overall insecurity of the economy added urgency. I was anxious to support their Sweet Home Chicago ordinance.

The number of tax-increment financing districts in the city had been increasing dramatically. Between the time the first TIF was established in the early 1980s and 2007, increments worth a total of over $440 million were received from 138 TIF districts. The teachers union was demanding that some of this increment be returned to the board of education to address the school district's own financial woes. Housing advocates were demanding a guarantee that 20 percent of the total increment collected each year be used for the development of low-income housing.

To further complicate matters, not all TIFs were equal. Some were in fast-growing areas of the city, others not so much. Without growth and an increase in property values, there would be no increment. Since money could only be moved (ported) from one TIF to another that it abutted, there were very few opportunities to transfer money from wealthy TIFs to poorer ones. This only served to heighten the already-unequal distribution of public resources going to underserved areas of the city.

The cornerstone of the Sweet Home Chicago Ordinance was the requirement that 20 percent of the total increment collected from all the TIFs in any given year be spent on affordable housing, coupled with a section that if this was not done, advocates could sue and the city would be on the hook for their legal fees.

While I was supportive of this idea, it wasn't actually allowed by the state law that had allowed for TIFs. This legislation required that when a TIF district was created, the local ordinance creating it had to state what its allowed uses would be, and that increment had to be spent in the TIF district from which the increment came. Since a good number of the TIFs in Chicago were created for strictly industrial or commercial uses (not mixed uses), housing could not be built in every TIF, nor could the increment a non-housing TIF received be used in another district unless it was one that abutted its boundaries.

Even if the legislation were passed, it was unlikely that the city would be able to reach the bar of 20 percent; therefore, it seemed to me that instead of spending money on housing we would be spending it on legal fees. While I'm sure that wasn't their intent, and while our conversations went on throughout my last term, we were never able to get to a place of agreement.

During the final budget process in which I would participate as an alderman, I made a last stab. In October 2010, after getting agreement from the mayor's Office of Intergovernmental Affairs, I proposed an alternative. Surprisingly, they had agreed to strengthen the affordable housing requirements, focusing their benefits on households at 80 percent and less of the median income (from 100 percent),[59] as well as assenting to provisions to increase the corpus of the Chicago Low-Income Housing Trust Fund (one of our best tools for housing low-income people) and to expand use of TIF funds for all allowable affordable housing expenses. If, in TIF districts, we amended the city's guidelines to allow TIF funds to be spent on HRAIL, EHAP, the so-called bungalow program, and all other housing-related programs that provide a capital improvement to any affordable housing units, we could expand what the city was able to do with these programs in areas of the city that were not TIFed.[60]

I suspect Intergovernmental Affairs agreed to all of this because they didn't really expect to get agreement on the real sticking point—the 20 percent requirement. My final proposed change had addressed this. It would have established the 20 percent as a goal—not a requirement—and would have deleted the section on legal action and court fees. In the end, however, we couldn't get over this hump. It would be one of my greatest regrets. It was regrettable and unnecessary that we lost this chance, which would have significantly improved Chicago's commitment to housing lower-income people, while stabilizing the housing for those who had a home.

My frustration and disappointment at this squandering of a well-fought-for opportunity—the result of the combined efforts of thousands for decades, as well as of the specific four-year effort that had brought us to this moment—has stayed with me. Ten years later, too many people

---

59 These percentages were based on the median income of people living in the larger Chicago Metropolitan Area. In 2009 Chicago's median income was much lower. Going by the area median income, a household earning as much as 125 percent of the median would qualify for the units pegged at 100 percent.

60 HRAIL is a program that provides limited home improvements for seniors at no cost to the homeowner or tenant; EHAP is an emergency housing program for low-income homeowners and allows up to $10,000 a unit in owner-occupied one-to-three-unit buildings for emergency repairs like a new furnace or a roof repair. The bungalow program does the same for Chicago's traditional bungalow stock.

in Chicago still live in substandard housing they can't afford. Too many have no home at all.

As time has gone by, I realize that perhaps my deepest regret is not having had any real impact on the police contracts with the city. From their inception, the contracts had a built-in bias that put the interests of the Fraternal Order of Police—anointed the union to represent all officers—above all others. This disavowed not only the interests of other police officers who disagreed with their persistent resistance to increasing the number of nonwhite or female officers on the force, but the very framework of their contract, which guaranteed a different legal standard for police officers than was tendered by police toward civilians.

When Freddrenna Lyle was appointed to the city council, replacing John Steele (who had become a circuit court judge), we agreed to insert ourselves into the Law Department's progress during contract negotiations. We were focused on the restrictions in the contract that prevented any information about an officer's past conduct that was more than six months old to be included in any review of complaints against that officer. While we had some minor impacts, in retrospect, the changes we were able to influence were paltry in nature—much too little and much too late.

A consistent theme of the work in Racine in the late 1960s and in Chicago in the '70s under the leadership of the Black Panther Party had been organizing for community control of policing. In my time in Chicago, I saw the creation of three different police accountability agencies, and each failed to change the culture of the Chicago Police Department. In fact, arguably the culture of the CPD rank and file moved further away from the culture and norms of the community over the last five decades. The impact of the Afro-American Patrolmen's League and other ethnic-based unions on the thought and analysis of the police dissipated, and every push for accountability brought retrenchment among the rank and file that was often backed up by most city leaders (even some progressive ones).

We had fought for community control of policing and, in 1974, won the creation of the Office of Professional Standards, hoping maybe with professional standards the rampant corruption might wane. It did not. When the Red Squad's out-of-control spying was exposed a year later and ultimately disbanded, we thought maybe police behavior would change. We were wrong. When Harold Washington moved the

Office of Professional Standards (OPS) out of police headquarters, we thought it would make a difference. It did not. When we pushed for and got community policing in the late 1980s and early '90s, we thought it would change the police and make them more responsive to the community. We were wrong again. The formation of the Independent Police Review Authority (IPRA) in my final term was meant to bring about some measure of accountability and change. It did not. After I left office, IPRA became the Civilian Office of Police Accountability (COPA), a consent decree was agreed to (a case my son worked on), and other reforms were implemented. And police violence and community violence continued unabated.[61]

During each decade from the 1970s to present, there have been numerous stories of police abuse, corruption, and neglect, accompanied by a culture of white supremacy in the department. No matter the efforts, the stories do not seem to change.

Despite all my attempts to get to the heart of how police misconduct was addressed by the city, it was impossible to unravel. Again and again the city council would be asked to support multimillion-dollar settlements filed to address police misconduct. Since I left the city council in 2011, the city has on average paid more than $50 million annually

---

61 On September 14, 2021, the city council approved a new eight-year contract with the FOP, expiring in 2025. As a result of a new state law, for the first time complaints of police misconduct may be submitted anonymously. The contract prohibits disclosure of the names of complainants to officers until immediately prior to their interview; prohibits officers who use force against a member of the public to revise their statement to investigators after reviewing audio and video recordings of the incident; and ends the practice of destroying disciplinary records (based on a 2020 ruling from the Illinois Supreme Court). However, the contract neglected to include many recommendations for reform. Among them are provisions delaying interviews in shooting cases for at least twenty-four hours to ensure that officers remain separated from their colleagues until all of them have given statements and a requirement that officers disclose whether they work a second job, how many hours they worked, and a cap on the number of hours officers may moonlight. In return for the reforms included, the agreement provides for a 20 percent pay increase for police officers over the life of the contract and the assignment of an officer (paid by the city) to union headquarters to administer a vaguely defined mental health program.

to settle these cases. And rarely if ever were the officers involved fired or even disciplined. In any other job, if your actions result in a major loss to your employer, let alone physical harm, you would be fired. Not here. The presumption I couldn't shake off or dent in any way was that the police officer is always right and the complainant is a liar or a criminal, or is protecting one.

The process for disciplining any officer for corruption, civil rights violations, or really any misconduct is intentionally complicated and drawn out. Depending on the nature of the misconduct, first it goes to COPA or to Internal Affairs and then to the superintendent, before making its way to the police board and then back to the superintendent.

Every budget season, I would ask the executive director of the police board the same questions. And every time I would leave the hearing feeling as uninformed as when I entered the room—at least until I started studying the police contract. The police board, consisting of nine civilian members appointed by the mayor for a term of five years, has four powers: first, to nominate three candidates to fill the position of superintendent and submit those names to the mayor whenever there is a vacancy in that position; second, to "adopt rules and regulations for the governance of the police department of the city";[62] third, to hear disciplinary action for all recommendations for suspension greater than thirty days and for the removal of officers or civilian employees of the police department; and fourth, to consider appeals of probationary officers who fail to pass their background investigation. Seems straightforward enough. But not once in twenty-four years could I get any police board executive director to even acknowledge a single rule or regulation for governance of the department that the board had taken up in that year.

The police board is required to hold a regular meeting at least once a month. Their members are expected to attend, and for this they receive a stipend. In addition, all disciplinary action that comes to the board is investigated by attorneys hired by their executive director, the results of which they must review; then, the board votes on whether to uphold the recommendation or reject it. It can be several years between the time the infraction occurred and the vote by the police board. Some of this time is eaten up while complaints are languishing at OPS (or IPRA or COPA). Some more is eaten up in the police department by the superintendent. A

---

62 Chicago Municipal Code.

good deal more is eaten up while being investigated by the police board. Then, after all that, their decision has been known to be overturned or ignored by the police superintendent. In 2022 the police board was budgeted $579,608, while the police department was allocated $1.75 billion.[63]

It is striking that most of our work when I first arrived in Uptown in 1972 was around the BPP's push for community control of policing, and that fifty years later, activists and community leaders are still searching for the same thing. There is nothing scarier than state-sanctioned and -protected violence. There is nothing more impactful on a community than state-condoned neglect and corruption. These corrosive activities, evinced by a department that is neither democratically controlled by the communities it polices nor effectively held accountable, are at the heart of all the other ills that harm our underserved communities.

If we don't have accountability from the agencies we expect to protect us, it should be no surprise that we don't have it elsewhere, either. Violence is not new to Chicago's neighborhoods: a quick glance at a chart of homicide rates between 1985 and 2016 shows a yo-yoing up and down, with a rise in the last few years that competes with one seen in the early 1990s.

In 2021, Chicago allocated 13 percent of its total budget to the Chicago Police Department. Meanwhile, the combined budgets of the Departments of Public Health, Housing, and Family and Support Services amounted to just 5 percent of the total. Pensions and health benefits are not included in either of these figures, nor is the judgment fund that pays for large settlements and court judgments resulting from police misconduct lawsuits. The 2021 annuity payment to the police pension fund alone was pegged at 6 percent of the budget—more than the human service departments combined.

---

63 Additionally, the police department expected to receive over $151 million in grants. None of these amounts includes allocations for police pensions, annuity funds, health care insurance paid by the city for police officers, payouts for settlements, and judgments for wrongful deaths and police misconduct that have come to average $50 million a year; nor does it include the budgets of the Office of Emergency Communications and the Public Safety Administration, whose combined budgets and expected grants come to just over $390 million in the 2022 city budget. While these departments do not deal exclusively with police officers, they do intertwine with the police department significantly.

After more than fifty years of lessons from failed reforms, I know firsthand that this dichotomy has to be turned on its head, and that in order to accomplish this, white-skin privilege and other lingering habits of privilege must be removed from the equation.

. . . .

77.

DO NO HARM

Over more than twenty years as an alderman, one of the most important lessons I learned was the importance of striving to "do no harm." Indeed, far too many of the ordinances proposed in the city council reacted to a problem in one place but had deleterious effects elsewhere.

To take an illustrative example: at some point, a South Side alderman was receiving complaints that hair salons in a part of her ward that were open overnight (primarily serving people that worked all day) were too loud, keeping nearby residents up at night. In response, the city council passed an ordinance requiring that anyone who wanted to open a salon in certain zoning designations and within one thousand feet of another licensed salon would have to get approval from the Zoning Board of Appeals. This became a citywide requirement, compliance with which would cost these small businesses thousands of dollars; and it would be virtually impossible to change because the majority of aldermen were afraid to give up the little power this gave them.

Young people and people of color were particular victims of such knee-jerk initiatives—especially when it came to petty crime and fighting the "war on drugs." Many of these well-intentioned ordinances ended up creating many more opportunities for interactions with the police that were unnecessary and that sometimes went bad—usually for the civilians involved.

Chicago also has a history of paying for its budget on the backs of hidden fees and fines without much consideration of the impacts. A lot of my time, and the time of my staff, was dedicated to ameliorating these impacts—aiming at small victories that would have big impacts (most often on marginalized people).

Following the snowstorm in 1979 that left most of the city paralyzed and led to the upset election of Jane Byrne, new parking restrictions were established. For many, the most onerous of these were new overnight parking restrictions for major thoroughfares throughout the city, which would be in effect (and enforced) between December 1 and March 31 each year. Cars parked on these streets during the overnight hours would be ticketed and towed. There were still several of these restricted zones in the Forty-Sixth Ward when I became alderman in 1987. We hadn't seen another snowstorm comparable to the one that had occurred in 1979, yet on perfectly clear nights when the streets were bereft of snow, hundreds if not thousands of cars were towed each night beginning on December 1.

The Forty-Sixth Ward is compact. We have high-rises and multifamily homes—many of which were built before requirements for parking were on anyone's radar. For many, overnight street parking was their only alternative. If they could afford it, residents began budgeting hundreds of dollars a month to cover their parking tickets and tow charges. Most could not. Cars were booted for having too many unpaid tickets, making them inaccessible to their owners, who in some cases lost their jobs because they were needed for work. Others went into debt. I went to war.

The Department of Transportation refused to budge on the rules; elected officials were afraid to act. The paranoia that a new storm would come and they'd be blamed reared its head at any mention of change. But this was insane. After all, there were already signs on each of these streets requiring drivers to move their cars if more than two inches of snow fell. The overnight restrictions appeared to be more about raising revenue than being prepared for a snowfall that comes once every ten years or so.

Block by block, I got the signs removed until there were no more in the boundaries of the Forty-Sixth Ward. This was no small feat, as it required an ordinance, the support of the Department of Transportation (to get out of the city council committee hearing the request), and a vote before the full city council. All the while, everyone seemed worried that this would somehow lead to blame and that they'd be the scapegoat.

Along the eastern boundaries of the Forty-Sixth Ward lived many cab drivers. Their cabs doubled as their personal cars, and they needed to park them overnight near their homes or apartments. This was illegal, and they often got ticketed. Some cab drivers had access to off-street parking, but not all. Why should they be treated differently than any other local residents? Again, I needed to get a solution passed by the city council. Ultimately it was agreed that cab drivers living in the Forty-Sixth Ward could purchase a permit to park on the streets in the vicinity of their home.

Another struggle around parking concerned street sweeping, which in 1987 occurred erratically. Paper warning signs would go up the day before, but sometimes they were only one on a block, or they would blow away, or someone was away that week and didn't know their street would be swept. Early on I insisted on a set schedule, which we published and distributed door to door throughout the ward. (This was before access to the internet and before anyone had a website.) The result: our streets were cleaned without the penalty of parking fines.

Traffic was a big deal at some of our intersections, tying up traffic for blocks. One street had become a major thoroughfare for people coming from miles west on their way to Lake Shore Drive, whose path to downtown swamped the area, which was regularly snarled in a major traffic jam where three streets came together (Montrose, Sheridan, and Broadway). I asked the Department of Transportation to do a traffic study. However, they came up with little useful information and seemed to have difficulty understanding the problem. I'm a visual person, so I asked the developer of a high-rise recently built at this intersection to shoot videos of the intersection at the worst times of congestion. Armed with these, we got the department's attention. Insisting they use new technologies available to monitor traffic and shift timelines for stop lights, we were finally able (after many attempts and several years) to get the problem greatly improved.

There are three locations in the Forty-Sixth Ward, and one farther north in what was then the Forty-Ninth Ward, where North Broadway and Sheridan Road cross. One of these is just south of the above intersection. Part of the problem that had to be solved was to direct traffic turning left from Broadway to Sheridan about two hundred feet south of Montrose. It was agreed that painting the path on the street for turning vehicles to follow should solve the problem. A job order was made. I drew a diagram for them to follow. A month or two later, I was informed that the job was done. The problem was that the lines had been painted on the other location in the ward—a typical two-way intersection where no clarification was needed. Lines would be drawn again on the northern intersection of these streets before the job was finally done where it was intended.

At some point, small pickup trucks became popular personal vehicles. My staff assistant Nora Hughes had one and used it exclusively for personal use. She became the poster child for my efforts to redirect the enforcement against trucks on Lake Shore Drive to be flexible enough to understand that a personal vehicle was not a commercial vehicle and should not be subject to the restriction of these vehicles from this very important means of travel.

Petty fines, with the stated intent to address any number of problems while the true effect has been to pad the city's coffers, have increased across the board for decades, with the only relief occurring during the Washington years. Taxes on necessities like gas and electricity, not to mention the city's steady increase of water rates, have made Chicago increasingly unaffordable.

The city's utility tax is tied to the amount of electricity or gas the consumer uses. Therefore, if the weather is colder in the winter and the cost of heating goes up, the city gets more revenue. Among many administrators, there is a deep-seated resistance to changing this tax because the city "can't afford to do so." Unfortunately, a rising number of residents cannot afford for the city *not* to.

Harold Washington had committed to changing this, and I wholeheartedly supported this intent. For the duration of my twenty-four years on the city council, I viewed most everything through the lens of affordability and the impact on Chicagoans' everyday struggle to survive. While I was not always successful, I strove to ensure that people on the margins and struggling to survive at least knew they were seen.

78.

LESSONS FROM MY YEARS
AS A BUREAUCRACY BUSTER

In the fall of 2010, Richard M. Daley announced he would not run for reelection. A month earlier, I had done the same. During the first four months of the new year, Daley held press conferences in most of the city's fifty wards, joining the respective aldermen and summarizing their joint accomplishments. Usually in attendance were any number of community residents, staff from various city departments, and the media. The Forty-Sixth Ward press conference took place in March along the lakefront, outside the restaurant nestled between the Park District's North Side golf course, soccer fields, and tennis courts, a stone's throw from Lincoln Park's iconic totem pole.

In advance, the mayor's staff had asked me to send them a list of what had been accomplished in the Forty-Sixth Ward around housing, city services, and crime. A number of my efforts over the years had concerned the city's response to crime, which had been constantly overstated, creating a hypersensitivity in the ward, a demonization of youth, and a perception that did not match the reality. I had adopted various strategies over the years to find honest solutions to the actual problems we faced. Among these were actions that would make people feel safer. To that end, using all available resources, I had made sure that every street and every alley in the ward had new street and alley lights complete with underground electric cables.[64]

---

64 As was true with much of Chicago's infrastructure, by the 1980s streetlights needed a lot of upgrading. Many streets in the city had just one or two streetlights on any given block—something that was particularly true throughout the South and West Sides but impacted numerous areas on the North Side, including Uptown. Most alleys in the city did not have lights at all. Additionally, electricity to the lights we did have had been installed with underground cables well over thirty years earlier with a twenty-five-year life span. The result was that most streetlights now received their electricity from overhead electric wires. These needed repairs, leaving the street dark. It was common for a live wire to be exposed, which was

In an effort to avoid a "war on crime" dialogue, the language I sent the mayor to describe how my ward had addressed crime focused, in part, on this re-lamping project—the point being that now our streets were well-lit during overnight hours, creating the sense, if not the reality, of safety. At the press conference, when he got to this sentence he read it, stopped for a minute, glanced at me curiously, and then, as if he had never heard of such a thing before, asked the reporters present, "Did you hear what I just said? She has new streetlights in every street and alley!" Adding something like, "Amazing."

When it was the media's turn to ask questions, the first one asked was "Mayor, how did you get Alderman Shiller to agree with you?" His answer was, "I didn't. She got me to agree with her."

I was as surprised as they were, but for different reasons. I'm pretty sure they were thinking that now that I was voting for the city's budgets, he had supported my initiatives in return—especially Wilson Yard. Many political pundits agreed with that assessment. They, like most, viewed power as being a transactional commodity.

For me, however, the definition of power that guided my actions actually came from Huey Newton: "Power is the ability to define phenomena and make it act in a desired manner." Unlike the more common (and more cynical) view, this notion of power is *empowering*. Rather than assume power as a commodity to be bartered and accumulated for personal benefit, this definition assumes a process that can lead to novel possibilities. It assumes that the dynamics of any situation can be changed. Instead of lamenting, "You can't fight city hall," it demands, "Dare to struggle, dare to win!"

As an activist, I demanded that those elected or appointed to positions of power used those positions to provide solutions to the problems we face. With fellow organizers, I had demanded housing that was livable, health care that made us well, an education that taught our children, and jobs that paid a living wage. When told to come up with a plan, we said, "That's your job!" while going about showing them how to do their job—serving breakfast to children who were otherwise going hungry and opening free health clinics with doctors and nurses who recognized our housing conditions were affecting the health of our families.

---

obviously dangerous, especially to children. When streets were dark, people were fearful—often for good reason.

As an elected official, I governed from the perspective of those most affected and with the objective of correcting power imbalances. Until I was in a governing position, I didn't really understand the true nature of power as a constantly changing dynamic. And sometimes, I found, in finite situations, those most affected and on the wrong side of the power dynamic are people who usually have privilege and are usually empowered. Governing sometimes led to unexpected and unwanted enemies and friends, many of them temporary. We found the best solutions when we approached a problem—pretty much any problem—from the point of view of those most affected (and, as I have mentioned, this was usually, but not always, those with fewer resources and/or those victimized by their race, gender, or sexual orientation), paid attention, and took seriously potential collateral impacts to each possible solution, starting with those most impacted but looking beyond to enlarge the understanding of who would be impacted and how.

As an activist I may have appreciated this approach (it did after all come from my experience), but my job would have been a different one. Indeed, this approach sometimes led to choices that as an activist I would not have appreciated nor necessarily understood.

I also learned just how fragile power is, and just how much power activists and community leaders have without realizing it. I learned just how much fear (and vulnerability) those in governing power often have, and how movable they really are when people are organizing in the streets. When a change in the status quo was necessary to accomplish a particular goal, I came to appreciate those campaigns where activists organized effectively, creating for me and others a "sea to swim in."

Whether it's an ordinance that has to be created or a problem that needs solving in the community or the city or world at large, circumstances are always changing, and real solutions (ones that actually get at the root of a problem) are almost always more complicated than we like to think. We all make decisions based on what we know in the moment and what we believe is best to accomplish our objectives in that moment. So do movements. Sometimes this can be complicated—especially when there are multiple interests that don't always coincide. Sometimes alliances change. Sometimes our policy goals evolve as new circumstances and information presents. Sometimes in our frustration we miss the growth and development that is occurring and fall victim to demonizing our perceived friends and enemies. Sometimes people are operating out of good intentions. Sometimes they are acting selfishly. In the end, we must ask ourselves: Are we moving forward? Are we having a material impact that advances us toward a just world?

THE BLACK PANTHER PARTY'S TEN-POINT PROGRAM

My activism in my early years was animated and guided by the Black Panther Party's Ten-Point Program, and as I have written this book I realize how much my governance as an elected official, in the decades after that, was as well. Points four, five, and seven became three of my most consistent fights. In many ways the *Program and Platform of the BPP* was simply a demand that the promises and ideals of democracy and justice, promised to white men who owned property when our country was founded, simply be finally applied to Black folk. There's nothing really radical about that—or maybe there still is.

Originally written by Huey Newton and Bobby Seale in 1966, the platform and program was revised in March 1972 and is reprinted below. The revised version acknowledged the role of technology, made the language gender inclusive, and expanded it to include all oppressed people and communities. It served us well in Uptown, where we were committed to organizing poor and working whites to join the Black-led struggle for liberation. After all, we all faced so many common problems. The BPP platform and program now included them. The racism we encountered was wedded to the white-skin privilege many held on to, and it was an ongoing and primary barrier. Our best tool was a vision of future changes worth fighting for by anyone willing and able to break the yoke of racism and white-skin privilege.

***

BLACK PANTHER PARTY PLATFORM AND PROGRAM

MARCH 29, 1972

WHAT WE WANT, WHAT WE BELIEVE

1. **We want freedom. We want power to determine the destiny of our Black and oppressed communities.**

   We believe that Black and oppressed people will not be free until we are able to determine our own destinies in our communities ourselves, by fully controlling all the institutions which exist in our communities.

2. **We want full employment for our people.**

   We believe that the federal government is responsible and obligated to give every person employment or a guaranteed income. We believe that if the American businessmen will not give full employment, the technology and means of production should be taken from the businessmen and placed in the community so that the people of the community can organize and employ all of its people and give a high standard of living.

3. **We want an end to the robbery by the capitalists of our Black and oppressed communities.**

   We believe that this racist government has robbed us and now we are demanding the overdue debt of forty acres and two mules. Forty acres and two mules was promised 100 years ago as restitution for slave labor and mass murder of Black people. We will accept the payment in currency which will be distributed to our many communities. The American racist has taken part in the slaughter of over 50 million Black people. Therefore, we feel this is a modest demand that we make.

4. **We want decent housing, fit for shelter of human beings.**

   We believe that if the landlords will not give decent housing to our Black and oppressed communities, then the housing and the land should be made into cooperatives so that the people in our communities, with government aid, can build and make decent housing for the people.

5. **We want education for our people that exposes the true nature of this decadent American society. We want education that teaches us our true history and our role in the present day society.**
   We believe in an educational system that will give to our people a knowledge of self. If you do not have knowledge of yourself and your position in society and the world, then you have little chance to know anything else.   .

6. **We want completely free health care for all Black and oppressed people.**
   We believe that the government must provide, free of charge, health facilities which will not only treat our illnesses, most of which have come about as a result of our oppression, but which will also develop preventative medical programs to guarantee our future survival. We believe that mass health education and research programs must be developed to give all Black and oppressed people access to advanced scientific and medical information, so we may provide ourselves with proper medical attention and care.

7. **We want an immediate end to POLICE BRUTALITY and MURDER of Black people, other people of color, and all oppressed people inside the United States.**
   We believe that the racist and fascist government of the United States uses its domestic enforcement agencies to carry out its program of oppression against Black people, other people of color and poor people inside the United States. We believe it is our right, therefore, to defend ourselves against such armed forces, and that all Black and oppressed people should be armed for self-defense of our homes and communities against these fascist police forces.

8. **We want an immediate end to all wars of aggression.**
   We believe that the various conflicts which exist around the world stem directly from the aggressive desires of the US ruling circle and government to force its domination upon the

oppressed people of the world. We believe that if the US government of its lackeys do not cease these aggressive wars that it is the right of the people to defend themselves by any means necessary against their aggressors.

9. **We want freedom for all Black and poor oppressed people now held in US federal, state, county, city and military prisons and jails. We want trials by a jury of peers for all persons charged with so-called crimes under the laws of the country.**

   We believe that the many Black and poor oppressed people now held in US prisons and jails have not received fair and impartial trials under a racist and fascist judicial system and should be free from incarceration. We believe in the ultimate elimination of all wretched, inhuman penal institutions, because the masses of men and women imprisoned inside the United States or by the US military are the victims of oppressive conditions which are the real cause of their imprisonment. We believe that when persons are brought to trial that they must be guaranteed, by the United States, juries of their peers, attorneys of their choice and freedom from imprisonment while awaiting trials.

10. **We want land, bread, housing, education, clothing, justice, peace and people's community control of modern technology.**

    When in the course of human events, it becomes necessary for one people to dissolve the political bonds which have connected them with another, and to assume among the powers of the earth, the separate and equal station to which the laws of nature and nature's god entitle them, a decent respect to the opinions of mankind requires that they should declare the causes which impel them to the separation.

We hold these truths to be self-evident, and that all men are created equal, that they are endowed by their creator with certain unalienable rights, that among these are life, liberty, and the pursuit of happiness. That to secure these rights, governments are instituted among men, deriving their just powers from the consent of the governed, that whenever any form of government becomes destructive of these ends, it is the right of the people to alter or abolish it, and to institute new government, laying its foundation on such principles and organizing its power in such a form as to them shall seem most likely to effect their safety and happiness. Prudence, indeed, will dictate that governments long established should not be changed for light and transient causes; and accordingly all experience hath shown that mankind are more disposed to suffer, while evils are sufferable, than to right themselves by abolishing the forms to which they are accustomed. But when a long train of abuses and usurpations, pursuing invariably the same object, evinces a design to reduce them under absolute despotism, it is their right, and their duty, to throw off such government, and to provide new guards of their future security.

10 POINT GUIDE TO ACTION

Taken from a speech by David Du Bois, Leading spokesperson of the Black Panther Party.

HAVE THE COURAGE TO STRUGGLE, HAVE THE COURAGE TO WIN!

1. Militant resistance to the power structure in this country cannot succeed unless it organizationally reflects the vanguard role of third world Americans, and foremost Black Americans.

2. We should fight against isolation from the people. Apply a circle of investigation which includes knowing the community, going to the community, listening to the community, learning from the community, becoming one with the community. Seek out honest community leaders, talk, listen, demonstrate humility. Find a basis for common action.

3. Pick the issues using the two way road: learn the real concerns of the community and apply your organizational understanding to these concerns. Use the four criteria in choosing the issue: the one closest to the human concern of the most people; the one least defensible for the power structure; the one closest to the democratic ideals and dreams of the American people; and the one whose resolution would cause the sharpest contradiction between reaction and honest belief.

4. Prepare carefully a protracted step by step campaign towards well defined step by step goals. Seize and keep the initiative. Know when to advance, when to retreat.

5. Identify the opposition and deepen the community's understanding of it. Actions must expose, confuse, put the enemy on the defensive; at the same time they must guarantee wider support, backing and involvement of people. We should clearly understand ourselves the interrelationship of our campaign to the

overall struggle against reactionary intercommunalism. We should plan action to help others grow in their understanding.

6. **For building coalitions:** we should let the community know what we're planning; let the community know we welcome participation; and, when participation comes around, listen to it, take and use its advice and let the community know and feel they are genuinely needed.

7. **Use People's politics.** Tie the campaign in with local politics and local politicians. Appeal to them for advice, participation and support, in that order. Expose them thoroughly when they don't comply, repeatedly, with larger and larger forces and finally replace them with peoples' candidates. Remember that the power is in our peoples' coalition, not in elected officials.

8. **Tie our issue to similar campaign in other areas.** Let them know what we are doing and keep them informed. Seek their declared support and publicize it. Don't depend on them and respect their priorities.

9. **On Knowledge and Patience:** Knowledge requires study, learning from people and trusting in your own judgment. Patience is built on the understanding that time is on our side and patience is necessary to plan and carry out step by step protracted struggle.

10. **On Discipline and Courage:** Discipline requires a constant personal and organizational struggle—In our own lives with our bodies kept strong and healthy, our minds kept open and growing in understanding, our behavior an example of service to the people, our appearance always mindful of the sensibilities of those we work to organize and move. In our organization with democratic centralism; political education as part of political work; system, order and organization in our administration; and well planned physical training and social activities.

Courage requires the understanding that we are in the belly of the monster. The people of all the world look to the American people to fulfill our responsibility. Their lives as well as ours depend on it.

INDEX

"Passim" (literally "scattered")
 indicates intermittent discussion
 of a topic over a cluster of pages.

ABOUT HAYMARKET BOOKS

Haymarket Books is a radical, independent, nonprofit book publisher based in Chicago. Our mission is to publish books that contribute to struggles for social and economic justice. We strive to make our books a vibrant and organic part of social movements and the education and development of a critical, engaged, international left.

We take inspiration and courage from our namesakes, the Haymarket Martyrs, who gave their lives fighting for a better world. Their 1886 struggle for the eight-hour day – which gave us May Day, the international workers' holiday – reminds workers around the world that ordinary people can organize and struggle for their own liberation. These struggles continue today across the globe—struggles against oppression, exploitation, poverty, and war.

Since our founding in 2001, Haymarket has published more than eight hundred titles. Radically independent, we seek to drive a wedge into the risk-averse world of corporate book publishing. Our authors include Angela Y. Davis, Arundhati Roy, Keeanga-Yamahtta Taylor, Eve Ewing, Aja Monet, Mariame Kaba, Naomi Klein, Rebecca Solnit, Olúfẹ́mi O. Táíwò, Mohammed El-Kurd, José Olivarez, Noam Chomsky, Winona LaDuke, Robyn Maynard, Leanne Betasamosake Simpson, Howard Zinn, Mike Davis, Marc Lamont Hill, Dave Zirin, Astra Taylor, and Amy Goodman, among many other leading writers of our time. We are also the trade publishers of the acclaimed Historical Materialism Book Series and of Dispatch Books.

ALSO AVAILABLE FROM HAYMARKET BOOKS

1919 and Electric Arches
Eve L. Ewing

The Billboard
Natalie Y. Moore, foreword by Imani Perry

Black Queer Hoe
Britteney Black Rose Kapri, foreword by Danez Smith

The Brother You Choose
Paul Coates and Eddie Conway Talk About Life, Politics, and The Revolution
Susie Day, afterword by Ta-Nehisi Coates

Haunted by Slavery
A Memoir of a Southern White Woman in the Freedom Struggle
Gwendolyn Midlo Hall, foreword by Pero G. Dagbovie

Mayor 1%: Rahm Emanuel and the Rise of Chicago's 99%
Kari Lydersen

My People Are Rising: Memoir of a Black Panther Party Captain
Aaron Dixon, foreword by Judson L. Jeffries

Palante: Young Lords Party
Young Lords Party, photography by Michael Abramson
Introduction by Iris Morales

The Torture Machine: Racism and Police Violence in Chicago
Flint Taylor

People Wasn't Made to Burn
A True Story of Housing, Race, and Murder in Chicago
Joe Allen

ABOUT THE AUTHOR

Helen Shiller, raised by migrant Jewish parents, was radicalized by the anti-war and civil rights movements. Shiller was in a collective of white people aligned with the Black Panther Party in Chicago. Beginning in 1987, Shiller was a radical Chicago alderperson for twenty-four years.